Ellen Hudson-Snyder

Automated
Software Testing

Automated Software Testing

Introduction, Management,

and Performance

Elfriede Dustin

Jeff Rashka

John Paul

ADDISON–WESLEY

Boston • San Francisco • New York • Toronto • Montreal
London • Munich • Paris • Madrid
Capetown • Sydney • Tokyo • Singapore • Mexico City

Many of the designations used by manufacturers and sellers to distinguish their products are claimed as trademarks. Where those designations appear in this book, and we were aware of a trademark claim, the designations have been printed with initial capital letters or in all capitals.

DISCOVER®, DISCOVER's Information Model™, DISCOVER Y2K™, and Tree Pattern Matching™ are trademarks of Software Emancipation Technology, Inc.

The authors and publisher have taken care in the preparation of this book, but make no expressed or implied warranty of any kind and assume no responsibility for errors or omissions. No liability is assumed for incidental or consequential damages in connection with or arising out of the use of the information or programs contained herein.

The publisher offers discounts on this book when ordered in quantity for special sales. For more information, please contact:

Pearson Education Corporate Sales Division
One Lake Street
Upper Saddle River, NJ 07458
(800) 382-3419

Visit AW on the Web: www.awl.com/cseng/

Library of Congress Cataloging-in-Publication Data

Dustin, Elfriede.
    Automated software testing : introduction, management, and
performance / Elfriede Dustin, Jeff Rashka, John Paul.
       p. cm.
    Includes bibliographical references.
    ISBN 0-201-43287-0
    1. Computer software—Testing—Automation. I. Rashka, Jeff.
II. Paul, John, 1968–   . III. Title.
    QA76.76.T48D87 1999
    005.1'4—dc21   99–25423
                                 CIP

Text printed on recycled and acid-free paper.

ISBN 0201432870

4 5 6 7 8 9 MA   03 02 01

4th Printing   February 2001

Contents

Part II
Introduction of Automated Testing to a Project

Part III

Test Planning and Preparation

Part IV
Test Execution and Review

Preface

Automated Software Testing addresses the challenge for today's software professionals who are faced with real schedule deadlines and need to introduce, manage, and perform automated testing on a project. The book addresses automated testing within a client-server or Web environment.

The focus of this book is the pragmatic concerns and information needed by the **software test engineer/manager** who faces the necessity of performing testing more thoroughly and quickly. By the same token, these same concerns may apply to the **software developer** who has the responsibility for development testing (that is, unit and integration testing) and, on some projects, system testing. The book also represents an informative guide that bolsters the ability of the **quality assurance engineer** to perform quality reviews on test design, test procedures, and the results of test activities.

The software **project manager**, who is responsible for the overall development effort, may also find this book useful. The text provides the project manager with guidelines concerning the goals and objectives of the testing effort and the decision about whether to automate testing. It also offers guidance on introducing automated testing on a project and outlines the processes for performing test planning, design, development, execution, and evaluation.

The authors have worked intimately with a number of automated testing professionals around the world, who were generous enough to share their problems and concerns. One primary concern voiced by these test engineers related to the fact that the test industry does not have the kind of structured methodologies that developers have traditionally enjoyed. Similarly, project managers, test managers, and test engineers may not be familiar with the kinds of approaches that are required to perform automated testing as opposed to the traditional test approach.

Clearly, the emphasis on automated testing represents a paradigm change for the software industry. This change does not simply involve the application of tools and the performance of test automation. Rather, it is pervasive across the entire test life cycle and the system development life cycle. The approach taken by project managers, test managers, software engineers, and test engineers is altered as a result. For software professionals to successfully make the leap to automated testing, structured approaches to testing must be embraced.

Automated Software Testing is revolutionary in that it promulgates a new structured, building-block approach to the entire test life cycle, while also providing relevant test automation and associated test management guidance needed by industry test professionals.

Automated Testing

Software project managers and software developers building today's applications face the challenge of doing so within an ever-shrinking schedule and with minimal resources. As part of their attempt to do more with less, organizations want to test software adequately, but as quickly and thoroughly as possible. To accomplish this goal, organizations are turning to automated testing.

Faced with this reality and realizing that many tests cannot be executed manually, such as simulating 1,000 virtual users for volume testing, software professionals are introducing automated testing to their projects. While needing to introduce automated testing, software professionals may not know what's involved in introducing an automated test tool to a software project, and they may be unfamiliar with the breadth of application that automated test tools have today. *Automated Software Testing* provides guidance in these areas.

The growth of automated test capability has stemmed in large part from the growing popularity of rapid application development (RAD), a software development methodology that focuses on minimizing the development schedule while providing frequent, incremental software builds. The objective of RAD is to engage the user early and throughout design and development of each build so as to refine the software, thereby ensuring that it more closely reflects the needs and preferences of the user. In this environment of continual changes and additions to the software through each software build, where requirements are encouraged to evolve, software testing takes on an iterative nature itself. Each new build is accompanied by a considerable number of new tests as well as rework to existing test scripts, just as there is rework on previously released software modules. Given the continual changes and additions to software applications, automated software testing becomes an important control mechanism to ensure accuracy and stability of the software through each build.

As noted above, a primary goal of RAD is to shorten the overall development schedule, by addressing the riskiest aspects of development in early builds. As a result, test activities are undertaken at the start of the initial RAD cycle and through each subsequent RAD cycle as well. As noted in Part III of this book, test design and development represent a complex undertaking. A test effort, in fact, may be as time-consuming as the effort required to develop the software application. When the project involves the integration of commercial off-the-shelf (COTS) products, for example, the test effort may even require more resources than software development. Instances where the test team does not participate in software specification or when test is not initiated soon enough pose a risk to the project. In these situations, potential outcomes include an incomplete software test effort, an insufficient test schedule, and an unplanned extension to the development schedule to accommodate testing.

Much of the test effort required on a project now needs to be supported by automated test tools. Manual testing is labor-intensive and error-prone, and it does not support the same kind of quality checks that are possible with an automated test tool. The introduction of an automated test tool can replace mundane manual test activities with a more efficient and repeatable automated test environment, which itself improves test engineer morale and retention.

Although some automated test tools began as capture and playback tools, the functionality and capabilities of automated test tool suites have been expanding. Automated test capabilities for software products include testing of the graphical user interface, requirements compliance, load performance, code coverage, Web interface, network communications, memory leakage, and more. New capabilities continue to be added to keep pace with the growing demand for test support.

ATLM—Automated Test Life-Cycle Methodology

This book concentrates on the concerns of the software test professional within the framework of an Automated Test Life-cycle Methodology (ATLM). ATLM is a structured methodology geared toward ensuring successful implementation of automated testing. The ATLM approach mirrors the benefits of modern, rapid application development efforts, where such efforts engage the user early in the development cycle. The end user of the software product is actively involved throughout analysis, design, development, and test of each software build, which is augmented in an incremental fashion.

The ATLM incorporates a multistage process consisting of six components. It supports the detailed and interrelated activities that are required to decide whether to acquire an automated testing tool. The methodology takes into account the process of introducing and optimizing an automated test tool and addresses test planning, analysis, design, development, execution, and management. The scope of the test program is outlined within the test plan, as a top-level description of test approach and implementation. The scope is further refined through the definition of test goals, objectives and strategies, and test requirements. Similar to software application development, test requirements are specified before test design is constructed. Likewise, the test program must be mapped out and consciously designed to ensure that the most efficient and effective tests for the target application are performed. Test design is developed through graphical portrayals of the test effort, so as to give project and test personnel a mental framework on the boundary and scope of the test program.

Test Training

The evolution of automated testing has given birth to new career opportunities for software engineers. In fact, while the demand for automated software test professionals has exploded, community colleges and universities have not produced a reciprocal response to help support industry demand.

Universities, corporations, and government operations already have been proactive in responding to changes in the software industry and have implemented software test and quality assurance courses. For example, George Mason University (GMU) provides software test and quality assurance courses (see the GMU Web site at http://www.isse.gmu.edu/ for more information). Kansas State University (KSU) offers students several courses on the subject of software test and quality assurance and other courses that touch on the subject (see the KSU Web site at http://www.ksu.edu/).

Purdue University offers two undergraduate courses in software engineering that cover software testing and reliability. Purdue also has established a software engineering research center (http://serc.uoregon.edu/serc/), in which faculty from eight universities and representatives from eleven companies participate. Among other areas this center supports software quality research. For more information, see the Purdue University Web site at http://www.purdue.edu/.

The North Seattle Community College has established one of the most progressive testing curricula in the country. The college offers three levels of software testing courses (introduction, automation, and leadership) and one- and two-year software testing programs. For more information about these courses and programs, visit its Web site at http://nsccux.sccd.ctc.edu/. Information concerning additional university and industry training resources is available on the authors' Web site at http://www.autotestco.com/. For corporate and other test training organizations, see Table C.3 in Appendix C.

Automated Software Testing is intended to help in classroom instruction on software testing that uses modern automated test tool capabilities. The book provides students with an introduction to the application and importance of software test, and it describes the different kinds of automated tests that can be performed. Instruction continues with the definition of the test approach, the roles and responsibilities of the test team, test planning, test design, test script development, test execution, defect tracking, and test progress reporting.

About the Authors

Automated Software Testing was developed by three software industry professionals.

Elfriede Dustin has performed as a computer systems analyst/programmer developing software applications and utilities, process and data modeling using CASE tools, and system design simulation models. She has experience supporting a variety of system application development projects, including health, financial, logistic, and enterprise information management systems. In addition, Elfriede has been responsible for implementing the entire development life cycle, from requirements analysis, to design, to development, to automated software testing. She has been a test manager and a lead consultant guiding the implementation of automated testing on many projects. Because of her automated test expertise, she has been sought out to help modify the capabilities of commercial test tool products, where her use of and feedback on test products have proved invaluable.

Jeff Rashka has managed a multitude of significant information system and systems integration projects. System applications on which he has served as manager include worldwide transportation asset management, enterprise information management, financial management, bar-coded inventory management, and shipboard information systems. Jeff also has process improvement management experience in implementing the guidelines contained within the Software Engineering Institute's Capability Maturity Model (CMM).

John Paul has worked as a senior programmer/analyst on financial and budgeting systems as well as a host of other information systems. His software development leadership responsibilities have included system analysis and design, application prototyping, and application development using a number of different methodologies and programming techniques. His software development responsibilities have included application testing using automated test tools. John has also assumed a lead role in the performance of year 2000 compliance testing.

The authors have applied their collective knowledge of software engineering, automated testing, and management to develop a book that addresses the pragmatic concerns and information needed by the software test engineer and manager. *Automated Software Testing* is designed to be a useful—and practical—guide for software engineers and software project managers who are responsible for software test activities.

Book Style and Organization

This book's organization correlates with the phases, tasks, and steps of the ATLM. The sequence of the book is fashioned in a purposeful way. It addresses the reader as if he or she had just been handed a note giving that individual the responsibility for automated software testing on a project. A first question might be, "What exactly is automated testing, and why do I need it?" Part I of the book answers this question and provides other fundamental instruction allowing the would-be test engineer to approach the new responsibility with confidence. The reader is then guided through the decision to automate testing as well as automated test tool selection and evaluation.

After receiving this fundamental instruction, the test engineer would have several more questions: "What is involved in setting up the tool?" "How do I get the test team in place?" "What early test planning is required?" Part II answers these questions. Specifically, the process for introducing an automated test tool is outlined and guidelines for structuring the test team are provided.

Part III focuses on automated test planning, analysis, design, and test automation (programming). This section of the book addresses test design techniques, which are comparable to the structured software design techniques introduced over the past 20 years. Specifically, it highlights the discipline required in the design of test automation. The goal is to give useful information on test design and test case development, so that the test engineer doesn't have to discover (by trial and error) how to put together a good test design and set of test procedures.

Part IV helps the reader address several additional questions: "What's involved in the performance of test?" "How do I manage my test schedule?" "How do I document and track defects?" This section provides guidelines pertaining to test execution, defect tracking, and test program status tracking. A set of best practices for the development and execution of automated test procedures is provided to assist test professionals in executing test activities in an efficient manner.

Overall, the book seeks to allay the concerns of the software test professional within the framework of the ATLM. ATLM is a structured methodology, and one that is geared toward ensuring successful implementation of automated testing. Readers with questions and comments may contact the authors via their home page at http://www.autotestco.com/. This Web site also provides more information on automated software testing and resources that are available to support automated software testing programs.

Acknowledgments

Special thanks to Oliver Jones and Chris Dryer for their enthusiasm and support of the book. Their encouragement, positive feedback, and valuable comments helped enhance the material presented here.

Thanks to all the testing professionals, such as Boris Beizer, for their test industry leadership and their persistent pursuit of software quality. We are especially grateful to all the individuals below whose contributions made this book possible.

- Brad Appleton
- Stacey Cornelius
- Matthias Daigl
- Chris Dryer
- Joyce Enos
- Robert L. Glass
- Sam Guckenheimer
- Dave Gustafson
- Richard J. Hedger
- Oliver Jones
- Anuradha Kare

- Bruce Katz
- Kirk Knoernschild
- Matthew Leahy
- Tilo Linz
- Ian Long
- Brett Schuchert
- Robert Schultz
- Andy Tinkham
- Will Tracz
- Chris Welch

ELFRIEDE DUSTIN
JEFF RASHKA
JOHN PAUL

Part I

What Is Automated Testing?

The Birth and Evolution of Automated Testing

An effective test program, incorporating the automation of software testing, involves a mini-development life cycle of its own. Automated testing amounts to a development effort involving strategy and goal planning, test requirement definition, analysis, design, development, execution, and evaluation activities.

1.1 | Automated Testing

"We need the new software application sooner than that." "I need those new product features now." Sound familiar?

Today's software managers and developers are being asked to turn around their products within ever-shrinking schedules and with minimal resources. More than 90% of developers have missed ship dates. Missing deadlines is a routine occurrence for 67% of developers. In addition, 91% have been forced to remove key functionality late in the development cycle to meet deadlines [1]. A Standish Group report supports similar findings [2]. Getting a product to market as early as possible may mean the difference between product survival and product death—and therefore company survival and death.

Businesses and government agencies also face pressure to reduce their costs. A prime path for doing so consists of further automating and streamlining business processes with the support of software applications. Business management and government leaders who are responsible for application development efforts do not want to wait a year or more to see an operational product; instead, they are specifying software development efforts focused on minimizing the development schedule, which often requires incremental software builds. Although these incremental software releases provide something tangible for the customer to see and use, the need to combine the release of one software build with the subsequent release of the next build increases the magnitude and complexity of the test effort.

In an attempt to do more with less, organizations want to test their software adequately, but within a minimum schedule. To accomplish this goal, organizations are turning to automated testing. A convenient definition of automated testing might read as follows: "The management and performance of test activities, to include the development and execution of test scripts so as to verify test requirements, using an automated test tool." The automation of test activities provides its greatest value in instances where test scripts are repeated or where test script subroutines are created and then invoked repeatedly by a number of test scripts. Such testing during development and integration stages, where reusable scripts may be run a great number of times, offers a significant payback.

The performance of integration test using an automated test tool for subsequent incremental software builds provides great value. Each new build brings a considerable number of new tests, but also reuses previously developed test scripts. Given the continual changes and additions to requirements and software, automated software test serves as an important control mechanism to ensure accuracy and stability of the software through each build.

Regression testing at the system test level represents another example of the efficient use of automated testing. Regression tests seek to verify that the functions provided by a modified system or software product perform as specified and that no unintended change has occurred in the operation of the system or product. Automated testing allows for regression testing to be executed in a more efficient manner. (Details and examples of this automated testing efficiency appear throughout this book.)

To understand the context of automated testing, it is necessary to describe the kinds of tests, which are typically performed during the various application development life-cycle stages. Within a client-server or Web environment, the target system spans more than just a software application. Indeed, it may perform across multiple platforms, involve multiple layers of supporting applications, involve interfaces with a host of commercial off-the-shelf (COTS) products, utilize one or more different types of databases, and involve both front-end and back-end processing. Tests within this environment can include functional requirement testing, server performance testing, user interface testing, unit testing, integration testing, program module complexity analysis, program code coverage testing, system load performance testing, boundary testing, security testing, memory leak testing, and many more types of assessments.

Automated testing can now support these kinds of tests because the functionality and capabilities of automated test tools have expanded in recent years. Such testing can perform in a more efficient and repeatable manner than manual testing. Automated test capabilities continue to increase, so as to keep pace with the growing demand for more rapid and less expensive production of better applications.

1.2 | Background on Software Testing

The history of software testing mirrors the evolution of software development itself. For the longest time, software development focused on large-scale scientific and Defense Department programs coupled with corporate database systems developed on mainframe or minicomputer platforms. Test scenarios during this era were written down on paper, and tests targeted control flow paths, computations of complex algorithms, and data manipulation. A finite set of test procedures could effectively test a complete system. Testing was generally not initiated until the very end of the project schedule, when it was performed by personnel who were available at the time.

The advent of the personal computer injected a great deal of standardization throughout the industry, as software applications could now primarily be developed for operation on a common operating system. The introduction of personal computers gave birth to a new era and led to the explosive growth of commercial software development, where commercial software applications competed rigorously for supremacy and survival. Product leaders in niche markets survived and computer users adopted the surviving software as de facto standards. Systems became increasingly on-line systems replacing batch-mode operation. The test effort for on-line systems required a different approach to test design, due to the fact that job streams could be called in nearly any order. This capability suggested the possibility of a huge number of test procedures that would support an endless number of permutations and combinations.

The client-server architecture takes advantage of specialty niche software by employing front-end graphical user interface (GUI) application development tools and back-end database management system applications as well as capitalizing on the widespread availability of networked personal computers. The term "client-server" describes the relationship between two software processes. In this pairing, the client computer requests a service that a server computer performs. Once the server completes the required function, it sends the results back to the client. Although client and server operations could run on one single machine, they usually run on separate computers connected by a network. Figure 1.1 provides a high-level graph of a client-server architecture.

The popularity of client-server applications introduces new complexity into the test effort. The test engineer is no longer exercising a single, closed application operating on a single system, as in the past. Instead, the client-server architecture involves three separate components: the server, the client, and the network. Inter-platform connectivity increases the potential for errors, as few client-server standards have been developed to date. As a result, testing is concerned with the performance of the server and the network, as well as the overall system performance and functionality across the three components.

Coupled with the new complexity introduced by the client-server architecture, the nature of GUI screens presents some additional challenges. The GUI replaces character-based applications and makes software applications usable by just about anyone by alleviating the need for a user to know detailed commands or understand the behind-the-scenes functioning of the software. GUIs involve the presentation of information in user screen windows.

The user screen windows contain objects that can be selected, thereby allowing the user to control the logic. Such screens, which present objects as icons, can be altered in appearance in an endless number of ways. The size of the screen image can be changed, for example, and the screen image's position on the monitor screen can be changed. Any object can be selected at any time and in any order. Objects can change position. This approach, referred to as an event-driven environment, is much different from the mainframe-based procedural environment.

Given the nature of client-server applications, a significant degree of randomness exists in terms of the way in which an object may be selected. Likewise, objects may be selected in several different orders. There are generally no clear paths within the application; rather, modules can be called and exercised through an exhausting number of paths. The result is a situation where test procedures cannot readily exercise all possible functional scenarios. Test engineers must therefore focus their test activity on the portion of the application that exercises the majority of system requirements and on ways that the user might potentially use the system.

With the widespread use of GUI applications, the possibility of screen capture and playback supporting screen navigation user scenarios became an attractive way

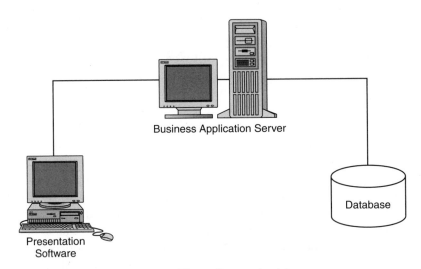

Business Application Server

Database

Presentation
Software

Figure 1.1   Client-Server Architecture

to test applications. Automated test tools, which perform this capability, were introduced into the market to meet this need and slowly built up momentum. Although test scenarios and scripts were still generally written down using a word-processing application, the use of automated test tools nevertheless increased. The more complex test effort required greater and more thorough planning. Personnel performing the test were required to be more familiar with the application under test and to have more specific skill requirements relevant to the platforms and network that also apply to the automated test tools being used.

Automated test tools supporting screen capture and playback have since matured and expanded in capability. Different kinds of automated test tools with specific niche strengths continue to emerge. In addition, automated software test has become increasingly more of a programming exercise, although it continues to involve the traditional test management functions such as requirements traceability, test planning, test design, and test scenario and script development.

1.3 | The Automated Test Life-Cycle Methodology (ATLM)

The use of automated test tools to support the test process is proving to be beneficial in terms of product quality and minimizing project schedule and effort (see "Case Study: Value of Test Automation Measurement," in Chapter 2). To achieve these benefits, test activity and test planning must be initiated early in the project. Thus test engineers need to be included during business analysis and requirements activities and be involved in analysis and design review activities. These reviews can serve as effective testing techniques, preventing subsequent analysis/design errors. Such early involvement allows the test team to gain understanding of the customer needs to be supported, which will aid in developing an architecture for the appropriate test environment and generating a more thorough test design.

Early test involvement not only supports effective test design, which is a critically important activity when utilizing an automated test tool, but also provides early detection of errors and prevents migration of errors from requirement specification to design, and thence from design into code. This kind of error prevention reduces cost, minimizes rework, and saves time. The earlier in the development cycle that errors are uncovered, the easier and less costly they are to fix. Cost is measured in terms of the amount of time and resources required to correct the defect. A defect found at an early stage is relatively easy to fix, has no operational impact, and requires few resources. In contrast, a defect discovered during the operational phase can involve several organizations, can require a wider range of retesting, and can

Table 1.1   Prevention Is Cheaper Than Cure

**Error Removal Cost Multiplies Over
System Development Life Cycle**

Phase	Cost
Definition	$1
High-Level Design	$2
Low-Level Design	$5
Code	$10
Unit Test	$15
Integration Test	$22
System Test	$50
Post-Delivery	$100+

cause operational downtime. Table 1.1 outlines the cost savings of error detection through the various stages of the development life cycle [3].

The Automated Test Life-cycle Methodology (ATLM) discussed throughout this book and outlined in Figure 1.2 represents a structured approach for the implementation and performance of automated testing. The ATLM approach mirrors the benefits of modern rapid application development efforts, where such efforts engage the user early on throughout analysis, design, and development of each software version, which is built in an incremental fashion.

In adhering to the ATLM, the test engineer becomes involved early on in the system life cycle, during business analysis throughout the requirements phase, design, and development of each software build. This early involvement enables the test team to conduct a thorough review of requirements specification and software design, more completely understand business needs and requirements, design the most appropriate test environment, and generate a more rigorous test design. An auxiliary benefit of using a test methodology, such as the ATLM, that parallels the development life cycle is the development of a close working relationship between software developers and the test engineers, which fosters greater cooperation and makes possible better results during unit, integration, and system testing.

Early test involvement is significant because requirements or use cases constitute the foundation or reference point from which test requirements are defined and against which test success is measured. A system or application's functional specification should be reviewed by the test team. Specifically, the functional specifications must be evaluated, at a minimum, using the criteria given here and further detailed in Appendix A.

- Completeness. Evaluate the extent to which the requirement is thoroughly defined.

- Consistency. Ensure that each requirement does not contradict other requirements.

- Feasibility. Evaluate the extent to which a requirement can actually be implemented with the available technology, hardware specifications, project budget and schedule, and project personnel skill levels.

- Testability. Evaluate the extent to which a test method can prove that a requirement has been successfully implemented.

Test strategies should be determined during the functional specification/ requirements phase. Automated tools that support the requirements phase can help produce functional requirements that are testable, thus minimizing the effort and cost of testing. With test automation in mind, the product design and coding standards can provide the proper environment to get the most out of the test tool. For example, the development engineer could design and build in testability into the application code. Chapter 4 further discusses building testable code.

The ATLM, which is invoked to support test efforts involving automated test tools, incorporates a multistage process. This methodology supports the detailed and interrelated activities that are required to decide whether to employ an automated

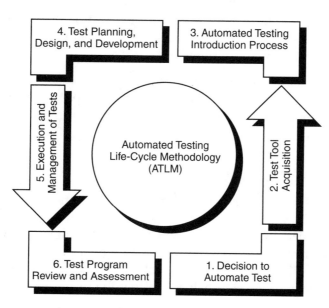

Figure 1.2   Automated Test Life-Cycle Methodology (ATLM)

testing tool. It considers the process needed to introduce and utilize an automated test tool, covers test development and test design, and addresses test execution and management. The methodology also supports the development and management of test data and the test environment, and describes a way to develop test documentation so as to account for problem reports. The ATLM represents a structured approach that depicts a process with which to approach and execute testing. This structured approach is necessary to help steer the test team away from several common test program mistakes:

- Implementing the use of an automated test tool without a testing process in place, which results in an ad hoc, nonrepeatable, nonmeasurable test program.

- Implementing a test design without following any design standards, which results in the creation of test scripts that are not repeatable and therefore not reusable for incremental software builds.

- Attempting to automate 100% of test requirements, when the tools being applied do not support automation of all tests required.

- Using the wrong tool.

- Initiating test tool implementation too late in the application development life cycle, without allowing sufficient time for tool setup and test tool introduction (that is, without providing for a learning curve).

- Involving test engineers too late in the application development life cycle, which results in poor understanding of the application and system design and thereby incomplete testing.

The ATLM is geared toward ensuring successful implementation of automated testing. As shown in Table 1.2, it includes six primary processes or components. Each primary process is further composed of subordinate processes as described here.

1.3.1 Decision to Automate Test

The *decision to automate test* represents the first phase of the ATLM. This phase is addressed in detail in Chapter 2, which covers the entire process that goes into the automated testing decision. The material in Chapter 2 is intended to help the test team manage automated testing expectations and outlines the potential benefits of automated testing, if implemented correctly. An approach for developing a test tool proposal is outlined, which will be helpful in acquiring management support.

Table 1.2   ATLM Process Hierarchy

Decision to Automate

1.1 Automated Test Expectations	Chapter 2
1.2 Benefits of Automated Test	Chapter 2
1.3 Acquiring Management Support	Chapter 2

Test Tool Acquisition

2.1 Review System Engineering Environment	Chapter 3
2.2 Review Tools Available on the Market	Chapter 3
2.3 Tool Research and Evaluation	Chapter 3
2.4 Tool Purchase	Chapter 3

Introduction of Automated Testing

3.1 Test Process Analysis	Chapter 4
3.2 Test Tool Consideration	Chapter 4

Test Planning, Design, and Development

4.1 Test Plan Documentation	Chapter 6
4.2 Test Requirements Analysis	Chapter 7
4.3 Test Design	Chapter 7
4.4 Test Development	Chapter 8

Execution and Management of Automated Test

5.1 Automated Test Execution	Chapter 9
5.2 Testbed Baseline	Chapter 8
5.3 Defect Tracking	Chapter 9
5.4 Test Progress Tracking	Chapter 9
5.5 Test Metrics	Chapter 9

Process Evaluation and Improvement

6.1 Post-Release: Test Process Improvement	Chapter 10

1.3.2   Test Tool Acquisition

Test tool acquisition represents the second phase of the ATLM. Chapter 3 guides the test engineer through the entire test tool evaluation and selection process, starting with confirmation of management support. As a tool should support most of the organization's testing requirements whenever feasible, the test engineer will need to review the systems engineering environment and other organizational needs. Chapter 3 reviews the different types of tools available to support aspects of the entire testing life cycle, enabling the reader to make an informed decision with regard to the types of tests to be performed on a particular project. It next guides the test engineer through the process of defining an evaluation domain to pilot the test tool. After completing all of those steps, the test engineer can make vendor contact to bring in the selected tool(s). Test personnel then evaluate the tool, based on sample criteria provided in Chapter 3.

1.3.3   Automated Testing Introduction Phase

The *process of introducing automated testing* to a new project team represents the third phase of the ATLM. Chapter 4 outlines the steps necessary to successfully introduce automated testing to a new project, which are summarized here.

Test Process Analysis.   *Test process analysis* ensures that an overall test process and strategy are in place and are modified, if necessary, to allow successful introduction of the automated test. The test engineer defines and collects test process metrics so as to allow for process improvement. Test goals, objectives, and strategies must be defined and test process must be documented and communicated to the test team. In this phase, the kinds of testing applicable for the technical environment are defined, as well as tests that can be supported by automated tools. Plans for user involvement are assessed, and test team personnel skills are analyzed against test requirements and planned test activities. Early test team participation is emphasized, supporting refinement of requirements specifications into terms that can be adequately tested and enhancing the test team's understanding of application requirements and design.

Test Tool Consideration.   The *test tool consideration* phase includes steps in which the test engineer investigates whether incorporation of automated test tools or utilities into the test effort would be beneficial to a project, given the project testing requirements, available test environment and personnel resources, the user environment, the platform, and product features of the application under test. The project schedule is reviewed to ensure that sufficient time exists for test tool setup and development of the requirements hierarchy; potential test tools and utilities are mapped to test requirements; test tool compatibility with the application and environment is verified; and work-around solutions are investigated to incompatibility problems surfaced during compatibility tests.

1.3.4   Test Planning, Design, and Development

Test planning, design, and development is the fourth phase of the ATLM. These subjects are further addressed in Chapters 6, 7, and 8, and are summarized here.

Test Planning.   The *test planning* phase includes a review of long-lead-time test planning activities. During this phase, the test team identifies test procedure creation standards and guidelines; hardware, software, and network required to support test environment; test data requirements; a preliminary test schedule; performance measurement requirements; a procedure to control test configuration and environment; and a defect tracking procedure and associated tracking tool.

   The test plan incorporates the results of each preliminary phase of the structured test methodology (ATLM). It defines roles and responsibilities, the project test schedule, test planning and design activities, test environment preparation, test risks and contingencies, and the acceptable level of thoroughness (that is, test acceptance criteria). Test plan appendixes may include test procedures, a description of the naming convention, test procedure format standards, and a test procedure traceability matrix.

   Setting up a test environment is part of test planning. The test team must plan, track, and manage test environment setup activities for which material procurements may have long lead times. It must schedule and monitor environment setup activities; install test environment hardware, software, and network resources; integrate and install test environment resources; obtain and refine test databases; and develop environment setup scripts and testbed scripts.

Test Design.   The *test design* component addresses the need to define the number of tests to be performed, the ways that test will be approached (for example, the paths or functions), and the test conditions that need to be exercised. Test design standards need to be defined and followed.

Test Development.   For automated tests to be reusable, repeatable, and maintainable, test development standards must be defined and followed.

1.3.5   Execution and Management of Tests

The test team must execute test scripts and refine the integration test scripts, based on a test procedure execution schedule. It should also conduct evaluation activities of test execution outcomes, so as to avoid false-positives or false-negatives. System problems should be documented via system problem reports, efforts should be made to support developer understanding of system and software problems and replication of the problem. Finally, the team should perform regression tests and all other tests and track problems to closure.

1.3.6   Test Program Review and Assessment

Test program review and assessment activities need to be conducted throughout the testing life cycle, thereby allowing for continuous improvement activities. Throughout the testing life cycle and following test execution activities, metrics need to be evaluated and final review and assessment activities need to be conducted to allow for process improvement.

1.4 | ATLM's Role in the Software Testing Universe

1.4.1   ATLM Relationship to System Development Life Cycle

For maximum test program benefit, the ATLM approach needs to be pursued in parallel with the system life cycle. Figure 1.3 depicts the relationship between the ATLM and the system development life cycle. Note that the system development life cycle is represented in the outer layer in Figure 1.3. Displayed in the bottom right-hand corner of the figure is the process evaluation phase. During the system life cycle process evaluation phase, improvement possibilities often determine that test automation is a valid approach toward improving the testing life cycle. The associated ATLM phase is called the decision to automate test.

During the business analysis and requirements phase, the test team conducts test tool acquisition activities (ATLM step 2). Note that test tool acquisition can take place at any time, but preferably when system requirements are available. Ideally, during the automated testing introduction process (ATLM step 3), the development group supports this effort by developing a pilot project or small prototype so as to iron out any discrepancies and conduct lessons learned activities.

Test planning, design and development activities (ATLM step 4) should take place in parallel to the system design and development phase. Although some test planning will already have taken place at the beginning and throughout the system development life cycle, it is finalized during this phase. Execution and management

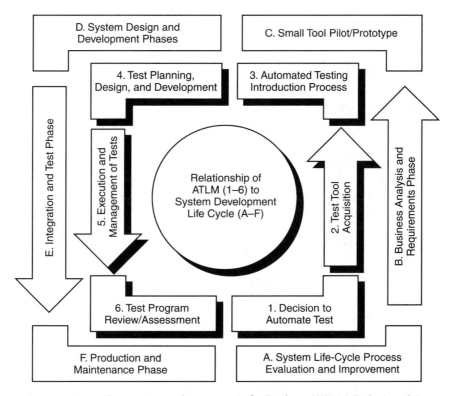

Figure 1.3 System Development Life Cycle—ATLM Relationship

of tests (ATLM step 5) takes place in conjunction with the integration and test phase of the system development life cycle. System testing and other testing activities, such as acceptance testing, take place once the first build has been baselined. Test program review and assessment activities (ATLM step 6) are conducted throughout the entire life cycle, though they are finalized during the system development production and maintenance phase.

1.4.2 Test Maturity Model (TMM)—Augmented by Automated Software Testing Maturity

Test teams that implement the ATLM will make progress toward levels 4 and 5 of the Test Maturity Model (TMM). The TMM is a testing maturity model that was developed by the Illinois Institute of Technology [4]; it contains a set of maturity levels through which an organization can progress toward greater test process maturity. This model lists a set of recommended practices at each level of maturity above level 1. It promotes greater professionalism in software testing, similar to the intention of the Capability Maturity Model for software, which was developed by the Software Engineering Institute (SEI) at Carnegie Mellon University (see the SEI Web site at http://www.sei.cmu.edu/).

1.4.2.1   Correlation Between the CMM and TMM

The TMM was developed as a complement to the CMM [5]. It was envisioned that organizations interested in assessing and improving their testing capabilities would likely be involved in general software process improvement. To have directly corresponding levels in both maturity models would logically simplify these two parallel process improvement drives. This parallelism is not entirely present, however, because both the CMM and the TMM level structures are based on the individual historical maturity growth patterns of the processes they represent. The testing process is a subset of the overall software development process; therefore, its maturity growth needs support from the key process areas (KPAs) associated with general process growth [6–8]. For this reason, any organization that wishes to improve its testing process throughout implementation of the TMM (and ATLM) should first commit to improving its overall software development process by applying the CMM guidelines.

Research shows that an organization striving to reach a particular level of the TMM must be at least at the same level of the CMM. In many cases, a given TMM level needs specific support from KPAs in the corresponding CMM level and the CMM level beneath it. These KPAs should be addressed either prior to or in parallel with the TMM maturity goals.

The TMM model adapts well to automated software testing, because effective software verification and validation programs grow out of development programs that are well planned, executed, managed, and monitored. A good software test program cannot stand alone; it must be an integral part of the software development process. Table 1.3 displays the levels 1 through 5 of the TMM in the first column, together with corresponding automated software testing levels 1 through 5 in the second column. Column 2 addresses test maturity as it specifically pertains to automated software testing.

The test team must determine, based on the company's environment, the TMM maturity level that best fits the organization and the applicable software applications or products. The level of testing should be proportional to complexity of design, and the testing effort should not be more complex than the development effort.

Table 1.3   Testing Maturity and Automated Software Testing Maturity Levels 1–5

TMM Level 1	Automated Software Testing Level 1
Initial. Testing is a chaotic process; it is ill defined and not distinguished from debugging. Tests are developed in an ad hoc way after coding is complete. Testing and debugging are interleaved to get the bugs out of the software. The objective of testing is to show that the software works [9]. Software products are released without quality assurance. Resources, tools, and properly trained staff are lacking. This type of organization would be at level 1 of the CMM developed by the Software Engineering Institute. There are no maturity goals at this level.	This level of automated software testing is referred to as "accidental automation." At the first level, automated testing is not done at all or only on an ad hoc basis. An automated test tool might be used on an experimental basis. With a capture/playback tool, automated test scripts are recorded and played back with only tool-generated scripts being used. Scripts are not modified for reusability or maintainability. No automated script design or development standards are followed. Resulting scripts are not reusable and difficult to maintain and must be recreated with each software build. This type of automation can actually increase testing costs by 125% or more—for example, 150% of manual test costs with each test cycle (see "Case Study: Value of Test Automation Measurement" in Chapter 2).

TMM Level 2	Automated Software Testing Level 2
Phase Definition. Testing is separated from debugging and is defined as a phase that follows coding. Although it is a planned activity, test planning at level 2 may occur after coding for reasons related to the immaturity of the test process. For example, at level 2 there is the perception that all testing is execution-based and dependent on the code, and therefore it should be planned only when the code is complete. The primary goal of testing at this level of maturity is to show that the software meets its specifications [10]. Basic testing techniques and methods are in place. Many quality problems at this TMM level occur because test planning takes place late in the software life cycle. In addition, defects propagate into the code from the requirements and design phases, as no review programs address this important issue. Post-code, execution-based testing is still considered the primary testing activity.	"At this level, testing is becoming a planned activity. This implies a commitment to the completion of testing activities. A project planning tool will aid the project manager in defining test activities, allocating time, money, resources, and personnel to the testing process" [11]. This level of automated software testing is referred to as "incidental automation." At the second level, automated test scripts are modified but no documented standards or repeatability exists. The types of tools used at this level can include project planning tools, capture/playback tools, simulators and emulators, syntax and semantic analyzers, and debugging tools. The introduction of automated test tools to a new project is not planned and a process is not being followed. Test design or development standards do not exist. Test schedules or test requirements are not taken into consideration or are not reliable when contemplating the use of an automated test tool. As with level 1, this type of test automation does not provide much return on investment and can actually increase the testing effort.

continued

continued from page 17

TMM Level 3

Integration. Testing is no longer a phase that follows coding; rather, it is integrated into the entire software life cycle. Organizations can build on the test planning skills they have acquired at level 2. Unlike level 2 (planning for testing at TMM), level 3 begins at the requirements phase and continues throughout the life cycle supported by a version of the V model [12]. Test objectives are established with respect to the requirements based on user and client needs and are used for test-case design and success criteria. A test organization exists, and testing is recognized as a professional activity. A technical training organization pursues a testing focus. Basic tools support key testing activities. Although organizations at this level begin to realize the important role of reviews in quality control, no formal review program has been established, and reviews do not yet take place across the life cycle. A test measurement program has not yet been established to qualify process and product attributes.

Automated Software Testing Level 3

This level of test maturity is referred to as "intentional automation." At the third level, automated testing becomes both well defined and well managed. The test requirements and the test scripts themselves proceed logically from the software requirement specifications and design documents.

Automated test scripts are created based on test design and development standards, yet the test team does not review automated test procedures. Automated tests become more reusable and maintainable. At this level of automated testing, the return on investment is starting to pay off and a break-even point can already be achieved by the second-regression test cycle (see "Case Study: Value of Test Automation Measurement" in Chapter 2). The types of tools used at this level include requirement management tools, project planning tools, capture/playback tools, simulators and emulators, syntax and semantic analyzers, and debugging tools.

TMM Level 4

Management and Measurement. Testing is a measured and quantified process. Reviews at all phases of the development process are now recognized as testing and quality-control activities. Software products are tested for quality attributes such as reliability, usability, and maintainability. Test cases from all projects are collected and recorded in a test-case database to test case reuse and regression testing. Defects are logged and given a severity level. Deficiencies in the test process now often follow from the lack of a defect-prevention philosophy and the porosity of automated support for the collection, analysis, and dissemination of test-related metrics.

Automated Software Testing Level 4

This level of test maturity, referred to as "advanced automation," can be achieved when adopting many aspects of the ATLM described in this book. This testing maturity level represents a practiced and perfected version of level 3 with one major addition—post-release defect tracking. Defects are captured and sent directly back through the fix, test creation, and regression test processes. The software test team is now an integral part of product development, and test engineers and application developers work together to build a product that will meet test requirements. Any software bugs are caught early, when they are much less expensive to fix. In addition to the tools mentioned at the previous testing levels, defect and change tracking tools, test procedure generation tools, and code review tools are used at this level.

continued

continued from page 18

TMM Level 5	**Automated Software Testing Level 5**
Optimization, Defect Prevention, and Quality Control. Because of the infrastructure provided by the attainment of maturity goals at levels 1 through 4 of the TMM, the testing process is now said to be defined and managed and its cost and effectiveness can be monitored. At level 5, mechanisms fine-tune and continuously improve testing. Defect prevention and quality control are practiced. The testing process is driven by statistical sampling and measurements of confidence levels, trustworthiness, and reliability. An established procedure exists for the selection and evaluation of testing tools. Automated tools totally support the running and rerunning of test cases, providing support for test-case design, maintenance of test-related items, defect collection and analysis, and the collection, analysis, and application of test-related metrics.	When incorporating the guidelines of the ATLM described in this book and using the applicable tools in an efficient manner, a TMM level 5 maturity can be achieved. Tools used at this highest level include the ones mentioned within previous levels plus test data generation tools and metrics collection tools, such as complexity and size measurement tools, coverage and frequency analyzers, and statistical tools for defect analysis and defect prevention. (All tools described at the various levels are discussed in detail in Chapter 3, and tool examples are provided in Appendix B.)

1.4.3 Test Automation Development

Modularity, shared function libraries, use of variables, parameter passing, conditional branching, loops, arrays, subroutines—this is now the universal language of not only the software developer, but also the software test engineer.

Automated software testing, as conducted with today's automated test tools, is a development activity that includes programming responsibilities similar to those of the application-under-test software developer. Whereas manual testing is an activity that is often tagged on to the end of the system development life cycle, efficient automated testing emphasizes that testing should be incorporated from the beginning of the system development life cycle. Indeed, the development of an automated test can be viewed as a mini-development life cycle. Like software application development, automated test development requires careful design and planning.

Automated test engineers use automated test tools that generate code, while developing test scripts that exercise a user interface. The code generated consists of third-generation languages, such as BASIC, C, or C++. This code (which comprises automated test scripts) can be modified and reused to serve as automated test scripts for other applications in less time than if the test engineer were to use the automated test tool interface to generate the new scripts. Also, through the use of programming techniques, scripts can be set up to perform such tasks as testing different data values, testing a large number of different user interface characteristics, or performing volume testing.

Much like in software development, the software test engineer has a set of (test) requirements, needs to develop a detailed blueprint (design) for efficiently exercising all required tests, and must develop a product (test procedures/scripts) that is robust, modular, and reusable. The resulting test design may call for the use of variables within the test script programs to read in the value of a multitude of parameters that should be exercised during test. It also might employ looping constructs to exercise a script repeatedly or call conditional statements to exercise a statement only under a specific condition. The script might take advantage of application programming interface (API) calls or use .dll files and reuse libraries. In addition, the software test engineer wants the test design to be able to quickly and easily accommodate changes to the software developer's product. The software developer and the software test engineer therefore have similar missions. If their development efforts are successful, the fruit of their labor is a reliable, maintainable, and user-capable system.

Again much like the software developer, the test engineer builds test script modules, which are designed to be robust, repeatable, and maintainable. The test engineer takes advantage of the native scripting language of the automated test tool so as to reuse and modify test scripts to perform an endless number of tests. This kind of test script versatility is driven largely by the fact that modern on-line and GUI-based applications involve job streams, which can be processed in nearly any order. Such flexibility translates into a requirement for test cases that can support an endless number of screen and data permutations and combinations.

Test scripts may need to be coded to perform checks on the application's environment. Is the LAN drive mapped correctly? Is an integrated third-party software application up and running? The test engineer may need to create separate, reusable files that contain constant values or maintain variables. Test script code, which is reused repeatedly by a number of different test scripts, may need to be saved in a common directory or utility file as a global subroutine, where the subroutine represents shared code available to the entire test team.

Maintainability is as important to the test engineering product (test scripts) as it is to the software developer's work product (that is, the application under test). It is a given that the software product under development will change. Requirements are modified, user feedback stipulates change, and developers alter code by performing bug fixes. The test team's test scripts need to be structured in ways that can support global changes. A GUI screen change, for example, may affect hundreds of test scripts. If the GUI objects are maintained in a file, the changes can be made in the file and the test team needs to modify the test in only one place. As a result, the corresponding test scripts can be updated collectively.

As noted earlier, the nature of client-server applications ensures a significant degree of randomness for which an object may be selected. There is just as much freedom in terms of the order in which objects are selected. No clear paths exist within the application; rather, modules can be called and exercised through an exhausting number of paths. As a result, test procedures cannot readily exercise all possible functional scenarios. Test engineers must therefore focus their test activity on the portion of the application that exercises the majority of system requirements.

Software tests, which utilize an automated test tool having an inherent scripting language, require that software test engineers begin to use analytical skills and perform more of the same type of design and development tasks that software developers carry out. Test engineers with a manual test background, upon finding themselves on a project incorporating the use of one or more automated test tools, may need to follow the lead of test team personnel who have more experience with the test tool or who have significantly more programming experience. These more experienced test engineers should assume leadership roles in test design and test script programming, as well as in the establishment of test script programming standards and frameworks. These same seasoned test professionals need to act as mentors for more junior test engineers. Chapter 5 provides more details on test engineers' roles and responsibilities.

In GUI-based client-server system environments, test team personnel need to be more like a system engineer as well as a software developer. Knowledge and understanding of network software, routers, LANs and various client/server operating systems, and database software are useful in this regard. In the future, the skills required for both the software developer and the software test engineer will continue to converge. Various junior systems engineering personnel, including network engineers and system administrators, may see the software test engineering position as a way to expand their software engineering capability.

1.4.4 Test Effort

"We have only one week left before we are supposed to initiate testing. Should we use an automated test tool?" Responding affirmatively to this question is not a good idea. Building an infrastructure of automated test scripts, for the purpose of executing testing in quick fashion, requires considerable investment in test planning and preparation. Perhaps the project manager has been overheard making a remark such as, "The test effort is not going to be that significant, because we're going to use an automated tool." The test team needs to be cautious when it encounters statements to this effect. As described in Table 1.3, ad hoc implementation of automated testing can actually increase testing costs by 125%—or even 150% of manual test costs with each test cycle.

Many industry software professionals have a perception that the use of automated test tools makes the software test effort less significant in terms of person-hours, or at least less complex in terms of planning and execution. In reality, savings accrued from the use of automated test tools will take time to generate. In fact, during the first use of a particular automated test tool by a test team, no or very little savings may be realized.

The use of automated tools may increase the scope and breadth of the test effort within a limited schedule and help displace the use of manual, mundane, and repetitive efforts, which are both labor-intensive and error-prone. Automated testing will allow test engineers to focus their skills on the more challenging tasks. Nevertheless, the use of automated testing introduces a new level of complexity, which a project's test team may not have experienced previously. Expertise in test script programming is required but may be new to the test team, and possibly few members of the test team may have had coding experience. Even when the test team is familiar with one automated test tool, the tool required for a new project may differ.

For a test engineer or test lead on a new project, it is important to listen for the level of expectations communicated by the project manager or other project personnel. As outlined in Chapter 2, the test engineer will need to carefully monitor and influence automated test expectations. Without such assiduous attention to expectations, the test team may suddenly find the test schedule reduced or test funding cut to levels that do not support sufficient testing. Other consequences of ignoring this aspect of test management include the transfer to the test team of individuals with insufficient test or software programming skills or the rejection of a test team request for formal training on a new automated test tool.

Although the use of automated test tools provides the advantages outlined in Section 1.1, automated testing represents an investment that requires careful planning, a defined and structured process, and competent software professionals to execute and maintain test scripts.

1.5 | Software Testing Careers

"I like to perform a variety of different work, learn a lot of things, and touch a lot of different products. I also want to exercise my programming and database skills, but I don't want to be off in my own little world, isolated from others, doing nothing but hammering out code." Does this litany of desirable job characteristics sound familiar?

Software test engineering can provide for an interesting and challenging work assignment and career. And, in addition, there is high demand in the marketplace for test engineering skills! The evolution of automated test capabilities has given birth to many new career opportunities for software engineers. This trend is further boosted by U.S. quality standards and software maturity guidelines that place a greater emphasis on software test and other product assurance disciplines. A review of computer-related job classified ads in the weekend newspaper clearly reveals the ongoing explosion in the demand for automated software test professionals. Software test automation, as a discipline, remains in its infancy stage, and presently the number of test engineers with automated test experience cannot keep pace with demand.

Many software engineers are choosing careers in the automated test arena for two reasons: (1) the different kinds of tasks involved and (2) the variety of applications for which they are introduced. Experience with automated test tools, likewise, can provide a career lift. It provides the software engineer with a broader set of skills and may provide this professional with a competitive career development edge. Likewise, the development of automated testing skills may be just the thing that an aspiring college graduate needs to break into a software engineering career.

"How do I know whether I would make a good test engineer?" you might ask. If you are already working as a software test engineer, you might pause to question whether a future in the discipline is right for you. Good software developers have been trained and groomed to have a mindset to make something work and to work around the problem if necessary. The test engineer, on the other hand, needs to be able to make things fail, but also requires a developer's mentality to develop work-around solutions, if necessary, especially during the construction of test scripts.

Test engineers need to be structured, attentive to detail, and organized, and, given the complexities of automated testing, they should possess a creative and planning-ahead type of mindset. Because test engineers work closely and cooperatively with software developers, the test engineer needs to be both assertive and poised when working through trouble reports and issues with developers.

Given the complexities of the test effort associated with a client-server or multi-tier environment, test engineers should have a broad range of technical skills. Test engineers and test teams, for that matter, need experience across multiple platforms, multiple layers of supporting applications, interfaces to other products and systems, different types of databases, and application languages. If this were not enough, in an automated test environment, the test engineer needs to know the script programming language of the primary automated test tool.

What might be a logical test career development path? Table 1.4 outlines a series of progressive steps possible for an individual performing in a professional test engineering capacity. This test engineer career development program is further described in Appendix C. This program identifies the different kinds of skills and activities at each stage or level and indicates where would-be test engineers should focus their time and attention so as to improve their capabilities and boost their careers. Individuals already performing in a management capacity can use this program as a guideline on how to approach training and development for test team staff.

Given that today's test engineer needs to develop a wide variety of skills and knowledge in areas that include programming languages, operating systems, database management systems, and networks, the ambitious software test engineer has the potential to divert from the test arena into different disciplines. For example, he or she might perform in the capacity of software development, system administration, network management, or software quality assurance.

Fortunately for the software test engineering professional, manual testing is gradually being replaced by tests involving automated test tools. Manual testing will not be replaced entirely, however, because some activities that only a human can perform will persist, such as inspecting the results of an output report.

As noted earlier, manual testing is labor-intensive and error-prone, and it does not support the same kind of quality checks that are possible through the use of an automated test tool. The introduction of automated test tools may replace some manual test processes with a more effective and repeatable testing environment. This use of automated test tools provides more time for the professional test engineer to invoke greater depth and breadth of testing, focus on problem analysis, and verify proper performance of software following modifications and fixes. Combined with the opportunity to perform programming tasks, this flexibility promotes test engineer retention and improves test engineer morale.

In the future, the software test effort will continue to become more automated and the kinds of testing available will continue to grow. These trends will require that software test engineering personnel become more organized and technically more proficient. The expansion of automation and the proliferation of multitier systems will require that test engineers have both software and system skills. In addition, software test engineering will offer many junior software engineers a place to start their software careers.

An article in *Contract Professional* magazine described a college student in Boston who learned an automated test tool while in school and landed a software test engineering position upon graduation. The student stated that she enjoyed her job because "you perform a variety of different work, learn a lot of things, and touch a lot of different products" [13]. The article also noted that software test engineers are in high demand, crediting this demand to the "boom in Internet development and the growing awareness of the need for software quality."

It is likely that more universities will acknowledge the need to offer training in the software test and software quality assurance disciplines. Some university programs already offer product assurance degrees that incorporate training in test engineering and quality assurance. The state of Oregon has provided funding of $2.25

Table 1.4   Test Career Progression

Career Progression	Description
Junior Test Engineer	An entry-level position for an individual with a computer science degree or an individual with some manual testing experience. Develops test scripts and begins to become familiar with the test life cycle and testing techniques.
Test Engineer/ Programmer Analyst	A test engineer or programmer who has one to two years of experience. Programs automated test scripts and provides early leadership in test programming. Further develops skills in programming languages, operating systems, networks, and databases.
Senior Test Engineer/ Programmer Analyst	A test engineer or programmer who has three to four years of experience. Helps to develop or maintain testing or programming standards and processes, leads peer reviews, and acts as a mentor to other, more junior test engineers or programmers. Continues to develop skills in programming languages, operating systems, networks, and databases.
Team Lead	A test engineer or programmer who has four to six years of experience. Responsible for the supervision of one to three test engineers or programmers. Has some scheduling and effort size/cost estimation responsibilities. Technical skills become more focused.
Test/Programming Lead	A test engineer or programmer who has six to ten years of experience. Responsible for the supervision of four to eight personnel. Responsible for scheduling, size/cost estimation, and delivery of product within schedule and budget targets. Responsible for developing the technical approach to the project. Provides some customer support and presentations. Develops technical expertise in a few particular areas.
Test/QA/Development (Project) Manager	Ten-plus years of experience. Responsible for the eight or more personnel performing on one or more projects. Full development life cycle responsibility within this area (test/QA/development). Provides some customer interaction and many presentations. Has cost, schedule, planning, and staffing responsibility.
Program Manager	Fifteen-plus years of development and support (test/QA) activity experience. Responsible for personnel performing on several projects and full development life cycle responsibility. Assumes project direction and profit/loss responsibility.

million to establish a master's degree program in quality software engineering in the greater Portland metropolitan area [14]. Additionally, the North Seattle Community College offers two-year and four-year degree programs in automated testing curricula, as well as individual courses on automated testing (see its Web site at http://nsccux.sccd.ctc.edu/).

For the next several years, the most prominent software engineering environments will involve GUI-based client-server and Web-based applications. Automated test activity will continue to become more important, and the breadth of test tool coverage will continue to expand. Many people will choose careers in the automated test arena—many are already setting off on this path today.

Chapter Summary

○ The incremental release of software, together with the development of GUI-based client-server or multitier applications, introduces new complexity to the test effort.

○ Organizations want to test their software adequately, but within a minimum schedule.

○ Rapid application development approach calls for repeated cycles of coding and testing.

○ The automation of test activities provides its greatest value in instances where test scripts are repeated or where test script subroutines are created, and then invoked repeatedly by a number of test scripts.

○ The use of automated test tools to support the test process is proving to be beneficial in terms of product quality and minimizing project schedule and effort.

○ The Automated Testing Life-cycle Methodology (ATLM) includes six components and represents a structured approach with which to implement and execute testing.

○ Early life-cycle involvement by test engineers in requirements and design review (as emphasized by the ATLM) bolsters test engineers' understanding of business needs, increases requirements testability, and supports effective test design and development—a critically important activity when utilizing an automated test tool.

○ Test support for finding errors early in the development process provides the most significant reduction in project cost.

○ Personnel who perform testing must be more familiar with the application under test and must have specific skills relevant to the platforms and network involved as well as the automated test tools being used.

○ Automated software testing, using automated test tools, is a development activity that includes programming responsibilities similar to those of the application-under-test software developer.

○ Building an infrastructure of automated test scripts for the purpose of executing testing in quick fashion requires a considerable investment in test planning and preparation.

○ An effective test program, incorporating the automation of software testing, involves a development life cycle of its own.

○ Software test engineering can provide for an interesting and challenging work assignment and career, and the marketplace is in high demand for test engineering skills.

References

1. CenterLine Software, Inc. Survey. 1996. CenterLine is a software testing tool and automation company in Cambridge, Massachusetts.

2. http://www.standishgroup.com/chaos.html.

3. Littlewood, B. *How Good Are Software Reliability Predictions? Software Reliability Achievement and Assessment.* Oxford: Blackwell Scientific Publications, 1987.

4. Burnstein, I., Suwanassart, T., Carlson, C.R. *Developing a Testing Maturity Model,* Part II. Chicago: Illinois Institute of Technology, 1996.

5. Ibid.

6. Paulk, M., Weber, C., Curtis, B., Chrissis, M. *The Capability Maturity Model Guideline for Improving the Software Process.* Reading, MA: Addison-Wesley, 1995.

7. Paulk, M., Curtis, B., Chrissis, M., Weber, C. "Capability Maturity Model, Version 1.1." *IEEE Software* July 1993: 18–27.

8. Paulk, M., et al. "Key Practices of the Capability Maturity Model, Version 1.1." Technical Report CMS/SEI-93-TR-25. Pittsburgh, PA: Software Engineering Institute, 1993.

9. See note 4.

10. Gelperin, D., Hetzel, B. "The Growth of Software Testing." *CACM* 1998;31:687–695.

11. See note 4.

12. Daich, G., Price, G., Ragland, B., Dawood, M. "Software Test Technologies Report." STSC, Hill Air Force Base, Utah, August 1994.

13. Maglitta, M. "Quality Assurance Assures Lucrative Contracts." *Contract Professional* Oct./Sept. 1997.

14. Bernstein, L. Pacific Northwest Software Quality Conference (1997). *TTN On-Line Edition Newsletter* December 1997.

Decision to Automate Test

If you want a high quality software system, you must
ensure each of its parts is of high quality.

—Watts Humphrey

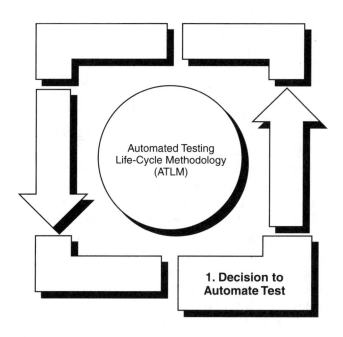

An organization has determined that its current testing program is not effective. An organizational need analysis has been conducted, and the outcome has shown that the current manual testing process requires improvement. The organization is looking for a more repeatable and less error-prone testing approach. An improvement analysis determines that automated testing should be introduced.

The organization's test lead has just been informed about the decision to introduce an automated testing, although a pilot project remains to be identified. Questions begin to surface immediately. Does the application being developed as part of the current project lend itself to automation? The test lead rounds up all information gathered during the improvement analysis regarding automated testing, searches the Web for more automated testing information, and contemplates the automated test tools that might apply to the current project. Yet, with regard to the decision about the best approach to automated testing, the test lead is not sure where to begin.

This chapter outlines a structured way of approaching the decision to automate test. Figure 2.1 depicts this step-by-step methodology. Between each step appears a decision point—that is, should the process continue or should it terminate with a decision not to automate test for that particular project?

The steps outlined in Figure 2.1 address the concerns of a test lead or manager facing a test effort on a new project. Which automated test tool should be used? How can management be convinced that automated testing is or is not beneficial to this project? At first, these issues may seem overwhelming. Manual testing may, in fact, be commonplace in the organization. Likewise, few or no test engineers in the organization may have been exposed to automated testing, and therefore few or no test automation advocates may exist.

How would the test engineer go about introducing a new concept such as automated testing? How can the test engineer determine whether the application lends itself to automated testing? The material outlined in this chapter and the structured approach it presents will help sort out these various issues. Step-by-step instructions will provide guidance regarding the decision about whether an application is suitable for automated testing.

The potential for unrealistic expectations of automated testing will also be examined, as some software engineers and managers perceive automated testing as a panacea for all quality-related problems. This chapter points out some of the misconceptions about automated testing and addresses ways to manage some of these "ivory tower" expectations. (Chapter 3 describes the types of tools available). The potential benefits of automated testing are outlined here, and guidance is provided on how to convince management that automated testing augments the quality of the product. Additionally, a structured approach for seeking resource commitment and acquiring management support is described.

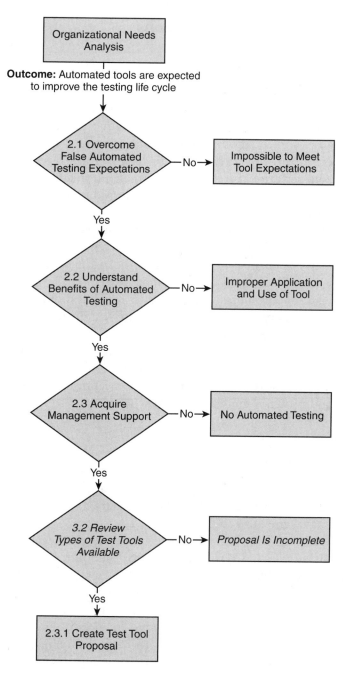

Figure 2.1   Automated Test Decision Process

2.1 | Overcoming False Expectations for Automated Testing

At a new project kick-off meeting, the project manager introduces you as the test lead. She mentions that the project will use an automated test tool and adds that, due to the planned use of an automated test tool, the test effort is not expected to be significant. The project manager concludes by requesting that you submit within the next week a recommendation for the specific test tool required plus a cost estimate for its procurement. You are caught by surprise by the project manager's remarks and wonder about her expectations with regard to automated testing. Clearly, any false automated testing expectations need to be cleared up immediately.

Along with the idea of automated testing come high expectations. Much is demanded from technology and automation. Some people believe that an automated test tool should be able to accomplish everything from test planning to test execution, without any manual intervention. Although it would be great if such a tool existed, no such capability is available today. Others believe—wrongly—that a single test tool can support all test requirements, regardless of environment parameters, such as the operating system or programming language used.

Some may incorrectly assume that an automated test tool will immediately reduce the test effort and the test schedule. Although automated testing can produce a return on investment, an immediate payback on investment is not always achieved. This section addresses some of the misconceptions that persist in the software industry and provides guidelines on how to manage some of the automated testing utopia.

2.1.1 Automatic Test Plan Generation

Currently, no commercially available tool can automatically create a comprehensive test plan, while also supporting test design and execution. This shortcoming may be a bitter pill for management to swallow.

Throughout the course of his or her career, a test engineer can expect to witness test tool demonstrations and review an abundant amount of test tool literature. Often the test engineer will be asked to give an overview of test tool functionality to a senior manager or a small number of managers. As always, the presenter must pay attention to the audience's identity. In this case, the audience may include individuals who have just enough technical knowledge to make them enthusiastic about automated testing, but who are not aware of the complexity involved with an automated test effort. Specifically, the managers may have obtained third-hand information about automated test tools and may have reached the wrong conclusions about capabilities of automated test tools.

The audience at the management presentation may be waiting to hear that the proposed tool automatically develops the test plan, designs and creates the test procedures, executes all test procedures, and analyzes the results automatically. Instead, you start the presentation by informing the group that automated test tools should be viewed as *enhancements to manual testing*, and that they will not automatically develop the test plan, design and create the test procedures, and execute the test procedures.

Soon into the presentation and after several management questions, it becomes very apparent how much of a divide exists between the reality of the test tool capabilities and the perceptions of the individuals in the audience. The term *automated test tool* seems to bring out a great deal of wishful thinking that is not closely aligned with reality. Such a tool will not replace the human factor necessary for testing a product. In fact, the services of test engineers and other quality assurance experts will still be needed to keep the testing machinery running. Thus a test tool can be viewed as an additional part of the machinery that supports the release of a good product.

2.1.2   Test Tool Fits All

Currently, not one single test tool exists that can be used to support all operating system environments. Thus a single test tool will not fulfill all testing requirements for most organizations. Consider the experience of one test engineer, Dave, who encountered this misconception. Dave's manager asked him to find a test tool that could automate all of the department's year 2000 tests. The department was using various technologies: mainframe computers and Sun workstations; operating systems such as MVS, UNIX, Windows 3.1, Windows 95, and Windows NT; programming languages such as COBOL, C, C++, MS Access, and Visual Basic; other client-server technologies; and Web technologies.

Expectations have to be managed. That is, the test lead must make it clear that no single tool currently on the market is compatible with all operating systems and programming languages. More than one tool is required to test the various technologies.

2.1.3   Immediate Test Effort Reduction

Introduction of automated test tools will not immediately reduce the test effort. Again, this issue may run counter to management's expectations.

A primary impetus for introducing an automated test tool as part of a project is to reduce the test effort. Experience has shown that a learning curve is associated with attempts to apply automated testing to a new project and to achieve effective use of automated testing. Test or project managers may have read the test tool literature and be anxious to realize the potential of the automated tools. They should be made aware that test effort savings do not necessarily come immediately.

Surprisingly, there is a good chance that the test effort will actually become more arduous when an automated test tool is first brought into an organization. The introduction of an automated test tool to a new project adds a whole new level of complexity to the test program. While a learning curve may exist for the test engineers to become familiar with and efficient in the use of the tool, manual tests must still be performed on the project. The reasons why an entire test effort generally cannot be automated are outlined later in this section.

The initial introduction of automated testing also requires careful analysis of the target application to determine which sections of the application are amenable to automation. In addition, test automation requires that the team pay careful attention to automated test procedure design and development. The automated test effort can be viewed as a mini-development life cycle, complete with the planning and coordination issues that come along with any development effort. Introducing an automated test tool requires the test team to perform the additional activities outlined in step 3 (automated testing introduction process) of the ATLM, which is discussed in detail in Chapter 4.

2.1.4   Immediate Schedule Reduction

Another misconception involves the expectation that the use of an automated testing tool on a new project will immediately minimize the test schedule. As the testing effort may actually increase, as described in Section 2.1.3, the testing schedule will not experience the anticipated decrease at first but may instead become extended. An allowance for schedule increase is therefore required when initially introducing an automated test tool. When rolling out an automated test tool, the current testing process must be augmented or an entirely new testing process must be developed and implemented. The entire test team and possibly the development team needs to become familiar with the new automated testing process (that is, ATLM) and learn to follow it. Once an automatic testing process has been established and effectively implemented, the project can expect to experience gains in productivity and turn-around time that have a positive effect on schedule and cost.

2.1.5   Tool Ease of Use

An automated tool requires new skills, so additional training is required. Plan for training and a learning curve!

Many tool vendors try to sell their tools by exaggerating the tools' *ease of use*. They deny that any learning curve is associated with the use of a new tool. Vendors are quick to point out that the tool can simply capture (record) test engineer keystrokes and (like magic) create a script in the background, which then can be reused for playback. In fact, efficient automation is not that simple. The test scripts that the tool generates automatically during recording must be modified manually, which requires tool scripting knowledge, so as to make the scripts robust, reusable, and maintainable. To be able to modify the scripts, the test engineer must be trained on the tool and the tool's built-in scripting language. Thus new training requirements and a learning curve can be expected with the use of any new tool.

2.1.6   Universal Application of Test Automation

As discussed earlier, automated testing represents an enhancement to manual testing, but it can't be expected that all of the tests on a project can be automated. For example, when an automated GUI test tool is first introduced, it is beneficial to conduct some compatibility tests on the target application to see whether the tool will be able to recognize all objects and third-party controls. Chapter 4 provides further discussion on compatibility testing.

The performance of compatibility tests is especially important for GUI test tools, because such tools have difficulty recognizing some custom-control features within the application. These features include the little calendars or spin controls that are incorporated into many applications, especially in Windows applications. These controls or widgets were once called VBXs, then became known as OCXs, and are now referred to as ActiveX controls in the Windows interface world. They are usually written by third parties, and most test tool manufacturers cannot keep up with the hundreds of clever controls churned out by the various companies.

A test tool might be compatible with all releases of Visual Basic and Power-Builder, for example, but if an incompatible third-party custom control is introduced into the application, the tool might not recognize the object on the screen. Perhaps most of the target application uses a third-party grid that the test tool does not recognize. The test engineer must then decide whether to automate this part of the application by finding a work-around solution or to test this control manually only. The incompatibility issues can be circumvented if the test engineer picks and evaluates the appropriate tool from the start that matches the project's needs, as noted in Chapter 3.

Other tests are physically impossible to automate, such as verifying a printout. The test engineer can automatically send a document to the printer, but then must verify the results by physically walking over to the printer to make sure that the document really printed. After all, the printer could have been off-line or out of paper.

Often associated with the idea that an automated test tool will immediately reduce the testing effort is the fallacy that such a tool can automate 100% of the test requirements of any given test effort. Given an endless number of permutations and combinations of system and user actions possible with *n*-tier (client/middle-layer/server) architecture and GUI-based applications, a test engineer does not have enough time to test every possibility.

Needless to say, the test team will not have enough time or resources to support 100% test automation of an entire application. As outlined earlier in this section, the complete testing of modern system applications has become an infinite task. It is not possible to test all inputs or all combinations and permutations of all inputs. Even on a moderately complex system, it is impossible to test exhaustively all paths. As a result, it is not feasible to approach the test effort for the entire application-under-test with the goal of testing 100% of the entire software application.

Another limiting factor is cost. Some tests can be more expensive to automate than to execute manually. A test that is executed only once is often not worth automating. For example, an end-of-year report for a health claim system might be run only once because of all the setup activity involved to generate it. As a result, it might not pay off to automate this specific test. When deciding which test procedures to automate, a test engineer must evaluate the value or payoff for investing the time in developing an automated script.

The test engineer should perform a careful analysis of the application when determining which test requirements warrant automation and which should be executed manually. When performing this analysis, the test engineer must also weed out redundant tests. This "manual versus automated test analysis" activity is further discussed in Chapter 7. The goal for test procedure coverage, using automated testing, is for each single test to exercise multiple items but to avoid duplication of tests.

2.1.7 One Hundred Percent Test Coverage

Even with automation, not everything can be tested. One major reason why testing has the potential to be an infinite task is that, to verify that no problems exist for a function, the function must be tested with all possible data—both valid and invalid. Automated testing may increase the breadth and depth of test coverage, yet there still will not be enough time or resources to perform a 100% exhaustive test.

It is impossible to perform a 100% test of all possible simple inputs to a system. The sheer volume of permutations and combinations is simply too staggering. Take, for example, the test of a function that handles verification of a user password. Each user on a computer system has a password, which is generally six to eight characters long, where each character is an uppercase letter or a digit. Each password must contain at least one digit. How many password character combinations are possible? According to Kenneth H. Rosen in *Discrete Mathematics and Its Application*, 2,684,483,063,360 possible variations of passwords exist. Even if it were possible to create a test procedure each minute or 60 test procedures per hour (that is, 480 test procedures per day), it would still take 155 years to prepare and execute a complete test. Therefore, not all possible inputs could be exercised during a test. With this type of rapid expansion, it would be nearly impossible to exercise all inputs; in fact, it has been proved to be impossible in general.

It is impossible to exhaustively test every combination of a system. Consider the test of the telephone system in North America. The format of the telephone numbers in North America is specified by a numbering plan. A telephone number consists of ten digits: a three-digit area code, a three-digit office code, and a four-digit station code. Because of signaling considerations, certain restrictions apply to some of these digits. To specify the allowable format, let X denote a digit that can take any of the values of 0 through 9 and let N denote a digit that can take any of the values of 2 through 9.

The formats of the three segments of a telephone number are NXX, NXX, and XXXX, respectively. How many different North American telephone numbers are possible under this plan? There are $8 \times 8 \times 10 = 640$ office codes with format NNX and $8 \times 10 \times 10 = 800$ with format NXX. There are also $10 \times 10 \times 10 \times 10 = 10{,}000$ station codes with format XXXX. Consequently, there are $800 \times 800 \times 10{,}000 = 6{,}400{,}000{,}000$ different numbers available. This number includes only valid numbers and inputs to the system; it does not even touch the invalid numbers that could be applied. Thus this example shows how it is impossible to test all combinations of input data for a system [1].

Clearly, testing is potentially an infinite task. In view of this possibility, test engineers often rely on random code reviews of critical modules. They may also rely on the testing process to discover defects early. Such test activities, which include requirement, design and code walkthroughs, support the process of defect prevention. (Defect prevention and detection technologies are discussed in detail in Chapter 4). Given the potential magnitude of any test, the test team needs to rely on test procedure design techniques, such as equivalence testing, that employ only representative data samples. (Test design techniques are described in Chapter 7).

2.2 | Benefits of Automated Testing

Automated testing can provide several benefits when it is implemented correctly and follows a rigorous process. The test engineer must evaluate whether the potential benefits fit the required improvement criteria and whether the pursuit of automated testing on the project is still a logical fit, given the organizational needs. Three significant automated test benefits (in combination with manual testing) have been identified: (1) production of a reliable system, (2) improvement of the quality of the test effort, and (3) reduction of the test effort and minimization of the schedule.

2.2.1   Production of a Reliable System

A strategic goal of the test effort is to find defects, thereby minimizing errors in the application so that the system runs as expected with very little downtime. Another major goal is to ensure that the system's performance requirements meet or exceed user expectations. To support these goals effectively, the test effort should be initiated during the development cycle's requirements definition phase, when requirements are developed and refined.

The use of automated testing can improve all areas of testing, including test procedure development, test execution, test results analysis, error status/correction monitoring, and report creation. It also supports all test phases including unit, integration, regression, system, user acceptance, performance, and stress and configuration testing, among others.

In all areas of the development life cycle, automated testing helps to build reliable systems, provided that automated test tools and methods are implemented correctly, and a defined testing process, such as the ATLM, is followed. Table 2.1 indicates the specific benefits that can be expected through the use of automated testing.

2.2.1.1   Improved Requirements Definition

As discussed previously, reliable and cost-effective software testing starts in the requirements phase, with the goal of building highly reliable systems. If requirements are unambiguous and consistently delineate all of the information that a test engineer needs in a testable form, the requirements are said to be test-ready or testable. Many tools on the market can facilitate the generation of testable requirements. Some tools allow the requirements to be written in a formal language such as LOTOS or Z [2] using a syntax-directed editor. Other tools allow for modeling requirements graphically. (Chapter 3 provides more details on the types of requirement tools available.)

Test-ready requirements minimize the test effort and cost. Requirements that are in test-ready condition help support the preparation of an efficient test design

---

Table 2.1   **Production of a Reliable System**

Improved requirements definition
Improved performance testing
Improved load/stress testing
Quality measurements and test optimization
Improved partnership with development team
Improved system development life cycle

and requirements to test design/test procedure traceability. This better traceability, in turn, provides the project team with greater assurance of test completeness. Refer to Appendix A for more information on test-ready requirements.

2.2.1.2   Improved Performance Testing

Performance data are no longer gathered with stopwatches. As recently as 1998, in one *Fortune* 100 company, performance testing was conducted while one test engineer sat with a stopwatch, timing the functionality that another test engineer was executing manually. This method of capturing performance measures is both labor-intensive and highly error-prone, and it does not allow for automatic repeatability. Today many *load-testing* tools are on the market that allow the test engineer to perform tests of the system functionality automatically, producing timing numbers and graphs and pinpointing the bottlenecks and thresholds of the system. A test engineer no longer needs to sit with a stopwatch in hand. Instead, he or she initiates a test script to capture the performance statistics automatically, leaving the test engineer now free to do more creative and intellectually challenging testing work.

In the past, a number of different computers and people would be required to execute a multitude of tests over and over again to produce statistically valid performance figures. New automated performance test tools allow the test engineer to take advantage of programs that read data from a file or table or that use tool-generated data, whether the information consists of one line of data or hundreds of lines. Still other programs can be developed or reused from test program libraries to support looping constructs and conditional statements.

The new generation of test tools enables the test engineer to run performance tests unattended, because they allow a time for the execution of the test to be set up in advance; a test script then kicks off automatically, without any manual intervention. Many automated performance test tools permit virtual user testing, in which the test engineer can simulate tens, hundreds, or even thousands of users executing various test scripts.

The objective of performance testing is to demonstrate that a system functions in accordance with its performance requirement specifications regarding acceptable response times, while processing the required transaction volumes on a production-size database. During performance testing, production loads are used to predict behavior and a controlled and measured load is used to measure response time. The analysis of performance test results helps support performance tuning.

2.2.1.3   Improved Stress Testing

A test tool that supports performance testing also supports stress testing. The difference between the two tests involves only how the tests are executed. Stress testing is the process of running client machines in high-volume scenarios to see when and where the application will *break* under the pressure. In stress testing, the system is subjected to extreme and maximum loads to find out whether and where the system breaks and to identify what breaks first. It is important to identify the weak points of the system. System requirements should define these thresholds and describe the system's response to an overload. Stress testing is useful for operating a system at its maximum design load to verify that it works properly. This type of testing also reveals whether the system behaves as specified when subjected to an overload.

It no longer takes ten or more test engineers to conduct stress testing. The automation of stress tests has benefits for all concerned. One story shared by a test engineer named Steve demonstrates this point. Steve was one of 20 test engineers supporting a large project. At the end of one week of testing, Steve's manager required that all 20 test engineers work on Saturday to support the stress testing effort. The manager emphasized that the whole test team needed to be present so that each test engineer could exercise the system at a high rate, which would "stress test" the system.

As the manager explained, each test engineer would execute the most complex functionality of the system at the same time. Steve and the other test engineers dutifully dragged themselves into work that Saturday morning. As each arrived at work, it quickly became apparent that the manager had omitted one small detail from the weekend plan. None of the employees had an access key for the building—and the facility did not have a security guard or magnetic access key readers. Each test engineer eventually turned around and went back home; the trip in to work that morning was a complete waste of time. As Steve put it, "I think that each one of us was personally being 'stress tested.'"

With an automated test tool, the test team does not need the extra resources and test engineers can often be spared from working after hours or on weekends. Likewise, managers can avoid paying overtime wages. With an automated *stress-testing* tool, the test engineer can instruct the tool when to execute a stress test, which tests to run, and how many users to simulate—all without user intervention.

It is expensive, difficult, inaccurate, and time-consuming to stress test an application adequately using purely manual methods. A large number of users and workstations are required to conduct the testing process. It is costly to dedicate sufficient resources to tests and difficult to orchestrate the necessary users and machines. A growing number of test tools provide an alternative to manual stress testing by simulating the interaction of many users with the system from a limited number of client workstations. Generally, the process begins by capturing user interactions with the application and the database server within a number of test scripts. The testing software then runs multiple instances of test scripts to simulate a large number of users.

Many automated test tools include a load simulator, which enables the test engineer to simulate hundreds or thousands of virtual users simultaneously working on the target application. No one need be present to kick off the tests or monitor them; timing can be set to specify when the script should be kicked off, and the test scripts can run unattended. Most such tools produce a test log output listing the results of the stress test. The tool can record any unexpected active window (such as an error dialog box), and test personnel can review the message contained in the unexpected window (such as an error message). An unexpected active window might arise, for example, when the test engineer records a test with window A open, but finds during script playback that window B is unexpectedly open as well.

Examples of stress testing include running a client application continuously for many hours or running a large number of different testing procedures to simulate a multiuser environment. Typical types of errors uncovered by stress testing include memory leakage, performance problems, locking problems, concurrency problems, excess consumption of system resources, and exhaustion of disk space.

2.2.1.4   Quality Measurements and Test Optimization

Automated testing will produce quality metrics and allow for test optimization. Its results can be later measured and analyzed. Indeed, the automated testing process itself can be measured and repeated. With a manual testing process, the steps taken during the first iteration of a test may not be the exact steps taken during the second iteration. As a result, it is difficult to produce any kind of compatible quality measurements with this approach. With automated testing, however, the testing steps are repeatable and measurable.

Test engineers' analysis of quality measurements supports the effort of optimizing tests, but only when tests are repeatable. As noted earlier, automation allows for repeatability of tests. For example, consider the situation where a test engineer manually executes a test and finds an error. The test engineer tries to recreate the test, but without any success. With an automated test, the script could have been played again and the test would have been both repeatable as well as measurable. The automated tool produces many metrics, usually creates a test log, and can accommodate automated metrics reporting.

Automated testing also supports optimization. For example, a test engineer can optimize a regression test suite by performing the following steps.

1.   Run the regression test set.
2.   If cases are discovered for which the regression test set ran acceptably, but errors surface later, the test procedures that uncovered those bugs in the regression test set can be identified.

3. By repeating these steps, the regression test suite of scripts is continuously optimized using quality measurements (in this case, the metric would be the amount and type of test procedure errors).

2.2.1.5 Improved Partnership with Development Team

When a test engineer named John was implementing automated testing at a *Fortune* 100 company, one of his many duties included mentoring other junior test engineers. John consulted or acted as a mentor for many project teams. On one project, he was asked to help a developer in a group with the use of an automated test tool. John installed the tool for the developer in approximately 15 minutes, and helped the developer begin a compatibility test between the automated test tool and the target application.

John gave the developer an overview of the major functionality of the tool, then started to conduct some compatibility tests. He observed that the tool could recognize some of the objects. Finally, the compatibility tests revealed that the automated test tool could not recognize one of the main third-party controls (widgets) used on each screen of the application under development. It was decided that the tool was not compatible with the target application. Later, the developer told John that he really appreciated John's support in learning about the tool. The developer shared a short story about his experience:

> I was working on this death-march (quote) project with a very tight schedule, when my boss walked over to me with the large box containing the XYZ automated test tool software and said, "here, use this automated test tool; it will speed up our testing." I put the box aside and was wondering when to get started using this tool, given the tight development schedule and the many other responsibilities for which I had been tasked. I asked myself, "when would I have the time to learn and understand the tool?"

The developer explained in great detail how he worried about trying to become proficient with the tool without any training, help, or guidance. He noted how John had unexpectedly entered into the picture and installed the tool for him, gave him an overview, showed him how it worked, and got him jump-started. It took John a fraction of time that it would have taken the developer to begin using the automated tool and to determine that the automated testing tool was incompatible with the target application. To the developer, John's dedication in helping him get on his feet with the tool was instrumental in fostering a close working relationship between the two.

Automated testing provides a convenient way for the test engineer and the application developer to work together. As the test engineer now needs to have similar software skills, more opportunities will arise for collaboration and for mutual respect. In the past, individuals who possessed only data entry skills often performed test program activities. In this type of environment, the developer did not view the person performing testing as a peer or confidant.

Because automated test tools are used to perform developmental testing, developers themselves will be working with these tools to carry out unit testing, memory leak testing, code coverage testing, user interface testing, and server testing. As a result, testers need to have the same qualifications—and the same career opportunities (remuneration, appreciation)—as developers. The respect between the application developer and the test engineer will continue to grow, and ideally the relationship will be viewed more as a partnership.

2.2.1.6   Improved System Development Life Cycle

Automated testing can support each phase of the system development life cycle. Today several automated test tools are available to support each phase of the development life cycle. For example, tools exist for the requirements definition phase that help produce test-ready requirements so as to minimize the test effort and cost of testing. Likewise, tools supporting the design phase, such as modeling tools, can record the requirements within use cases. Use cases represent user scenarios that exercise various combinations of system level (operational-oriented) requirements. These use cases have a defined starting point, a defined user (can be a person or an external system), a set of discrete steps, and a defined exit criteria.

Tools also exist for the programming phase, such as code checkers, metrics reporters, code instrumentors, and product-based test procedure generators. If requirement definition, software design, and test procedures have been prepared properly, application development may be the easiest activity of the bunch. Test execution will surely run more smoothly given these conditions.

Many other tools are available that can support the test effort, including performance test tools and capture/playback tools. The many different test tools contribute in one way or another to the overall system development life cycle and the final quality of the end product. Although each different tool has its purpose, it is not likely that all the tools have the same utility for a given project, nor is it likely that the organization will have every tool on hand.

2.2.2   Improvement of the Quality of the Test Effort

By using an automated test tool, the depth and breadth of testing can be increased. Specific benefits are outlined in Table 2.2.

2.2.2.1   Improved Build Verification Testing (Smoke Test)

The smoke test (build verification test) focuses on test automation of the system components that make up the most important functionality. Instead of repeatedly

Table 2.2   Improved Quality of the Test Effort

Improved build verification testing (smoke testing)

Improved regression testing

Improved multiplatform compatibility testing

Improved software compatibility testing

Improved execution of mundane tests

Improved focus on advanced test issues

Execution of tests that manual testing can't accomplish

Ability to reproduce software defects

Enhancement of business expertise

After-hours testing

retesting everything manually whenever a new software build is received, a test engineer plays back the smoke test, verifying that the major functionality of the system still exists. An automated test tool allows the test engineer to record the manual test steps that would usually be followed in software build/version verification. By invoking the use of an automated test tool, tests can be performed that confirm the presence of all major functionality, before any unnecessary manual tests are performed.

The automated test tool supports the smoke test by allowing the test engineer to play back the script. The script will automatically walk through each step that the test engineer would otherwise have performed manually, again reducing test effort. During the time that the script replays, the test engineer can concentrate on other testing issues, thereby enhancing the capabilities of the entire test team.

Smoke testing ensures that no effort is wasted in trying to test an incomplete build. At one large company, a test engineer named Mary Ellen had the following experience performing test on a new software version/build:

1. The business users were called to come from the fifth floor to the fourth-floor testing room to verify that specific problem reports had been fixed in the new software build. The business users were often asked to drop what they were doing to perform a regression test on a new version/build. Sometimes they would start testing and immediately find a *show-stopper* bug (a bug that does not allow the system to be exercised any further). They would report the error and then return upstairs, because they couldn't continue testing until the fix was incorporated into the build. Just finding one bug wasted at least an hour of time for five people.

2. During manual test execution, a newly introduced defect to previously working functionality might not be found until hours into the regression testing cycle. As a result, even more time was wasted, as the entire new build had to be redone and then retested. That case was observed often, because test personnel would become complacent, thinking, "I've tested this functionality the last time already and it worked fine; instead, I will concentrate on the things that didn't work last time."

With a smoke test, when a developer has created a new software version or build, the developer or independent test engineer merely replays the test to verify that the major functionality, which worked in the previous version of code, still works with the latest release. Configuration management personnel can also benefit by using this test to verify that all versions of the build have been checked out correctly. The configuration management specialist also can immediately ascertain whether a version of the build or part of the build is missing. Thus a smoke test can save developers, configuration management personnel, business users, and test engineers much valuable time.

2.2.2.2   Improved Regression Testing

A regression test is a test or set of tests that is executed on a baselined system or product (baselined in a configuration management system) when a part of the total system product environment has been modified. The objective is to verify that the functions provided by the modified system or product match the specifications and that no unintended change in operational functions has been made. An automated test tool provides for simplified regression testing. Automated regression testing can verify in an expedient manner that no new bugs were introduced into a new build. Experience shows that modifying an existing program is a more error-prone process (in terms of errors per statements written) than writing a new program [3].

Regression testing should occur after each release of a previously tested application. The smoke test described in Section 2.2.2.1 is a smaller, rapid regression test of major high-level functionality. Regression testing expands on the smoke test to include all existing functionality that has already been proved viable. The regression test suite represents a subset of the overall test procedures that exercise the basic functionality of the application. It may include test procedures that have the highest probability of detecting the most errors. This type of testing should be performed via an automated tool because it is usually lengthy and tedious and thus prone to human error.

Executing a test shell or wrapper function containing a complete set of system test scripts is an example of the efficient use of automated scripts during regression testing. A test shell is a test procedure that calls or groups several test procedures, then plays them back in a specific, predefined sequence. Such a procedure allows the test engineer to create and execute a comprehensive test suite and subsequently store the results of the test in a single log output.

2.2.2.3   Improved Multiplatform Compatibility Testing

Another example of the savings attributable to the use of automated testing is the reuse of test scripts to support testing from one platform (hardware configuration) to another. Changes in computer hardware, network versions, and operating systems can cause unexpected compatibility problems with the existing configuration. Prior to a production rollout of a new application to a large number of users, the execution of automated test scripts can provide a clean method of ensuring that these changes did not adversely affect current applications and operating environments.

Prior to the advent of automated testing, a test engineer would have to repeat each manual test required for a Windows 95 environment step by step when testing in a Windows NT environment, for example. Now when the test engineer creates the test scripts for an application-under-test on a Windows 95 platform, he or she can simply execute the same test scripts on the Windows NT platform, using multiplatform-compatible tools, such as Rational's TestStudio or AutoScriptor Inferno. (Refer to Appendix B for more information on these tools.)

2.2.2.4   Improved Software Configuration Testing

The same principle that drives multiplatform compatibility testing applies to software configuration testing. Software changes (such as upgrades or the implementation of a new version) can cause unexpected compatibility problems with existing software. The execution of automated test scripts can provide a clean method of ensuring that these software changes did not adversely affect current applications and operating environments.

2.2.2.5   Improved Execution of Mundane Tests

An automated test tool will eliminate the monotony of repetitious testing. Mundane repetitive tests are the culprits that allow many errors to escape detection. A test engineer may get tired of testing the same monotonous steps over and over again. One test engineer named Jo Ann was responsible for performing year 2000 testing using an automated test tool. Jo Ann's test scripts put in hundreds of dates on as many as 50 screens, with various cycle dates, and with some having to be performed repeatedly. The only difference was that during one cycle Jo Ann would add rows of data to include the dates. During another cycle, she would delete the data; in another, she would perform an update operation. In addition, the system date had to be reset to accommodate high-risk year 2000 dates.

The same steps were repeated over and over again, with the only change from one to the other being the kind of operation (add, delete, update) that was being performed. An end user performing acceptance testing would have become tired very quickly when executing these mundane and repetitive tests and might omit some, hoping that the system would execute properly. An important testing issue such as year 2000 verification can't be short-circuited, however. The tests were therefore automated in Jo Ann's case. This instance is another good example when automation pays off, because a test script does not care whether it has to execute the same monotonous steps over and over again and can automatically validate the results.

2.2.2.6 Improved Focus on Advanced Test Issues

Automated testing allows for simple repeatability of tests. A significant amount of testing is conducted on the basic user interface operations of an application. When the application is sufficiently operable, test engineers can proceed to test business logic in the application and other behavior. With both manual and automated regression testing, the test teams repeatedly expend effort in redoing the same basic operability tests. For example, with each new release, the test team would need to verify that everything that worked in the previous version still works in the latest product.

Besides delaying other testing, the tedium of these tests exacts a very high toll on manual testers. Manual testing can become stalled due to the repetition of these tests, at the expense of progress on other required tests. Automated testing presents the opportunity to move on more quickly and to perform a more comprehensive test within the schedule allowed. That is, automatic creation of user interface operability tests gets these tests out of the way rapidly. It also frees up test resources, allowing test teams to turn their creativity and effort to more complicated problems and concerns.

2.2.2.7 Execution of Tests That Manual Testing Can't Accomplish

Software systems and products are becoming more complex, and sometimes manual testing is not capable of supporting all desired tests. As discussed in the introduction to this section, many kinds of testing analysis simply cannot be performed manually today, such as decision coverage analysis or cyclomatic complexity metrics collection. Decision coverage analysis verifies that every point of entry and exit in the program has been invoked at least once and that every decision in the program has taken on all possible outcomes at least once [4]. Cyclomatic complexity, which is derived from an analysis of potential paths through the source code, was originally published by Tom McCabe and is now part of the IEEE *Standard Dictionary of Measures to Produce Reliable Software*. It would require many man-hours to produce the cyclomatic complexity of the code for any large application. In addition, manual test methods employed to perform memory leakage tests would be nearly impossible.

Today, tools on the market can test that the application's Web links are up and running in a matter of seconds. Performing these tests manually would require many hours or days.

2.2.2.8   Ability to Reproduce Software Defects

How many times has a test engineer, in the course of performing manual tests, uncovered a defect, only to discover that he or she cannot recall the steps exercised that led to the error? Automated testing eliminates this problem. With an automated test tool, the manual steps taken to create a test are recorded and stored in a test script. The script will play back the exact same sequence of steps that were initially performed. To simplify matters even further, the test engineer can inform the appropriate developer about the defect, and the developer has the option of playing back the script to experience firsthand the sequence of events that produced the software bug.

2.2.2.9   Enhancement of Business Expertise

Many test managers have probably experienced a situation where the one resident functional expert on the test team is absent from the project for a week during a critical time of testing. A test engineer named Bill went through one such dilemma. Bill was shocked to learn one day that the primary business area expert designated to support the test was on vacation. Clearly, communication among project members was a problem. For many areas of the target application, only the business area expert had the requisite knowledge. Fortunately for Bill and the rest of the test team, the business area expert had scripted all of the business functionality of his expertise into automated test scripts.

Another business user was assigned to replace the one who had left on vacation. This business area expert, however, was not equally familiar with the application. Nonetheless, the new business user was able to play back the business test scripts that the expert had created. The use of these test scripts allowed the test team to verify that the original functionality still behaved in the correct manner. It also prevented the test team from worrying about the fact that the resident expert had left for a week to the sunny beaches of Hawaii. At the same time, the new business user learned more about the "other side" of the business functionality of the application-under-test by watching the script play back the exact sequence of steps required to exercise the functionality.

2.2.2.10   After-Hours Testing

As noted previously, automated testing allows for simple repeatability of tests. As most tools allow scripts to be set up to kick off at any specified time, automated testing allows for after-hours testing without any user interaction. The test engineer can set up a test script program in the morning, for example, to be initiated automatically by the automated test tool at 11 P.M., while the test team is at home sound asleep. When the test team returns to work the next day, it can review the test script output (log) and conduct analysis.

Another convenient time for kicking off a script is when the test engineer goes to lunch or attends a meeting, or just before he or she departs for home at the end of the work day. Initiating tests at these times makes maximum use of the test lab and time.

2.2.3   Reduction of Test Effort and Minimization of Schedule

As outlined in Section 2.1, a test team may not immediately experience an immediate or huge reduction in the testing effort. Initially, it may even see an increase in effort using automated test tools in some ways because of the need to carry out setup tasks, as explained in Section 2.1. While the testing effort will likely increase at first, a payback on test tool investment will appear after the first iteration of the implementation of an automated test tool, due to improved productivity of the test team. The use of an automated test tool can minimize both the test effort and the schedule. The case study at the end of this section entitled "Value of Test Automation Measurement" provides more details on how the test effort may be reduced through the use of test automation. The specific benefits that are associated with the more efficient testing are described here.

A benchmark comparison conducted by the Quality Assurance Institute analyzed the specific difference in effort, measured in man-hours, to perform testing using manual methods as compared with using automated test tools. The study showed that the total test effort using automated testing consumed only 25% of the number of man-hours required to perform testing using manual methods [5].

Test effort reduction perhaps has the biggest impact on shortening the project schedule during the test execution phase. Activities during this phase typically include test execution, test result analysis, error correction, and test reporting. The benchmark study showed that manual testing required nearly seven times more effort than automated testing.

Table 2.3 gives the results of this benchmark comparison of manual and automated testing effort for various test steps, as conducted by the Quality Assurance Institute in November 1995. The testing involved 1,750 test procedures and 700 errors. The figures in Table 2.3 reflect an overall 75% reduction in test effort achieved through the benefits of test automation.

Test Plan Development—Test Effort Increase.   Before the decision is made to introduce an automated test tool, many facets of the testing process must be considered.

Table 2.3   Manual Versus Automated Testing

Test Steps	Manual Testing (hours)	Automated Testing (hours)	Percentage Improvement with Tools
Test plan development	32	40	–25%
Test procedure development	262	117	55%
Test execution	466	23	95%
Test result analysis	117	58	50%
Error status/correction monitoring	117	23	80%
Report creation	96	16	83%
Total duration	1090	277	75%

A review of the planned application-under-test (AUT) requirements should be conducted to determine whether the AUT is compatible with the test tool. The availability of sample data to support automated test needs to be confirmed. The kinds and variations of data required should be outlined, and a plan should be developed for obtaining and/or developing sample data. For scripts to be reusable, test design and development standards must be defined and followed. The modularity and reuse of test scripts needs to be given thought and consideration. Automated testing therefore necessitates its own kind of development effort, complete with its own mini-development life cycle. The planning required to support the automated test development life cycle, operating in parallel with an application development effort, has the effect of adding to the test planning effort. For further details on test planning, see Chapter 6.

Test Procedure Development—Test Effort Decrease.   In the past, the development of test procedures was a slow, expensive, and labor-intensive process. When a software requirement or a software module changed, a test engineer often had to redevelop existing test procedures and create new test procedures from scratch. Today's automated test tools, however, allow for the selection and execution of a specific test procedure with the click of an icon. With modern automated test procedure (case) generators (see Chapter 3 for more details), test procedure creation and revision time is greatly reduced relative to manual test methods, with some test procedure creation and revision taking only a few seconds. The use of test data generation tools (also described in Chapter 3) contributes to the reduction of the test effort.

Test Execution—Test Effort/Schedule Decrease.   Manual performance of test execution is labor-intensive and error-prone. A test tool allows test scripts to be played back at execution time with minimal manual interference. With the proper setup and in the ideal world, the test engineer simply kicks off the script and the tool executes unattended. The tests can be performed as many times as necessary and can be set up to kick off at a specified time and run overnight, if necessary. This unattended playback capability allows the test engineer to focus on other, higher-priority tasks.

Test Results Analysis—Test Effort/Schedule Decrease. Automated test tools generally include some kind of test result report mechanism and are capable of maintaining test log information. Some tools produce color-coded results, where green output might indicate that the test passed, while red output indicates that the test failed. Most tools can distinguish between a passed or failed test. This kind of test log output improves the ease of test analysis. Most tools also allow for comparison of the failed data to the original data, pointing out the differences automatically, again supporting the ease of test output analysis.

Error Status/Correction Monitoring—Test Effort/Schedule Decrease. Some automated tools on the market allow for automatic documentation of defects with minimal manual intervention after a test script has discovered a defect. The information documented in this way might include the identification of the script that produced the defect/error, identification of the test cycle that was being run, a description of the defect/error, and the date/time that the error occurred. For example, the tool TestStudio allows for creation of the defect report as soon as a script has detected an error, by simply selecting to generate a defect. The defect can then be automatically and dynamically linked to the test requirement, allowing for simplified metrics collection.

Report Creation—Test Effort/Schedule Decrease. Many automated test tools have built-in report writers, which allow the user to create and customize reports tailored to a specific need. Even those test tools that do not include built-in report writers might allow for import or export of relevant data in a desired format, making it a simple task to integrate the test tool output data with databases that support report creation.

Another benefit concerns the use of automated test tools to support the test engineer in the performance of test methods and techniques that previously had been performed manually. As noted earlier, automated test tools cannot completely eliminate the need to perform manual tests. Some test activities still must be performed manually by the test engineer. For example, many test setup activities must be conducted in a manual fashion. As a result, both manual test expertise and expertise in the use of automated test tools are necessary to execute a complete test and produce a system that meets the requirements of the end user. Automated test tools, therefore, cannot be viewed as a panacea for all test issues and concerns.

Case Study
Value of Test Automation Measurement

The example of test automation value outlined here reflects a research effort conducted in Europe to collect test automation measurements with the purpose of studying the benefits of test automation versus manual test methods. The study was conducted by the company imbus GmbH, and was sponsored by the European Commission [6]. The European Systems and Software Initiative (ESSI) Initiative of the European Commission promoted the imbus Process Improvement Experiment (PIE) of Automated Testing of Graphical User Interfaces (PIE No. 24306). The PIE consisted of two parts: the baseline project and the experiment.

The *baseline project* refers to the project for which the companies' software development (among other system development activities) was performed. It consisted of the development of an integrated PC software tool (called RBT) used for maintaining radio base station equipment. This application provided a graphical user interface for commissioning, parameter definition, hardware diagnostics, software downloading, equipment database creation, and in-field and off-line diagnostics of multiple types of base stations for GSM radio communication, including a full-graphics editor for equipment definition.

In the *experiment* itself, a new method of conducting tests was performed—automated testing. To find out whether this new method represented an improvement, its performance was compared with that of the old method—manual testing, which was used in addition to automated testing in parallel to the baseline project.

The goal of this project was to optimize the GUI testing process and to heighten the degree of test automation by using applicable tools. This project began in March of 1997 and concluded in March 1998. To obtain performance figures for comparison, the researchers conducted tests using manual methods in one example and tests using automated methods in a second example. The test requirements, which were defined in the test specification, were executed manually by a test engineer in the baseline project. Simultaneously, the PIE team used the test requirements to develop automated test procedures and then executed tests and regression tests using the automated tool, WinRunner.

To determine how much more economical automated GUI testing is compared to manual testing, the study measured and compared the expenditures for both methods during the PIE. The primary question that the study addressed centered on the number of times that a specific test had to be repeated before automated testing became less expensive than manual testing. The results of the process improvement experiment are highlighted in Table 2.4.

Table 2.4 Break-Even Point of GUI Test Automation

Test	Preparation V Manual	Preparation V Automated	Execution D Manual	Execution D Automated	N	Expenditure E for n Automated Tests 1	5	10	20
Test 1	16	56	24	1	1.74	143%	45%	26%	15%
Test 2	10	14	2	0.1	2.11	118%	73%	50%	32%
Test 3	10	16	4.5	0.2	1.40	112%	52%	33%	20%
Test 4	20	28	1.5	0.2	6.15	131%	105%	86%	64%
Test 5	10	15	1	0.1	5.56	137%	103%	80%	57%
Test 6	10	15	1.5	0.1	3.57	131%	89%	64%	43%
Test 7	10	11.5	0.75	0.1	2.31	108%	87%	71%	54%
Test 8	10	11.5	0.5	0.1	3.75	110%	96%	83%	68%
Test 9	10	14	3	0.1	1.38	108%	58%	38%	23%
Test 10	10	10.6	0.5	0.1	1.50	102%	89%	77%	63%
Total	116	191.6	39.25	2.1	2.03	125%	65%	42%	26%

Test *i:* Tests specified within baseline projects test specification.

V_m: Expenditure for test specification.

V_a: Expenditure for test specification + implementation.

D_m: Expenditure for single, manual test execution.

D_a: Expenditure for test interpretation after automated testing. The time for the test process was not counted because it was executed without supervision via a CR tool.

V and D are given in terms of hours of work.

$E_n = A_a/A_m = (V_a + n{*}D_a)/(V_m + n{*}D_m)$

N = "break-even" point

The test requirements specification of "Testing Software Download," where "Software Download" was one feature of the product accessible by the "DOWN-LOAD" button, took 10 hours to prepare (*V* Manual in the Test 2 row in Table 2.4). Programming these tests took 4 additional hours, which resulted in a complete test automation preparation time (*V* Automated) of 14 hours (see the Test 2 results). Manual execution of these tests then took 2 hours (*D* Manual) as opposed to 0.1 hour (*D* Automated), as the tester needed to inspect and analyze the test tools reports generated by the automated test run. Taking these single-test-run measurements, one can calculate a projection of the expenditure that would be needed for retesting 5, 10, or 20 times. In our example, 5 automated test runs will decrease the testing expenditure compared with manual testing by the following factor:

$$E_5 = A_a / A_m$$
$$= (V_a + 5*D_a) / (V_m + 5*D_m)$$
$$= (14 + 5*0.1) / (10 + 5*2)$$
$$= 14.5/20 = 0.725 = 73\%$$

In Table 2.4, this break-even point in general is represented by the N factor, in accordance with the equation $E_n = A_a/A_m = 100\%$, where E is relative expenditure and A is absolute expenditure. (A_a = absolute automated expenditure; A_m = absolute manual expenditure) and N is the "break-even" point, V is preparation, and D is execution.

The measurements undertaken within these experiments show that a break-even point can already be attained by the second regression test cycle (n_{total} = 2.03). This break-even, however, has two prerequisites: (1) the tests must run completely without human interaction (for example, as overnight test runs), and (2) no further test script modifications are necessary to rerun the tests in later releases of the product. As already mentioned, this prerequisite is not easy to achieve. If the purchase of a tool is followed by the immediate initiation of test procedure capturing, testing costs will increase to 125% (see total E_1) or more—for example, 150% of manual testing costs within each test cycle.

The reason is that the additional test preparation costs (191/116 = 165%; totals from the Preparation V column) will not be paid back (the prerequisite given earlier). The poor initial test programming forces test script maintenance with each repeated test run. On the other hand, if the test team establishes a complete framework for GUI test automation (where the CR tool is a cornerstone and not the complete solution), then a decrease of cost down to about 40% for a typical product test cycle (E_{10}) is realistic.

2.3 | Acquiring Management Support

Whenever an organization tries to adopt a new technology, it faces a significant effort to determine how to apply the technology to its needs. Even with completed training, organizations wrestle with time-consuming false starts before they become adept with the new technology. For the test team interested in implementing automated test tools, the challenge is how to make the best case for implementation of a new test automation technology to the management team.

Test engineers need to influence management's expectations for the use of automated testing on projects. They can help to manage these expectations by forwarding helpful information to the management staff. Bringing up test tool issues during strategy and planning meetings can also help develop a better understanding of test tool capabilities among everyone involved on a project or within the organization. For example, a test engineer might develop training material on the subject of automated testing and advocate to management that a seminar be scheduled to train staff members.

The first step in moving toward a decision to automate testing on a project requires that the test team influence management's understanding of the appropriate application of this technology for the specific need at hand. The test team, for example, needs to check whether management is cost-adverse and would be unwilling to accept the estimated cost of automated test tools for a particular effort. If so, test personnel need to convince management about the potential return on investment by conducting cost-benefit analysis.

In some instances, management is willing to invest in an automated test tool, but is not able or willing to staff a test team with individuals having the proper software skill level or provide for adequate test tool training. The test team will then need to point out the risks involved and may need to reconsider a recommendation to automate testing.

Assuming that management has appropriate expectations on the use and execution of automated testing, then the test team can move on to the next step in the decision to automate test, which pertains to defining the objectives of this type of testing. What does the test team intend to accomplish, and which need will be met, by using automated testing tools?

Management also needs to be made aware of the additional cost involved when introducing a new tool—not only in terms of the tool purchase itself, but also the initial schedule/cost increase, additional training costs, and costs for enhancing an existing testing process or new testing process implementation.

Test automation represents a highly flexible technology, and one that provides several ways to accomplish an objective. Use of this technology requires new ways of thinking, which amplifies the problem of test tool implementation. Many organizations can readily come up with examples of technology that failed to deliver on its potential because of the difficulty of overcoming the "now what?" syndrome. The potential obstacles that organizations must overcome when adopting automated test systems include the following:

- Finding and hiring test tool experts
- Using the correct tool for the task at hand
- Developing and implementing an automated testing process, which includes developing automated test design and development standards
- Analyzing various applications to determine which are best suited for automation

- Analyzing the test requirements to determine which are suitable for automation
- Training the test team on the automated testing process, including automated test design, development, and execution
- Dealing with the initial increase in schedule and cost

2.3.1 Test Tool Proposal

As a test engineer for a new project, you will have followed the structured approach outlined in the previous sections to obtain several results. You will have aligned management expectations to be consistent with the actual potential and impact of automated test on the project. Analyses associated with the automated test decision process will have been performed, and you will have worked through each of the decision points (quality gates). You also will need to gain an understanding of the types of tools available to determine which ones match the testing needs (see Section 3.2, which covers testing life-cycle support tools). The next step involves the development of a test tool proposal to present to project management. Management must support the decision to bring in a test tool by providing a tangible commitment to its use. The test tool proposal needs to convince management that a positive cost benefit is associated with the purchase of an automated test tool.

The test tool proposal effort is aimed at persuading management to release funds to support automated test tool research and procurement, as well as test tool training and implementation. The proposal may also serve the long-range budget planning requirements of the organization. Typically, organizations forecast budget requirements for one or more years out from the present fiscal year. As a result, funds such as those needed to support the procurement of automated test tools and training on such tools can be factored into the budget process early in the game.

The development of a test tool proposal helps to outline in detail the cost of test tool procurement and training requirements. The proposal also documents plan phases, where test tool licenses are procured incrementally over a period of time. In addition, it may help document the need for a phased buildup of a test engineering staff as well as the desired skills sought for the bolstered test team.

The test engineer needs to ascertain whether sufficient funding has been allocated within the organization's budget for the purchase of software development support tools. Although funding may not be set aside specifically for automated test tools, perhaps management wants the test team to provide a proposal (or plan) that outlines the organization's test tool investment requirements. Often it is the test team's responsibility to define the test tool requirements of the organization and provide an associated cost estimate.

The test tool proposal should identify the benefits and give an idea of the features of the proposed automated test tool or tools. It should indicate the potential evaluation domain that will include the best software applications on which to exercise the test tool. When identifying these target applications, it is important to review the associated development schedules to ensure that they provide adequate time for the introduction of one or more automated test tools. Chapter 3 discusses pilot/evaluation domain selection criteria.

It is also important to verify that the associated project teams have the requisite skills to successfully utilize the automated test tool. Where skills are insufficient, the possibility of training must be examined. Most importantly, the team should follow the automated test tool introduction process discussed in Chapter 4.

In short, resource commitment from management is necessary to procure and introduce an automated test tool and successfully use the tool. Eventually, the test engineer will need to develop a budget that includes reasonable and accurate estimates for hardware and software procurement, personnel training, and other acquisition and administration costs. Chapter 3 helps the test team further define the features of the tool, and Chapter 5 helps the team define its roles and responsibilities. To win management backing for the resources needed, the test tool proposal should ideally contain the elements depicted in Table 2.5.

2.3.1.1 Estimated Improvement Opportunities

At the end of the test life cycle, the test team needs to conduct a test program review (as discussed in detail in Chapter 9). Through an organizational needs analysis or the review of lessons learned, it may become apparent to the organization that a need exists for the introduction of automated test tools. In other situations, a test team may turn to automated testing after reviewing industry literature that highlights its potential advantages. In this case, it is especially important to identify a

Table 2.5   Test Tool Proposal

Estimated improvement opportunities
Approach for selecting the correct tool
Tool cost range
Additional time to introduce tool
Tool expertise
Tool training cost
Tool evaluation domain
Tool rollout process

measure that shows the potential range of gain (hours saved) through the implementation of a particular automated tool. Sometimes an automated tool sounds like the perfect solution to a problem, but further analysis fails to reveal a specific gain. It is often beneficial to implement the suggested changes via a small prototype/pilot, thereby allowing the test team to make a valid estimate of suggested corrective action/improvement gains.

Table 2.6 provides an example of a simplified improvement table, produced as a result of an automated testing capability research. The third column labeled "Gain M" reflects gains in productivity achieved through the use of manual test methods, while the column labeled "Gain A" reflects gains in productivity achieved through the use of automated test methods. This table depicts productivity gain estimates, which are expressed in terms of percentage of test effort saved through the application of an automated test tool.

The organization may require one or more automated test tools, with each test tool having its own features and strengths. These tools may support unique test interests and have special niche values. This consideration can be especially important when the type of test supported is of special interest to the end user or when the type of test has particular value because of the type of system or application being supported. Management needs to be well aware of the functionality and value of each test tool. A list of tool benefits needs to be provided within the proposal, as discussed in Section 2.2.

2.3.1.2 Criteria for Selecting the Correct Tool

The return on investment obtained by using an automated test tool largely depends on the appropriate selection of a test tool. Automated test tools can vary from ones having simple functionality to those offering complex functionality, and their performance can vary from mediocre to excellent. A test tool with only minimal functionality will often cost less than a tool with extensive functionality. The challenge for the test engineer is to select the best test tool for the organization and/or the particular test effort and to understand what types of tools are available that could meet these needs. For example, a requirements management tool such as DOORS can also be employed as a test management tool, even though DOORS is not advertised as such. With regard to selecting a test tool, the test engineer needs to outline the most important criteria for tool selection.

The criteria definition guidelines given here are provided for the purpose of supporting budget planning; they are covered in detail within Section 3.1:

- Gather third-party input from management, staff, and customers regarding tool needs.
- Select tool criteria to reflect the organization's system engineering environment.

Table 2.6   Gain Estimates

Test Activity	Current Method	Gain M	Use of Tool A	Gain A	Basis of Estimate for Gain A
Integration of testing tool with requirements management tool	Excel spread-sheet	0	Tool is integrated with requirements management tool and allows for auto-mated traceability between test require-ments and business requirements	30%	Estimated time usually expended in manually creating and maintaining a traceability matrix
Integration of testing tool with configuration management tools	Manual (using XYZ CM tool)	0	Tool is not integrated with CM tool	5%	Estimated time usually spent trying to resolve compat-ibility issues between testing products and the CM tool
Preparation of test procedures	Manual	0	Tool allows for automated test procedure generation based on code	20%	Estimated time saved because tool automatically creates test procedures (it is understood that additional manual test procedures have to be created)
Test execution	Manual	0	Tool allows for recording/playback of test scripts, includ-ing automatic success/failure reporting with traceability to test requirements	60%	Estimated time saved as gathered from literature
Preparation of test data	Manual	0	Tool can generate test data	10%	Estimated time saved as gathered from literature
Stress/load testing	Manual	0	Tool allows for virtual user stress/load testing	80%	Estimated time saved by not con-ducting stress and load testing manually
Defect tracking	Home-grown Access database	0	Tool is integrated with defect tracking tool	20%	Estimated time saved because tool allows for automatic generation of defects, once a defect has been found

- Specify tool criteria based on long-term investment assumptions.
- Ensure that the tool will be usable in many testing phases.

It is important to point out in the proposal that determining the tool requirements and researching and evaluating the various tools will require personnel resources, time, and money.

2.3.1.3   Tool Cost Estimate

After describing the benefits of the proposed automated test tools, it is necessary to estimate their cost. It may be necessary to outline a phased implementation of the test tools so that costs can be spread over a period of time. For larger purchases, pricing discounts may be available. A good resource for obtaining tool feature and cost information quickly is the World Wide Web.

Once the test team has identified the prospective cost for an initial automated test tool purchase, it is valuable to perform a quick mental evaluation about whether this cost is in line with management's expectations. Recall that, in the steps described in Section 2.1, the test team did some investigative research to ascertain and help shape management expectations. Did management·express a tolerable range for cost at that stage? Does the estimate for an initial tool purchase lie within this range? Again, a plan for the phased implementation of the test tools may need to be modified to align the short-term implementation strategy with the budget reality. Another option is to make a case for augmenting the budget so as to align the budget reality with the test performance requirements of the organization. A cost-benefit analysis should be conducted, with the test team ensuring that funding is available to support this analysis.

Providing that management expectations, tool purchase budgets, and test tool costs are consistent, then it is beneficial to organize a demonstration of the proposed test tool by the vendor for management, complete with a presentation that reiterates the tool's benefits to the organization. The presentation may also need to revisit tool cost. Costs associated with the implementation of the test tool may include costs necessary to upgrade hardware to meet performance requirements, any necessary software maintenance agreements, hotline support, and requirements for tool training.

If, at the test tool proposal stage, the test team members are unsure of which specific tool they prefer, it may be necessary to estimate tool costs by providing a cost range for each kind of automated test tool of interest. If the test team has identified a very capable test tool that meets the organization's requirements but is significantly more costly than the planned budget allows, several options are available. First, the test team could select a less expensive tool that supports test requirements adequately for the near term. Second, it could outline the cost savings or performance enhancing benefits in a way that convinces management that the tool is worth the upfront investment. Third, it could scale down the implementation of the test tool and plan for additional implementation during the next budget period.

2.3.1.4 Additional Time to Introduce Tool

A major concern when selecting a test tool focuses on its impact and fit with the project schedule. Will there be enough time for the necessary people to learn the tool within the constraints of the schedule? If there isn't sufficient time to support implementation of a sophisticated tool, can the team deploy an easy-to-use tool? The scope of automated testing might be reduced, but the effort might nevertheless benefit from the use of this type of tool. This approach may not be advisable in instances where money for software support tools is difficult to obtain. Spending the money for a less expensive, easy-to-use tool that offers minimal functionality may put at risk the test team's ability to follow up later with the procurement of a tool that better supports the organization's long-term outlook.

Where the project schedule does not include enough time for introducing an appropriate test tool for the organization, it may be advisable to decide against implementing an automated testing tool. By postponing the introduction of a test tool until a more opportune time, the test team may avoid the risk of applying the right tool on the wrong project or selecting the wrong tool for the organization. In either case, the test tool likely will not be received well, and those who might otherwise become champions for the use of automated test tools may instead turn into their biggest opponents.

Provided the project schedule permits the introduction of an appropriate test tool for the organization, then the test team needs to ensure that the tool is launched in a manner that leads to its adoption. After all, if no one in the organization uses the tool, the effort to obtain and incorporate it will have been wasted.

2.3.1.5 Tool Expertise

When introducing automated testing tools, many believe—incorrectly—that the test team skill set does not need to include technical skills. In fact, the test team skill profile needs to include personnel with technical expertise on the operating system, database management system, network software, hardware device drivers, and development support software, such as configuration and requirements management tools. In addition to these skills, a proficiency in the scripting language of the automated test tool is necessary.

Some members of the test team should have a technical or software development background, ensuring that the features of the automated tool will be exercised sufficiently. Likewise, the test team needs to maintain its manual testing expertise.

When the test team consists of nontechnical individuals, it may need to obtain commitment from management to augment the test group with additional test tool experts. For example, the team might hire new personnel, borrow personnel from other projects, or use outside consultants. If enough lead time exists, a software professional might be retained to become more proficient in the use of the tool. This individual may then be able to provide tool leadership to others on the test team. (Chapter 5 further discusses test team composition strategies.)

The introduction of a new test tool to the project or organization adds short-term complexity and overhead. Additional effort is expended to support tool evaluation and implementation, as well as to conduct test planning and development. The appropriate test team composition may help mitigate performance risk, especially when the team is populated with individuals who have a strong technical background.

2.3.1.6   Tool Training Cost

The increased use of automated test tools on software application efforts has subsequently reduced the amount of manual test activity. Even though the know-how and analytical skills that pertain to manual testing will always be needed on the test effort, expertise with automated test tools and test automation must be developed. Test engineers, as a result, need to transition their skill set to include more technical skills and more experience with automated test tools. Some test engineers may take the initiative on their own to obtain additional technical training. These individuals may also volunteer their time on projects involving automated test tools so as to obtain further experience with such tools.

Managers supporting project planning or project start-up for an effort involving automated testing must carefully consider the test team's composition. Do members of the test team need refresher training on the pertinent automated test tools? Do some members of the team lack automated test experience all together?

The test tool proposal should specify the cost of training required to successfully implement the automated test tool. The test team, in turn, needs to identify each individual who requires training and specify the kind of training necessary. Such training may include refresher courses on a specific test tool, introductory training on a specific tool for the individual who does not have experience with it, or more advanced test design and development training that could have application to a wide variety of test tools.

Once a shopping list of training needs has been developed, the test team should identify organizations that offer the desired training. Cost estimates from several sources should be obtained for each type of training required. Organizations that offer such training include test tool manufacturers and test consulting organizations.

Test teams may also wish to consider the temporary use of test consultants as mentors on the project. Such consultants may be able to provide helpful guidance to the members of the test team in areas such as test design and test development. Note, however, that the test team should not depend entirely upon consultants for the execution of the test program. If it does, once the consultants leave and are no longer available to provide support, test program repeatability on behalf of the remaining test organization will decrease and automated script maintenance could become difficult.

The automated test tool proposal should list the costs associated with various sources of training and mentoring that will be required for a specific project or organization. These costs may be rough estimates based upon information obtained from Web sites or from telephone conversations with training organizations.

In summary, the test team must develop test tool expertise if it is to take advantage of the powerful time-saving features of the tool. Training may be required at different levels. For instance, training may be required for the test engineer who has a manual test background and who has automated test tool experience but not on the specific tool being applied, or it may be needed for a business user or other professional who is being temporarily assigned to the test team.

2.3.1.7   Tool Evaluation Domain

As part of the test tool proposal, consideration should be given to the method with which the test tool or tools will be evaluated. For example, the test tool will need to be exercised during the evaluation against a particular application and a particular operating environment. This evaluation itself may carry a cost that must be factored into the proposal. In addition, it may require advanced coordination and approvals from several different managers. These cost and logistics factors should be made apparent in the test tool proposal.

The particular application and the particular operating environment utilized to support test tool evaluation may, in fact, be the first project on which the test team seeks to implement the test tool. Chapter 3 provides a set of pilot application selection guidelines that a test team can follow when picking a pilot application and listing the findings of the pilot in the test tool proposal.

When selecting an evaluation domain, it is beneficial to pick an application-under-test within the organization that has high visibility. A long-term goal for the test team is for the organization testing expertise to be held with high regard. If one or more success stories become known, other test teams within the organization will have an easier time advocating and implementing automated testing. Likewise, interest in automated testing will spread throughout the organization's application developers.

When first implementing a test tool on a high-visibility project, the benefits of success are great—but so is the downside of failure. It is important that the test team follow a defined process when introducing automated test tools to a new project team. Chapter 4 includes a further discussion on the process of introducing automated test tools.

2.3.1.8   Tool Rollout Process

Another concern for the test proposal involves the method by which the test tool is implemented or rolled out within the organization. Once a test tool has successfully passed through the decision points of initial selection, tool evaluation, and final management approval, the test team needs to execute a plan to roll out the tool to the target project or projects.

The test team may advocate that a particularly strong application developer or test engineer be assigned the responsibility to review the test tool, develop simplified implementation procedures, and then teach or mentor members of the test team on the tool's use. This person can become the tool champion. Alternatively, the test team may assign a selected tool to different developers who then learn the function, streamline access, and teach other developers.

Experience has shown that the best rollout strategy involves the use of a separate test team to implement the tool. Under this strategy, a separate test team evaluates the new tool, gains expertise in its use, and then assists project teams in rolling out the tool. The use of such an independent test team represents a structured approach that generally eliminates many frustrating weeks of inefficient concurrent trial-and-error learning by application developers. For more information on the setup of test teams, see Chapter 5; for more information on test tool rollout strategies, see Chapter 4.

In addition, the test team may wish to use test tool presentations and demonstrations so as to increase tool buy-in and interest throughout the project or organization. It might also post information about one or more automated test tools on the organization's intranet—it is, after all, important to advertise the potential benefits of the various tools. The test team might consider organizing a test tool user group within the organization so as to transfer knowledge about the tool.

If the test tool proposal is accepted and funded by management, the test team then needs to obtain permission to proceed with test automation. It should next complete test tool selection and evaluation as outlined in Chapter 3, and follow the guidelines in Chapter 4 on rolling out an automated test tool on a new project.

Chapter Summary

- The steps outlined within the automate test decision process provide a structured way of approaching the decision to automate testing. These step-by-step instructions guide the test engineer toward making a decision on whether the software application is suitable for automated testing.

- One step in moving toward a decision to automate testing on a project requires that the test team make sure that management understands the appropriate application of automated testing for the specific need at hand.

- Another step in moving toward a decision to automate testing on a project requires that the test team decide how much of the test effort can be supported using an automated test tool given the type of application being developed, the hardware environment, and the project schedule.

- The benefits of automated testing (when implemented correctly) may include a reduction in the size of the test effort, a reduction of the test schedule, the production of a reliable system, and the enhancement of the test process.

- With the proper planning, an appropriate test tool, and a defined process with which to introduce automated testing, the total test effort required with automated testing represents only a fraction of the test effort required with manual methods.

- An automated test tool cannot be expected to support 100% of the test requirements of any given test effort.

- Automated testing may increase the breadth and depth of test coverage, yet there is still not enough time or resources to perform a 100% exhaustive test.

- The optimal value of test automation is obtained through the proper match of a test tool with the technical environment and the successful application of the Automated Test Life-cycle Methodology (ATLM).

- To obtain management backing for the resources needed, it is beneficial to develop an automated test tool proposal. This proposal should define the organization's test tool requirements and benefits and provide a cost estimate. The test tool proposal may be especially helpful in persuading management to set aside future budget dollars for test tool support.

References

1. Rosen, K.H. *Discrete Mathematics and Its Application,* 2nd ed. New York: McGraw-Hill, 1991.
2. Poston, R. *A Guided Tour of Software Testing Tools.* San Francisco: Aonix, 1988. www.aonix.com.

3. Myers, G.J. *The Art of Software Testing*. New York: John Wiley and Sons, 1979.

4. RTCA. "Software Considerations in Airborne Systems and Equipment Certification." Document No. RTCA/DO-178B, prepared by: SC-167. December 1, 1992.

5. Quality Assurance Institute. *QA Quest*. November 1995. See http://www.qaiusa.com/journal.html

6. Linz, T., Daigl, M. *GUI Testing Made Painless. Implementation and Results of the ESSI Project Number 24306*. 1998. www.imbus.de.

Automated Test Tool Evaluation and Selection

> If the only tool you have is a hammer, you tend to see every problem as a nail.
>
> **—Abraham Maslow**

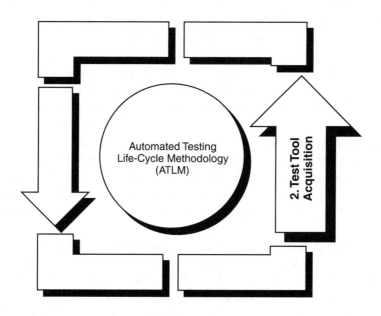

Automated Testing
Life-Cycle Methodology
(ATLM)

2. Test Tool Acquisition

Frequently, the selection of an automated test tool is accomplished long after the development platform and development tools have been determined. In an ideal situation, the organization's test team would be able to select a test tool that fits the criteria of the organization's system engineering environment as well as a pilot project that is in the early stages of the system development life cycle. In reality, a project often has a detailed system design in place before the concern for software test is addressed.

Regardless of the particular situation, test tool cost and the formal and on-the-job training for the tool received by test team personnel represent an investment by the organization. Given this fact, the selected tool should fit the organization's entire systems engineering environment. This approach allows the entire organization to make the most use of the tool. To accomplish this goal, the test team needs to follow a structured approach for performing test tool evaluation and selection.

This chapter systematically steps the test engineer through pertinent evaluation and selection criteria. Figure 3.1 provides a high-level overview of the automated test tool selection process. As a test engineer concerned with the selection of an automated test tool, you should have followed the process for supporting a decision to automate testing outlined in Chapter 2. Specifically, you should have developed a test tool proposal for management that outlined the test tool requirement and the justification for the tool. Test tool proposal development and its acceptance by management are intended to secure management's commitment for the resources needed to properly implement the test tool and support the automated testing process.

Once management has approved the proposal and a commitment for resources has been obtained, the test engineer needs to take a methodical approach toward identifying the tool best suited for the situation. He or she must review the organization's systems engineering environment or, when not feasible, review the systems engineering environment for a particular project, as outlined in Section 3.1. In this way, the test engineer becomes familiar with the system and software architectures for each of the various projects within the organization. Next, the test engineer defines the criteria for a tool evaluation domain based upon review of the system and software architectures supported by the defined system engineering environment.

The test engineer then identifies which of the various test tool types might apply to a particular project. Section 3.2 outlines the types of automated test tools available to support the testing effort throughout the various development life-cycle phases. The test engineer must assess the automated test tools available on the market, ascertaining which can support the organization's systems engineering environment. A determination needs to be made whether the defined system requirements can be verified through the use of one or more test tools.

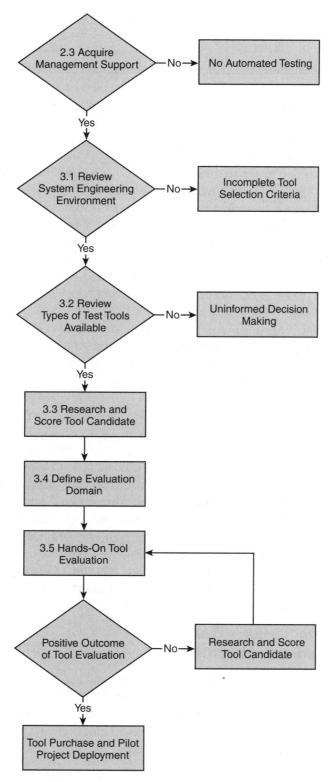

Figure 3.1   Automated Test Tool Selection Process

Next, the test engineer matches the test tool requirements with the types of test tools available so as to derive a list of candidate test tools. When one or more test tools exists within a single test type category, the test engineer needs to determine which of the candidate tools is the best option. He or she scores the candidate test tools using functional evaluation criteria, which reflects defined tool requirements. A sample evaluation form is provided in Section 3.3.

Once one or more automated test tools have been chosen to support the organization's test efforts, the test engineer must identify an evaluation domain or a pilot project with which to apply the tool and develop some experience and lessons learned. Section 3.5 outlines evaluation domain and pilot project considerations. Once the technical environment in which the automated test tool will operate has been defined, the test engineer can work with test tool candidate vendors. He or she should request an evaluation copy of the software, as described in Section 3.5. Pricing, support, and maintenance information on the test tool can also be obtained and reviewed.

After screening the test tool for its functional capabilities and reviewing the pricing, support, and maintenance information, the test engineer should conduct a hands-on evaluation of the tool in an isolated test environment and produce an evaluation report, as outlined in Section 3.5. Providing that the test tool performs satisfactorily in the isolated test environment, it can then be installed to support the pilot project. The process for automated test tool selection may be an iterative one, as a particular test tool selection could fail at numerous decision points, requiring the test engineer to reenter the selection process with a different tool.

Section 2.3 outlined the development process for a test tool proposal, which is aimed at persuading management to release funds to support automated test tool procurement and automated test tool training. The test tool proposal should have estimated the cost of the resources needed to research and evaluate the tool and to procure the tool. At this stage, it is assumed that management has approved the proposal and is aware of the benefits of planned test tool implementation. In addition, management should have set aside appropriate funding to support the test tool implementation and should be visibly supportive of automated test efforts.

3.1 | The Organization's Systems Engineering Environment

Once management is committed to providing the required resources, the test engineer reviews the organization's systems engineering environment. He or she will want to ensure that the tool is compatible with as many operating systems, programming languages, and other aspects of the technical environment used within the organization as possible. The test engineer reviews the organization's system engineering environment by addressing the questions and concerns described in this section and documenting his or her findings.

3.1.1 Third-Party Input from Management, Staff, and End Users

It is valuable to survey management, project staff, and end-user customers to understand their expectations pertaining to automated testing. Such a survey allows the test engineer to ascertain and document the functionality that needs to be provided by the test tool. This activity ensures that all personnel potentially involved understand and support the automated test tool's requirements and goals.

The following questions should be addressed as part of a data-gathering exercise, assuring that the desired tool functionality is defined adequately:

- How will the tool be used within the organization?
- Will other groups and departments use the tool?
- What is the most important function of the tool?
- What is the least important function of the tool?
- How will the tool mainly be used?
- How portable must the tool be?

During the survey, the test engineer identifies the database architecture and technical application architecture, including any middleware, databases, and operating systems most commonly used within the organization or on a particular project. The test engineer also identifies the languages used to develop the GUI for each application. Additionally, he or she needs to gain an understanding of the detailed architecture design, which can affect performance requirements. A review of prevalent performance requirements—including performance under heavy loads, intricate security mechanisms, and high measures of availability and reliability for a system—is beneficial. In particular, the test engineer should inquire about whether a majority of the applications support mission-critical operations.

The test team needs to understand the data managed by the application under test and define how the automated test tool supports data verification concerns. A primary purpose of most applications is the transformation of data into meaningful information. The test team should understand how this transformation takes place for the application, so that test strategies can be defined to support data verification and to validate that this transformation occurs correctly.

From the survey, the test engineer obtains an overall idea of the organization's engineering environment, so that the organization's tool needs can be properly identified. If the organization develops mainframe and client-server applications, but most of the system's trouble reports pertain to client-server applications, then the test tool requirements should focus on the client-server environment. If the organization's client-server applications experience primarily performance problems, then test tool selection efforts should concentrate on performance-monitoring tools.

The test team responsible for implementing a test tool must also account for its own expectations. As a single tool will not generally satisfy all organizational test tool interests and requirements, the tool should at a minimum satisfy the more immediate requirements. As the automated test tool industry continues to evolve and grow, test tool coverage for system requirements is likely to expand and the chance that a single tool can provide most desired functionality may improve. At present, one tool might be perfect for GUI testing, another tool might be needed for performance testing, and a third tool might support unit testing. Thus the use of multiple test tools needs to be considered, and expectations for the use of the tools must be managed. Likewise, the significance of tool integration should be assessed. The test engineer needs to document the inputs received from the test tool survey and compare these inputs with the features of the tools being considered.

The test tools applied to an automated test effort should accurately reflect customer quality concerns and priorities. The test engineer needs to clearly state customers' needs and expectations to ensure that the proper breadth and scope of testing can be performed. Some customers may wish to apply the test tool used during system testing to the acceptance test effort.

3.1.2   Tool Criteria Reflecting the Systems Engineering Environment

Next, the test engineer should review the system and software architectures that pertain to the majority of the projects and environments within the organization (depending on the size of the organization). These other projects and environments may have a different set of test goals and objectives, and many types of tests can be performed. To which phase of the software development life cycle does the test team wish to apply automated testing? How will the test tool be used in the organization? Is there interest in a requirements management tool that could be applied during the requirements definition phase? Is there interest in performing usability testing during the design phase?

Section 3.2 describes the various types of test tools that are available for the different system development phases. The test engineer must identify which types of test tools are the most applicable. Ideally, an automated tool is used in support of each phase of the software development life cycle. It is generally not the test team's responsibility to identify an automated tool to support each software engineering activity; rather, a software engineering manager or a process improvement group takes on this responsibility. Preferably, the tools will be integrated, allowing the output of one tool to be used as input to another tool.

With regard to the review of system requirements, several questions need to be posed. Do you want to concentrate the automated test effort during the development phase? Do you need a tool that supports memory leak testing? A memory leak tool analyzes a computer program to determine which part does not use memory effectively. Some tools support module complexity analysis—that is, they map the program module interdependencies in a given system. This capability may be useful in identifying computer programs that need to be structured or separated into two or more programs. Complexity information may also be helpful in identifying program code that warrants more detailed code inspection. Again, these types of issues might already have been identified in an organizational needs analysis.

The test team will generally concentrate its review on those test tools that have the greatest applicability to the testing phase. It is important to analyze the need for tools that support regression, stress, or volume testing. The test engineer needs to understand the importance of system performance requirements and determine which technical criteria are most important during the testing phase. These criteria might include the ability to maintain software test scripts and the ability to perform regression testing quickly and thoroughly. The level of sophistication inherent within an automated test tool is an important factor to consider when selecting a tool. (Questions and concerns pertaining to test tool sophistication are outlined later in this chapter in Table 3.2).

The specific selection criteria for any given effort will depend on the applicable system requirements of the target applications. If the test team might be able to take advantage of one or more automated test tools for several projects or applications, then it might be necessary to narrow the selection criteria to the most significant applications-under-test within the organization. Ideally, you should not limit the automated test tool selection criteria to a single project. Such a constraint may lead to an investment good only for that project alone, with the test tool becoming shelfware after the immediate project has been completed.

3.1.3 Level of Software Quality

When considering an automated test tool, the test engineer should define the level of software quality expected for the project and determine which aspects of the software development are the most crucial to a particular project or effort. He or she should inquire about whether the organization is seeking to comply with industry quality guidelines, such as ISO 9000 or the Software Engineering Institute's Capability Maturity Model (CMM). The test engineer should also gain insight into the size of the planned application development effort. If the application development effort involves the use of five full-time developers, for example, over the duration of the project, then extensive use of a variety of test tools would likely prove too expensive given the size of the project. For projects involving as many as 30 or more developers, however, the size and complexity of the effort would justify the use of a greater variety of test tools.

The test engineer also needs to define the crucial aspects of the organization's primary applications. A high level of software quality would be critical, for example, for a company that develops patient monitors, the electronic devices that monitor the physiological parameters (ECG, heart rate, blood pressure, oxygen saturation) of critically ill patients in real time. On the other hand, the quality criteria for an organization that develops noncritical software would not be as extensive. At financial institutions, which employ systems that manage the flow of millions of dollars each day, high availability of hardware and software is a critical concern.

3.1.4 Help Desk Problem Reports

When an application or version of an application is in operation, the test team can monitor help desk trouble reports so as to review the history of the most prevalent problems of the application. If a new version of the application is being developed, the team can focus its effort on the most prevalent problems of the operational system, identifying a test tool that supports this kind of testing.

3.1.5 Budget Constraints

When the test engineer has obtained management commitment for a test tool and must satisfy a large number of organizational test tool requirements on a limited budget, he or she must be both selective and cost-conscious when looking for one or more tools to support requirements. The test engineer may need to purchase a single tool that meets a majority of the requirements or one that best satisfies the most important requirements.

3.1.6 Types of Tests

As many types of tests can be performed on any given project, it is necessary to review the types of testing of interest. The types of tests to consider include regression testing, stress or volume testing, and usability testing. What is the most important feature needed in a tool? Will the tool be used mainly for stress testing? Some test tools specialize in source code coverage analysis; that is, they identify all possible source code paths that need to be verified through testing. Is this capability required for the particular project or set of projects? Other test tool applications might include support for process automation or bulk data loading through input files. Consider what the test team is trying to accomplish with the test tool. What is the goal? What functionality is desired?

3.1.7 Long-Term Investment Considerations

The use of one or more automated test tools should be contemplated for a longer period than just one year. As a result, the tool should be viewed as a long-term investment, involving multiple tool upgrades. Test tool selection criteria should therefore include the staying power of the tool. Who is the vendor? Does the product have a good track record? What is its industry acceptance? Ideally, the test tool vendor should be available to answer questions and should provide regular upgrades to keep up with technological development.

Another element to consider is the potential for the tool to be more widely used within the organization. This issue represents another reason why the test engineer should examine the entire organization's system engineering make-up.

3.1.8 Test Tool Process

When evaluating a test tool, keep in mind that the test team will need to introduce the test tool within the organization. Thus the test engineer needs to verify that management is willing to commit adequate resources to support the test tool introduction process. Provided enough room exists in the project schedule to permit the introduction of an appropriate test tool for the organization, the test team needs to ensure that the tool is implemented in a manner that promotes its adoption. After all, if no one in the organization is using the tool, the effort to obtain and incorporate the tool will have been wasted. An appropriate test tool introduction process should be followed, as outlined in Chapter 4, and all stakeholders in the tool should receive education on the use of the tool and become involved in its implementation.

3.1.9 Avoiding Shortcuts

To determine the test tool requirements, the test engineer will have to address additional questions such as, "Will I be supporting a large testing effort?" Again, when considering the requirements for a project involving a small testing effort, it is beneficial to consider the future application of the test tool on other projects. Remember to think of test tool selection as a long-term investment!

Another concern when selecting a test tool is its impact and fit with the project schedule. Will there be enough time for the necessary people to learn the tool within the constraints of the schedule? Given a situation where the project schedule precludes the introduction of an appropriate test tool for the organization, it may be advisable not to introduce an automated test tool. By postponing the introduction of a test tool until a more opportune time, the test team may avoid the risk of rushing the launch of the right tool on the wrong project or choosing the wrong tool for the organization. In either case, the test tool likely will not be received well, and potential champions for the use of automated test tools may become their biggest opponents.

3.2 | Tools That Support the Testing Life Cycle

When performing an organizational improvement or needs analysis, it is important to become familiar with the different types of tools available on the market. This section provides an overview of tools that support the various testing life-cycle phases. This tool section is not intended to be comprehensive, but instead provides a sample set of tools that improve the test life cycle. Table 3.1 lists tools that support each phase of the testing life cycle. In addition to testing tools, other tools are included in the table because they support the production of a testable system. Even though some tools are used throughout various phases (such as defect tracking tools, configuration management tools, and test procedure generation tools), the table lists only the tools in the first phase used. Appendix B provides examples and details of the tool types listed here, and it gives examples of other tool information sources.

The tools listed in Table 3.1 are considered valuable in improving the testing life cycle. Before an organization selects a particular tool to purchase, however, it should

Table 3.1   Test Life-Cycle Tools

Life-Cycle Phase	Type of Tool	Tool Description
Business analysis phase	Business modeling tools	Allow for recording definitions of user needs and automating the rapid construction of flexible, graphical, client-server applications
	Configuration management tools	Allow for baselining of important data repositories
	Defect tracking tools	Manage system life-cycle defects
	Technical review management	Facilitates communication and automates the technical review/inspection process
	Documentation generators	Automate document generation

continued

continued from page 76

Life-Cycle Phase	Type of Tool	Tool Description
Requirements definition phase	Requirements management tools	Manage and organize requirements; allow for test procedure design; allow for test progress reporting
	Requirements verifiers	Verify syntax, semantics, and testability
	Use case generators	Allow for creation of use cases
Analysis and design phase	Database design tools	Provides a solution for developing second-generation enterprise client-server systems
	Application design tools	Define software architecture; allow for object-oriented analysis, modeling, design, and construction
	Structure charts, flowcharts, and sequence diagrams	Help manage processes
	Test procedure generators	Generate test procedures from requirements or design of data and object models or cause-effect diagrams.
Programming phase	Syntax checkers/ debuggers	Allow for syntax checking and debugging capability; usually come with built-in programming language compilers
	Memory leak and run-time error detection tools	Detect runtime errors and memory leaks
	Source code testing tools	Verify maintainability, portability, complexity, cyclomatic complexity, and standards compliance
	Static and dynamic analyzers	Depict quality and structure of code
	Various code implementation tools	Depending on the application, support code generation, among other things
	Unit test tools	Automates the unit testing process
Metrics tools	Code (test) coverage analyzers or code instrumentors	Identify untested code and support dynamic testing
	Metrics reporters	Read source code and display metrics information
	Usability measurements	Provide user profiling, task analysis, prototyping, and user walkthroughs

continued

continued from page 77

Life-Cycle Phase	Type of Tool	Tool Description
Other testing life-cycle support tools	Test data generators	Generate test data
	Prototyping tools	Allow for prototyping of application, using high-level programming languages like Visual Basic
	Stub routine generation tools	Allow for stub routine generation when all modules have not been programmed yet, but parts of the code need to be tested as stand-alone units
	File compare utilities	Allow for searching for discrepancies between files that should be identical in content
	Simulation tools	Simulate applications to measure for scalability, among other tasks
Testing phase	Test management tools	Allow for test management
	Network testing tools	Allow for monitoring, measuring, testing, and diagnosis of performance across the entire network
	GUI testing tools (capture/playback)	Allow for automated GUI tests; capture/playback tools record user interactions with on-line systems, so they may be replayed automatically
	Non-GUI test drivers	Allow for automated execution of tests for products without GUIs
	Load/performance testing tools	Allow for load/performance and stress testing
	Environment testing tools	Testing tools for various testing environments to include MVS, UNIX, and X-Windows, as well as the World Wide Web
Year 2000 (Y2K) testing tools	Management and Y2K test planning tools	Allow for test management and metrics reporting
	Code parsers, inventory, code analysis	Parse and report on mainframe or client-server source code for date impact
		Analyze Excel spreadsheets and Access databases
		Scan Solaris and Sun OS for date-related system calls
		• nm: Displays symbol table information for Solaris binaries
		• ar: Used to check library dependencies
	Baseline test data generation	Support the baseline creation of Y2K test data
	Data agers	Allow for automatically setting the values of date fields in test data forward or backward to allow for Y2K testing
	Date simulation	Allow for date simulation and simulate Y2K test environment

78

conduct a needs/improvement analysis. The organization needs to determine which tools could be most beneficial in improving the system development process. This assessment is made by comparing the current process with a target process and evaluating the improvement indicator and by conducting a cost-benefit analysis. Before purchasing a tool to support a software engineering activity, a tool evaluation should be performed for the tool, similar to the automated test tool evaluation process described in this chapter.

3.2.1 Business Analysis Phase Tools

Numerous tools on the market support the business analysis phase. Some tools support various methodologies, such as the Unified Modeling Language (UML). Other business analysis tools have the ability to record process improvement opportunities and allow for data organization capabilities, thus improving the testing life cycle. For more details on each of the tools listed in this phase, refer to Appendix B.

3.2.1.1 Business Modeling Tools

Business modeling tools support the creation of process models, organization models, and data models. They allow for recording definitions of user needs and for automating the rapid construction of flexible, graphical client-server applications. Some business modeling tools integrate with other phases of the system/testing life cycle, such as the data modeling phase, design phase, programming phase, and testing and configuration management phase. These tools can be very valuable in supporting the testing effort. Using these tools correctly and efficiently will enhance process modeling throughout the system life cycle, while simultaneously supporting the production of testable systems.

3.2.1.2 Configuration Management Tools

Configuration management tools should be deployed early in the life cycle, so as to manage change and institute a repeatable process. Although this tool category is depicted as part of the business analysis phase in Table 3.1, configuration management tools are actually used throughout the entire life cycle. The final outputs of each system life-cycle phase should be baselined in a configuration management tool.

3.2.1.3 Defect Tracking Tools

Just as it is important to use configuration management tools throughout the testing life cycle, so it is also important to use defect tracking tools from the beginning and throughout the testing life cycle. All defects or software problem reports encountered throughout the system life cycle should be documented and managed to closure. The identification of defects is the primary goal of testing and quality assurance activities. For defects to be removed successfully from the application, they must be identified and monitored until their elimination.

3.2.1.4   Technical Review Management Tools

One of the best defect detection strategies relies on technical reviews or inspections, because such reviews allow defects to be discovered early in the life cycle. Reviews and inspections represent a formal evaluation technique applicable to software requirements, design, code, and other software work products. They entail a thorough examination by a person or a group other than the author.

Technical review management tools allow for automation of the inspection process, while facilitating communication. They also support automated collection of key metrics, such as action items discovered during a review.

3.2.1.5   Documentation Generation Tools

Documentation generation tools can simplify the testing life cycle by reducing the effort required to manually produce software documentation. Again, they are helpful throughout the entire testing life cycle.

3.2.2   Requirements Definition Phase Tools

Software needs to be assessed relative to an understanding of what the software is intended to do. This understanding is encapsulated within requirements specifications or use case definitions. The quality of defined requirements can make the test (and, of course, development) effort relatively painless or extremely arduous.

When a requirements specification contains all of the information needed by a test engineer in a usable form, the requirements are said to be test-ready. Testable requirements minimize the effort and cost of testing. If requirements are not test-ready or testable, test engineers must search for missing information—a long, tedious process that can significantly prolong the test effort. See Appendix A for more information on testable requirements.

3.2.2.1   Requirements Management Tools

Requirements management tools permit requirements to be captured quickly and efficiently. Requirements can be recorded in a natural language, such as English, using a text editor within a requirements management tool. They can also be written in a formal language such as LOTOS or Z [1] using a syntax-directed editor. Additionally, requirements can be modeled graphically, using tools such as Validator/ Req (see Appendix B for more details on this tool).

One method of modeling requirements involves use cases. The use case construct defines the behavior of a system or other semantic entity without revealing the entity's internal structure. Each use case specifies a sequence of actions, including variants, that the entity can perform by interacting with actors of the entity.

Many requirements management tools support information traceability. Traceability involves more than just tracking requirements. Linking all information together—such as links forged between requirements/use cases and either design, implementation, or test procedures—is a critical factor in demonstrating project compliance and completeness. For example, the designer might need to trace the design components to the detailed system requirements, while the developer needs to trace the code components to the design components. The test engineer needs to trace the system requirements to test procedures, thereby measuring how much of the test procedure creation is complete. Requirements management tools can also automatically determine which test procedures are affected when a requirement is modified.

In addition, requirements management tools support information management. Regardless of whether the project involves software, hardware, firmware, or a process, data must be managed and traced to ensure compliance with requirements through all phases of development. Tools such as these can be used to support *lessons learned* review activities (discussed in Chapter 10 in detail) and to facilitate the management of issues and defects.

3.2.2.2 Requirements Verifiers

Requirements recorders are well-established tools that continue to be updated with new features and methods, such as use cases. Requirements verifiers [2], on the other hand, are relatively new tools. Before requirements verifiers appeared on the market, recorded requirements information could be checked in two ways: (1) by using another function, available in some requirements analysis tools, to verify that information conformed to certain methodology rules, or (2) by performing manual reviews on the information. Neither of these verifications, however, could assure that the requirements information represented a testable product.

To be testable, requirements information must be unambiguous, consistent, quantifiable, and complete. A term or word in a software requirements specification is unambiguous if it has one, and only one, definition. A requirements specification is consistent if each of its terms is used in one, and only one, way. Consider, for example, the word *report*. Within a requirements specification, *report* must be used as either a noun or a verb. To use the word *report* as both a name and an action, however, would make the specification inconsistent.

From a test engineer's point of view, completeness means that the requirements contain necessary and sufficient information for testing. Every action statement must have a defined input, function, and output. Also, the tester needs to know that all statements are present. If any statement is incomplete or if the collection of statements known as the requirements specification is incomplete, testing will be difficult. Worse, some organizations have no requirement specifications, making testing impossible. For more details on testable requirements, see Appendix A.

Requirements verifiers quickly and reliably check for ambiguity, inconsistency, and statement completeness. An automated verifier, however, cannot determine whether the collection of requirement statements is complete. The tool can check only what is entered into it—not what *should* be entered. Checking the completeness of the requirements specification must therefore be performed manually.

Most testing and development tools used later in the software life cycle depend on the availability of reliable requirements information, so a requirements verifier can prove valuable in creating this sound foundation. Unlike most test tools, which are packaged separately, requirements verifiers are usually embedded within other tools.

3.2.3   Tools for the Analysis and Design Phase

A requirements specification defines *what* a software system is expected to do, while the design phase determines *how* these requirement specifications will be implemented.

3.2.3.1   Visual Modeling Tools

Visual modeling tools, which are used during the business analysis phase, may also prove helpful during the design phase. These tools, such as Rational Rose, allow developers to define and communicate a software architecture, which accelerates development, by improving communication among various team members; improves quality, by mapping business processes to software architecture; and increases visibility and predictability, by making critical design decisions explicit visually.

Additionally, the information gathered via the requirements management tools during the requirements phase can be reused in the design phase. A detailed design is generated from these detailed systems requirements, use cases, and use case diagrams. In addition to deploying the tools classified under earlier system life-cycle phases during the design phase, specific database design tools and application design tools can enhance the design effort and thus the testing phase. Structure charts, flowcharts, and sequence diagrams may support process management. For more details on these types of tools, see Appendix B.

3.2.3.2   Test Procedure Generators

The requirements management tools discussed in Section 3.2.2 may be coupled with a specification-based test procedure (case) generator. A requirements management tool will capture requirements information, which the generator then processes to create test procedures. A test procedure generator creates test procedures by statistical, algorithmic, or heuristic means. In statistical test procedure generation, the tool chooses input structures and values to form a statistically random distribution, or a distribution that matches the usage profile of the software under test. In algorithmic test procedure generation, the tool follows a set of rules or procedures, commonly called test design strategies or techniques. Most often test procedure generators employ action-, data-, logic-, event-, and state-driven strategies. Each of these strategies probes for a different kind of software defect. When generating test procedures by heuristic or failure-directed means, the tool employs information from the test engineer, such as failures that the test team discovered frequently in the past. The tool then becomes knowledge-based, using the knowledge of historical failures to generate test procedures.

In the past, test engineers primarily focused on the creation and modification of test procedures. Coming up with test procedures was a slow, expensive, and labor-intensive process. If one requirement changed, the tester had to redo many existing test procedures and create new ones. With modern test procedure generators, however, test procedure creation and revision time can be reduced to a matter of CPU seconds [3].

These types of tools can be used during the design and development phases and during the testing phases. For example, Interactive Development Environments (IDE) has announced that a version of its StP/T tool will be made available to software development teams. This tool allows developers to automatically test software code against the functionality specified in the analysis and design stages. IDE's test procedure generation tool links the testing process to the initial analysis and design. As a result, developers can create test-ready designs from the start, thereby slashing the time and costs associated with multiple design iterations. Through its link to analysis and design tools, StP/T builds test cases directly from specifications outlined in the application's data and object models.

3.2.4 Programming Phase Tools

During the business analysis and design phases, the modeling tools used often allow code generation from the models created in the earlier phases. If these setup and preparation activities have been carried out correctly, programming can be simplified. Thus programmers should follow standards and convey much of what a system can do through the judicious choice of names for methods, functions, classes, and other structures. Also, programmers should include extensive preambles or comments in their code that describe and document the purpose and organization of the program. In addition, application developers should create program logic and algorithms that support code execution.

The preambles, algorithms, and program code can serve as inputs to testing tools during the test automation development phase. These inputs make it easier for a test engineer to design a test. Preambles may be envisioned as requirements descriptions for the small units of software code that the programmer will develop. The test tools employed during the requirements phase may be reused to test these units of software code.

Tools such as the metrics reporter, code checker, and instrumentor may also support testing during the programming phase. Sometimes these tools are classified as static analysis tools, because they check code while it is not being executed and is in a static state. They are discussed in Section 3.2.5.

3.2.4.1 Syntax Checkers/Debuggers

Syntax checkers and debuggers are usually bundled within a high-level language compiler. These tools support the testability of the software and therefore are important in improving the testability of software during the programming phase. Debugging can include setting breakpoints in the code to allow the executing program to be stopped for debugging, inserting a stop condition, allowing source code to be viewed during debugging, and allowing program variables to be viewed and modified.

3.2.4.2 Memory Leak and Runtime Error Detection Tools

Memory leak and runtime error detection tools can check for memory leaks, showing where memory has been allocated but to which no pointers exist; such memory can never be used or freed. Runtime errors may be detected in third-party libraries, shared libraries, and other code. Memory leak and runtime error detection tools can identify problems such as uninitialized local variables, stack overflow errors, and static memory access errors, just to name a few. These tools are very beneficial additions to the testing life cycle.

3.2.4.3 Source Code Testing Tools

An early code checker test tool, called LINT, was provided to application developers as part of the UNIX operating system. LINT is still available in today's UNIX systems. Many other code checkers are now offered to support other operating systems as well.

The name "LINT" was aptly chosen, because the code checker goes through code and picks out all the "fuzz" that makes programs messy and error-prone. This type of tool looks for misplaced pointers, uninitialized variables, and deviations from standards. Application development teams that utilize software inspections as an element of static testing can minimize the static test effort by invoking a code checker to help identify miniscule problems prior to each inspection [4]. Code checkers such as Abraxas Software's Codecheck measure maintainability, portability, complexity, and standards compliance of C and C++ source code.

3.2.4.4   Static and Dynamic Analyzers

Some tools allow for static and dynamic analysis of code. Tools such as LDRA (see Appendix B for more details) perform static analysis, assessing the code in terms of programming standards, complexity metrics, unreachable code, and much more. These tools also support dynamic analysis, which involves the execution of code using test data to detect defects at runtime, as well as detection of untested code, analysis of statement and branch execution, and much more. These types of products analyze the source code, producing reports in both textual and graphical form.

3.2.5   Metrics Tools

Metrics tools, which are used during the unit and integration testing phases, can identify untested code and support dynamic testing. These types of tools provide coverage analysis to verify that the code is tested in as much detail as possible.

3.2.5.1   Metrics Reporter

The metrics reporter tool [5] has been around for years and remains valuable. This tool reads source code and displays metrics information, often in graphical format. It reports complexity metrics in terms of data flow, data structure, and control flow. It also provides metrics about code size in terms of modules, operands, operators, and lines of code. Such a tool can help the programmer correct and groom code and help the test engineer determine which parts of the software code require the most test attention.

3.2.5.2   Code Coverage Analyzers and Code Instrumentors

Measurement of structural coverage gives the development team insight into the effectiveness of tests and test suites. For example, tools such as McCabe's Visual Test Tool can quantify the complexity of the design, measure the number of integration tests required to qualify the design, produce the desired integration tests, and measure the number of integration tests that have not been executed.

Other tools, such as Hindsight, measure multiple levels of test coverage, including segment, branch, and conditional coverage. The appropriate level of test coverage will depend upon the importance of the particular application. (For more detail on these tools, see Appendix B.)

3.2.5.3   Usability Measurement

These types of tools evaluate the usability of a client/server application. Please see Appendix B for more detail.

3.2.6   Other Testing Life-Cycle Support Tools

3.2.6.1   Test Data Generators

Many tools now on the market support the generation of test data and populate database servers. Such test data can be used for all testing phases, especially during performance and stress testing, simplifying the testing process. For examples of test data generators, see Appendix B.

3.2.6.2   File Compare Utilities

File compare utilities search for discrepancies between files that should be identical in content. Such comparisons are useful in validating that regression tests produce the same output files as baselined information, before code fixes were implemented. File compare utilities are often functions of capture/playback tools.

3.2.6.3   Simulation Tools

Simulation modeling tools can simulate the behavior of application-under-test models, using various modifications of the target application environment as part of "what-if" scenarios. These tools provide insight into the performance and behavior of existing or proposed networks, systems, and processes. For examples of simulation modeling tools, see Appendix B.

3.2.7   Testing Phase Tools

3.2.7.1   Test Management Tools

Test management tools support the testing life cycle by allowing for planning, managing, and analyzing all aspects of it. Some tools, such as Rational's TestStudio, are integrated with requirement and configuration management tools, thereby simplifying the entire testing life-cycle process. For more details on test management tools, see Appendix B.

3.2.7.2   Network Testing Tools

The advent of applications operating in a client-server, multitier, or Web environment has introduced new complexity to the test effort. The test engineer is no longer exercising a single closed application operating on a single system, as in the past. Instead, the client-server architecture involves three components: the server, the client, and the network. Interplatform connectivity also increases the potential for errors. As a result, testing must focus on the performance of the server and the network, as well as the overall system performance and functionality across the three components. Many network test tools allow the test engineer to monitor, measure, test, and diagnose performance across the entire network. For more details on network test tools, see Appendix B.

3.2.7.3   GUI Application Testing Tools (Record/Playback Tools)

Many automated GUI test tools are on the market. These tools usually include a record and playback feature, which allows the test engineer to create (record), modify, and run (play back) automated tests across many environments. Tools that record the GUI components at the widget level (and not the bitmap level) are most useful. The *record* activity captures the keystrokes entered by the test engineer, automatically creating a script in a high-level language in the background. This recording is a computer program, which is referred to as a test "script." The use of only the capture/playback features usually takes advantage of 10% of a test tool's capacity. To get the best value from a capture/playback tool, it is necessary to work with its inherent scripting language. The test engineer will need to modify the script to create a reusable and maintainable test procedure (see Chapter 8 on automated test development guidelines). This script will become the baseline test and can later be played back on a new software build for comparison.

Test tools that provide a recording capability are usually bundled with a *comparator*, which automatically compares actual outputs with expected outputs and logs the results. The results can be compared pixel by pixel, character by character, as the tool automatically pinpoints the failure between the expected and actual result. In the case of the Rational Robot test tool, a positive result is logged in the Test Log Viewer as a *pass* and depicted on the screen using a green color, while a *fail* is represented using a red color.

3.2.7.4   Load/Performance/Stress Testing Tools

Performance testing tools, such as Rational's PerformanceStudio, allow for load testing, where the tool can be programmed to run a number of client machines simultaneously to *load* the client/server system and measure response time. Load testing typically involves various scenarios to analyze how the client/server system responds under various loads.

Stress testing involves the process of running the client machines in high-stress scenarios to see when and if they break.

3.2.7.5   Environment Testing Tools

Numerous types of tools are available to support the numerous environments (mainframe, UNIX, X-Windows, and Web). The number of test tools supporting Web applications is increasing. Specific Web testing tools are now on the market geared toward testing Web applications, as noted in Appendix B.

3.2.7.6   Year 2000 (Y2K) Testing Tools

A number of tools on the market support Y2K testing. Such tools parse and report on mainframe or client-server source code regarding the date impact. Some Y2K tools support the baseline creation of Y2K data; others allow for data aging for Y2K testing. Still other Y2K tools provide data simulation and simulate the Y2K testing environment.

3.2.7.7   Product-Based Test Procedure Generators

The product-based test procedure generator has been known since the 1970s [6]. It reads and analyzes source code, and then derives test procedures from this analysis. This tool tries to create test procedures that exercise every statement, branch, and path (structural coverage). While attaining comprehensive structural coverage is a worthwhile goal, the problem with this tool is that it tries to achieve structural coverage by working from the code structure rather than from the requirements specification.

Criticism of this kind of test method springs from the fact that program code structure represents only what a software product does—not what the system was intended to do. Program code can have missing or incorrect functions, and a test tool utilizing the code structure has no way of compensating for such errors. Because it cannot distinguish between good program code and bad program code, the test tool attempts to generate test procedures to exercise every part of all program code. Thus it will not warn the test engineer that some of the program code may be faulty.

When utilizing a product-based test procedure generator, the determination of whether program code is good or bad is left up to the test engineer. As discussed earlier, the test engineer makes such a determination by comparing actual behavior of the code to its specified or expected behavior. When written requirements specifications are not available and test engineers must work from their recollection of specifications, then the test team will be inclined to trust the product-based test procedure generator. After all, the test engineers have no other reference point to support the test effort. In this situation, the test team mistakenly places its faith in reports showing high structural coverage. In contrast, test engineers with written or modeled specifications have the definitive reference point required to perform complete software testing. As a result, he or she does not need to test software against itself, and therefore has no need for a product-based test procedure generator.

3.3 | Test Tool Research

The information given in Section 3.2 will assist the test engineer in fashioning a test tool feature "wish list" that supports the organization's systems engineering environment. It outlines the various types of test tools to consider. Next, the test engineer must translate the need for a test tool type into one or more specific test tool candidates.

Based on test tool requirements, the test team needs to develop a test tool specification and evaluation form. The organization may already have a standard form to support tool evaluation. It is beneficial to check the organization's process or standards library to obtain any existing guidelines and forms.

It is important that the test tool functionality that you require, as the test engineer responsible for implementing a test tool, be factored into the evaluation process. The test engineer should investigate whether a requirements management tool will be used, or any other tool that can potentially be integrated with a testing tool. A features checklist should be developed for each type of tool needed during the various system life-cycle phases, as each phase will have different tool requirements and needs.

Several questions need to be posed. Do you need a capture/playback tool or a code coverage tool, or both? What are you trying to accomplish with the test tool? Do you need a tool for test management? Do you plan to use the tool for load testing or only regression testing? Test tool goals and objectives will need to be considered when outlining the criteria and desired features of the test tool. Table 3.2 provides an example of an evaluation scorecard for an automated GUI test tool.

3.3.1 Improvement Opportunities

At the end of the test life cycle, test program review activities are performed, as discussed in Chapter 10. The outcome of these activities might suggest the need for automated testing tools and identify those processes or products that need improvement as well as outline how an automated tool could be expected to help improve the process or product. The test engineer needs to incorporate the results of test program review activities when selecting the criteria for a new test tool.

Armed with documented expectations of the functionality that the test tools should provide, the test engineer begins to research the tools that fit the specific needs. A thorough evaluation requires a rich field of candidate vendors and products. A number of ways exist to identify candidates. A multitude of information is available on the World Wide Web and in software testing publications. Read magazines—especially software and database application development publications—looking for

Table 3.2   Evaluation Scorecard—Automated GUI Testing (Record/Playback) Tool

Test Tool Characteristic	Weight (1–10)	Score (1–5)	Value (1–50)
Ease of Use			
Learning curve	7	5	35
Easy to maintain the tool	5	5	25
Easy to install—tool may not be used if difficult to install	5	3	15
Tool Customization			
Can the tool be customized (can fields maintained by tool be added or deleted)?	7	4	28
Does the tool support the required test procedure naming convention?	8	4	32
Platform Support			
Can it be moved and run on several platforms at once, across a network (that is, cross-Windows support, Win95, and WinNT)?	8	4	32
Multiuser Access			
What database does the tool use? Does it allow for scalability?	8	5	40
Network-based test repository—necessary when multiple access to repository is required	8	5	40
Defect Tracking (For more detail on evaluating defect tracking tools, see Chapter 8)			
Does the tool come with an integrated defect-tracking feature?	10	3	30
Tool Functionality			
Test scripting language—does the tool use a flexible, yet robust scripting language? What is the complexity of the scripting language: Is it 4 GL? Does it allow for modular script development?	9	5	45
Complexity of scripting language	9	5	45
Scripting language allows for variable declaration and use; allows passing of parameters between functions	9	5	45
Does the tool use a test script compiler or an interpreter?	9	5	45
Interactive test debugging—does the scripting language allow the user to view variable values, step through the code, integrate test procedures, or jump to other external procedures?	8	4	32
Does the tool allow recording at the widget level (object recognition level)?	10	5	50

continued

continued from page 90

Test Tool Characteristic	Weight (1–10)	Score (1–5)	Value (1–50)
Does the tool allow for interfacing with external .dll and .exe files?	9	5	45
Published APIs—language interface capabilities	10	4	40
ODBC support—does the tool support any ODBC-compliant database?	10	4	40
Is the tool intrusive (that is, does source code need to be expanded by inserting additional statements)?	9	4	36
Communication protocols—can the tool be adapted to various communication protocols (such as TCP/IP, IPX)?	9	3	27
Custom control support—does the tool allow you to map to additional custom controls, so the tool is still compatible and usable?	10	3	30
Ability to kick off scripts at a specified time; scripts can run unattended	9	5	45
Allows for adding timers	10	5	50
Allows for adding comments during recording	7	5	35
Compatible with the GUI programming language and entire hardware and software development environment used for application under test (i.e., VB, Powerbuilder)	10	5	50
Can query or update test data during playback (that is, allows the use of SQL statements)	10	4	40
Supports the creation of a library of reusable function	10	5	50
Allows for wrappers (shells) where multiple procedures can be linked together and are called from one procedure	10	5	50
Test results analysis—does the tool allow you to easily see whether the tests have passed or failed (that is, automatic creation of test results log)?	10	3	30
Test execution on script playback—can the tool handle error recovery and unexpected active windows, log the discrepancy, and continue playback (automatic recovery from errors)?	5	3	15
Allows for synchronization between client and server	5	10	50
Allows for automatic test procedure generation	8	5	40
Allows for automatic data generation	8	5	40
Y2K compliance	10	5	50

Reporting Capability

Ability to provide graphical results (charts and graphs)	8	5	40
Ability to provide reports	8	5	40
What report writer does the tool use?	8	5	40
Can predefined reports be modified and/or can new reports be created?	8	5	40

continued

continued from page 91

Test Tool Characteristic	Weight (1–10)	Score (1–5)	Value (1–50)
Performance and Stress Testing			
Performance and stress testing tool is integrated with GUI testing tool	9	5	45
Supports stress, load, and performance testing	10	3	30
Allows for simulation of users without requiring use of physical workstations	10	3	30
Ability to support configuration testing (that is, tests can be run on different hardware and software configurations)	10	3	30
Ability to submit a variable script from a data pool of library of scripts/data entries and logon IDs/password	10	3	30
Supports resource monitoring (memory, disk space, system resources)	10	3	30
Synchronization ability so that a script can access a record in database at the same time to determine locking, deadlock conditions, and concurrency control problems	10	5	50
Ability to detect when events have completed in a reliable fashion	9	5	45
Ability to provide client to server response times	10	3	30
Ability to provide graphical results	8	5	40
Ability to provide performance measurements of data loading	10	5	50
Version Control			
Does the tool come with integrated version control capability?	10	4	40
Can the tool be integrated with other version control tools	8	3	24
Test Planning and Management			
Test planning and management tool is integrated with GUI testing tool	8	5	40

continued

in-depth articles, technical reviews, and vendor advertisements. Use software programs such as Computer Select, which catalogs and indexes tens of thousands of articles from hundreds of magazines. Tool vendors often have their success stories published in industry periodicals. In addition, many software-related magazines research and rate test tools on the market. Another option is to use the research services of companies such as the Gartner Group.

Talk to associates and ask them to recommend tools and vendors. Join testing newsgroups and testing discussion groups, and obtain tool feedback and other expert opinions.

continued from page 92

Test Tool Characteristic	Weight (1–10)	Score (1–5)	Value (1–50)
Test planning and management tool is integrated with requirements management tool	8	5	40
Test planning and management tool follows specific industry standard on testing process (such as SEI/CMM, ISO)	7	4	28
Supports test execution management	10	5	50
Allows for test planning—does the tool support planning, managing, and analyzing testing efforts? Can the tool reference test plans, matrices, and product specifications to create traceability?	10	5	50
Allows for measuring test progress	10	5	50
Allows for various reporting activities	9	4	36
Pricing			
Is the price within the estimated price range?	10	4	40
What type of licensing is being used (floating, fixed)?	7	3	21
Is the price competitive?	9	4	36
Vendor Qualifications			
Maturity of product	8	4	32
Market share of product	8	4	32
Vendor qualifications, such as financial stability and length of existence. What is the vendor's track record?	8	4	32
Are software patches provided, if deemed necessary?	8	4	32
Are upgrades provided on a regular basis?	8	5	40
Customer support	10	3	30
Training is available	9	4	36
Is a tool Help feature available? Is the tool well documented?	9	5	45
Availability and access to tool user groups	8	4	32
Total Value			2,638

Narrow down the search by eliminating tools that don't meet the minimal expectations, and focus additional research on the tools that fulfill at least the minimal requirements. Many questions need to be asked to ascertain whether the tool provides the required functionality. How will the tool be used in the organization? What is its most important function? How portable must the tool be to support multiple platforms? With which system life-cycle phases should the tool integrate?

The test team needs to research whether other groups or departments within the organization are already using specific tools and can share good insight about the tools. Once the test engineer has narrowed the search for a particular type of test tool down to two or three lead candidates, the evaluation scorecard depicted in Table 3.2 can be used to determine which tools best fit the particular requirements.

As the weighted values for the test tool characteristics will vary with each type of test tool, the test team may wish to develop an evaluation scorecard form for each type of test tool required. In Table 3.2, an automated GUI test tool (capture/playback) candidate is evaluated against the desired test tool characteristics. The total value of 2,638 for this candidate must then be compared with the total values derived for the other two candidates. As noted in the sample scorecard summary below, Candidate 3 achieved a rating of 75.3% in being able to provide coverage for all the desired test tool characteristics:

Candidate	Score	Rating
Candidate 1	2,360	67.4%
Candidate 2	2,530	72.3%
Candidate 3	2,638	75.3%

An optional evaluation scoring method involves sizing up the three candidates using only the most important test tool characteristics. Note that 12 of the characteristics were assigned a weight of 10. Table 3.3 reflects the scores for the three test tool candidates using a preferred scorecard form based upon product information obtained from each vendor.

Using this model for scoring, Candidate 2 achieves a higher rating than Candidate 3, which had posted the highest rating using the evaluation scorecard method. Candidate 2 achieved a rating of 90.0% for being able to provide coverage for the highest-priority test tool characteristics.

Candidate	Score	Rating
Candidate 1	97	74.6%
Candidate 2	117	90.0%
Candidate 3	103	79.2%

The evaluation for each kind of test tool being considered for an organization or project will differ, because each type of test tool has its own peculiar desired characteristics and necessitates a different weight scheme for the tool's desired characteristics. The guidelines of what to look for and weigh when evaluating a GUI test tool, for example, will be different from guidelines of how to evaluate a network monitoring tool.

Table 3.3   Preferred Scorecard—GUI Record/Playback Tool

Test Tool Characteristic	Candidate 1 (1–5)	Candidate 2 (1–5)	Candidate 3 (1–5)
Integrated defect-tracking feature	3	5	3
Recording at the widget level	5	5	5
Published APIs—Language interface capabilities	4	5	4
ODBC support—tool supports ODBC-compliant databases	4	4	4
Custom control support	3	5	3
Allows for adding timers	4	5	5
Compatible with GUI language/ development environment	5	5	5
Can query or update test data during playback	4	4	4
Supports the creation of a library of reusable functions	4	4	5
Allows for wrappers (shells)	4	5	5
Test results analysis	3	5	3
Y2K compliance	5	5	5
Supports stress, load, and performance testing	3	5	3
Allows for simulation of users	3	5	3
Supports configuration testing	3	3	3
Ability to use variable scripts	3	4	3
Supports resource monitoring	3	4	3
Synchronization ability	4	5	5
Client to server response times	3	4	3
Performance measurements of data loading	3	4	3
Version control	4	4	4
Supports test execution management	5	4	5
Allows for test planning	4	3	5
Measuring test progress	5	5	5
Price is within estimated range	3	5	4
Customer support	3	5	3
Total Value	97	117	103

3.4 | Evaluation Domain Definition

Even though the test tool vendor may guarantee a test tool's functionality, experience shows that often tools don't work as expected within the particular environment. It is worthwhile to develop an evaluation test plan that outlines in detail how to test the tool, so as to verify whether it fits particular system requirements and whether it is compatible with the target environment. The scope of the test plan for evaluating the product is highly dependent on the length of time that is available to review the test tool product.

To evaluate one or more candidate test tools, it is advantageous to first test the tool in an isolated test environment (test lab) before applying the test tool on a pilot project (target evaluation domain). Ideally, the test environment will be similar enough to the pilot project environment to provide assurance that the test tool will perform satisfactorily on the pilot project. Both the isolated test environment and the pilot project environment constitute evaluation domains. Evaluation within the test environment is aimed at proving the claims of test tool product literature and supporting a first-hand evaluation of the actual test tool itself. Evaluation within the pilot project environment is aimed at assessing the test tool's actual performance on a first project.

The hardware/software configuration within the test lab, together with the end-user application selected to support testing, constitutes the test environment. If the hardware/software configuration will be used for only a single application, then the isolated test environment is simple to construct. If a broader evaluation domain is preferred, however, the automated test tool should be evaluated against the needs of several projects.

In support of a broader evaluation domain, the test environment needs to be expanded to include a number of applications, provided that such applications and the resources to test the applications are available. Larger evaluation domains not only establish better and broader selection requirements, but also can enhance partnerships across sections or departments within the organization. This broader base can be helpful in expanding the acceptance of the selection process. It might include a test of the tool within a multitude of operating system environments and a test with applications developed in several programming languages. By making the selection process as inclusive as possible, later automated test tool introduction will be viewed as voluntary rather than forced.

The test team may be able to select an application development project as a pilot for applying the test tool; on other occasions, however, the test team must select a test tool to support a specified project. Table 3.4 provides one set of guidelines for selecting an application development project as a pilot when a record/playback tool candidate is being applied.

Table 3.4   Pilot Project Selection Guidelines— Record/Playback Tool [7]

Application Architecture Consists of a Two-Tiered, Client-Server Architecture

Application to be used to support testing has been developed using a major development tool (such as PB, VB, or Gupta) or a common language (such as C, C++, or Java)

Application to be used to support testing has been developed using RAD or OO (Object Oriented) technology (or equivalent) and a RAD or OO development life cycle

Hardware/software configuration is typical of the type of environment used within the organization

Application to be used to support testing is typical of the type of application commonly developed or used by the organization

Application to be used to support testing is under development and is still early in the software development life cycle, although a prototype or early build is expected to be available

Application to be used to support testing is being fully developed in-house, meaning that the developers who are developing the code for the application are on site or within easy access

Application to be used to support testing is not viewed as a business-sensitive application for which details about the application would not be open for discussion; the application is readily available and accessible for purposes of presentations, analysis, and demos

Guidelines for an Unsuitable Pilot Project

Application Consists of a GUI Client Interface Supporting a Mainframe Application Accessed via a Terminal Emulator

Application to be used to support testing represents a specialized application, which is not typical of the type of application commonly developed or used by the organization

Application is developed or purchased from a third party (except when the third party is developing on site)

Application is new and unknown to the test engineers, and is already in the last stages of the development life cycle

Application's schedule dictates that it must be completed and deployed in the very near future (within four to six weeks of the engagement)

Along with the evaluation domain, the organizational structure of the testing team will need to be considered. In particular, you should identify as early as possible whether the organization intends to establish a centralized test team. Such a test team would carry out all testing functions required for the multiple application development groups. An alternative way of structuring the test organization is to develop a distributed organization in which the different application development project groups are responsible for the test of their own application, with only limited cross-application requirements.

The structure of the test organization affects the characteristics of the desired test tool. A centralized test team will want to utilize a more powerful automated test tool that offers tremendous flexibility, programming language capabilities, and growth potential. A decentralized organization will be better served by an easy-to-use tool that minimizes the cost and time associated with learning how to use it. Chapter 5 provides more details on how the test team can be structured within the organization.

While the hardware and software configuration of the test lab is important, as is the identification of an application to be used to support testing, it is also critical to identify the individuals who will perform the evaluation of the test tool in the test lab. In addition, it will be necessary to define the role that each test engineer will play in the test tool evaluation process. See Chapter 5 for further discussion of these roles and responsibilities.

3.5 | Hands-on Tool Evaluation

As the test engineer responsible for selecting an automated test tool, you have now performed several of the steps necessary to support test tool evaluation and selection. The test engineer has become familiar with the system and software architectures of the application projects within the organization by surveying the systems engineering environment. The test group has reviewed the different types of test tools available on the market, used an evaluation scorecard to grade each candidate test tool against desired test tool characteristics, identified an isolated test environment, defined a target evaluation domain, and identified the individuals who will perform a hands-on evaluation of the test tool in the test environment.

Now, with a lead test tool candidate in mind, the test engineer needs to contact the test tool vendor to request a product demonstration. During the demonstration, the test engineer should note any questions or uncertainties and follow up with the vendor on any questions that cannot be answered during the demonstration. When working with a vendor representative, the test engineer should consider the professionalism demonstrated by the representative. It is important to assess whether the vendor representative will be supportive and easy to work with following the actual procurement of the test tool.

The test engineer should ask for a test tool evaluation copy from the vendor. Nearly all vendors have programs for allowing potential customers to try products for some specified period of time without an obligation to buy. The duration of this trial period may range from two weeks to 30 days. Some may extend the evaluation period even longer. The test engineer must clearly understand the duration specified, as failure to return the product within the vendor's specified timeframe may automatically obligate its purchase.

Some vendors may want a purchase order prepared prior to shipping their products for a no-obligation product evaluation. The test engineer should avoid this kind of arrangement if possible. Ideally, the evaluation process should not take more than two months. Of course, this length will depend on the number of tools with which to evaluate. If the timeframe to make a test tool decision is limited, the test team will likely need to have more than one test tool installed within the evaluation domain at the same time. In such a case, it is important to make sure that enough resources are dedicated to perform the evaluations. The evaluators should also understand the required functions of each candidate test tool. For each type of test tool required, a test plan should be created. Remember—the goal is to ensure that the test tool performs as advertised and that the tool works within the required environment.

3.5.1 Evaluation Report

During the test tool demonstration (or exercise of the test tool evaluation copy), the test engineer should compare the test tool's performance with its rating on desired test tool characteristics documented using the evaluation and preferred scorecard forms (see Tables 3.2 and 3.3). If the test tool's rating significantly differs from the baseline score developed as part of the test tool research exercise outlined in Section 3.3, then the test engineer may need to reconsider whether that test tool represents the best product for the particular requirement.

Following the conclusion of the evaluation process, an evaluation report should be prepared that documents the results of the first-hand examination of the test tool [8]. This report is produced only when the evaluation process is complete—that is, after a test tool demonstration by the tool vendor and exercise of the test tool evaluation copy in an isolated test environment.

The evaluation report formally outlines the evaluation results using clear, precise language and is targeted toward addressing management concerns. The distribution for the report should include all functional areas that participated in the evaluation process or otherwise will be affected by the tool's introduction. The report should contain background information, technical findings, product summaries, and a conclusion. It should also include a summary of the questions and answers addressed during the test tool demonstration, notes about the tool's performance documented during a test tool evaluation period, and an updated evaluation scorecard.

An example of a typical evaluation report document outline is provided here. The test team will want to tailor this format to suit the particular needs for its own organization.

1.0 Introduction. The introduction identifies the document, describes its purpose and scope, and provides some background information. For example, it is important to document whether the scope of the test tool evaluation is geared toward 32-bit, Visual Basic applications or some other applications. If this information is omitted, someone could look at the report a year later and assume it also covers mainframe applications. Within the introduction (and conclusion), it would be politically correct to acknowledge the individuals within the functional areas that participated in the evaluation process or otherwise will be affected by the introduction of the tool.

2.0 Summary.   Summarize the process that has taken place as well as the roles and participation of particular groups. Identify any assumptions that were made during the selection process, such as the anticipated organization structure of the project, preferred operating systems, and certain technical requirements. The summary is the area where the test team will want to allay any management concerns. How will this tool help? Where is the return on the investment?

3.0 Background Information.   Include names, addresses, and contact information for all potential vendors, including information pertaining to test tools that were not formally evaluated. The list should be extensive enough to demonstrate that the test team conducted a thorough search. For those companies and products that did not pass early screening, list the names of the products and indicate why they were rejected. Describe the test environment utilized to evaluate the test tool or tools, and describe the application(s) used to support testing. Be brief, but be sure that the team articulates that it understands the applications used to evaluate the tool.

4.0 Technical Findings.   Summarize the results and highlight points of particular interest. Note which product received the best score and why. This section is an overview of technical findings only; don't attempt to address each evaluation criteria in this area.

5.0 Product Summaries.   This section should summarize the results of the evaluation of each vendor and its product. The focus is on the company and the tool, rather than on the requirements. Provide the results of the evaluation scorecard for each test tool and present the findings in descending order of their scores, from best to worst. Raise issues that go beyond the absolute score. Although the process should be objective, "gut feelings" and instincts, if pertinent, should be mentioned. A table of the prices, such as the base tool, hotline support, maintenance, training, and other costs, would be a nice addition to this section. If a price table is included, make sure that anticipated quantities required are noted as well as the unit cost and total cost.

6.0 Conclusion.   Reiterate the objective and the evaluation team's recommendation. Be brief. In addition to the Introduction, the Conclusion could also be a good place in which to acknowledge test personnel who performed well.

3.5.2 License Agreement

Once a decision has been made to use a particular test tool, the test engineer needs to ensure that the resulting purchase (license) agreement satisfies operational requirements. The test engineer can also potentially reduce the organization's costs by working out arrangements for site licenses for the tools or volume (purchase) discounts.

The test engineer needs to review the license agreement before it is accepted by the organization's Purchasing Department. He or she needs to fully understand the license agreement, as the test team will be required to comply with it. Even though the initial agreement is written to protect the licenser (the tool vendor), not the licensee, it does not mean that the test team must accept it as written. The topics below can be considered when negotiating a test tool license agreement. (Note that this discussion is not to be construed as legal advice.)

Named Users versus Concurrent Users. Modify the agreement to allow for the concurrent use of the tool, regardless of location. Normally, test tool software is licensed to run on a single desktop computer. To install the test tool on another desktop computer requires that the tool be removed from the initial desktop computer. This transferral could be a logistical nightmare if the environment is large and dynamic. A *concurrent users* stipulation may alleviate this problem by limiting the test team's organization to the number of copies that can be run simultaneously, not the number of desktop computers on which it can be installed.

Extended Maintenance. Maintenance agreements will usually renew automatically each year unless the test team explicitly terminates the agreement sufficiently ahead of time. Consider changing the maintenance agreement so that the positive act of payment (or notification of payment) extends the maintenance contract, and nonpayment terminates the extended maintenance.

Be aware, though, that vendors generally access a penalty to reinstate maintenance if the maintenance agreement is allowed to lapse. If the licenser grants itself the right to cancel the extended maintenance, have this text removed from the maintenance agreement. (As long as you pay for the service, the right to end it should remain with you.) Finally, be sure that the license agreement explicitly caps the amount that the maintenance cost may increase from one year to the next.

Termination. If the contract mentions termination due to "material breach," make sure that the licenser specifies what this phrase specifically entails or cites a governing law, for example. Some licenses indicate that the laws of a particular state will govern all disputes. Consider changing the license agreement to the more favorable locations of New York or Delaware.

Upgrades.   During the evaluation process, the vendor may indicate that certain functionality will be released in a later version. Consider having an addendum attached that requires the vendor to commit to a specific date that the new functionality (or beta releases) will be available and have them commit to providing the upgrades [9].

Chapter Summary

o   In an ideal situation, the organization's test team will select a test tool that fits the criteria of the organization's system engineering environment, when feasible, and will select a pilot project that is in the early stages of the system development life cycle.

o   With an understanding of the systems engineering environment, the test engineer needs to identify which of the various test tool types might potentially apply on a particular project. A determination needs to be made whether the defined system requirements can be verified with one or more test tools. The test tool requirements need to be matched with the types of test tools available so as to derive a list of candidate test tools.

o   When considering each test tool type, the test engineer should define the level of software quality that is expected from the project, and determine which aspects of the software development are the most crucial to a particular project or effort.

o   The test engineer narrows down the test tool search by eliminating tools that fail to meet minimal expectations and focuses additional research on the tools that fulfill at least the minimal requirements.

o   Once the test engineer has narrowed down the search for a particular type of test tool to two or three lead candidates, an evaluation scorecard can be used to determine which tool best fits the particular requirements.

o   An optional evaluation scoring method involves sizing up the candidates using only the most important test tool characteristics.

o   With a lead test tool candidate in mind, the test engineer needs to contact the test tool vendor to request a product demonstration and ask for an evaluation copy. Even though the test tool vendor may guarantee a test tool's functionality, experience has shown that tools do not always work as expected in the specific environment. It is worthwhile to develop an evaluation test plan that outlines in detail how to test the tool, allowing the test team to verify whether it fits the particular system requirements and whether it is compatible with the target environment.

○ Following the conclusion of the evaluation process, an evaluation report should be prepared that documents the results of the first-hand examination of the test tool. This report is produced only when the evaluation process is complete—that is, after a demonstration by the tool vendor and exercise of the test tool evaluation copy in an isolated test environment.

References

1. Poston, R. *A Guided Tour of Software Testing Tools.* San Francisco: Aonix, 1988. www.aonix.com.

2. Ibid.

3. Ibid.

4. Ibid.

5. Ibid.

6. Ibid.

7. Adapted from SQA Process "Cust_Chk.doc," January 1996. See www.rational.com.

8. Greenspan, S. "Selecting Automated Test Tools During a Client/Server Migration." Paper presented at STAR conference, Orlando, Florida, May 13–17, 1996.

9. Used with permission of Steven Greenspan. "Selecting Automated Test Tools During a Client/Server Migration." Paper presented at STAR conference, Orlando, Florida, May 13–17, 1996.

Part II

Introduction of Automated Testing to a Project

A t the start, a new candidate for (a) para-digm (change) may have few supporters, and on occasions the supporters' motives may be suspect. Nevertheless, if they are competent, they will improve it, explore its possibilities, and show what it would be like to belong to the community guided by it. And as that goes on, if the paradigm is one destined to win its fight, the number and strength of the persuasive arguments in its favor will increase.

—Thomas Kuhn,

***The Structure of Scientific Revolution* [1]**

Automated Testing
Introduction Process

A tool is only as good as the process being used to
implement the tool. How a tool is implemented and
used is what really matters.

—Anonymous

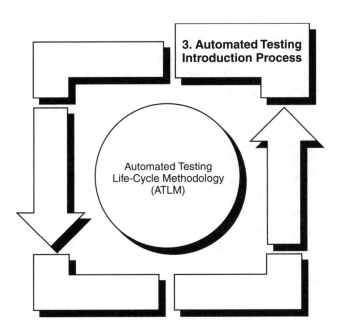

107

A new technology is often met with skepticism—and software test automation is no exception. How test teams introduce an automated software test tool on a new project is nearly as important as the selection of the most appropriate test tool for the project.

Over the last several years, test teams have largely implemented automated testing tools on projects without having a process or strategy in place describing in detail the steps involved in using the tool productively. This approach commonly results in the development of test scripts that are not reusable, meaning that the test script serves a single test string but cannot be applied to a subsequent release of the software application. In the case of incremental software builds and as a result of software changes, these test scripts need to be recreated repeatedly and must be adjusted multiple times to accommodate minor software changes. This approach increases the testing effort and brings subsequent schedule increases and cost overruns.

Perhaps the most dreaded consequence of an unstructured test program is the need for extending the period of actual testing. Test efforts that drag out unexpectedly tend to receive a significant amount of criticism and unwanted management attention. Unplanned extensions to the test schedule may have several undesirable consequences to the organization, including loss of product market share or loss of customer or client confidence and satisfaction with the product.

On other occasions, the test team may attempt to implement a test tool too late in the development life cycle to adequately accommodate the learning curve for the test tool. The test team may find that the time lost while learning to work with the test tool or ramping up on tool features and capabilities has put the testing effort behind schedule. In such situations, the team may become frustrated with the use of the tool and even abandon it so as to achieve short-term gains in test progress. The test team may be able to make up some time and meet an initial test execution date, but these gains are soon forfeited during regression testing and subsequent performance of test.

In the preceeding scenarios, the test team may have had the best intentions in mind, but unfortunately was simply unprepared to exercise the best course of action. The test engineer did not have the requisite experience with the tool or had not defined a way of successfully introducing the test tool. What happens in these cases? The test tool itself usually absorbs most of the blame for the schedule slip or the poor test performance. In fact, the real underlying cause for the test failure pertained to the absence of a defined test process, or, where one was defined, failure to adhere to that process.

The fallout from a bad experience with a test tool on a project can have a ripple effect throughout an organization. The experience may tarnish the reputation of the test group. Confidence in the tool by product and project managers may have been shaken to the point where the test team may have difficulty obtaining approval for use of a test tool on future efforts. Likewise, when budget pressures materialize, planned expenditures for test tool licenses and related tool support may be scratched.

By developing and following a strategy for rolling out an automated test tool, the test team can avoid having to make major unplanned adjustments throughout the test process. Such adjustments often prove nerve-wracking for the entire test team. Likewise, projects that require test engineers to perform tests manually may experience significant turnover of test personnel.

It is worth the effort to invest adequate time in the analysis and definition of a suitable test tool introduction process. This process is essential to the long-term success of an automated test program. Test teams need to view the introduction of an automated test tool into a new project as a process, not an event. The test tool needs to complement the process, not the reverse. Figure 4.1 depicts the test tool introduction process that should be used to avoid false starts.

Following the analysis of the overall test process and the development of test goals, objectives, and strategies (as outlined in Section 4.1), the test team will need

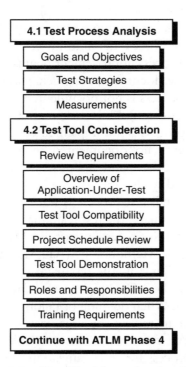

Figure 4.1   Test Tool Introduction Process

to verify that an automated test tool supports most of the project's specific test needs. Recall that the selection criteria in Chapter 3 stated that a really useful automated test tool will meet the needs of the system engineering environment of the organization. This selection criteria is the basis for purchasing a particular test tool.

Section 4.2 outlines the steps necessary to verify that the test tool meets the project's specific test needs and provides guidelines for determining whether it is feasible to introduce an automated testing tool, given the project schedule and other criteria. This section also seeks to ensure that automated test tool expertise is in place and that team members understand who is responsible for rolling out the testing tool and who will design, create, and execute the automated test scripts.

Once the test team has concluded that the test tool is appropriate for the current project, it continues with the ATLM by performing Test Planning (Chapter 6), Test Analysis and Design (Chapter 7), and Test Development (Chapter 8). The outcomes of the activities described in Sections 4.1 and 4.2 need to be recorded as part of the test planning activities that are documented within the formal test plan.

4.1 | Test Process Analysis

The test team initiates the test tool introduction process by analyzing the organization's current test process. Generally, some method of performing test is in place, and therefore the exercise of process definition itself may actually result in process improvement. In any case, process improvement begins with process definition.

The test process must be documented in such a way that it can be communicated to others. If the test process is not documented, then it cannot be communicated or executed in a repeatable fashion. If it cannot be communicated or is not documented, then often a process is not implemented.

In addition, if the process is not documented, then it cannot be consciously and uniformly improved. On the other hand, if a process is documented, it can be measured and therefore improved.

If the organization's overall test process is not yet documented, or it is documented but outdated or inadequate, the test team may wish to adopt an existing test process or adopt an existing test process in part. The test team may wish to adopt the Automated Test Life-cycle Methodology (ATLM) outlined in this book as the organization's test process. Similarly, the test team may wish to adopt the ATLM with modifications, tailoring the ATLM to accommodate the test goals and interests of its particular organization. When defining or tailoring a test process, it may prove useful for the test engineer to review the organization's product development or software development process document, when available.

When defining a test process for an organization, the test team should become familiar with the organization's quality and process improvement objectives. Perhaps the organization is seeking to comply with industry quality and process maturity guidelines, such as the Software Engineering Institute's Capability Maturity Model (CMM). The CMM for software was established as a guide for providing software development organizations with a structured way of instilling discipline into their process for creating and maintaining software. This model instructs organizations to implement this discipline in an evolutionary manner, where levels or plateaus of maturity are reached and then surpassed.

Implementation of CMM guidelines is intended to create an infrastructure of people and proven practices that enable the organization to produce quality products, achieve customer satisfaction, and meet project objectives. Consistent with the CMM, the test team will want to define and refine test process inputs, outputs, and process-specific metrics. The test team should not be content to know that the overall organization is performing in a mature manner, if test procedures are not defined and test documentation is not being produced in a consistent manner. Only when the test process has been documented and metrics have been defined, collected, and analyzed can the test team make effective improvements to the test process.

To further support process objectives, the test team will want to maintain a repository of objective evidence that documents performance of testing in accordance with the defined test process. Should the organization undergo an assessment of its compliance with CMM guidelines, the assessment team will attempt to verify that the test team's activities match the activities defined within the test process. The assessment team will also check whether process outputs or artifacts produced comply with the defined test process.

The purpose of analyzing the organization's test process is to identify the test goals, objectives, and strategies that may be inherent in the test process. These top-level elements of test planning serve as the cornerstones for a project's test program. The purpose of documenting the test tool introduction process is to ensure that the test team has a clearly defined way of implementing automated testing, thereby allowing the team to fully leverage the functionality and time-saving features of the automated test tool.

The additional time and cost associated with the documentation and implementation of a test tool introduction process sometimes emerges as a contentious issue. In fact, a well-planned and well-executed process will pay for itself many times over by ensuring a higher level of defect detection and fielded software fixes, shortening product development cycles, and providing labor savings. A test team that is disciplined in defining test goals and reflects the test goals in its definition of processes, selection of skills for test team staff, and the selection of a test tool will perform well. This kind of discipline, exercised incrementally, supports the test team's (and the entire organization's) advancement in quality and maturity from one level to the next.

4.1.1 Process Review

As noted earlier, the test engineer needs to analyze the existing development and test process. During this analytical phase, he or she determines whether the current testing process meets several prerequisites:

- Testing goals and objectives have been defined.
- Testing strategies have been defined.
- The tools needed are available to implement planned strategies.
- A testing methodology has been defined.
- The testing process is communicated and documented.
- The testing process is being measured.
- The testing process implementation is audited.
- Users are involved throughout the test program.
- The test team is involved from the beginning of the system development life cycle.
- Testing is conducted in parallel to the system development life cycle.
- The schedule allows for process implementation.
- The budget allows for process implementation.

This section provides information to help the test engineer determine whether the testing process meets this criteria, outlines what to look for during the evaluation of the test process, and supports the test process enhancement or implementation effort. Test goals and objectives are discussed along with strategies that can help to achieve these goals and objectives. As depicted in Figure 4.2, it is important to document the outcome of each test tool introduction phase in the test plan.

A successfully implemented test process will minimize the schedule, achieve high defect detection efficiency, improve software quality, and support the development of reliable systems that will keep the users happy. This section describes proven practices to apply when reviewing or revising the organization's test process.

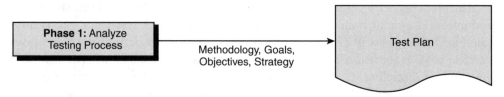

Figure 4.2   Documenting the Results of Test Process Analysis

4.1.1.1 Early Involvement of Test Team

The test process should be initiated at the beginning of the system development life cycle. Early test team involvement is essential. During the business analysis phase, the test team augments its understanding of business rules and processes, and it obtains greater understanding of customer needs. During the requirements phase, the test team verifies the testability of requirements. Early test involvement also permits earlier detection of errors and prevents migration of errors from requirements specification to design, and from design into code.

4.1.1.2 Repeatable Process

The organization's test process should be repeatable. A repeatable test process can be measured, fine-tuned, and improved. This process should also result in quality and efficiency whenever it is undertaken. Such a process will be measurable, reliable, and predictable. A repeatable process can be achieved by *documenting every step of the process.* When a test process is thoroughly documented, then testing can be controlled and implemented uniformly.

In addition to documentation, *automation of tests* is the most efficient means of achieving repeatability. Conventional test design techniques should be supplemented with automated static and dynamic analysis. A repeatable process can be further augmented through the application of *reusable test scripts.* Chapter 8 provides detailed information on how to create such reusable test scripts.

Collection and analysis of measurements also need to be part of the test process. Within many organizations, a quality assurance group is responsible for performing audits to ensure that activities are being performed in accordance with defined processes. As a result, the test team needs to verify that the ATLM process has been properly implemented. To this end, the test team should review criteria by which the ATLM process can be measured. Several such criteria measures are as follows [2]:

- **Performance of the process.** Obtain a measure of product attributes that result from the ATLM process, then measure the attributes of the process itself.

- **Repeatability.** Would someone else be able to repeat the measurements and obtain the same results?

- **Product traceability.** Measure the traceability of products to standards and products to process.

- **Stability of process.** Are products on schedule according to plan? Are variations predictable and unexpected results rare? Does the process need to be improved to produce better and higher-quality products?

Table 4.1   Process Compliance Measures

Fitness to Execute Process		Use of Defined Process	
Are all the requisites for successful process execution in place (for example, personnel, skills, experience, training, facilities, tools, documented procedures)?		Is the process being executed faithfully? Are tools, methods, practices, and work plans being used?	
Entities	**Attributes**	**Entities**	**Attributes**
People	Skills, experience, training, quantity	People	Effort, time
Tool	Accessibility, adequacy, utility, skills	Tool	Use: how widely, frequently, long
Procedures	Coverage, sufficiency, quality, documentation	Procedures	Awareness use: how widely, frequently, long
Facilities	Space, computers, technical support, sufficiency	Facilities	Use: how widely, frequently, long
Work Plan	Targets, work breakdown structure applicability, understandable, doable	Work Plan	Awareness use: how widely, frequently, long

- **Compliance of process.** Actual performance must be consistent with the defined test process. Table 4.1 outlines entities and attributes that can be measured to address process compliance.

- **Fitness to execute process.** Are project personnel aware of, trained in, or given the tools needed for executing the process? Are tools and procedures effective in accomplishing what was intended?

- **Use of defined process.** Consistent execution of process is required. Is the process being executed as defined?

- **Capability of process.** When a process is stable and conforming to requirements, it is termed capable.

4.1.1.3   Continuous Improvement

Another best practice to apply when maintaining a test process involves continuous process improvement. The primary goal is continuous refinement and improvement of the test process. To achieve process improvement, it is necessary to document lessons learned and QA audit findings throughout the testing life cycle and take corrective action before it is too late. It is also beneficial to document lessons learned at the end of the application development life cycle. The purpose of this effort is to identify needed improvement activities and ensure that mistakes are not repeated in the next test phase, during the next incremental software delivery, or on the next project. Chapter 10 discusses these lessons learned.

Determining and documenting the benefits reaped as a result of utilizing an automated test tool and making this information available to everyone in the organization also support continuous process improvement. Likewise, this information enhances the project team's understanding of the benefits of using such tools. Chapter 9 discusses these benefits.

Surveys represent another way of determining how the process can be improved. The test team can send out a survey that asks project team personnel to give their impressions of the test process and the outputs produced by that process. The survey can also seek to identify ways in which the process could be improved. Project team personnel may include application developers, functional analysts/business users, and test engineers.

Process assessments and audits are very valuable in verifying that processes are being implemented correctly, thus supporting continuous improvement. The quality assurance department usually conducts these activities.

Root-cause analysis is another way of figuring out why a defect was introduced. Chapter 9 describes this type of analysis.

4.1.1.4 Safeguarding the Integrity of the Automated Test Process

To safeguard the integrity of the automated test process, the test team needs to exercise new releases of an automated test tool in an isolated environment; it can also validate that the tool performs up to product specifications and marketing claims. The test team should verify that the upgrades will run in the organization's current environment. Although the previous version of the tool may have performed correctly and a new upgrade may perform well in other environments, the upgrade might adversely affect the team's particular environment. The verification of the test tool upgrade should be performed in an isolated environment, as described in Chapter 3. Additionally, using a configuration management tool to baseline the test repository will help safeguard the integrity of the automated testing process.

Although process definition, metric-gathering, and process improvement activities can be expensive and time-consuming, the good news is that creating and documenting standards and procedures for an automated test program may be no more expensive than the same activities for a manual test program. In fact, use of an automated test tool with scripting, test identification, and automatic documentation capabilities can reduce costs by providing some of the framework and content required.

Following performance of the test process analysis as outlined so far, the test team must decide whether the process needs to be revised or whether the team can proceed with the existing test process. Once a test process has been defined, reviewed, and then updated through a couple of iterations to shake out the bugs, the test team is ready to define test goals, objectives, and the test strategies for a particular project of product development effort.

4.1.2   Goals and Objectives of Testing

What does the test effort hope to accomplish? Testing in general is conducted to verify that the software meets specific criteria and satisfies the requirements of the end user or customer. The high-level goal of testing is to identify defects in the application, thereby permitting the prevention, detection, and subsequent removal of defects and the creation of a stable system.

The primary goal of testing is to increase the probability that the application-under-test will behave correctly under all circumstances and will meet defined requirements, thus satisfying the end users by detecting (and managing to closure) as many defects as possible. One objective of automated testing is to support manual testing efforts intended to achieve this testing goal. Automated testing, when implemented correctly, promotes faster, better, and more efficient testing. It eventually can lead to a reduction in the size of the test effort, a reduction of the test schedule, the production of a reliable system, and the enhancement of a repeatable test process.

Testing verifies that software programs work according to the specifications. A program is said to work correctly when it satisfies the following criteria:

1. Given valid input, the program produces the correct output.
2. Given invalid input, the program correctly and gracefully rejects the input.
3. The program doesn't hang or crash, given either valid or invalid input.
4. The program keeps running correctly for as long as expected.
5. The program behaves as specified.

In addition to verifying that software programs work correctly and without any major defects, the test team, together with quality assurance personnel, seeks to verify that other outputs of the application development life cycle are correct or work as required. These criteria include requirement specifications, development and development support procedures, project documentation, test design and test procedures, and other output specific to a particular development effort. Testing also serves the purpose of finding defects so that they can be fixed. In addition, the test effort helps define "quality" when criteria exist for deciding when software is ready to be deployed.

Once test goals are defined and understood by the test team, these personnel must define more tangible or specific objectives that should be achieved during the test effort. Achievement of the test goals requires satisfaction of the test objectives. Once clear test objectives have been established, the test team needs to outline the test strategies required to attain test objectives. Test strategies include very specific activities that will be performed by the test team. The different test strategies that support the development life cycle are described in further detail in Chapter 7.

As an example of test goal and objective definition, consider the experience of a test engineer named Erika. A major redesign effort was under way for the largest application at her company. The application comprised many parts and incorporated a multitude of functionality. The system was supposed to be redesigned from scratch, but because it was a mission-critical system, it could be redesigned only in small fragments that collectively represented an upgrade of a major functionality.

As a result, the system was upgraded incrementally. Each incremental release had its own catchy name, such as Skywalker and Chewy. Erika needed to quantify the test goal in terms that reflected the mission of the application effort. Erika's test could be stated as follows:

- Increase the probability that all applications that make up the final system can be integrated with the existing production system into a working system, while meeting all system requirements and acceptance criteria, by detecting as many defects as possible and managing them to closure.

Her test objectives included the following points:

- Ensure that each incremental application release will meet its specific requirements without any major defects, while producing a repeatable integration process that meets all system requirements.

- Incorporate an automated test tool that can record a baseline of reusable scripts to be played back repeatedly for regression, performance, and stress testing once the new modules have been integrated with the existing operational system.

- Create and maintain a baseline of reusable test scripts to streamline future test efforts.

The specific test objectives can vary from one test phase to the next, so the test engineer needs to ask several questions. What is the test team trying to accomplish during this test phase? What is the purpose of the software being tested? Section 4.1.3 provides further detail on how the concerns of the various test phases can affect the choice of a defect detection strategy.

Test objectives can also vary according to system requirements. Test objectives for a commercial-off-the-shelf (COTS) tool, for example, will be different than the test objectives applicable to an in-house developed system. When testing a COTS tool, a primary objective would be the integration of the COTS tool with the rest of the system, and the corresponding test objective would be based on black-box testing. On the other hand, when testing a homegrown system, the test team will be concerned with the application's internal workings, which necessitates white-box testing, and the integration with other systems, which involves black-box testing.

With white-box testing, the individual performing the test can see into the program code and checks for defects related to the execution path, coverage, decision points, loops, and logic constructs. Black-box testing focuses on the external behavior of inputs and related outputs, and assesses the software's ability to satisfy functional requirements. Chapter 7 provides more information on white-box and black-box testing.

Finally, test objectives may vary by test phase. A test objective that is pertinent during stress testing may not be relevant during functional requirement testing. During stress testing, the test objective is to establish an environment where multiple machines can access one or multiple servers simultaneously so as to obtain measurements of client and server response times. During functional requirements testing, the test objective is to determine whether the system meets business requirements.

Test objectives should be outlined early in the planning process and need to be clearly defined. It is a common practice to list test objectives within the Introduction section of the test plan. Table 4.2 provides sample test process analysis docu-

Table 4.2   Test Process Analysis Documentation

Process Review

- Test process. The project will utilize the organization's standard test process, which adopts the ATLM.
- Test tool introduction. To support a smooth implementation of the automated test tool, the project team will verify that goals, objectives, and strategies are defined and compatible with automated testing. A test tool consideration phase will be conducted before continuing with phase 4 of the ATLM and executing each subsequent ATLM phase.

Test Goals

- Increase the probability that the application-under-test will behave correctly under all circumstances
- Increase the probability that the application-under-test meets all defined requirements
- Execute a complete test of the application within a short timeframe

Test Objectives

- Ensure that the system complies with defined client and server response times
- Ensure that the most critical end-user paths through the system perform correctly
- Ensure that user screens perform correctly
- Ensure that database changes have not had an adverse affect on existing software modules
- Incorporate a test design that minimizes test rework following changes to the application
- Incorporate the use of automated test tools whenever feasible
- Perform test activities that support both defect prevention and defect detection
- Incorporate the use of automated test design and development standards so as to create reusable and maintainable scripts

mentation, which would be reflected within the Introduction of the project test plan. This documentation is generated as a result of the test team's process review together with its analysis of test goals and objectives.

Case Study
Test Objectives and Strategies

As an example of test objective definition, consider the experience of a test engineer named Jake, who was assigned the responsibility for testing a database management system (DBMS) redesign project. The database was redesigned to accommodate additional data requirements related to a system upgrade. As a result of the upgrade, new tables were added and some tables were deleted. Additionally, a new version of Sybase was introduced.

Jake defined his test goal as follows: Verify that the application will behave correctly following the database change. What would logically be his test objectives? Jake jotted down some notes to help him analyze the situation. The GUI of the target application had not changed, but he still needed to test the data output. In addition, he needed to verify that the edit boxes and data controls on the GUI screens continued to display data correctly. Although the testing was data-driven, performance and stress test measures were nevertheless required. Jake ultimately developed the following list of test objectives:

- After data conversion, ensure that data were successfully converted from the old to the new database.

- After data conversion, ensure that database changes did not have an adverse effect on existing software modules and that the data managed by the system were not compromised by addition, deletion, updating, restoration, or retrieval processing.

- After data conversion, ensure that the application development team can successfully upgrade to a new database management system (DBMS) release.

- Ensure that the system still complies with defined client and server response times.

- Ensure that end-user paths through the system and user screens perform correctly.

Jake needed to define the test strategies to be implemented to support testing. That is, he needed to review his test objectives and identify suitable strategies that could fulfill these objectives. He then developed the following list of test strategies. (More information on test strategy development is provided in Section 4.1.3.)

Data Conversion and Data Integrity Testing Record a baseline of test scripts developed against the initial system, verifying their accuracy. After data conversion, play back the baseline test scripts against the updated system containing the new database schema. If the data output is the same and the baseline test scripts execute successfully, then the updated system is performing correctly.

Database Version Upgrade After data conversion testing, verify that the updated system performs correctly by using the old DBMS release, then allowing the database version to be upgraded. Next, play back the baseline test scripts against the updated system containing the new DBMS release. If the data output is the same and the baseline test scripts execute successfully, then system is performing correctly.

Performance Testing Record a baseline of performance test scripts developed against the initial system. After data conversion and upgrade of the new database, play back the baseline performance test scripts against the updated system. Following this test, compare the results of the new test with the test of the baseline system. Inspect the results to ensure that the system has not experienced degradation. Verify that the system meets the new performance requirements.

Regression Testing Play back the baseline regression test scripts against the updated system containing the new database schema and the new DBMS release. If the data output is the same and the baseline test scripts execute successfully, then end-user paths and user screens are performing correctly.

4.1.3 Test Strategies

A multitude of test strategies can be implemented to support defined test goals and objectives. A careful examination of goals, objectives, and constraints should culminate with the identification of a set of systematic test strategies that produce more predictable, higher-quality test results and that support a greater degree of test automation. Test strategies can be lumped into two different categories: defect prevention technologies and defect detection technologies. Table 4.3 lists selected test strategies.

Defect prevention provides the greatest cost and schedule savings over the duration of the application development effort. Given the complexity of systems and the

Table 4.3   Test Strategies and Techniques

Defect Prevention Technologies (Section 4.1.3.1)

Examination of constraints
Early test involvement
Use of process standards
Inspections and walkthroughs
Quality gates

Defect Detection Technologies (Section 4.1.3.2)

Inspections and walkthroughs	
Quality gates (see Figure 4.2)	
Testing of product deliverables	
Designing testability into the application	
Use of automated test tools	
Unit test phase	Condition coverage, path coverage, fault insertion, memory leak, error handling, string test, statement coverage, decision coverage, cyclomatic complexity, data flow coverage
Integration test phase	Integration testing
System test phase	Subtypes of system testing: stress, regression, replication, data integrity, configuration, performance, functional, security, alpha/beta, acceptance, compatibility/conversion, benchmark, usability, error guessing, backup and recoverability, operational readiness, random (discussed in Chapter 7)
Acceptance test phase	Same as system test phase
Following a test process	
Risk assessment	
Strategic manual and automated test design	
Execution and management of automated test	
Test verification method	
User involvement	

various human factors involved, defect prevention technologies, by themselves, cannot always prohibit defects from entering into the application-under-test. Therefore defect detection technologies are best applied in combination with defect prevention technologies.

The specific test strategies required on a particular project will depend upon the test goals and objectives defined for that project. The test engineer should therefore review these test objectives and then identify suitable strategies for fulfilling them.

4.1.3.1   Defect Prevention Strategies

The Testing Maturity Model (TMM) that was developed by the Illinois Institute of Technology lists the highest maturity as level 5: optimization, *defect prevention*, and quality control [3]. The existence of defect prevention strategies not only reflect a high level of test discipline maturity, but also represent the most cost-beneficial expenditure associated with the entire test effort. The detection of defects early in the development life cycle helps to prevent the migration of errors from require-ment specification to design, and from design into code.

Recognition that testing should take place at the earliest stages of the applica-tion development process is clearly a break from the general approach to testing pursued over the last several decades. In the past, the test effort was commonly con-centrated at the end of the system development life cycle. It focused on testing the executable form of the end product. More recently, the software industry has come to understand that to achieve best system development results, the test effort needs to permeate all steps of the system development life cycle. Table 1.1 on page 8 lists some of the cost savings that are possible with early life-cycle involvement by the test team.

Examination of Constraints.   Testing at program conception is intended to verify that the product is feasible and testable. A careful examination of goals and con-straints may lead to the selection of an appropriate set of test strategies that will pro-duce a more predictable, higher-quality outcome and support a high degree of automation. Potential constraints may include a short time-to-market schedule for the software product or the limited availability of engineering resources on the project. Other constraints may reflect the fact that a new design process or test tool is being introduced. The test team needs to combine a careful examination of these constraints, which influence the defect prevention technology, with the use of defect detection technologies to derive test strategies that can be applied to a particular application development effort.

Early Test Involvement.   The test team needs to be involved in an application development effort from the beginning. Test team involvement is particularly criti-cal during the requirements phase. A report from the Standish Group estimates that a staggering 40% of all software projects fail, while an additional 33% of projects are completed late, over budget, or with reduced functionality. According to the report, only 27% of all software projects are successful. The most significant factors for cre-ating a successful project are requirements-related. They include user involvement, clear business objectives, and well-organized requirements. Requirements-related management issues account for 45% of the factors necessary to ensure project devel-opment success [4].

During the requirements definition phase, the test effort should support the achievement of explicit, unambiguous requirements. Test team involvement in the requirements phase also needs to ensure that system requirements are stated in terms that are testable. In this context, the word *testable* means that given an initial system state and a set of inputs, a test engineer can predict exactly the composition of system outputs.

Appendix A provides a detailed discussion of requirements testing. The test of system requirements should be an integral part of building any system. Software that is based on inaccurate requirements will be unsatisfactory, regardless of the quality of the detailed design documentation or the well-written code that makes up the software modules. Newspapers and magazines are full of stories about catastrophic software failures that ensued from vendor failure to deliver the desired end-user functionality. The stories, however, usually do not indicate that most of the failed systems' glaring problems can be traced back to wrong, missing, vague, or incomplete requirements. In recent years, the importance of ensuring quality requirements has become more thoroughly understood. Project and product managers now recognize that they must become familiar with ways to implement requirements testing before they launch into the construction of a software solution.

During the design and development phases, test activities are intended to verify that design and development standards are being followed and other problems are avoided. Chapter 3 discusses the various automated testing tools that can be used during these stages.

Use of Standards.   Many reasons exist for using standards. Coherent standards development will help prevent defects. Use of standard guidelines also facilitates the detection of defects and improves the maintainability of a software application.· Test activities are interdependent, requiring a significant amount of teamwork among project personnel. Teamwork, in turn, requires rules for effective interaction. Standards provide the rules or guidance governing the interaction of the project personnel.

A multitude of different standards have been developed. There are standards for software design, program coding, and graphical user interfaces. There are standards issued by product vendors such as Microsoft, others issued by software industry organizations, and standards promulgated by the U.S. Department of Defense. There are communication protocol standards, safety standards, and many more. In addition, many large companies define and promote their own internal standards.

A software design standard may require the development of structure charts, and a coding standard may require that each software module have a single point of entry and a single exit point. The coding standard may specify that software code employ maximum cohesion (intramodule relationship) and minimum coupling (intermodule relationship). Typically, such standards promote the modularity of code in an effort to create functional independence. In some companies, the test team may take the lead in ensuring that the developers follow software design standards. This approach may be applied when the QA team does not exist or is understaffed (for example, during inspections, unit tests, and system tests). Any particular application development project will likely be bound to conform to a number of development standards. The test team needs to obtain a listing of these standards—perhaps from the project plan, where one exists.

The test team may also be responsible for promulgating standards for the performance of testing within the overall organization. It may decide to advocate the use of standard test tools or adopt the ATLM (discussed in Chapter 1) as the organization's standard test process. Because standards represent methodologies or techniques that have proved successful over time, adherence to such standards supports the development of quality software products. Test activities therefore need to verify that the application-under-test adheres to required standards. Similarly, the development of test procedures should be performed in accordance with a standard.

Inspections and Walkthroughs.   Inspections and walkthroughs represent formal evaluation techniques that can be categorized as either defect prevention or defect detection technology, depending upon the particular scope of the activity. The technology of using inspections and walkthroughs is listed as one of the principal software practices by the Airlie Software Council [5].

Walkthroughs and inspections provide for a formal evaluation of software requirements, design, code, and other software work products, such as test procedures and automated test scripts. They entail an exhaustive examination by a person or a group other than the author. Inspections are intended to detect defects, violations of development standards, test procedure issues, and other problems. Walkthroughs address the same work products as inspections, but perform a more cursory review.

Examples of defect prevention activities include walkthroughs and inspections of system requirements and design documentation. These activities are performed to avoid defects that might crop up later within the application code. When requirements are defined in terms that are testable and correct, then errors are prevented from entering the system development pipeline, which would eventually be reflected as defects of the overall system. Design walkthroughs can ensure that the design is consistent with defined requirements, conforms to standards and applicable design methodology, and contains few errors.

Walkthroughs and inspections have several benefits: They support the detection and removal of defects early in the development and test cycle; prevent the migration of defects to later phases of software development; improve quality and productivity; and reduce cost, cycle time, and maintenance efforts. These types of technical reviews and inspections have proved to be the most effective forms of defect detection and removal. As discussed in Chapter 3, technical review management tools are available to automate this process.

Quality Gates.　　Successful completion of the activities prescribed by the test process (such as walkthroughs and inspections) should be the only approved gateway to the next phase of software development. Figure 4.3 depicts typical quality gates that apply during the testing life cycle. Quality gates also exist throughout the entire development life cycle after each iterative phase.

　　The test team needs to verify that the output of any one stage represented in Figure 4.3 is fit to be used as the input for the next stage. Verification that output is satisfactory may be an iterative process, and this goal is accomplished by comparing the output against applicable standards or project specific criteria.

　　The results of walkthroughs, inspections, and other test activities should adhere to the levels of quality outlined within the applicable software development standards.

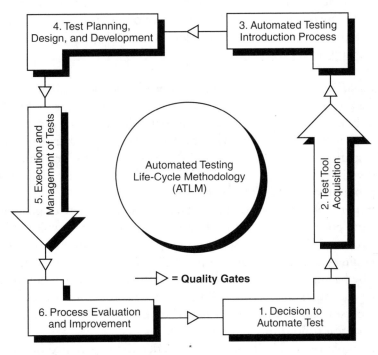

Figure 4.3　Testing Life Cycle and Quality Gates

Test team compliance with these standards, together with involvement of the test team early in the development life cycle, improves the likelihood that the benefits of defect prevention will be realized.

4.1.3.2   Defect Detection Strategies

Although the defect prevention methodologies described in Section 4.1.3.1 are effective, they cannot always prevent defects from entering into the application-under-test. Applications are very complex, and it is difficult to catch all errors. Defect detection and subsequent removal techniques complement the defect prevention efforts. The two methodologies work hand in hand to increase the probability that the test team will meet its defined test goals and objectives.

Defect detection strategies seek to exercise the application so as to find previously undiscovered errors. Further detection and removal of errors increase the developers' confidence that the system will satisfy the user requirements and perform correctly. As a result, end users of the system can entrust the operation of their business to the system. In the final analysis, thoroughly tested systems support the needs of end users, reduce the nuisance factors that are associated with misbehaving systems, and reduce the system maintenance cost and effort.

Defect tracking is very important during the defect prevention and detection stages. Everyone involved in the testing and development life cycle must keep track of defects found and maintain a log of defect status. Chapter 7 provides additional details concerning defect tracking.

Inspections and Walkthroughs.   As previously noted, the performance of inspections and walkthroughs can be categorized as either defect prevention or defect detection technology, depending upon the particular scope of the activity. Defect prevention activities focus on eliminating errors prior to the start of coding; defect detection activities concentrate on eliminating errors after program coding has begun. Inspections and walkthroughs associated with defect detection include reviews of program code and test procedures.

A *code walkthrough* consists of a top-level or cursory review of program code to ensure that the code complies with relevant standards. It will typically involve the use of a checklist, which ensures that the most important guidelines addressed within the coding standard are being applied. A *code inspection* examines the code in more detail by having the programmers narrate their code and orally work through sample test procedures as a group. Similarly, a *test procedure walkthrough* is performed at a cursory level, while a *test procedure inspection* involves a more detailed examination of test procedures and test scripts.

As an example of a code inspection, consider the experience of an application developer named Jason, who developed some program code and now must attend his first code inspection. Jason has been informed by the development manager that the code inspection team will review his work in detail, and that Jason will be expected to explain the structure and workings of his code. Jason understands that he must outline the logic of his program, statement by statement. The development manager further explains that the code inspections are conducted with a group of people in attendance to include his programmer peers, a software quality assurance engineer, and a software test engineer. The group will analyze his program by comparing it with a list of common programming errors. During the code inspection, the group will mentally execute test procedures of his program by talking them out. Jason learns that usually three or more people attend a code inspection. The defined roles for the code inspection are as follows:

Moderator. The moderator distributes the program code before the actual meeting, schedules the meeting, leads the meeting, records the meeting minutes, and follows up on any resulting actions.

Programmer. Each programmer is responsible for narrating his or her code from beginning to end.

Test Lead. The test lead should come prepared with several test procedures to talk through with the group.

Peers. Programmers help review code developed by others and provide objective feedback.

Even though the code inspection detects errors in Jason's program, no solutions to the errors are provided. Instead, the moderator of the meeting records the errors in his program. Jason is informed that corrective actions resulting from the inspection will be gathered by the moderator, who will then pass them to the development manager for final disposition. (Jason will probably end up fixing the coding errors, unless the corrective action involves other areas of the system development life cycle.)

Testing Product Deliverables.   Another effective defect detection strategy involves the review of product deliverables. Deliverables consist of the work products resulting from the development effort that include documentation of the system. Documented work products may actually be delivered to the end user or customer, or the work product may represent an internal document deliverable. Product deliverables may include requirement specifications, design documentation, test plans, training material, user manuals, system help manuals, system administration manuals, and system implementation plans. Product deliverables may consist of hard-copy documents or on-line system documentation.

The test team should review product deliverables and document suspected errors. For example, following the review of test procedures, errors relating to requirement issues, implementation issues, and usability issues may be discovered. Product deliverables may be reviewed in isolation or in comparison with other product deliverables. For example, an effective way to detect errors is to compare a user manual deliverable against the actual application under test. When differences are detected, which is in error? When such differences are discovered, the test engineer needs to investigate further to ascertain which of the two items is correct.

Designing Testability into the Application.   Defect detection becomes more effective when the concern for system testability is factored into the development process. Incorporating testability into the application is a global process that begins at project or product conception. The *IEEE Standard Glossary of Software Engineering Terminology* defines "testability" as: (1) the degree to which a system or component facilitates the establishment of test criteria and the performance of tests to determine whether those criteria have been met, and (2) the degree to which a requirement is stated in terms that permit establishment of test criteria and performance of tests to determine whether those criteria have been met [6].

Product or project mission statements should be defined in such a way that they can be traced to end-user requirements statements. End-user requirements, in turn, should be concise and clearly understood (see Appendix A for more detail on this point). These requirements should then be transformed into system requirements specifications, which need to be stated in terms that can be tested or verified.

The documentation of the system requirements specifications is often a critical juncture for the development effort. As outlined in Section 1.3, a poor requirements specification is one of the primary culprits in failed projects. When specified requirements are not testable, then neither development personnel nor end users can verify that a delivered system application will properly support the targeted business operation.

Incorporating testability into the system design is important to increase the likelihood of effective development. Structured and object-oriented design methodologies provide a means to structure or modularize design components in the form of structure charts or objects. This transformation facilitates the review of design components. Design documentation, which is considered to be testable, uses design components that permit the dissection of output and the analysis of complete threads of functionality. It is more productive to inspect and change graphical design documentation than it is to correct errors in code later, as code-based errors might have migrated as a result of poor design. By incorporating testability within design documentation, the number of logic and structural errors that can be expected within program code is reduced. Additionally, program code resulting from design documentation, which has incorporated testability, requires less debugging.

Testability must be factored into development strategies as well. If program modules are small and functionally associative (cohesive), they can be developed with fewer internal logic and specification errors. If program modules are linked only by required data (loosely coupled), then fewer opportunities exist for one module to corrupt another. Following these two development strategies reduces the number of severe error types. As a result, the remaining errors within the program modules will consist primarily of syntax and other minor error types, many of which can be caught by a compiler or program analyzer.

Another development strategy that incorporates testability is called application partitioning. In this strategy, applications are separated into several layers, which include the user interface, application-specific logic, business rules (or remote logic), and data access logic. The GUI and application-specific logic should reside on the client; the business rules (remote logic) and data access logic should reside on a server ("a server" here means possibly both database and application servers). The testing advantage of layered application design derives from the fact that it results in far more reusability, easier performance tuning, and expedited and more isolated debugging [7].

Many of the same characteristics that make a program testable make it maintainable as well. Following coding standards, for example, represents another way of incorporating testability within the program code. The use of such coding standards reduces the cost and effort associated with software maintenance and testing. For example, the use of preambles or comments in front of code that describe and document the purpose and organization of a program make the resulting program more readable and testable. Such preambles can become test requirement inputs during the test automation development phase.

Both application developers and test engineers must bear in mind that the guidelines promulgated within standards should not be overenforced. Even the most mature guidelines sometimes need to be adjusted or waived for a particular development effort. Although the use of standards facilitates later quality reviews and maintainability objectives, standard compliance should not obstruct the overall project goal—that is, creating an effective product.

Custom controls, widgets, or third-party add-on products, whether in Visual Basic or any other such programming language, often cause an application to be incompatible with the testing tool, thus decreasing the application's automated testability. To counter this problem, test engineers should produce a list of custom controls (provided by the vendor) for which the test tool is compatible. The use of the controls in this list should be made a standard, thereby making the developers aware of controls that are compatible with the test tool and ensuring that they will use only supported third-party controls. Senior management should also be required to approve exceptions to using third-party controls that support the organization's automated testing tool. By implementing such a standard, chances are good that the resulting applications will have the same look and feel and that test engineers will not have to continuously create work-around solutions to incompatibility problems caused by the use of an unapproved third-party control.

Another testability issue to consider is whether the application-under-test has been installed on the test machines in the exact same way that it will be installed on end-user machines. A good installation procedure, and one that is consistently followed throughout the entire application life cycle, will improve testability.

Use of Automated Test Tools.   In addition to the manually intensive review and inspection strategies outlined earlier in this section, automated test tools can be applied to support the defect detection process. Increasingly, software testing must take advantage of test automation tools and techniques if the organization hopes to meet today's challenging schedules and adequately test its increasingly complex applications.

Code testing, for example, can generate statistics on code complexity and provide information on what types of unit tests to generate. Code coverage analyzers examine the source code and generate reports, including statistics such as the number of times that a logical branch, path, or a function call is executed during a test suite run.

Test tools are being applied to generate test data, catalog the tests in an organized fashion, execute tests, store test results, and analyze data. (Chapter 3 describes the various test tools now available.) These tools broaden the scope of tests that can be applied to a development effort. Because so many specialty tools and niche testing capabilities are now available, the use of automated test tools itself can be considered a strategy that supports the achievement of test goals and objectives.

Project schedule pressures are another reason why the use of automated test tools should be viewed as a strategy for achieving test goals and objectives. Test automation is the only way that software test engineers can keep pace with application developers and still test each new build with the same level of confidence and certainty as previous builds.

Traditional Testing Phases.   The various test techniques that are commonly applied during the traditional test phases represent the most widespread defect detection test strategies. In the book, *Software System Testing and Quality Assurance*, Boris Beizer identifies three phases of testing: unit, integration, and system testing. Commonly, acceptance testing appears in project schedules as an extension to system testing. During acceptance testing, feedback is gathered from end users for a specified time following the performance of system testing.

Unit testing, also known as module or component testing, involves testing of the smallest unit or block of program code. A software unit is defined as a collection of code segments that make up a module or function.

The purpose of the *integration testing* is to verify that each software unit interfaces correctly with other software units.

System testing seeks to test all implementation aspects of the system design. It relies on a collection of testing subtypes, including regression, load/stress, volume, and performance testing, among many other types of testing.

These various testing phases and subtypes are described in detail in Chapter 7.

Adherence to a Test Process.   The test team's adherence to a test process can serve as an effective defect detection strategy. Faithful adherence helps to ensure that the requisite activities of an effective test program are properly exercised. Following the required steps in the proper sequence and performing all of the necessary activities guarantees that test resources are applied to the maximum extent within given constraints. The end result is a software application product that is as correct and as responsive to defined requirements as possible, given the limitations of the project schedule and available manpower. Test team adherence to the defined test process makes it possible to identify and refine the defined process, thereby permitting continual process improvement.

As outlined in Section 4.1, the test team's test goals, objectives, and strategies for a particular test effort should be reflected in the defined test process. These top-level elements of test planning represent the cornerstone on which a project's test program is developed.

Risk Assessment.   An important part of a testing strategy involves risk assessment. The principle here is simple. The test engineer identifies the parts of a project that pose the greatest risk and the functionality that is most likely to cause problems. The test engineer then develops tests for these parts first. Test goals and objectives generally include some considerations of minimizing the risk of failure, where "failure" is defined in terms of cost overruns, schedule slippage, critical software errors, and the like. The test team therefore needs to weigh the risk that system requirements cannot be successfully supported.

Risk assessments should include a determination of the probability that a defined risk will happen, as well as an estimate of the magnitude or impact of the consequence should the risk be realized. Risk mitigation strategies should be defined for those system requirements that are deemed the most critical. Chapters 6 and 8 discuss test planning and test development initiatives that further address risk management.

Strategic Manual and Automated Test Design.   An effective test strategy specifies the way in which test design is approached. When tests are designed to incorporate reusability and maintainability, defects can be repeatedly identified. A test design that incorporates critical success functionality is also important in eliminating defects within the most critical component of the software application. This critical component may represent the part of the software that gets the most use or the part that is most important. In either case, the most critical component should be as close to error-free as possible. Test design is discussed in more detail in Chapter 7.

Development of Automated Tests.   Another part of an effective test strategy involves the development of automated test development guidelines. If tests are to be uniform, repeatable, maintainable, and effective, the test team must follow its test development guidelines. Chapter 8 discusses examples of automated test development guidelines.

Execution and Management of Automated Tests.   The way that automated software test is executed and managed can also serve as a defect detection strategy. Once again, the test team needs to realize that often the project schedule is tight and limited project resources are available for the testing effort. Invoking the proper elements of test execution and performing these elements in the correct manner (that is, with the proper management) help to ensure that the test effort will produce the maximum results. The end result should be a software application product that operates correctly and performs in accordance with defined requirements. Part IV addresses test execution, test script configuration management, defect tracking and reporting, test progress monitoring, and test metrics.

Test Verification Method.   The test verification method is another part of a testing strategy. With this strategy, a test qualification method is employed to verify that the application satisfies all system requirements. This method involves the creation of a test verification summary matrix, which outlines the various system requirements and identifies a specific method for testing each one. In this matrix, each system requirement is assigned a testability indicator, otherwise known as a test verification method. Verification methods include demonstration, analysis, inspection, and test. Section 6.2 discusses verification methods.

User Involvement.   Test team interaction with prospective end users is likely the most important strategy for ensuring that defect prevention or defect detection becomes incorporated into the test process. As noted earlier, the test team should participate in the requirements phase. Specifically, the test engineers should work closely with end users to ensure that system requirements are stated in testable terms.

User involvement with the test team continues as part of a defect detection strategy. The test team needs to obtain end-user or customer buy-in for the test plan, which outlines the overall testing strategy, and for the test procedures and scripts, which define the actual tests planned. This buy-in consists of end-user concurrence that the test plan and test scripts will satisfy the end user's system functionality and performance concerns. What better way is there to ensure success of the test effort and to obtain end-user acceptance of the application than to involve the end user through the entire testing life cycle?

This section has introduced many testing strategies that a test team could potentially follow. The particular test strategies applied to a particular project will depend upon the application development environment as well as the test objectives and requirements. A successful, cost-effective testing strategy requires a clear vision of the project goals and the kinds of constraints that may be encountered along the way. Be careful to select a testing strategy that applies to the specific project and one that will be most useful to the test team. Remember, no one solution will fit all situations. Communication and analysis are key considerations in selecting the right mix of test strategies to support the accomplishment of test goals and objectives.

4.2 | Test Tool Consideration

As a test engineer seeking to outline a test program in support of the next project and considering the use of automated test tools as part of that effort, you will have followed the course outlined in Chapters 2 and 3 to get started. These two chapters laid out a plan for performing a preliminary assessment intended to determine whether the test team should incorporate the use of automated test tools in a specific project and for identifying the potential benefits inherent in the use of these tools. In Chapter 3, the test team evaluated a host of prospective test tools, finding one or more that support all of the operating environments and most of the GUI languages that apply. Now let's assume that the next project requiring test support has been identified.

After following the guidance outlined in Section 4.1, the test engineer has reviewed the test process and defined test goals, objectives, and strategies. With this understanding, he or she can decide whether to continue pursuing the use of an automated test tool. Specifically, the test engineer seeks to verify that the previously identified automated test tools will actually work in the environment and effectively meet the system requirements. Figure 4.4 depicts the various steps involved in test tool consideration.

The first step in test tool consideration is to review the system requirements. The test team needs to verify that the automated test tool can support the user environment,

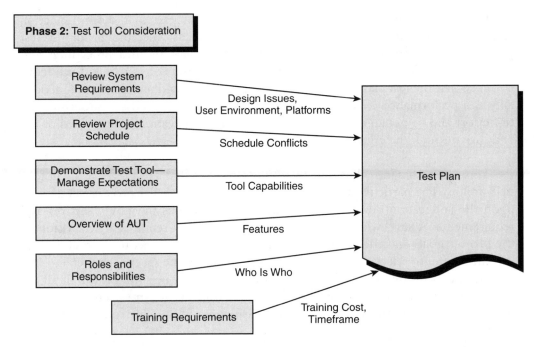

Figure 4.4   Test Tool Introduction Process (Phase 2)—Test Tool Consideration

computing platform, and product features. If a prototype or part of the application-under-test (AUT) already exists, the test team should ask for an overview of the application. An initial determination of the specific sections of the application that can be supported with automated testing can then be made.

Next, the test schedule should be reviewed. Is there sufficient time left in the schedule or allocated within the schedule to support the introduction of the test tool? Remember, automated testing should ideally be incorporated from the beginning of the development life cycle. The project schedule may need to be adjusted to include enough time to introduce an automated testing tool.

During test tool consideration, the automated test tool should be demonstrated to the new project team, enabling all pertinent individuals to gain an understanding of the tool's capabilities. Project team personnel in this case should include application developers, test engineers, quality assurance specialists, and configuration management specialists. Remember that software professionals on the project may have a preconceived notion of the capabilities of the test tool, which may not match the tool's actual application on the project.

If part of the application exists at the time of test tool consideration, conduct a test tool compatibility check. Install the testing tool in conjunction with the application and determine whether the two are compatible. One special concern relates to the availability of memory to support both the application and the automated test tool. Another concern is the compatibility of third-party controls used in the application. Once a compatibility check has been performed and a few problems arise, the test team will need to investigate whether work-around solutions are possible.

The use of automated test tools with a particular application requires the services of a test team that has the appropriate blend of skills needed to support the entire scope of the test effort. Roles and responsibilities of these people need to be clearly defined, and the skills and skill levels of test team personnel need to be considered carefully.

Another element of test tool consideration relates to the need to determine whether the test team has sufficient technical expertise to take advantage of all of the tool's capabilities. If this technical expertise is not resident within the test team, individuals who can mentor the test team on the advanced features of the test tool might be applied to the project on a short-term basis. Another possibility is test tool training for all test team personnel. Section 4.2.7 discusses training considerations.

After completing the test tool consideration phase, the test team can perform the final analysis necessary to support a decision of whether to commit to the use of an automated test tool for a given project effort.

4.2.1 Review of Project-Specific System Requirements

Section 3.1 discussed the organization's systems engineering environment and touched on the overall organization's requirements. During the test tool consideration phase for a specific project, the test engineer is interested in the specific project's requirements. Before he or she can effectively incorporate and use an automated test tool on a project, the test engineer needs to understand the requirements for the AUT. Once project-specific system requirements have been set, the test team can be more certain that the test tool will satisfy the particular needs of the specified project.

The test team must understand the user environment, computing platforms, and product features of the application-under-test, collectively referred to as the system architecture. For example, a client-server project can require a DBMS, application builder, network operation system, database middleware, source code control software, installation utility, help compiler, performance modeling tools, electronic distribution software, help-desk call tracking, and possibly systems management software to enforce security and track charge-backs. For a decision support system (perhaps as a replacement for an application builder), a project might also include a DSS front end tool (such as one geared toward Excel with the Microsoft EIS toolkit) and possibly some local temporary tables to expedite queries from previously downloaded data. For a high-volume, on-line transaction-processing system, the project may use a transaction-processing (TP) monitor and remote procedure call software. For a lookup or browsing-intensive application the project might use a variety of database back ends and simply create a front-end browser using an integrated shell; alternatively, it might employ data-mining tools [8].

The team then needs to analyze and provide a preliminary determination of whether a particular test tool is compatible with the specific system/software architecture and the system requirements of the AUT. The potential benefits of using the particular test tool for a project should be defined and documented as part of the test plan.

It is critically important that the test team develop an understanding of the primary business tasks addressed by the application. Several questions should be posed. For example, what are the transactions or scenarios that are performed to fulfill the tasks? What sort of data does each transaction or scenario require?

When the test team is involved on a project from the beginning of the development life cycle, it should investigate whether the development team plans to use a tool-incompatible operating environment or tool-incompatible application features, such as incompatible widgets. If such an incompatibility exists, the test team can negotiate recommended changes. If the incompatibility cannot be resolved, the test team can investigate the use of a different test tool or consider abandoning plans for the use of an automated test tool on the project.

The test team should determine the types of database activity (add, delete, change) that will be invoked, and identify when these transactions will occur within the application. It is beneficial to determine the calculations or processing rules provided by the application, as well as the time-critical transactions, functions, and conditions and possible causes of poor performance. Conditions that pose a stress to the system, such as low memory or disk capacity, should be identified. The test team should become familiar with the different configurations employed for the particular application, and should identify additional functions that are called to support the application-under-test. Other concerns include the plan for installing the application-under-test and any user interface standards, rules, and events.

Once the test team has found answers to these questions and addressed all relevant concerns, a decision needs to be made about whether to move forward with the particular test tool. The test team may have some leeway to consider using the selected test tool on a different project. The whole effort associated with reviewing system requirements is meant to verify that a particular automated test tool can support a specific set of test needs and requirements.

When attempting to perform a system requirements review, the team should identify the operational profile and user characteristics of the application-under-test. That is, it needs to understand the frequency of use for each system requirement as well as the number, type, and knowledge of users (that is, the user type) for each requirement. It is also beneficial to understand whether any conditions are attached to each system requirement. Obtaining operational profiles and user characteristics is a very difficult and time-consuming task, and one that requires management approval.

4.2.2 Application-Under-Test Overview

If it has adopted an automated test tool as a standard for the general systems engineering environment for an organization, the test team still needs to verify that the particular tool will be compatible with a specific application development effort. If parts of the AUT are already available or a previous release exists, the test team members—if not already familiar—should familiarize themselves with the target application. They should request an overview of the specific application as part of test tool consideration phase, as noted earlier. This overview may consist of a system prototype when only parts of the system application are available. Indeed, it could take the form of a user interface storyboard, if only a detailed design exists.

Technical aspects of the application now need to be explored. What is the GUI language or development environment? Is the application being developed to operate in a two-tier or a multitier environment? If it is intended for a multitier environment, which middleware is being used? Which database has been selected?

The test team should also review the application to determine which section or part can be supported with an automated test tool. Not all system requirements can be supported via automated testing, and not all system requirements can be supported with a single tool. The best approach to take is to divide and conquer the system requirements. That is, *determine which automated test tool can be used for which system requirement or section of the application.*

As tools differ and a variety of tests may be performed, the test team needs to include test engineers who have several types of skills. In support of the GUI test, a capture/playback tool, such as Rational's TestStudio, may be applied. In support of the back-end processing, a server load test tool, such as Rational's Performance Studio, may prove beneficial. UNIX system requirements may be fulfilled by UNIX shell script test utilities. Performance monitoring tools, such as Landmark TMON, can satisfy database system testing requirements. An automated tool may also support network testing. Chapter 3 offers more details on the various tools available.

The benefits of this step of the test tool consideration phase include the identification of potential design or technical issues that might arise with the use of the automated test tool. If incompatibility problems emerge during test tool consideration, then work-around solutions can be considered and the test design effort can focus on alternative test procedure approaches.

4.2.3   Review of Project Schedule

As noted earlier, an automated test tool is best introduced at the beginning of the development life cycle. Early introduction assures that lead time is adequate for the test team to become familiar with the tool and its advanced features. Sufficient lead time also ensures that system requirements can be loaded into a test management tool, test design activities can adequately incorporate test tool capabilities, and test procedures and scripts can be generated in time for scheduled test execution.

Beware of development project managers who invite test team participation near the end of the development life cycle! The project manager may be frantic about testing the particular application and desperate to obtain test engineering resources. This scenario presents some glaring problems. The test engineers have not become familiar with the application. The quality of the system requirements may be questionable. No time is available to assess the test design or cross-reference this design to the system requirements. The test team may not be able to determine whether its standard automated test tool is even compatible with the application and environment. Generation of test procedures and scripts may be rushed. Given these and other obstacles to test performance, test team personnel who step in to bail out the project will likely face a significant amount of scrutiny and pressure. It should not come as a great surprise if a few test engineers on the team leave the organization to seek greener pastures.

Clearly, a decision to incorporate automated testing at the end of the development life cycle carries risks. The test team is exposed to the risk of executing a test effort that does not catch enough application defects. On the other hand, it may perform sufficient testing but exceed the allocated schedule, thereby delaying a product from being released on time.

Deploying products on schedule has a multitude of implications. Product market share—and even the organization's ability to survive—may hang in the balance. As a result, test teams need to review the project schedule and assess whether sufficient time is available or has been allocated to permit the introduction of an automated test tool.

Even when the test team is involved at the beginning of the development life cycle, it is important for team members to make sure that the automated test tools are made available and introduced early. In situations when an automated tool is an afterthought and does not become available until the end of the development process, the test team and project manager may both be in for a surprise. They may discover that insufficient time has been allocated in the schedule for a test process that incorporates the new tool.

When utilizing an automated test tool and exercising an automated testing process, a majority of the test effort will involve test planning, design, and development. The actual performance of tests and the capture of defects account for a much shorter period of time. It is imperative, therefore, that automated test be introduced in parallel to the development life cycle, as described in Figure 1.3 on page 15.

During the test tool consideration phase, the test team must decide whether the project schedule permits the utilization of an automated test tool and the performance of an automated testing process. It may be able to avoid an embarrassing and painful situation by reviewing and commenting on the feasibility of the project schedule. At a minimum, testing personnel must clearly understand the specific timeframes and associated deadline commitments that are involved. If potential schedule conflicts are minor, they might be resolved with judicious project management. The results of this project review—including identification of issues, updated schedules, and test design implications—should be documented within the test plan.

Without a review of the project schedule, the test team may find itself in a no-win situation, where it is asked to do too much in too little time. This kind of situation can create animosity between the test team and other project personnel, such as the development team, who are responsible for the development and release of the software application. In the heated exchange and the blame game that become inevitable, the automated test tool becomes the scapegoat. As a result of such a bad situation, the automated test tool may develop a poor reputation within the organization and become shelfware. The organization may then abandon the use of the particular test tool, perhaps even shunning automated testing in general.

4.2.4 Test Tool Compatibility Check

In Section 4.2.2, the usefulness of an application overview was discussed. During the application overview exercise, the test team may have identified some compatibility issues. Nevertheless, it still needs to conduct a hands-on compatibility check, provided that a part of the application or a prototype exists, to verify that the test tool will support the AUT.

In particular, the test group needs to install the test tool on a workstation with the application resident and perform compatibility checks. It should verify that all application software components that are incorporated within or are used in conjunction with the application are included as part of the compatibility check. Application add-ins such as widgets and other third-party controls should come from the organization's approved list. Most vendors will provide a list of the controls that are compatible with the particular tool.

Some tools can be customized to recognize a third-party control. In this situation, the vendor should provide a list of compatible controls together with instructions on how to customize the tool to recognize the third-party tool. Depending on these requirements, the test engineer might want to verify that the resulting tool is still compatible with the application by conducting the following tests:

1. Presentation layer calling the database server

2. Presentation layer calling the functionality server

3. End-to-end testing (presentation calling functionality server, calling database server)

4. Functionality server calling another functionality server

5. Functionality server calling the database server

Beware of the vendor that does not offer full disclosure for its tool. Gather information on industry acceptance of the vendor and its tools.

When tool conflicts occur with the application, work-around solutions should be investigated. The potential requirement for these solutions is another reason to introduce the automated test tool early in the development life cycle. When time permits, the test team might install and test the test tool on a variety of operating systems that the tool supposedly supports.

In addition, the test team should verify that it has access to the application's internal workings, such as hidden APIs and protocols.

The compatibility check offers another benefit. Once the test tool has been installed, the test team can verify that the targeted hardware platform is compatible with the tool. For example, the test engineer can verify that disk space and memory are sufficient. The results of the compatibility check should be documented within the test plan.

4.2.5 Demonstration of the Tool to the Project Team

It is important to ensure project-wide understanding and acceptance of the automated test tool. Such positive feelings may prove valuable later should the test team encounter difficulties during the test effort. When other project personnel, such as managers and application developers, understand the usefulness and value of the automated test tool, then they are generally more patient and supportive when problems arise.

A demonstration of the proposed test tool or tools can help to win such support. It is especially useful when the tool will perform developmental testing during the unit test phase. Tools that may be employed in the unit test phase include code coverage, memory leakage, and capture/playback test tools, among others.

It is valuable for project personnel to see the tool first-hand. A demonstration will provide them with a mental framework on how the tool works and can be applied to support the needs of the project. Without such a demonstration, people may confuse other tools with the particular test tool being applied to the effort or fail to fully grasp its capabilities.

Some people expect a test tool to do everything from designing the test procedures to executing them. It is important that members of the project team understand both the capabilities *and* the limitations of the test tool. Following the test tool demonstration, the test team can gauge the level of acceptance by reviewing any issues raised and noting the tone of the discussion about the tool. The test group then must decide whether to continue with the demonstrated test tool or to pursue another tool. If it chooses to pursue another tool, the test team should document the reasons for abandoning the demonstrated test tool.

Project managers and other software professionals often assume that a testing tool necessarily automates and speeds up the entire test effort. In fact, automated test scripts generally reduce the required timeframe for test execution and really pay off on the second release of software, where scripts can be reused—but not during initial setup of test scripts with the initial release. Automated test scripts may also provide benefits with the initial release when performing load testing and regression testing. Further information about the benefits of automated testing is provided in Chapter 2.

4.2.6 Test Tool Support Profile

An important factor to consider when making a final determination on a test tool is the availability of test team personnel who have sufficient experience with the tool to plan, prepare, and execute testing. Another question to pose is whether any individual on the test team has enough experience with the tool to leverage the tool's more advanced features. The test team may have received a slick test tool demonstration by tool professionals during a marketing demonstration, and the tool may have looked easy to use on the surface, but once heavily into the test process the team may discover that its skills with the tool are insufficient.

The test team manager should map out a staffing profile of each of the team members to ascertain the team's strengths and weaknesses. Upon review of this staffing profile, the manager can determine whether there is sufficient coverage for all system requirements areas as well as sufficient experience to justify the use of the automated test tool. On a team of five test engineers, for example, all should have general experience with the tool or at least had introductory level training on the test tool and its capabilities.

On a five-person test team, at least one test engineer should be able to provide leadership in the area of test automation. This test automation leader should have advanced experience with the tool, have attended an advanced training course on the tool, or have a software programming background. Skills that are generally beneficial for the automated test engineer include familiarity with SQL, C, UNIX, MS

Access, and Visual Basic. Preferably, the test team would include two test engineers with advanced skills, in the event that the one advanced-skill test engineer had to leave the project for some reason.

Table 4.4 provides a sample test tool support profile. In this example, the test team is considering the use of the automated test tool called Rational's TestStudio.

Table 4.4   Test Tool Support Profile

	Test Tool Experience	Advanced Tool Training	Advanced Tool Experience
Test Team Manager			
Skills include: Rational's TestStudio, Purify, WinRunner, MS Project, MS Access, UNIX, C, SQL, Oracle	✓		
Test Team Lead			
Skills include: QA Partner, Rational's Performance Studio, Visual Basic, MS Access, UNIX, C, SQL, Sybase	✓	✓	✓
Test Engineer 1			
Skills include: C, C++, Visual Basic, MS Access, MVS, COBOL, Fortran			
Test Engineer 2			
Skills include: C, UNIX, HTML, Java, Powerbuilder, Novell Netware			
Test Engineer 3			
Skills include: Visual Test, C, C++, PVCS, Visual Basic, MS Access, SQL, Oracle	✓		
Test Engineer 4			
Skills include: Visual Test, C, C++, Visual Basic, MS Access	✓		

The second column indicates whether the test team member has at least some experience with Rational's TestStudio or a similar kind of test tool. The third and fourth columns indicate whether the individual has advanced Rational's TestStudio tool training or advanced tool experience with other similar test tools. If team members have sufficient experience with the automated test tool, then they can proceed to adopt the test tool. If not, the test team manager can entertain work-around solutions, such as general or advanced training to shore up the team's capability with the tool. Another option is to hire a part-time consultant to mentor the test team through test design, development, and execution.

If the test team is not able to place personnel experienced with the designated test tool on the project and the right levels of training are not available, the test team will need to either consider an alternative test tool or an alternative test method, such as manual testing.

It may be worthwhile to document the desirable skills for test team members within the application's test plan, then ensure that the staffing profile matches the desired skill set. Roles and responsibilities of the test team are further defined in Chapter 5.

4.2.7 Review of Training Requirements

The test tool consideration phase also must account for the need to incorporate training into the project schedule. To determine whether such training may be necessary, the manager may review the test tool support profile, such as the one depicted in Table 4.4.

It is important to develop test process expertise among those individuals involved in software test. It is not sufficient for the test team to have a well-defined test process; the test engineers must also be familiar with and use the process. Likewise, test team members should develop expertise in one or more automated test tools through training, knowledge transfer achieved as a result of attending user group meetings, membership in a user group Web site, or participation in a software quality assurance organization.

Test teams that find themselves short of needed experience may become frustrated and actually abandon the use of the automated test tool so as to achieve short-term gains in test progress, only to experience a protracted test schedule during actual and regression testing. Often the tool draws the blame for inadequate testing, when in reality the test process was not followed closely or was nonexistent.

Chapter Summary

o   How test teams introduce an automated software test tool into a new project is nearly as important as the selection of the appropriate test tool for the project.

o   The purpose of analyzing the organization's test process, which is required as part of the test analysis phase, is to ascertain the test goals, objectives, and strategies that may be inherent in the test process.

o   Test process analysis documentation is generated through the test team's process review and its analysis of test goals and objectives. This documentation outlines test goals, test objectives, and test strategies for a particular effort. It is a common practice to include this information within the Introduction section of the project's test plan.

o   Test strategies can be classified into two different categories: defect prevention technologies and defect detection technologies. Defect prevention provides the greatest cost and schedule savings over the duration of the application development effort.

o   Defect prevention methodologies cannot always prevent defects from entering into the application-under-test, because applications are very complex and it is impossible to catch all errors. Defect detection techniques complement defect prevention efforts, and the two methodologies work hand in hand to increase the probability that the test team will meet its defined test goals and objectives.

o   Unit testing is often performed by the developer of the unit or module. This approach may be problematic because the developer may not have an objective viewpoint when testing his or her own product.

o   The test strategies that apply to a particular project depend on the application development environment as well as the test objectives and requirements.

o   One of the most significant steps in the test tool consideration phase requires that the test team decide whether the project schedule will permit the appropriate utilization of an automated test tool and whether an automated testing process can offer value under the particular circumstances.

o   The compatibility check is intended to ensure that the application will work with the automated testing tool and, where problems exist, to investigate work-around solutions.

o   The test team manager must determine whether the test team has sufficient skills to support the adoption of the automated test tool.

References

1. Kuhn, T. *The Structure of Scientific Revolutions, Foundations of the Unity of Science,* Vol. II. Chicago: University of Chicago, 1970.

2. Florac, W.A., Park, R.E., Carleton, A.D. *Practical Software Measurement: Measuring for Process Management and Improvement.* Guidebook CMU/SEI-97-HB-003. Pittsburgh, PA: Software Engineering Institute, Carnegie Mellon University, April 1997.

3. Burnstein, I., Suwanassart, T., Carlson, C.R. *Developing a Testing Maturity Model,* Part II. Chicago: Illinois Institute of Technology, 1996.

4. Standish Group. http://www.standishgroup.com/chaos.html.

5. A Best Practices initiative created by the U.S. Department of Defense in late 1994 brought together a group of consultants and advisors, dubbed the Airlie Software Council after its meeting place in the Virginia countryside. Yourdon, E. "The Concept of Software Best Practices." http://www.yourdon.com/articles/BestPractice.html.

6. Voas, J., and Miller, K. *"Software Testability: The New Verification,"* IEEE Software, page 3. May 1995. http://www.rstcorp.com/papers/chrono-1995.html

7. Corporate Computing Inc. *Corporate Computing's Top Ten Performance Modeling Tips.* Monroe, LA, 1994.

8. Corporate Computing Inc. *Corporate Computing's Test to Evaluate Client/Server Expertise.* Monroe, LA, 1994.

Test Team Management

> Clarifying expectations sometimes takes a great deal
> of courage. It seems easier to act as though differ-
> ences don't exist and to hope things will work out than
> it is to face the differences and work together to arrive
> at a mutually agreeable set of expectations.
>
> **—Steve Covey**

Automated test tools are effective in providing solutions only when the problem at hand is adequately understood. Once the problem is understood, the challenge becomes identifying the individuals who will be responsible for solving it. Test efforts are complex and require a diverse set of skills. The test team needs to include members with the specific expertise necessary to comprehend the scope and depth of the required test effort and to develop a strategy to execute and implement the test program.

To execute a successful test program, the test team composition needs to be designed, the test team assembled, and the team members' roles and responsibilities defined and assigned. Experienced people are needed to conduct test planning and write test procedures for manual and automated testing. To ensure that everyone on the test team is aware of what needs to be done and who will take the lead on a task, it is important to document the roles and responsibilities assigned to the various test team members.

The roles and responsibilities should be communicated both verbally and in written form and made available to everyone on the team. By identifying the assigned roles of each test team member on the project, everyone will have a clear understanding as to the individual responsible for each particular area of the project. Also, new team members can quickly determine whom to contact if a problem arises.

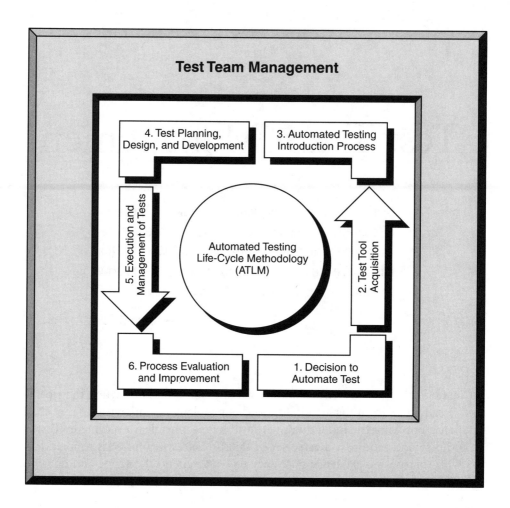

To get a clear picture of the individuals who are needed to support a particular task, a task description should be created. Once the scope of the task is understood, then assigning the specific talent to the task becomes easier. To help ensure successful execution of the task, work packages can be developed and distributed to the individuals involved in the task. Such packages typically detail the task organization, technical approach, task schedule, allocation of hours for each individual, and applicable standards and processes.

Along with members of the quality assurance department, the test team typically takes responsibility for an assortment of test and quality-related tasks, including the enforcement of development standards and code inspection standards on the project. If such project-specific standards are not available, the test team should inquire about organization-level standards that can be adopted or tailored to the project. Other sources for applicable standards, depending on the organizational needs, include the Software Engineering Institute (SEI), IEEE, ISO, and military standards organizations, among others. By the same token, the test team should be responsible for knowledge transfer of testing processes, methodologies, and test tools. For further detail on test team roles and responsibilities, see Section 5.5.

When test activities will span the entire development life cycle, the test team is in a position to facilitate communication among project development and test groups. This goal can be accomplished by conducting meetings to discuss and analyze the testing process, discuss the life-cycle approach to testing, provide test tool overviews, and conduct training.

Test teams need to inform project team members about the test approach defined for the project, allowing these personnel to be aware of the full scope of the test activities and to support the test process appropriately. This orientation can be both formal and informal in nature. For example, the test team might provide a presentation on the capabilities of the test tool being used in the test process. Test program orientation might also include test team participation in technical interchange meetings with end-user customers, if this type of communication is not already a standard practice.

As emphasized in the ATLM, the test team should attend requirements and design walkthroughs so that it can verify that requirements are testable, code is designed for testability, and traceability between requirements and design is possible. The test team may also decide to post test tool and process information on the organization's intranet, together with appropriate links, such as those referring project personnel to the test tool vendor's Web site.

The test team needs to work closely with the development group. It is beneficial to identify one lead contact from the development team and to have the test team work one on one with the development group whenever feasible. The test team should also be proactive in soliciting developer involvement in test activities. Lead test engineers, for example, should have a vision of test end goals in mind and communicate these goals to the development team.

Depending on the organization, the test team can be structured in a variety of ways. The potential organizational structures are discussed in the following section.

5.1 | Organizational Structure of a Test Team

The structure of the test team will vary from organization to organization. Its depth and makeup also depend on the kind of product being tested and the mission of the test team. Several different organizational structures may be imposed on the test team that will be responsible for performing test activities and for introducing automated testing to a project. The flexibility that a test manager may have in designing a test team, however, will likely depend upon the organization's culture and its influence on project team composition. Software testing is performed most often by testing staff who are divided among application groups (44%) rather than by a single, centralized software test department (39%) [1].

Some organizations hire and assign test engineers in response to the birth and retirement of projects. Within these organizations, long-term testing capability is not consciously managed. Job descriptions, which are developed for hiring purposes, are based entirely upon the particular needs of a specific project. Once the project goes away, the test engineers who worked on the project may leave, taking with them the experience gained with the application-under-test, test tools, lessons learned, and process and procedural insights. For purposes of discussion, we will call these structures *stovepipe test teams*.

Other organizations view professional software testing capability as a strategic investment. These organizations deploy *centralized test teams*. They seek to attract professional test engineers by offering career development paths within a centralized software test department, training and development in automated test tools, mentoring opportunities with more senior test engineers, increased job security by having the test engineer rotate between projects, and increased professional development opportunities achieved by the diversity of technology and tools experienced over a multitude of projects.

Besides test team organization strategies based along distributed or centralized organizational concepts, test team structure may also differ based on the team's mission. Some organizations view testing as a last-ditch, stop-gap effort occurring at the end of the development cycle and classify it as an independent verification and validation (IV&V) effort. Test engineers assigned to an *IV&V test team* perform an

Table 5.1 Test Team Profiles

Stovepipe Team (small)	Stovepipe Team (large)	Centralized Team	IV&V Team	SMT Group
Test Lead	Test Manager	Test Director	IV&V Manager	SMT Manager
Test Engineers (1–4)	Test Leads (1–2)	Test Manager	IV&V Lead	Process Lead
	Test Engineers (4–8)	Test Leads (3–5)	IV&V Specialists (1–4)	Test Lead
		Test Engineers (10–20)		Test Engineers (1–4)
				Engineers (1–3)

acceptance test of the software application and review software documentation to validate product quality. Other test teams are seen as a nucleus of internal quality, testing, and process engineering, with consultants being made available to the various projects within the organization. In these organizations, testing is carried out by *system methodology and test (SMT) groups.*

Table 5.1 suggests sample compositions for each of these different types of test organizations.

5.1.1 Stovepipe Test Team

A manager responsible for a particular project will likely interview candidates for the test team and make the hiring decision. Given all of the various project start-up activities that demand the project manager's attention, the test team may not be assembled until well into the project. The test plan document for the project may therefore be developed by the project manager prior to the assignment of test engineers.

A stovepipe test team typically includes two to five test engineers. These test team members do not belong to a separate testing organization entity but instead report to a task manager on the project or the actual project manager. One of the test engineers will act as a test lead, and the other test engineers will perform test development and execution activities.

Once in place, the test team will likely be introduced to the test tool, which was chosen during early project conception, or asked to perform a quick review of test tools so that the right tool can be procured and installed. In some situations, the project manager may inform the test team that no budget has been provided for a test tool, hand a copy of the test plan to the lead test engineer, and ask the team to begin developing test procedures.

The test lead develops a test design for the development of test procedures and then makes assignments for this development effort. After the test effort ends, the engineers may find themselves in the precarious position of not knowing where they will be assigned next. Once the project has concluded, no formal mechanism is available to ensure that the test effort's lessons learned are retained. Likewise, the organization has no formal way to transfer test process, methodology, or automated tool knowledge and expertise.

5.1.2 Centralized Test Team

Some organizations view professional software testing capability as a strategic investment. They recognize that testing professionals possess skills with automated test tools, skills with network operations, functional knowledge of certain types of applications, and skills in software programming. In summary, they see the software testing professional as very versatile and as an important asset for the organization.

The centralized test team boasts a roster of test professionals who collectively support a number of projects. Each test engineer may work on one or more projects at a given time. As the test team may include 10 to 30 test engineers, the centralized test organization may need to be headed up by a test director. The test director has the full-time responsibility of maintaining the professionalism and technical expertise of the group. He or she must ensure that test activities are being performed correctly and within schedule on several projects. To fulfill this mission, the test director needs to ensure that the centralized test organization retains the services of test professionals with a variety of technical skills and a mix of skill levels.

During the start-up phase for a new project, the centralized test team can often supply personnel on a part-time basis to perform a number of activities that otherwise would be left to the project manager. These activities might include test effort sizing, development of test engineer job descriptions, test engineer interview support, test automation decision support (see Chapter 2), test tool evaluation and selection support (see Chapter 3), and test tool introduction support (see Chapter 4). The centralized test team generally provides an individual to develop the test plan for the project.

The centralized test team may be able to assign one or more full-time test engineers to the project from the outset. These engineers can help with the start-up activities and initiate full life-cycle support (the full range of tasks required for this step are discussed in Section 5.2).

The organization may find that the centralized test team offers a great deal of flexibility by being able to perform on a variety of projects. For instance, a test engineer could be assigned to a new project on a part-time basis to support the review of software requirements to ensure that the requirements are stated in testable terms. This part-time help may prove valuable when the test engineers slated for the project have not yet been hired or started working. In other situations, the centralized test team may provide additional test engineers during the project's peak activity periods. On still other occasions, the project may require the services of a test engineer with a specialized test expertise for a limited period of time.

The fact that an organization has a centralized test team may in itself motivate a talented software test professional to join the organization. The test engineer will likely view the centralized test team as an organizational hierarchy within which it is possible to advance. He or she may also appreciate the mentoring opportunities possible with the team's senior engineers. Other perceived benefits associated with the establishment of a centralized test team may include the availability of training, the diversity of technology and tools across projects, information sharing and technology transfer among the test engineers, and increased job security.

In some organizations, the centralized test team may be part of a larger organization responsible for implementing key software management and performance disciplines on projects. The larger organization may be referred to as a systems engineering support (SES) center or department. The SES organization commonly is responsible for implementing the level 2 and 3 key process areas outlined within the Software Engineering Institute's (SEI's) Capability Maturity Model (CMM). (For more information on the SEI's CMM, see http://www.sei.cmu.edu/.) Its composition would likely include personnel who would perform tasks outside the test engineering discipline, such as those related to requirements management, risk management, quality assurance, and configuration management. (The composition of the centralized test team given in Table 5.1 focused only on the testing discipline; it does not reflect support for these other areas.)

Once the project has concluded, the test engineers performing on the project would report back to the centralized test team for their next assignments. Lessons learned from the test effort on the project are likely to be retained within a database maintained by the centralized test team. Likewise, the team probably maintains a repository of test processes, methodologies, procedures, test tool evaluation results, and test automation code libraries.

5.1.3 IV&V Test Team

Another possible structure for a test team is the independent verification and validation (IV&V) group. This type of team may consist of personnel who are assigned to a separate group within the software development organization or it may be a group that exists outside of the software development organization, such as a subcontractor. Often the IV&V group will decide whether a new software build is ready and acceptable for release. Its responsibilities are to participate in walkthroughs, verify that standards are being followed, perform quality assurance reviews of software documentation, and carry out other testing tasks. The IV&V group usually focuses on system testing (see Chapter 7 for more details on system testing) and is not concerned with the application's internal processing.

The IV&V group is not responsible for the development of a project test plan but rather for ensuring that the test plan is thorough and complete, complies with standards, and supports appropriate system requirements and derived test requirements. It could therefore be seen as the first and most demanding user, meaning that business knowledge combined with technical knowledge is a must for an IV&V group member.

This type of organizational structure is fitting for a company that, for example, performs a significant amount of work in a particular business such as financial, logistics management, or space satellite control systems. The IV&V group structure may also prove advantageous for a large commercial software development organization or a company that maintains and possibly markets large financial services software programs. Within such an environment, it is beneficial for the organization to retain its investment by holding on to the expertise of the IV&V personnel.

Once a project has concluded, IV&V specialists report to a IV&V group manager or some other organization manager for their next assignments. Lessons learned from the IV&V test effort on the project may be retained, and the organization may maintain a repository of IV&V processes and procedures.

5.1.4 Systems Methodology and Test Team

In some organizations, the test technology transfer responsibility is assigned to a separate group within the same organization called the system methodology and test (SMT) team. This group's reporting chain is kept separate from the immediate project organization. This test group is often responsible for carrying out test program start-up activities for a multitude of applications being simultaneously developed by the organization.

An SMT team is generally viewed as a group of internal consultants within the organization. The SMT staff is responsible for promoting knowledge transfer of methodologies and standards, promulgating guidelines for development and testing, developing and refining test techniques, performing evaluations and training on automated testing tools, and introducing test tools on projects. Team members should work one on one with the various project development team leads to perform the knowledge transfer and other activities.

The SMT team should include software professionals who have proven testing capabilities and a cerebral talent for conceptualizing, organizing, and planning. The process and methodology work require a disciplined approach to ensure that procedural steps explicitly cover all required actions and that the output of one step satisfies the input requirements for the next step. The capabilities required of SMT team members include an understanding of the complete testing life cycle and the software skills necessary to support test design, development, automation, and execution activities.

SMT personnel are usually heavily involved in project start-up activities as well as test planning and design activities, but take lesser roles during test development and execution. Their duties are not to perform testing on a project, but rather to consult, train, and mentor the project personnel who will actually carry out test development and execution.

Once a project's test development effort begins to take off, the SMT test engineer generally returns to more routine SMT activities, which may include researching new test methodologies and tools, attending test tool conferences, maintaining the organization's software and test process assets, maintaining a software project "lessons learned" database, and maintaining a repository of test tool evaluation results and test automation code libraries.

5.1.5 Test Team Summary

The structure of a test team depends on several variables, including the culture of the organization. The most important consequence of test team organization pertains to the likelihood of continual improvement in process maturity and software test capability. Structures that persist after a project end have the means to retain and improve upon the organization's processes, procedures, and tool knowledge, as well as to transfer this knowledge to new projects. Table 5.2 describes the advantages and disadvantages for different test organizations.

Table 5.2 Test Team Comparison

Test Team	Advantages	Disadvantages
Stovepipe Test Team	Complete control over the test effort is retained within the project organization.	The test start-up effort is inefficient.
	Consultants can be applied on a short-term basis to provide support.	There is a limited depth of test skill resources on team.
		The test effort is often not initiated early in development life cycle.
		No formal way exists for the organization to improve upon the test process.
		The organization has a limited ability to transfer process and test tool expertise.
Centralized Test Team	An individual within the organization is identified to maintain the expertise of the test team.	Increased management oversight is required to rotate test engineers between projects.
	A roster of test professionals is maintained who have a variety of software/test skills.	The organization has an increased cost to retain test engineers on staff between projects.
	A centralized team can often supply personnel to a project on a part-time basis.	
	Test professionals can be applied to the project to support project start-up.	

continued

continued from page 155

Test Team	Advantages	Disadvantages
	Senior test engineers can mentor junior test engineers.	
	Test engineers enjoy exposure to a diversity of technology and tools across projects.	
	Information sharing and technology transfer among test engineers are facilitated.	
	Increased long-term job security is available.	
	A repository of test processes, test tool evaluation results, and test automation code libraries is maintained.	
	Less turnover and improved retention of test engineers occur.	
IV&V Team	A depth in niche IV&V skills is developed for the organization.	The test engineer career path can become narrowly focused on IV&V expertise.
	Consultants can be applied on a short-term basis to provide support.	The test engineer's software skills can become outdated.
SMT Group	SMT staff become proficient in the latest processes, tools, and techniques.	Maintaining SMT staff is more costly to the organization than pursuing a simple stovepipe test team organization.
	Broad experience across a number of different projects strengthens the test engineer's skills and capability.	
	A repository of test processes, test tool evaluation results, and test automation code libraries is maintained.	
	Improved test effort ramp-up on new projects is possible due to training and assistance by SMT staff.	
	Information sharing and technology transfer among test engineers are facilitated.	
	The SMT group provides continuous consulting to all project teams within the organization.	
	Less personnel turnover and improved retention of personnel occur.	
	Maintaining SMT staff is less costly than the centralized team approach.	

The top 10 ingredients for a successful test group (all organization types) are as follows:

1. **Business knowledge.** Test engineers need to have business knowledge and work closely with the users and customers of the system.

2. **Technical knowledge.** Applications are more complex and, to understand the technical intricacies of the application, both automated test tools and a technical background are required.

3. **Task separation.** Business tasks are kept separate from technical tasks.

4. **Resource management.** Business and technical resources can be combined.

5. **Relationship with development team.** Test engineers work hand in hand with the developers.

6. **Early life-cycle involvement.** The test team becomes involved from the beginning of the development life cycle.

7. **Defined test methodology.** Methods, standards, and processes need to be in place, implemented, or modified as necessary.

8. **Flexibility/adaptability.** Each application is different. A testing strategy that has proven itself successful on one project might fail on another.

9. **Metrics.** The team can learn which metrics to collect and then use these metrics to improve the testing process. Metrics are collected throughout the development life cycle.

10. **Process improvement.** The team can strive for continuous improvement of the defined test methodology.

5.2 | Test Program Tasks

Table 5.3 describes the different types of test tasks that can be performed. The work breakdown structure (WBS) depicted in the table can be used in conjunction with timekeeping activities to develop a historical record of the effort expended to perform the various activities on projects. The maintenance of such historical records is valuable in the test effort sizing exercise, which seeks to estimate the test effort required for a new project. The test program work breakdown structure will be helpful in determining the earned value metric of the test program, as discussed in Chapter 9.

Test teams may wish to further break down elements 8.7 and 9.3 in Table 5.3 so as to delineate test procedure/script development and execution according to the various testing subtypes. The possible test subtypes may include functional requirements testing, server performance testing, user interface testing, performance testing,

Table 5.3   Test Program Work Breakdown Structure

No.	Work Breakdown Structure (WBS) Element

1   Project Start-Up

1.1   Process improvement. Review lessons learned and suggested improvement activities from previous similar projects. Decide which improvement activities to implement.
1.2   Process. Gather understanding of automated test life-cycle methodology (ATLM).
1.3   Scope. Outline preliminary test goals and objectives.
1.4   Sizing. Test effort sizing.
1.5   Team composition. Test team composition analysis and test engineer job description development.
1.6   Recruiting. Development of test engineer recruiting advertisements and conduct of interviews.

2   Early Project Support

2.1   Goals/objectives. Further define test goals and objectives and review goals/objectives with project management, development group, and test engineers to develop understanding and acceptance of test goals and objectives.
2.2   Constraint examination. Review project constraints such as short time to market and limited resources.
2.3   Testability review. Assure that testability is designed into the application.
2.4   Requirements review. Ensure that requirements are specified in testable terms.
2.5   Review of standards. Identify and become acquainted with applicable standards. Decide whether standards need to be adjusted based on lessons learned. Define missing standards.
2.6   Test process analysis. Analyze organization's current test process.
2.7   Customer involvement. Assure customer involvement from beginning to end of testing life cycle.

3   Decision to Automate Test

3.1   Test objectives/strategies. Refine definition of test objectives for the project and develop test strategies.
3.2   Test tool value. Outline the expected value/benefits derived from incorporating an automated test tool.
3.3   Test tool proposal. Develop a test tool proposal to acquire management support.

4   Test Tool Selection and Evaluation

4.1   Systems engineering environment. Review organization's systems engineering environment.
4.2   Test tools available. Review types of test tools available.
4.3   Test tool candidates. Research, evaluate, and score test tool candidates.
4.4   Define evaluation domain.
4.5   Conduct hands-on tool evaluation.

continued

continued from page 158

4.6   Test tool evaluation report. Report and document tool selection and the results of evaluations.

4.7   Test tool purchase. Develop purchase order in coordination with the purchasing department.

5   Test Tool Introduction

5.1   Test process. Implement (or modify existing) testing process, methodologies, and "life-cycle" approach to testing to allow for the introduction of automated testing tools. Assure that test effort is scheduled to perform in parallel with development effort. Maintain test tool introduction process (see ATLM).

5.2   Defect removal activities. Attend inspections and walkthroughs and conduct other defect removal activities.

5.3   Test tool expertise. Have test engineers participate in formal test tool training, review test tool tutorials, and practice with test tool. Hire tool experts, if deemed necessary.

5.4   Test tool validation. Validate new test tool releases to ensure that the tool performs according to specification and that the tool works in a particular operating environment.

5.5   Test consultation. Test engineer supports a test support hotline, answering questions within the organization pertaining to the test process and tools. Document all tool issues and solutions for future reference. Provide mentoring and coaching on automated software test discipline.

5.6   Test tool orientations. Test engineer provides presentations and demonstrations to orient project personnel on the use and application of test tools.

5.7   Relationship building. Develop a working relationship with development group and facilitate communications among project team members.

5.8   Network environment setup. Consult on the setup of an automated test tool repository on the local area network. Request additional network storage space where necessary.

5.9   Defect management process. Establish a process (workflow) for defect reporting and resolution for a project. Outline applicable standards and formats.

5.10   Defect management training. Provide training on the process for defect reporting and resolution.

5.11   Test tool reporting. Determine the types of automated test reports that are applicable for a project.

6   Test Planning

6.1   Test requirements. Document the application-under-test test requirements, as derived from the system requirements.

6.2   Examination of constraints. Identify and outline constraints such as short time to market and limited engineering resources.

6.3   Test goals/objectives. Document goals and objectives for test (such as scalability and regression) within the test plan. Include goals pertaining to end-user involvement in the test process.

6.4   Test strategy. Document the test strategies and the types of test tools that apply on the project.

continued

continued from page 159

6.5   Test program activities. Develop a test strategy that incorporates test activities early within the development life cycle.

6.6   Deliverables. Identify the product deliverables on the project that will be reviewed or tested by test personnel.

6.7   Critical success functions. Work with the project team and business users to identify critical success functions and document them within the test plan.

6.8   Test program parameters. Define test program parameters such as assumptions, prerequisite activities, system acceptance criteria, and test program risks, and document them within the test plan.

6.9   Level of quality. Work with the project team and business users to determine the level of quality for the project and document it within the test plan.

6.10   Test process. Document the test process within the test plan, including considerations related to the test tool introduction process and the defect management process.

6.11   Test training. Document test training requirements and plans within the test plan.

6.12   Decision to automate test. Document the assessment outlining the benefit of using an automated test tool on the project and the ability to incorporate an automated test tool given the project schedule.

6.13   Technical environment. Document the technical environment in which the application-under-test will be developed and eventually operate. Identify potential application design or technical automated testing tool issues that may need to be resolved.

6.14   Test tool compatibility check. Document the results of the test tool compatibility check. Where an incompatibility problem occurs, document work-around solutions and alternative test methods.

6.15   Quality gates. Plan for the incorporation of quality gates and checks.

6.16   Risk assessments. Perform risk assessments in support of project management reviews and reporting requirements.

6.17   Test readiness reviews. Perform planning and analysis activities necessary for supporting test readiness reviews. Develop presentation slides and perform presentations where required.

6.18   Test plan document. Assemble and package the test planning documentation into a test plan. Incorporate changes to the test plan as a result of test plan reviews by project management and end-user customers. Maintain the test plan document throughout the test life cycle.

6.19   Test data. Document test data requirements and plans for developing and maintaining a test data repository.

6.20   Test environment. Identify requirements for a test laboratory or test environment and identify personnel responsible for setting up and maintaining this environment.

6.21   Reporting requirements. Define reporting requirements and document them within the test plan.

6.22   Roles and responsibilities. Define and document team members' roles and responsibilities for the test effort.

6.23   Test tool system administration. Define all tools used during the testing life cycle. Outline the requirements for setting up and maintaining the automated test tools and environment and identify personnel responsible for setting up and maintaining the test tools. Administrative tasks include the setup of tool users and various privilege groups.

continued

continued from page 160

7	**Test Design**
7.1	Prototype automated environment. Prepare and establish a test laboratory environment to support test design and development.
7.2	Techniques and tools. Identify test techniques/strategies and automated tools to be applied to the project application and its interfaces.
7.3	Design standards. Prepare and establish test procedure design standards.
7.4	Test procedure/script design. Develop a list and hierarchy of test procedures and test scripts. Identify which procedures and scripts are to be performed manually and which are supported by an automated test tool. Decide on and define other test verification methods (such as analysis and demonstration).
7.5	Test procedure/script assignments. Assign test team personnel to the various test procedures and scripts.
7.6	Inputs/outputs. Develop test procedure/script design inputs and expected outputs.
7.7	Test automation script library. Identify test automation scripts contained with the organization's script library that can be applied to the project.

8	**Test Development**
8.1	Best practices/standards. Develop/tailor best practices and standards for testing of the project.
8.2	Test procedure development standards. Implement test procedure development standards (for example, provide comments on each automated testing tool scripting step, fill in test procedure header file information, enforce modularity, and so on).
8.3	Script execution standards. Implement test procedure execution standards (for example, a consistent environment, test database backup, and rollback).
8.4	Test setup. Implement test procedure scripts during various testing phases (for example, during the regression test phase or performance test phase).
8.5	Test procedure pseudocode. Prepare step-by-step pseudocode for the test procedures. Consider including test procedure pseudocode as an appendix to the test plan.
8.6	Work-around solutions. Develop work-around solutions for tool/application-under-test incompatibility problems.
8.7	Develop test procedures/scripts for various testing phases and testing subtypes.
8.7.1	Unit test phase test procedures/scripts. Witness execution of unit test procedures and scripts.
8.7.2	Integration test phase test procedures/scripts. Witness execution of integration test procedures and scripts.
8.7.3	System test phase test procedures/scripts. Develop test procedures and automate scripts that support all phases of the system test cycle (that is, regression, performance, stress, backup, and recoverability).
8.7.3.1	Develop a test procedure execution schedule.
8.7.3.2	Conduct automated test reuse analysis.
8.7.3.3	Conduct analysis to determine which tests to automate.
8.7.3.4	Develop a modularity relationship matrix.
8.7.4	Acceptance test phase test procedures/scripts. Develop and maintain test procedures and scripts.

continued

continued from page 161

8.8   Database group coordination. Work together with database group to develop test database environment. Baseline and maintain test data to support test execution.

8.9   Test procedure peer reviews. Compare test procedures with design and development standards (comments for each test tool scripting step, header file information, modularity, and so on). Document and manage defects and action items to closure.

8.10   Reuse library. Develop and maintain a test procedure reuse library for the project.

8.11   Test utilities. Support the creation/modification of in-house test support utilities that improve test effort efficiency.

9   Test Execution

9.1   Environment setup. Develop environment setup scripts.

9.2   Testbed environment. Develop testbed scripts and perform testbed development logistics.

9.3   Test phase execution. Execute the various test phases—strategic execution of automated testing. Monitor software defects to closure.

9.4   Test reporting. Prepare test reports.

9.5   Issue resolution. Resolve daily issues regarding automated test tool problems. If necessary, contact the test tool vendor for support.

9.6   Test repository maintenance. Perform test tool database backup/repair and troubleshooting activities.

10   Test Management and Support

10.1   Process reviews. Perform a test process review to ensure that standards and defined test process are being followed.

10.2   Special training. Seek out training for test engineers for special niche test requirements that become apparent during the test life cycle. Continue to develop technical skills of test personnel.

10.3   Testbed configuration management (CM). Maintain the entire testbed/repository (that is, test data, test procedures and scripts, software problem reports, and so on) in a CM tool. Define test scripts for the CM process and ensure that test personnel work closely with the CM group to assure test process reusability.

10.4   Test program status reporting. Identify mechanisms for tracking test program progress. Develop periodic reports on test program progress. Reports should reflect estimates to complete tasks in progress (earned value measurements).

10.5   Defect management. Define defect tracking workflow. Perform defect tracking and reporting. Attend defect review meetings.

10.6   Metrics collection and analysis. Collect and review all metrics to determine whether changes in the process are required and to determine whether the product is ready to be shipped.

11   Test Process Improvement

11.1   Training materials. Develop and maintain test process and test tool training materials.

11.2   Test process assets. Maintain a repository of test process assets, such as standards, processes, and procedures, test tool proposals, tool evaluation reports, historical test

continued

continued from page 162

effort sizing records, test effort lessons learned database, test automation script library, and test effort metrics and analysis reports.

11.3 Lessons learned. Conduct "lessons learned" sessions throughout the testing life cycle and gather test life-cycle benefits information.

11.4 Metrics analysis and reporting. Perform analysis of test process metrics across the organization and report the results of this analysis.

11.5 Test team intranet. Develop/maintain a test team intranet Web site to communicate with the rest of the organization.

11.6 Customer support surveys. Conduct surveys for projects supported by the test team to identify ways to improve test process and test team support.

11.7 Continuous process improvement. Refine test process assets based upon lessons learned, survey feedback, metrics analysis, and experience with new test tools. Verify that improvement suggestions are implemented.

11.8 Test conferences and professional associations. Participate in test tool user groups, test conferences, and meetings of other professional associates that promote information sharing and professional networking.

program module complexity analysis, program code coverage testing, system load performance testing, boundary testing, security testing, memory leak testing, and response time performance testing, among others.

5.3 | Test Effort Sizing

The test effort applied to a given project depends on a number of variables, such as the culture or test maturity of the organization, the scope of test requirements defined for the project, the skill levels of the individuals performing testing, and the type of test team organization supporting the test effort. The Test Maturity Model (TMM) addresses the level of test effort required on a project in relation to the testing maturity of the organization. The human resources costs vary according to the organization's test maturity, as defined by TMM [2].

Level 1 Test Maturity. At test maturity level 1, testing is often limited to debugging. A programmer writes and debugs the product's software until everything appears to work correctly. Because only the programmer is involved, testing costs often remain hidden within the cost of development. Likewise, the potential benefits of better test practices are hidden in field-support and product-upgrade costs. Historical costs pertaining to level 1 testing may be difficult to ascertain.

Level 2 Test Maturity. In level 2 software test programs, testing is recognized as a separate function. Test plans and scripts are generally developed by experienced product users or support personnel. These individuals may or may not have test automation (programming) experience. In any case, the individuals performing the testing must understand the software requirements and design specifications well enough to develop a comprehensive test plan and associated test scripts. Once the test scripts exist, they are provided to test engineers, who run them and record the results.

At level 2, the test team may consist of a group of more junior, relatively inexperienced end users or individuals with relevant functional knowledge. These individuals are given the job of trying to break the system as well as making sure that it works correctly. At level 2, the test effort may also include the services of one or more high-level support people who coordinate test writing, supervise the test engineers, and edit the results. Although a one-time set-up cost is incurred in implementing a capture/playback tool, this investment more than pays for itself when a number of test cycles are involved. During the later cycles, test scripts are reused and automatically played back, providing a huge labor saving with regard to script development and execution.

Levels 3–5 Test Maturity. At higher levels of testing maturity, the test engineer responsible for developing the test plan should participate in product development meetings with design engineers to help build testability into the product. The test engineer's programming background combined with his or her familiarity with the product will promote the subsequent creation of efficient tests that address the weakest aspects of the product. If the test tool has white-box test capabilities, the test engineer uses his or her knowledge of the system's internal workings to specify tests for functions that cannot be tested manually. The test plan serves to document the results of the test design. The test design, in turn, provides the guidance necessary for test engineers to develop the test script programs.

The test script development effort may be performed by either a team of test engineers or the application programmers. The level of programming experience required to develop test scripts depends on the test tool being used and the complexity of the tests. Generally, the most versatile tools employ scripts that are written in a common programming language, such as C. Other tools may use simplified languages. In any case, at least one member of the test team must have experience in developing a structured set of programming instructions. Automated tools are used to automatically generate test logs, document defects, and produce test status outputs. These tools provide significant labor savings with regard to test execution and management.

5.3.1 Test Team Sizing Methods: An Overview

Several methods are commonly used to determine the size of the test team needed to support a test effort. Historically, software development programs have focused on estimating the required development effort and overall project effort. Efforts related to product quality assurance, such as software testing, have then been sized in relation to the amount of anticipated development effort or overall project effort.

Commercial estimation tools such as COCOMO, PriceS, and SLIM require the input of various parameters associated with development size, productivity input, and the scope of project management activities. The accuracy of the output generated by these commercial tools, not surprisingly, reflects the quality of the input data. Few of these tools account for the growing importance and complexity of product-quality-assurance-related disciplines such as software testing by incorporating these considerations in the set of input factors used to generate resource and cost estimates.

The level of test effort required to support a given project depends on a number of variables, which can be used as input to complex estimation models to develop test team resource estimates. Other, simpler estimation models can be employed when values for a number of input parameters are lacking. Given the predominant focus within the industry on estimating the scope of the software development effort, attempts to size a test program often rely on the results of software development estimation, as reflected in the development ratio method.

5.3.2 Development Ratio Method

A quick and easy way to gauge the level of effort required to support a test program is to determine how many test engineers are needed based upon the number of software developers assigned to the project. The size of the test team is calculated by designating a desired ratio of developers on a project to test engineers. The term "developers" in this case includes those personnel dedicated to performing design, development, compilation, and unit-level test activities. Even though some developers' roles may extend beyond traditional development activities, for purposes of using this ratio method, the classification of the developer is limited to these specific activities. This classification excludes those personnel performing (on a full-time basis) functional analysis, requirements management, configuration management, quality assurance, process improvement, project management, software test, training material development, and user manual documentation.

The developers-to-test engineers ratio will vary depending on the type of software development effort, as noted in Table 5.4. The ratios in Table 5.4 (which are derived from the authors' experience) also assume that the scope of the test effort will involve functional and performance testing at the integration and system test

Table 5.4   Development Ratio Method

Development Type	Developers Planned	Ratio	Test Team Size
Commercial Product (Large Market)	30	3:2	20
Commercial Product (Small Market)	30	3:1	10
Application Development for Individual Client	30	6:1	5
Development and Heavy COTS Integration for Individual Client	30	4:1	7
Government (Internal) Application Development	30	5:1	6
Corporate (Internal) Application Development	30	4:1	7

levels. The values in the columns labeled "Developers Planned" and "Test Team Size" are expressed in terms of number of people.

Some mission-critical software projects may employ a higher number of test engineers than developers. The ratio between the number of application developers and test engineers, therefore, may reflect the roles defined for developers and test engineers. The figures in Table 5.4 assume that test engineers are involved only in executing testing life-cycle activities and do not perform any direct development work.

5.3.3   Percentage Method

Another quick way to estimate the level of effort required to support a test program is to use the percentage method, outlined in Table 5.5. This method considers the number of people planned to support a project in calculating the size of the test team. The test team size factor values given in Table 5.5 assume that the scope of the test effort will involve functional and performance testing at the integration and system test levels.

Also represented in Table 5.5 is sizing factor for a product assurance (PA) team. Organizations performing software development in accordance with maturity guidelines outlined within the CMM would require the services of individuals who support the various key process areas promulgated by the CMM. The PA team composition indicated in Table 5.5 includes both the test team personnel and personnel who undertake requirements management, configuration management, quality assurance, and process improvement. In this context, "process improvement" means that personnel supervise the effort to tailor organization processes to the specific project, provide project personnel with requisite training, and collect and analyze project performance metrics.

Table 5.5   Percentage Method

Development Type	Project Staffing Level	Test Team Size Factor	Test Team Size (People)	Product Assurance Team Size Factor	Product Assurance Team Size
Commercial Product (Large Market)	50	27%	13	37%	18
Commercial Product (Small Market)	50	16%	8	28%	14
Application Development for Individual Client	50	10%	5	20%	10
Development and Heavy COTS Integration for Individual Client	50	14%	7	23%	11
Government (Internal) Application Development	50	11%	5	20%	10
Corporate (Internal) Application Development	50	14%	7	23%	11

5.3.4   Test Procedure Method

Another way to estimate the level of effort required to support a test program is to use the number of test procedures planned for a project. The organization will need to develop a historical record of its development projects and their associated development sizing values, number of test procedures required, and the resulting test effort measured in terms of man-hours. Development sizing values may be documented in terms of lines of code (LOC), lines of code equivalent, function points, or number of objects produced.

Once this historical record exists, the test team could determine the past relationship between the sizing values and the number of test procedures developed, and then estimate the number of test procedures required for a new project. Once the number of test procedures was estimated, the test team could determine the historical relationship between the number of test procedures and the number of test team man-hours expended. This factor would then be used to estimate the number of man-hours or full-time equivalent personnel needed to support the test effort on the new project. The historical values are assumed to reflect the culture or test maturity of the organization and a correlation is presumed between the number of test procedures applied to a project and the scope of test requirements.

Table 5.6   Test Procedure Method

	Number of Test Procedures	Factor	Man- Hours	Per- formance Period	Test Team Size (People)
Historical Record (Similar Project)	860	6.16	5,300	9 months (1,560 hours)	3.4
New Project Estimate	1,120	6.16	6,900	12 months (2,080 hours)	3.3

Table 5.6 gives an example of the use of the test procedure method, where a test team has estimated that a new project will require 1,120 test procedures. The team reviewed historical records, finding that a previous test effort involving 860 test procedures required a total of 5,300 hours. On this previous effort, the ratio of hours to test procedures was 6.16. The 5,300 hours were expended over a nine-month period giving a full-time equivalent of 3.4 test engineers for the project. Given the historical ratio of 6.16 for number of hours/number of test procedures, the test team calculates that it will take 6,900 hours to complete testing on the 1,120-test procedure project. As the new project is scheduled to be developed over 12 months, the test team calculates that 3.3 test engineers will be needed. This figure is calculated by dividing the total number of hours (6,900) by the number of hours per person (2,080) for the given period of performance (12 months).

5.3.5   Task Planning Method

Another way to estimate a test program's level of effort required involves the review of historical records with regard to the number of man-hours expended to perform test program tasks for a similar type of test effort. The test team would need to perform time recording in accordance with a work breakdown structure like that depicted in Table 5.3. Historical records would then be developed that highlight the effort required to perform the various tasks. Next, the estimated number of test procedures (1,120) for the new project is compared with the historical sizing baseline, as shown in Table 5.7. The historical baseline indicates that the total number of man-hours for a project involving 860 test procedures is 5,300 hours, which represents a factor of 6.16. This factor is then used to estimate the number of hours required to perform a test effort involving 1,120 test procedures. This same historical comparison appeared in Table 5.6.

The test team then reviews the historical makeup of the expended hours associated with the various test program tasks included in the work breakdown structure depicted in Table 5.3. Table 5.8 sums the hours needed for each WBS element.

Table 5.7　New Project Man-Hours Estimation

	Number of Test Procedures	Factor	Man-Hours
Historical record (similar project)	860	6.16	5,300
New project estimate	1,120	6.16	6,900

Table 5.8　Task Planning Method

No.	WBS Element	Historical Value	Percentage	Preliminary Estimate	Adjusted Estimate
1	Project startup	140	2.6	179	179
2	Early project support	120	2.2	152	152
3	Decision to automate test	90	1.7	117	—
4	Test tool selection and evaluation	160	3	207	—
5	Test tool introduction	260	5	345	345
6	Test planning	530	10	690	690
7	Test design	540	10	690	690
8	Test development	1,980	37	2,553	2,553
9	Test execution	870	17	1,173	1,173
10	Test management and support	470	9	621	621
11	Test process improvement	140	2.5	173	—
	Project Total	5,300	100%	6,900	6,403

The test team develops a preliminary estimate of the hours for each WBS element using the historical percentage factor. Given that the new project has been mandated to use a particular automated test tool, the test effort is revised as indicated in the far right-hand column in Table 5.8. The test team had also been advised that the project would not be provided with any funding to cover test process

Table 5.9   Test Team Size

	Number of Test Procedures	Man-Hour Estimate	Adjusted Estimate	Per-formance Period	Test Team Size
New Project Estimate	1,120	5.71	6,403	12 months (2,080 hours)	3.1

improvement activities. The far right-hand column in Table 5.8 is therefore further adjusted.

Next, the test team computes the test team size based on the adjusted man-hour estimate of 6,403 hours as depicted in Table 5.9. The test team size is calculated to be equivalent to 3.1 test engineers over the 12-month project. In the event that the test team is staffed with exactly three full-time test personnel throughout the duration of the test effort, the team will need to achieve a slightly higher level of productivity than that of previous test teams so as to complete the test effort within the given schedule. It could implement a different staffing approach, applying two full-time test personnel and the fractional time of two other test engineers. The fractional time could be split a number of ways to include 50% of one person and 60% of a second person. Under this plan, it would be best for the two fractional-time personnel to be consistently used to perform a particular type of testing or test a particular functionality.

5.3.6   Test Effort Sizing Factors

The following factors should be considered when developing test effort sizing estimates:

1. **Organization.** This factor includes the culture or test maturity of the organization.
2. **Scope of test requirements.** Tests to be performed can include functional requirements testing, server performance testing, user interface testing, program module performance testing, program module complexity analysis, program code coverage testing, system load performance testing, boundary testing, security testing, memory leak testing, response time performance testing, and usability testing. Chapter 8 provides more information on the different kinds of testing.
3. **Test engineer skill level.** This factor encompasses the technical skill levels of the individuals performing the testing.

4. **Test tool proficiency.** The use of automated testing introduces a new level of complexity that a project's test team may not have previously experienced. Test script programming is a required expertise that may be new to the test team, and few members of the test team may have had experience in performing coding. Even if the test team has had experience with one kind of an automated test tool, the tool required on the new project may be different.

5. **Business knowledge.** Test team personnel must have familiarity with the application business area.

6. **Test team organization.** This factor includes the type of test team organization supporting the test effort. Section 5.1 provides more information on test team organization types.

7. **Scope of test program.** An effective automated test program amounts to a development effort complete with strategy and goal planning, test requirements definition, analysis, design, and coding.

8. **Start of test effort.** Test activity and test planning should be initiated early in the project, which means that test engineers should be involved in analysis and design review activities. These reviews can serve as effective testing components, preventing analysis/design errors. Such involvement allows the test team to more completely understand the project's requirements and design, develop the most appropriate test environment, and generate a more thorough test design. Early involvement not only supports effective test design, which is a critically important activity when utilizing an automated test tool, but also enables early detection of errors and prevents migration of errors from requirements specification to design, and from design into code.

9. **Number of incremental software builds planned.** Many industry software professionals assume that the use of automated test tools makes the software test effort less significant in terms of man-hours or less complex in terms of planning and execution. In reality, savings accrued from the use of automated test tools will take time to generate. At the first use of a particular automated test tool by a test team, very little savings may be realized. Instead, savings are realized in subsequent builds of a software application.

10. **Process definition.** Test team utilization of defined (documented) processes can improve the efficiency of test engineering operations. A lack of defined processes has an opposite effect, translating into a longer learning curve for junior test engineers.

11. **Mission-critical applications.** The scope and breadth of testing for mission-critical software applications, where a software failure poses a risk to human life or is crucial to the success of an organization, will be greater than that for software

applications that do not pose a high risk. For example, testing of software that will control a heart monitor in a hospital setting is more critical than testing of the performance of game software.

12. **Test development/execution schedule.** Short timeframes to perform test development and execution may interject inefficiency into test engineering operations and require that additional test engineering effort be applied.

5.4 | Test Engineer Recruiting

A test manager who faces the challenge of staffing and executing a test program on a project needs to recruit the right kind of test engineering talent. The manager likely has several questions in mind. What kind of person makes a good test engineer? What kind of skills should the test engineer have? How do I know which test engineer candidates are the best for the job?

Good software developers will have been trained and groomed to have a mindset to make something work and to develop a work-around solution, if necessary. Test engineers, on the other hand, need a capacity to be able to make things fail and a developer's mentality to develop work-around solutions, if necessary, especially during the construction of test scripts.

Test engineers should be analytical, attentive to detail, and organized, and, given the complexities of automated testing, possess a creative and planning-ahead mindset. Because test engineers must work closely and cooperatively with software developers, they should be both assertive and poised when working through trouble reports and issues with developers. In addition, test engineers need a broad range of technical skills and experience across multiple platforms, operating systems, layers of supporting applications, interfaces to other products and systems, databases, and application languages. It is beneficial for them to be familiar with the script programming language of the primary automated test tool.

5.4.1 Test Engineer Qualities

The test engineer will be asked to carry out the various test program tasks listed in Table 5.3. This software professional should therefore be comfortable performing a variety of different tasks, often in parallel. The test engineer needs to be able to pick up new technology quickly. She should also have good conceptual skills to be able to understand the technical intricacies of the application.

The test engineer may perform testing on a mainframe application on one project and then test a client-server application on the next project. An automated test expert must be familiar not only with development techniques, but also with network, database, and middleware issues.

The skills required by the test team will depend on the kinds of tests performed and the test tools applied. For GUI testing, the test engineer may need to be familiar with Visual Basic, MS Access, SQL Server, and Windows-based operating systems. For server testing, he or she may need the ability to use C, C++, SQL, UNIX, and/or UNIX scripting and an understanding of remote procedure calls (RPCs). Applications operating in client-server environments depend on RPCs to bridge the gap between the processes in the different layers. Because the processing can be distributed across multiple platforms, the data must be delivered to the target platform in a form that can be read on that platform. Using RPCs makes the delivery and translation processes transparent to both client and server. The client program can receive the results of a server call as if the server were a compatible local procedure.

Qualities and skills to consider when recruiting for a test engineer are listed below. It may be worthwhile to document the skills desired of test team members within the application's test plan.

1. Adaptability—able to perform in a variety of different technical environments, and familiar with different processes, tools, and methodologies.

2. Quick learner—enjoy performing a variety of different kinds of tasks, learning new things, and touching many different products.

3. Conceptual skills—aptitude for conceptualizing complex activities and articulating thoughts and ideas.

4. Organizational skills—understand complex test requirements and be able to formulate test planning and design approaches to support requirements; able to perform multiple responsibilities concurrently.

5. Problem solving—be able to develop work-around solutions to problems encountered during test development and execution.

6. Creativity—mindset to be able to think of a multitude of ways to exercise a system or application to ensure that it works in all circumstances; able to identify all conditions under which the software or system could fail.

7. Analytical/programming skills—training, experience, and skill to be able to develop automated test scripts.

8. Application business area knowledge—familiarity or understanding of the required functionality of the business application.

9. Diplomatic/cooperative—able to work closely and effectively with software developers; includes strong verbal communication skills.

10. Software professional—proficient at exercising the system and skillful in identifying and communicating problems to the developer.

11. Technical expertise—ability to set up and evaluate test tools; develop and maintain test data; control the test configuration and environment; and understand network, database, and middleware issues.

12. Test experience—level of test program experience. An effective test program incorporating the automation of software testing will involve a development life cycle of its own. The test engineer should have experience with test strategy and goal planning, test requirements definition, and test design, development, and execution.

13. Detail-oriented—pays attention to detail so as to identify difficult-to-find glitches and has a strong interest in improving the quality of a software product.

14. Process-oriented—skilled in the ability to understand inputs, logical sequences of steps, and expected output.

15. Writing/grammar skills—ability to effectively evaluate and improve requirements specifications and software design documentation.

5.4.2 Test Team Composition

To be able to recruit test engineers for a test program, it is necessary to understand the target composition of the test team. The test team, as a whole, will be responsible for fulfilling all test requirements for a project and performing all test program tasks. The effective execution of a test program requires a team with enough resident expertise to leverage the adopted test process and the applied test tools. The team will need enough familiarity and experience with the test tool to adequately plan, prepare, and execute test. The composition of the test team should be outlined within a test team profile like that depicted in Table 5.10.

The test team profile in Table 5.10 portrays the composition of a team responsible for a test program involving the use of an automated test tool called QA Partner. The project involves the development of a client-server health care patient-scheduling and resource-management application operating on Windows client computers and servers running UNIX. The application is being developed in Visual Basic and C++ with a SQL Server back end. The scope of testing on the particular project involves functional requirements, server performance, the user interface, memory allocation, and system load testing.

The team described in Table 5.10 consists of a test manager, test lead, three test engineers, and a junior test engineer. This test team profile suggests that the test manager would need to have at least six years of software testing experience, including one to two years of test leadership experience. Ideally, the test leadership experience would include personnel supervision. In reality, the test manager's experience might include both software development and software testing experience. Ideally,

Table 5.10 Test Team Profile

Position	Duties/Skills	Test Experience (years)	SQA Tool (years)
Test manager	Duties: Responsible for test program, customer interaction, recruiting, test tool introduction, staff supervision, test planning/design/development and execution Skills: MS Project, C/C++, SQL, MS Access, UNIX, test tool experience	6+	1+
Test lead	Duties: Supports customer interaction, recruiting, test tool introduction, staff supervision, cost/progress status reporting, test planning/design/development and execution Skills: QA Partner, Purify, SQL, SQA Basic, UNIX, MS Access, C/C++, SQL Server	4+	2+
Test engineer	Duties: Responsible for performing test planning/design/ development and execution Skills: Test tool experience, health care system experience	2+	Some
Test engineer	Duties: Responsible for performing test planning/design/ development and execution Skills: Test tool experience, health care system experience	2+	Some
Test engineer	Duties: Responsible for creating and controlling test tool environment, network and middleware testing, and performing test planning/design/development and execution Skills: Visual Basic, SQL, CNE, UNIX, C/C++, SQL Server	1+	—
Junior test engineer	Duties: Responsible for performing test planning/design/ development and execution Skills: Visual Basic, SQL, UNIX, Java, CGI/Perl, HTML, MS Access	—	—

the test manager would also have at least one year of experience with the primary test tool planned for the project as well as some exposure to other test tools on the market. It would also be beneficial for this manager to be familiar with various software tools that support the management of the test effort or help team members navigate their way around the testbed environment.

While the test manager is responsible for the overall effort and focuses on long-term and strategic concerns, the test lead is responsible for the technical execution of the test program. The test team profile in Table 5.10 suggests that the test lead should have at least four years of test experience and at least two years of experience with the QA Partner test tool. The ideal skill set for the test lead includes abilities in the use of the Purify test tool and several programming languages, as well as familiarity with SQL Server relational databases.

The example test team profile also requires three test engineer positions. While all three would perform general test activities, two would ideally have experience in the relevant business area and one would have a proficiency in network engineering and administration. This proficiency might be reflected in network experience as well as credentials as a certified network engineer (CNE).

Rounding out the test team might be a very junior test engineer—right out of college or having only one or two years of software development experience. The junior test engineer supports the test team in a utility capacity. He would initially perform simple tasks, such as verifying the user manual and help files. The junior test engineer would gradually become more familiar with the test life cycle, the test tools being applied on the project, and the business application itself. It would be beneficial for this team member to have a variety of software skills, including training and academic experience in new software tools and programming languages.

5.4.3 Job Requisition

Armed with an understanding of the desired qualifications for a test engineer candidate as well as a mental framework for the composition of the test team, the test manager can initiate the recruiting process. For most organizations, a form must be completed to advertise for an open job position. This form may be referred to as a job requisition, position description, or recruiting request. Its purpose is to define the nature of the position, by indicating the required skills and credentials necessary to perform the job. The form is usually distributed within the organization and released to equal-opportunity employment offices and state or local employment agencies. For purposes of discussion, this chapter will call this form a job requisition.

The contents of the job requisition are fairly standard. The job requisition usually contains a posting date, position title, work location, and position identification number. It outlines duties to be performed in the position as well as required and desired skills. It will usually stipulate the level of education and number of years of experience required.

For each position identified within the test team profile outlined in Table 5.10, a job requisition would need to be created. A sample job requisition for the test lead position is provided in Figure 5.1.

Job Requisition

Title: Test lead		**FT/PT:** Full-time	
Date: (today's date)		**Job Req#:** 10068	
Salary Range: (minimum–maximum)		**Location:** Fairfax, Virginia	
Division: 002		**Manager:** John Smith	

Qualifications Required:

- Bachelor's degree in computer science, information systems, engineering, business, or other related scientific or technical discipline
- 4 years experience in software testing
- 1 year experience with an automated test tool
- Test plan development experience
- Familiarity with entire software development life cycle

Qualifications Desired:

- Experience with the automated test tools WinRunner and Purify
- Familiarity with RDBMS/SQL Server software
- Experience with systems integration/software programming/QA responsibility
- Familiarity with C or C++, UNIX shell scripts, Visual Basic, or Powerbuilder
- Strong communication skills and the ability to work in a fast-paced environment
- Ability to work well in a team environment and be able to interact effectively with senior management

Description/Duties:

- Supports customer interaction, recruiting, test tool introduction, staff supervision, cost/progress status reporting, test planning/design/development and execution
- Responsible for test engineering tasks to include: analyzing systems requirements for testability; deriving test requirements and test strategy; evaluating automated test tools; verifying automated test tool compatibility with application-under-test; planning for test tool introduction on project; finding work-around solutions to test tool incompatibility problems; planning test activities; identifying the kinds of tests to be performed; planning, tracking, and managing test environment setup activities; developing test designs; developing and executing test procedures; developing and managing test data; controlling the test configuration and environment; fostering a close working relationship between software developers and test engineers; performing test readiness reviews; documenting, tracking, and obtaining closure on trouble reports

Figure 5.1 Job Requisition

5.4.4   Recruiting Activities

The ability of an organization to effectively recruit a quality test engineer differs based upon the type of test team employed by the organization. Organizations that use the stovepipe test team organization (see Section 5.1) recruit and hire test professionals on a project-by-project basis. In this type of scenario, the organization responsible for the project assigns a project manager to oversee the start-up and execution of the project. During project start-up, this manager investigates and evaluates tools for the project, develops job requisitions for the types of personnel desired, interviews candidates for the various positions, and makes personnel hiring decisions. This project manager may have had limited experience with professional software testing programs and may not know how to define, recruit, or recognize the types of skills needed for the test team.

Other test team organizations, such as the centralized and SMT types outlined in Section 5.1, possess infrastructures that support the managed rotation of test engineering personnel between projects. These test organizations can generally draw on a network of test engineer professionals in the event that the team needs to be augmented with an additional test professional. By definition, these test organizations have professional test engineers on staff who are available to put together a job requisition, provide input for a recruitment advertisement, and interview test engineer candidates. They enjoy several advantages over stovepipe test organizations when it comes to attracting the candidate to join the organization, as noted in Section 5.1. Given that the demand for professional software test engineers has exceeded the supply in recent years—a trend that is expected to continue—successful recruiting and retention of test engineers may require a special effort. Employers may need to offer comprehensive compensation packages, training opportunities, flexible work hours, attractive job titles, and signing bonuses. Another important consideration is the availability of modern software engineering development and support tools, as well as the use of current technology computer equipment.

Centralized and SMT organizations often seek to attract professional test engineers by offering career development paths within a centralized software test department, training and development in automated test tools, mentoring opportunities with more senior test engineers, increased job security by having the test engineer rotate between projects, and increased professional development opportunities achieved by the diversity of technology and tools experienced over a multitude of projects.

5.4.5   Locating Test Engineers

Regardless of the type of test team organization, the individual responsible for screening and hiring test engineers must know how to locate job candidates. He or she must also be able to distinguish a superior test engineer candidate from a mediocre test engineer candidate during an interview.

Résumés for test engineers can be solicited or located via several means. One approach is to review the organization's recruiting or résumé repository. Alternatively, one can solicit résumés in a job advertisement in a newspaper or magazine. A more proactive and potentially more cost-beneficial avenue is to query Internet résumé sources or to advertise open positions with test tool user groups or test-related newsgroups. Employee referral programs, when offered, are beneficial to solicit résumés of test engineers as well, and special promotions, such as those offering trips to exotic places, may be helpful.

Following the effort to retrieve or solicit test engineer résumés, the hiring manager needs to whittle the pile of prospective résumés down to a handful or so of those that most closely resemble the manager's specific requirements. The manager must then screen the candidates in person.

5.4.6 Test Engineer Interviews

In preparation for test engineer interviews, the hiring manager should develop a list of relevant questions intended to confirm that the candidate has the resident expertise at the level of proficiency required. Once these questions have been prepared, they should be distributed to all staff members participating in the interview process.

The individuals conducting an interview should document or summarize the responses to each question. The interviewer should also jot down notes pertaining to observations about the candidate. This documentation will be helpful later when making a decision about whether to offer the position to a candidate or when trying to decide between two candidates. Where possible, the candidate should be interviewed by two or more people.

Some introductory questions to consider at the start of the interview are as follows:

1. It's good to start the interview off with an *open-ended question* that allows the candidate to talk for a while. During this timeframe, the interviewer can assess the candidate's communication skills and ability to organize his or her thoughts. Example: "Could you summarize your test background and interest in the test profession?"

2. A good second question will ask that the test engineering candidate to talk about their *problem-solving ability*. Example: "Could you describe how you've overcome technical problems and the kinds of results that you have had?"

3. The test engineer should be familiar with the *test life cycle*. Example: "Could you outline your perspective of the test engineering life cycle?"

Specific topics to consider when interviewing a test engineer are described below. The interviewer should ask the candidate about his or her experience regarding each topic. Depending on the qualification level of the test engineer being hired, these questions can be reduced or increased.

1. Analyzing system requirements for testability. Give examples of testable and nontestable requirements, and have the candidate define which requirements are deemed to be testable and which ones are not (for example, "the system shall allow for the addition of an unlimited amount of accounts" is a nontestable requirement).

2. Understanding the testing life cycle. The test engineer should know that the testing life cycle takes place in parallel with the development life cycle.

3. Deriving test requirements and test strategies. Ask the candidate to give examples.

4. Using an automated testing tool.

5. Evaluating an automated test tool.

6. Modifying automated test scripts. The candidate should have some development experience.

7. Verifying automated test tool compatibility with the application-under-test.

8. Finding work-around solutions to test tool incompatibility problems.

9. Planning for test tool introduction on a project.

10. Planning test activities.

11. Planning, tracking, and managing test environment setup activities.

12. Understanding the importance of baselining the testbed and test environment.

13. Identifying the kinds of tests to be performed.

14. Developing a test design.

15. Developing test data and refreshing the test database during test execution.

16. Performing data validation tests.

17. Inserting comments when recording scripts with an automated test tool.

18. Performing test readiness reviews.

19. Being able to break the system or make the application fail, and identifying and communicating the problem to the developer.

20. Documenting, tracking, and obtaining closure on trouble reports.

21. Fostering a close working relationship between developers and test engineers.

22. Performing test activities within the technical environment planned for the project.

23. Demonstrating the technical skills required for the position as reflected in the published job requisition.

24. Performing a variety of different kinds of tasks, learning new technologies, and performing multiple responsibilities concurrently.

25. Understanding the required functionality of the business application.

26. Working closely and effectively with software developers and users.

27. Understanding that users need to be involved from the beginning of and throughout the system development life cycle.

28. Understanding common network, database, and middleware issues.

29. Being familiar with the project-specific operating system, database, network, and development language.

30. Understanding metrics collection and metrics analysis.

5.4.7 Distinguishing the Best Candidate

Aside from reviewing the candidate's personal qualities and his or her test engineering and technical skills, a hiring manager can take several steps to ensure that the test engineering candidate will successfully perform in the particular position:

1. Assess how the candidate asked questions and took the initiative during the interview.

2. Determine whether the candidate listened well and showed interest in the position and the company.

3. Listen for comments and responses that indicate that the candidate is a team-oriented person.

4. Listen for comments and responses that indicate that the candidate is a hard worker and committed to doing an excellent job.

5. Assess for how well the candidate is able to make important distinctions and share important insights with regard to an effective test process, design, and execution.

6. Assess how well the candidate answers questions. Are the answers brief and to the point, or do they go off on tangents, becoming incoherent or disorganized?

7. Inquire about how well the candidate performs programming. For junior candidates, find out what kind of grades they received in academic programming

courses. A computer science degree offers some assurance that the candidate is analytical, intuitive, and persistent enough to successfully perform as a test engineer. Programming skills are important because they enable the test engineer to modify scripts so as to make them reusable and maintainable, minimizing the time required to regenerate test scripts.

8. Note whether the candidate speaks with respect about the testing profession.

9. Note whether the candidate speaks with respect about a previous boss, college professors, and members of college projects teams. Although technical skills are important, it is also crucial to select people who will work effectively with others, as the test engineer will need to advise developers about defects. The test engineer must be patient enough to stick with the project and with the organization through obstacles and tough challenges encountered on the project.

10. Don't hire a test engineer who didn't make it as a developer. Remember, a bad developer does not make a good test engineer.

11. Consider how well the test engineer's personality fits with the rest of the test team. The test team needs to be populated with both leaders and warriors. A team mix including all of one type and none of the other may present a problem. If too many strong-headed or stubborn technicians (warriors) work on the project, they will likely be at odds with one another and the resulting friction may hamper test performance. If the project includes too many leaders, disagreements may arise regarding which direction to take, and the test team may lack enough technician strength to persevere through tough challenges.

5.5 | Roles and Responsibilities

This section describes the major roles and responsibilities of individuals who perform test activities as well as those who typically have a close working relationship with test engineers. These roles and responsibilities should be tailored to the particular project and documented within the project test plan.

The number of test engineering roles required on a project may outnumber the number of actual test team positions. As a result, a test engineer may be responsible for more than one role—that is, she may "wear different hats." The different test engineering roles required for the various test program tasks were listed in Table 5.3. To ensure that test roles are properly carried out, several practices may need to be considered, such as using consultants on a part-time or short-duration basis. Consideration should also be given to assigning an existing test engineer within the organization to act as a mentor for a more junior test engineer. In addition, the organization should cross-train test engineers across projects, different technical environments, and different test tools.

Table 5.11 lists the responsibilities and roles of the participants in the testing process.

Test teams that plan to use automated test tools should have personnel on staff who have software development skills, as automated testing differs from manual testing in the way that test scripts are developed, executed, and managed. As a result, the skills and activities pertinent to test engineers who will perform manual testing differ from the skills and activities of test engineers who will perform automated software testing. Manual test roles are therefore listed separately in the defined roles and responsibilities in Table 5.11.

It is important that the correct roles be assigned to the appropriate person. Assess and leverage current strengths and assign accordingly. Organize and manage the test effort to take maximum advantage of the specialized skills of each member of the team and the specific purpose of each element of the test program.

Table 5.11   Testing Team Responsibilities and Roles

Responsibilities	Skills
Test Manager	
• Responsible for customer and test tool vendor interaction, recruiting, test tool introduction, staff supervision, and staff training • Test plan development, including development of test goals, objectives, and strategy • Cohesive integration of test and development activities • Acquisition of hardware and software • Test environment and test product configuration management • Test process definition, training, and continual improvement • Test program oversight and progress tracking • Use of metrics to support continuous test process improvement	• Familiar with test program concerns, including test data management, trouble reporting and resolution, test design, and development • Understands application business area and application requirements • Skilled at developing test goals, objectives, and test strategy • Familiar with different test tools and their use • Good at all planning aspects, including personnel management, facilities, and schedule

continued

continued from page 183

Responsibilities	Skills

Test Lead

• Technical leadership for the test program, including the test approach • Customer interaction, recruiting, test tool introduction, test planning, staff supervision, and cost/progress status reporting • Test requirement definition, test design, test script and test data development, test automation, test environment configuration, test script configuration management, and test execution • Interaction with test tool vendor to identify best ways to leverage test tool on project • Staying current on latest test approaches and test tools and transfers this knowledge to test team • Test procedure walkthroughs • Implementation of test process improvements resulting from lessons learned and benefits surveys • Testing of traceability matrix • Test process implementation • Review of test product documentation	• Understands application business area and application requirements • Familiar with test program concerns such as test data management, trouble reporting and resolution, test design, and development • Expertise in a variety of technical skills, including programming languages, database technologies, and computer operating systems • Familiar with different test tools and their use

Usability Test Engineer

• Design and development of usability testing scenarios, administration of testing process • Definition of criteria for those performing usability testing, analysis of results of testing sessions, presentation of results to development team • Development of test product documentation and reports • Definition of usability requirements and interaction with customer to refine usability requirements • Test procedure walkthroughs	• Proficient in designing test suites • Skilled in test facilitation • Excellent interpersonal skills • Proficient in GUI design standards

continued

continued from page 184

Responsibilities	Skills

Manual Test Engineer

- Development of test procedures and cases based upon requirements
- Manual execution of the test procedures
- Test procedure walkthroughs
- Conduct of tests and preparation of reports on test progress and regression
- Adherence to test standards

- Good understanding of GUI design—usability errors are often uncovered during QA testing
- Proficient in software testing
- Proficient in designing test suites
- Proficient in the business area of the application-under-test
- Proficient in GUI design standards

Automated Test Engineer

- Development of test procedures and cases based upon requirements
- Design, development, and execution of reusable and maintainable automated scripts
- Adherence to test design standards
- Test procedure walkthroughs
- Execution of tests and preparation of reports on test progress and regression
- Attendance at test tool user group meetings to stay abreast of test tool capabilities

- Good understanding of GUI design—usability errors are often uncovered during QA testing
- Proficient in software testing
- Proficient in designing test suites
- Proficient in the test tool
- Programming skills
- Proficient in GUI design standards

Network Test Engineer

- Network, database, and middleware testing
- Research on network, database, and middleware performance monitoring tools
- Implementation of performance monitoring tools on an ongoing basis

- Network, database, and system administration skills
- Expertise in a variety of technical skills, including programming languages, database technologies, and computer operating systems
- Product evaluation and integration skills

continued

continued from page 185

Responsibilities	Skills

Test Environment Specialist

• Installation of test tools and establishment of test tool environments • Creation and control of the test environment via environment setup scripts • Maintenance of a test database • Maintenance of a requirements hierarchy within the test tool environment	• Network, database, and system administration skills • Expertise in a variety of technical skills, including programming languages, database technologies, and computer operating systems • Test tool experience • Product evaluation and integration skills

Test Library and Configuration Specialist

• Test script change management • Test script version control • Maintenance of a test script reuse library	• Network, database, and system administration skills • Expertise in a variety of technical skills, including programming languages, database technologies, and computer operating systems • Configuration management tool expertise • Test tool experience

Business Analyst

• Analysis of business relative to the application's goals • User interviews and review of current business • Definition of processes to gather requirements and determination of the need for reengineering • Creation of requirements specifications • Coordination with the usability test engineers	• Experience in the business area • Interviewing skills • "People" skills • Proficient in user and task analysis • Understands the GUI usability process

Chief User Liaison

• Primary user representative • Communication of business and user requirements to the development team	• Excellent interpersonal skills • Expertise in the business area

Chapter Summary

- The test team needs to possess the specific expertise necessary to comprehend the scope and depth of the required test effort and be able to develop a strategy to execute and implement the test program. Test team composition needs to be designed, the test team assembled, and the roles and responsibilities of the test team defined.

- Several organizational structures are possible for the test team. Potential approaches include stovepipe test team, centralized test team, IV&V test team, and systems methodology and test team organizations.

- The most important consequence of test team organization pertains to the opportunities for continual improvement in process maturity and software test capability. Test team structures that persist after a project ends can readily retain and improve upon the organization's processes, procedures, and tool knowledge, as well as transfer this knowledge to new projects.

- The different types of test tasks involved in a test program are commonly outlined within a work breakdown structure. This structure is then used in conjunction with timekeeping activities to develop a historical record of the effort expended to perform various test activities.

- Several methods are commonly employed to determine the size of the test team required to support a test effort. Size estimation approaches include the development ratio, percentage, test procedure, and task planning methods.

- A test engineer needs to possess the ability to discover defects. He needs a developer's mentality to develop work-around solutions to incompatibility problems that may arise when using an automated test tool. The ideal test engineer is analytical, attentive to detail, and organized and, given the complexities of automated testing, has a creative and planning-ahead mindset. A test engineer also needs to be both assertive and poised when working through issues with software developers.

- Given the complexities of the test effort associated with a client-server or multi-tier environment, test engineers need a broad range of technical skills. They should possess experience across multiple platforms, operating systems, layers of supporting applications, interfaces to other products and systems, databases, and application languages. They also need to know the script programming language of the primary automated test tool.

- To recruit test engineers for a test program, the hiring manager should understand the target composition of the test team. The effective execution of a test program requires that a test team have enough resident expertise to leverage the adopted test process and the applied test tools. The composition of the test team should be outlined within a test team profile.

o   In preparation of test engineer interviews, the hiring manager should develop a list of questions intended to confirm that the candidate has the appropriate expertise at the level of proficiency required. All individuals involved in the interview process should document or summarize each candidate's responses to each question.

o   The major roles and responsibilities of individuals who perform test activities on a project need to be defined and documented within the project test plan.

References

1. "Survey Provides Software Testing Industry Snapshot." *Software Testing Newsletter* Fall/Winter 1995–1996.

2. Burnstein, I., Suwanassart, T., Carlson, C.R. *Developing a Testing Maturity Model,* Part II. Chicago: Illinois Institute of Technology, 1996.

Part III

Test Planning and Preparation

If software defects were gold, then software testing would be gold mining. Test planning would be the geologist's surveys and preparation activities done before mining takes place: The geologist establishes a plan and strategy, increasing the probability that digging at particular spots using a particular strategy would prove to be successful.

—Reliable Software Technologies*

*Adapted from Reliable Software Technologies. "Testability." *IEEE Software*, May 1995.

Test Planning: Smart
Application of Testing

Failing to plan is a plan to fail.

—Effie Jones

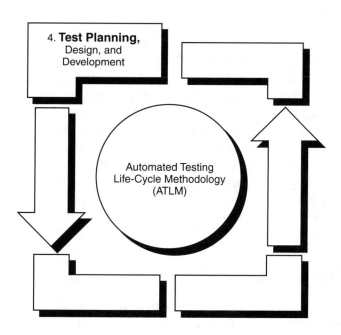

Table 6.1   ATLM Process Hierarchy

Incorporate ATLM into Test Plan

Decision to automate (Chapter 2)

Test tool acquisition (Chapter 3)

Introduction of automated testing (Chapter 4)

Test team management (Chapter 5)

Test planning, design, and development (Chapters 6–8)

Execution and management of automated test (Chapter 9)

The cornerstone of an effective test program is test planning. The test planning element of the Automated Testing Life-cycle Methodology (ATLM) encompasses the review of all activities that will be required for the test program and the verification that processes, methodologies, techniques, people, tools, and equipment (hardware/middleware/software) are organized and applied in an efficient way.

For each test program, test goals and objectives must be defined and test requirements must be specified. Test strategies aimed at supporting test requirements need to be defined. The main events and primary activities of the test program should be entered into a schedule. The products (including deliverables) to be created by the test team during the execution of the test program must be identified as well. Finally, all pertinent information should be captured and kept up-to-date in a test plan document.

Planning activities occur and planning information is captured throughout the various phases of the ATLM, as depicted in Table 6.1. The test planning phase of the ATLM focuses attention specifically on the identification of test program documentation, the planning required to achieve the test objectives and support the test environment, and the development of the test plan document. These particular activities are addressed within this chapter; the other test planning activities are covered in the various chapters of this book, as noted in Table 6.1.

6.1 | Test Planning Activities

The efficient use of automated test tools requires considerable investment in test planning and preparation. The test plan contains a wealth of information, including much of the testing documentation requirements for the project. The test plan will outline the team's roles and responsibilities, project test schedule, test design activities, test environment preparation, test risks and contingencies, and acceptable level of thoroughness. Test plan appendixes may include test procedures, a naming convention description, and requirements-to-test procedure traceability matrix. The test plan also needs to incorporate the outcome of each phase of the ATLM.

Given that much of the documentation developed throughout the various ATLM phases needs to find its way into the test plan, it is beneficial to briefly review this documentation and understand its relationship to the test plan. This mapping is summarized in Figure 6.1.

At the beginning of the test plan, an Introduction section typically defines the purpose of the test plan, the background of the project, a system description, and a project organization chart. Early in the test plan, all relevant documentation available related to the test effort is listed, such as the business requirements, design specifications, user manual, operations manual, GUI standards, code standards, system certification requirements, and other project information. The test team should review the various project plans to ascertain information needed to complete the background, documentation, system description, and project organization sections. Such project plans might include the software development plan, system evolution plan, migration plans, systems engineering management plan, and project management plan.

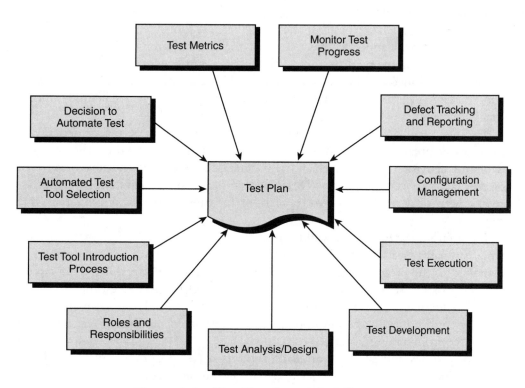

Figure 6.1   Test Plan Source and Content

An early planning exercise involves the inquiry into whether automated testing will be beneficial for the particular project given its testing requirements, available test environment and personnel resources, the user environment, platform, and product features of the target application. The test engineer follows the guidance outlined in Chapter 2 pertaining to deciding whether to automate the testing. An outcome of this planning exercise is the documentation of the reasons for applying automated test tools, which should be captured within the test plan.

Another early planning exercise pertains to the effort of evaluating and selecting automated test tools to support test efforts (see Chapter 3). An outcome of this exercise includes the documentation of the reasons for selecting one or more automated test tools. A "tools" section should be included in the test plan, listing the applicable tools, their functionality, their purpose on the project, and the reason for their selection.

Test planning also includes the performance of a test process analysis exercise, as described in Chapter 4. Test process analysis documentation is generated as a result of the test team's process review plus the analysis of test goals and objectives. An outcome of this analysis includes the refinement of test goals, objectives, and strategies of the test program.

The test team then verifies that the particular test tools will actually work in the project environment and effectively support the test requirements for a particular test effort before implementing them. The test team utilizes the test tool introduction process outlined in Chapter 4 to support this verification. A test tool consideration exercise is performed to review test requirements and test schedule, among other activities.

The test plan must identify the scope of test activities to be performed. Typically, a work breakdown structure (WBS) is developed that identifies the categories of test activities at one level and the detailed activities at the next level (see Chapter 5 for an example). The WBS is commonly used in conjunction with time-keeping activities (see Chapter 9) to account for time spent performing each test activity.

In addition, the test plan should reflect the results of test effort sizing exercises. Sizing estimates (see Chapter 5) may specify the number of test team personnel to be applied to the project in terms of total hours or in terms of people, given a constant level of effort for some specified timeframe. Other sizing estimates, which should be documented in the test plan, when available, include the estimated number of test procedures to be developed and the estimated number of test scripts to be adopted from a reuse library.

The qualities and skills required to support a test program should be documented. The test engineer qualities and skills commonly required are described in Chapter 5. The composition of the test team, which should match the required qualities and skills, can be indicated in a test team profile. A sample profile is depicted in Table 5.10 on page 175.

Individuals assigned to the test team may not have all necessary skills and experience, however. The test manager therefore needs to assess the difference between skill requirements and team members' actual skills to identify potential areas for training. The test planning effort, in turn, should document training requirements. Planned training should be reflected in the test schedule so that the timeframes for concurrent test activities can be adjusted.

The roles and responsibilities of test team personnel (see Chapter 5) need to be defined and documented in the test plan as well. These roles and responsibilities should be tailored for the particular project.

The test planning phase—the focus of this chapter—concentrates on the definition and documentation of test requirements, the identification of test program documentation, the planning required to support the test environment, and the development of the test plan document. Related to the documentation of test requirements is the need to define the requirements storage mechanism used to manage the test requirements.

As discussed in this chapter, every test program should have a defined scope, reflecting the fact that the test effort has limitations in terms of personnel, person-hours, and schedule. A system description or overview should define the components of the system being tested. Test program assumptions, prerequisites, and risks need to be defined and documented within the test plan. This definition includes any events, actions, or circumstances that might prevent the test program from meeting the schedule, such as the late arrival of test equipment or delays in the availability of the software application.

Associated with the system description is the need to identify critical success functions and the highest-risk functions of the system. Not everything can be tested and not everything can be automated. As noted in this chapter, identification of the highest-risk functionality ensures that the test team will focus its efforts on the critical success functions as a first priority.

A requirements traceability matrix allows the test team to keep track of test procedure coverage of requirements. This matrix is generally provided as part of the test plan and can be included as an appendix or separate section. As described later in this chapter, each system requirement is assigned a verification method. Verification methods include demonstration, analysis, inspection, and testing and certification.

The test plan will also need to identify hardware, software, and network requirements to support a test environment that mirrors the AUT environment, as described in this chapter. The procurement, installation, and setup activities for various test environment components must be carefully planned and scheduled. When unusual test environment requirements exist, the test team may need to increase the total test program sizing estimate, which is measured in terms of total person-hours. Test environment plans should identify the number and types of individuals who will need to use the test environment and verify that a sufficient number of computers is available to accommodate these individuals.

The overall test design approach is another component of the test plan. Methods for modeling the design of the (dynamic) test program are detailed in Chapter 7. A graphical representation of the test design identifies the test techniques that will be employed on the test effort, including white-box and black-box test techniques.

In addition, the test plan needs to document the various test procedures required, as outlined in Chapter 7. Documentation of the test procedure definition involves the identification of the suite of test procedures that must be developed and executed as part of the test effort. The design exercise involves the organization of test procedures into logical groups and the definition of a naming convention for the suite of test procedures.

Test planning will identify test data requirements and identify the means to obtain, generate, or develop test data. As explained in Chapter 7, the test plan should identify the mechanism for managing the integrity of the testbed, such as refreshing the test database to an original baseline state, so as to support regression testing. The test plan should indicate the names and locations of the applicable test databases necessary to exercise software applications.

The test development architecture is documented within the test plan. As noted in Chapter 8, it provides the test team with a clear picture of the test development preparation activities (building blocks) necessary to create test procedures. A graphical illustration depicts the test development architecture by showing the major activities to be performed as part of test development.

The test procedure development/execution schedule is prepared by the test team as a means to identify the timeframe for developing and executing the various tests. As noted in Chapter 8, this schedule takes into account any dependencies between tests and includes test setup activities, test procedure sequences, and cleanup activities.

The test plan incorporates the results of modularity relationship analysis. A modularity relationship matrix is presented (see Chapter 8) that specifies the interrelationship of the various test scripts. This graphical representation allows test engineers to quickly identify opportunities for script reuse in various combinations using the wrapper format, thereby minimizing the effort required to build and maintain test scripts.

Another element of test planning involves the identification of procedures for baselining test scripts. A configuration management tool should be specified for the project. The test plan needs to address the means for controlling the test configuration and environment, as discussed in Chapter 8. As test procedures are being developed, the test team needs to ensure that configuration control is performed for test design, test scripts, and test data, as well as for each individual test procedure.

Next, the test team needs to identify the test procedure development guidelines that will apply to the various test development activities. Test procedure development guidelines should be available for both manual test procedures and automated test procedures, as outlined in Table 8.5 on page 309.

The test plan needs to address the test execution activities, including the development of a test schedule and the transition from one testing phase to another. Execution and management topics are discussed in Chapter 9, where we provide a set of best practices pertaining to the development and execution of automated test procedures.

Chapter 9 also discusses the identification of a defect tracking tool as part of test planning. Likewise, defect tracking procedures and defect workflow should be defined and documented, and the test engineers need to be trained regarding these procedures.

The test plan should also define and document the test metrics that will be collected throughout the testing life cycle. Test metrics (see Chapter 9) provide the test manager with key indicators of the test coverage, progress, and quality.

During the early test planning stages, a preliminary test schedule should be created that complements the development schedule. Once test activities have been analyzed and plans documented in more detail within the test plan, the test schedule must be refined and augmented. The test team will need to review any updates to the project development schedule to ensure that the test schedule is consistent.

The development of a test plan is not a simple task, but rather takes a considerable amount of effort. The test team should begin its development by locating a test plan template and then customizing the outline as necessary. (A sample test plan outline is provided in Appendix D.) Once a test plan has been constructed and refined to fully document the test program approach, it will become the guiding instrument for ensuring the success of the test program.

6.2 | Test Program Scope

This section outlines the primary activities necessary to define the scope of the test program. The scope of the test program is formulated through the definition of test goals, objectives, and strategies and the definition of test requirements. These definitions can be developed once the test team has a clear understanding of the system, has identified which automated tools will support the test program, and has documented several test program parameters.

A preliminary step in the process of defining the test program scope, as noted in Table 6.2, involves a test team review of system requirements or use cases and, when

Table 6.2   Test Program Scope Definition

Step	Description
1	Review system requirements or use cases/design documentation (business/functional requirements or design specifications)
2	Review existing project plans and develop a system description definition for the test plan
3	Develop a system-critical function/high risk function definition
4	Develop test goals, objectives, and strategies
5	Identify automated tools to be applied in support of the test program
6	Outline test program parameters, including the scope, assumptions, prerequisites, system acceptance criteria, and risks
7	Identify verification methods associated with the system requirements or use cases
8	Test requirements definition

available, design documentation. Next, the test engineer reviews the system's mission description and identifies critical and high-risk system functions. He must have a clear definition of the system and an understanding of system requirements or use cases to be able to define test goals, objectives, and strategies.

Automated tools to be applied to the project then need to be identified. Next in the process is the documentation of test program parameters, including any assumptions made when defining test goals, objectives, and strategies. This phase also includes the listing of prerequisite events, documentation, and products required to support various test program activities. System acceptance criteria are defined, and test program risks are assessed and mitigation plans developed. Finally, test requirements are defined. The outcomes of these various activities are all documented within the test plan.

6.2.1   System Description

To define a test program, the test engineer needs to have a clear understanding of the system being tested. A system description or overview needs to be obtained or developed and eventually documented within the test plan. This description may be derived from a system mission description or from the introductory material provided within the system requirements or use cases or a design document. The system description should define the user environment, computing platforms, and product features of the application-under-test.

In addition to describing the system, it is important to bound the system with regard to the test effort. Within a client-server or Web environment, the system under test spans more than just a software application. It may perform across multiple platforms, involve multiple layers of supporting applications, interact with a host of commercial off-the-shelf (COTS) products, utilize one or more different types of databases, and necessitate both front-end and back-end processing. It is important to identify the specific elements of the system that will be tested, including both software hardware and network components. The test engineer should also determine which software components will be supported by COTS products and which will be supported by newly developed software. It may also be necessary to specify whether the software is developed in-house or outsourced to a different organization.

6.2.2   Critical/High-Risk Functions

The test team needs to identify the critical success and high-risk functions of the system, listing them in the test plan in order of severity. These functions include those most critical to the mission of the system and those functions that could help mitigate the greatest risk to successful system operation. The test team then needs to solicit end-user feedback to validate and refine the priority ranking. Ranking system functions helps the test team prioritize test activities and address the most critical and high-risk system functions early.

6.2.3   Test Goals, Objectives, and Strategies

Once the boundary for the system under test has been established and the critical and high-risk functions of the system have been identified, the test team is ready to define the scope of the test program. It needs to perform a test process review and an analysis of test goals and objectives, as outlined within the test process analysis exercise discussed in Chapter 4. Test process analysis documentation is then generated that reflects the refinement of test goals, objectives, and strategies.

6.2.4   Test Tools

The test team should clearly specify which test tools will be applied on the project. When the team is still contemplating the use of an automated test tool, it should follow the process outlined in Chapter 2 to determine whether to automate the testing process. An outcome of this planning exercise is the documentation of the reasons for applying automated test tools. The evaluation and selection of automated test tools for the particular project were discussed in Chapter 3. A Tools section should be included within the test plan, listing the applicable tools, their functionality, their purpose on the project, and the reason for their selection. The test team should undertake the test tool consideration exercise outlined within Chapter 4 to verify that the particular test tools actually work in the project environment. The results of the test tool compatibility checks are documented in the test plan.

6.2.5 Test Program Parameters

Test program parameters defined may include the scope, assumptions, prerequisites, system acceptance criteria, and risks, depending on the testing phase. The test program scope noted in the test plan should provide a top-level description of the anticipated test coverage. It should identify the system application to be tested and indicate whether the test effort will include the network, hardware, and databases in addition to the software application.

The scope must state whether tests will address nondevelopmental items, such as integrated COTS products. When the system is being developed in accordance with a life-cycle methodology, such as the incremental build model, the team should specify whether system-level testing will involve regression test of existing software modules from an earlier implementation. The incremental build model, by definition, involves the performance of development activities in a series of builds, each incorporating more capabilities, until the system is complete.

The unit test plan should indicate whether stubs and drivers are to be used in unit testing. In particular, the unit testing schedule should account for whether these stubs must be developed to allow for unit testing.

The acceptance testing strategies need to be identified as well. When individual site acceptance tests are planned, the team should note whether these tests will involve a complete set of acceptance test procedures or some subset.

In its development of test goals, objectives, and strategies, the test team will undoubtedly make certain assumptions, which need to be documented in the test plan. Listing these assumptions has the benefit of flagging the need for potential test program redirection when any of these assumptions are not realized during the course of project execution.

It is also beneficial to clearly define dependencies between various test program activities as well as between test activities and other activities being performed on the project. Situations where the performance of a test activity depends on a prerequisite action or activity being performed on the project should be clearly noted in the test plan. For example, performance testing cannot be performed accurately unless the production configuration is in place. Prerequisites may include actions, activities, events, documentation, and products. Documenting these prerequisites may protect the test team from unwarranted blame for schedule slips and other project anomalies. Explicitly identifying event or activity dependencies also aids in the formulation of the test program schedule.

In addition to listing assumptions and prerequisite activities, the test team needs to define a test program boundary. This boundary represents the limit of the test program effort and the team's responsibility. The test team should define the point when testing will be considered complete. The test team achieves this definition through the development of clear system acceptance criteria. The definition of such criteria will help to prevent various project team personnel from having different expectations for the test program. For example, the acceptance criteria might include a statement saying that all defined test procedures must be executed successfully without any significant problems. Other criteria may state that all fatal, high-priority, and medium-priority defects must have been fixed by development team and verified by a member of the test team. The test plan may also list an assumption stating that the software will probably be shipped with the existence of known low-priority defects and certainly with some unknown defects.

Developers need to be made aware of the system acceptance criteria. The test team should therefore communicate the list of acceptance criteria to the development staff prior to submitting the test plan for approval. System acceptance criteria for the organization should be standardized, where possible, based upon proven criteria used in several projects.

Because the budget and number of test engineers allocated to the test program are limited, the scope of the test effort must have limits as well. When acceptance criteria are stated in ambiguous or poorly defined terms, then the test team will not be able to determine the point at which the test effort is complete. The test team also needs to highlight any special considerations that must be addressed, such as the test of special technologies being implemented on the project or special attention that should be paid to mission-critical functions.

Test program risks should also be identified within the test plan, assessed for their potential impact, and then mitigated with a strategy for overcoming the risks should they be realized. A test program risk might involve an element of uncertainty on the project. For example, a software application development effort might involve a significant amount of COTS software integration, and the amount and depth of COTS software component testing may still be under negotiation. Meanwhile, budgets and schedules are in place based upon certain assumptions. The final resolution to the COTS testing issue may involve the performance of test activities well beyond those planned and budgeted. The potential impact of this test program risk therefore includes a cost overrun of the test program budget or an extension of the test schedule, possibly resulting in the project missing its targeted completion date.

Given this risk and the potential impacts, the test team would need to develop and define a risk mitigation strategy that can either minimize or alleviate the impact of the risk should it be realized. One possible strategy might involve a contingent agreement with one or more COTS vendors to support the test effort on a limited basis in the event that large-scale COTS testing is required. This approach may be especially helpful in instances where one or two large vendors have a significant stake in the successful outcome of the product integration effort and accompanying tests. Such a risk mitigation strategy may have the effect of reducing cost expenditures as well as minimizing the schedule extension.

6.2.6   Verification Methods

The test team should construct a requirements traceability matrix so as to keep track of system requirements or use cases and test procedure coverage of requirements. The traceability matrix explicitly identifies every requirement that will undergo examination by the test team, ensuring that all requirements have been successfully implemented.

The term "examination" in this context means that the test team will perform a verification (or qualification) of the system implementation. The ways that this examination can be performed are known as verification methods. Verification methods include demonstration, analysis, inspection, test (automated or manual), and certification, as outlined in Table 6.3 [1].

Demonstration, for example, would be used to test the following statement: "Allow on-line queries to all enrollment records by case number." The test input would consist of a query to the database using a case number. The test engineer would then observe the results displayed on the workstation. This method is appropriate for demonstrating the successful integration, high-level functionality, and connectivity provided by nondevelopmental (NDI), COTS, and government off-the-shelf (GOTS) products.

Analysis and inspection often do not require code execution of the application-under-test. Nevertheless, analysis can sometimes be used to verify that inputs produce the required outputs. For example, the test engineer would compare the input data to a process with the report generated by the system as a result of processing that input data. The test engineer would verify that the output corresponded with the input data. Inspection is used to examine graphical user interface (GUI) screens for compliance with development standards or to examine code for logic errors and compliance with standards. The test method is used when code must be modified or generated to simulate an unavailable input or output. The certification method is employed if the application-under-test needs to meet specific certification requirements. Consider the example of a financial system that requires certification by the Federal Reserve Bank. Such a system needs to meet specific requirements and pass specific tests before it can be moved into a production environment.

Table 6.3   Verification/Qualification Methods

Verification Method	Description
Demonstration	Verification by observation of expected external behavior during system operation. Demonstration verifies conformance to requirements by exercising a sample of observable functional operations.
Analysis	Analysis verifies conformance to requirements by technical evaluation, processing, review, or study of accumulated data. It can include a review of test outputs versus test inputs, technical evaluation, mathematical evaluation, and simulation.
Inspection	Inspection verifies conformance to requirements by visual examination, reviewing descriptive documentation, and comparing characteristics with predetermined criteria.
Manual Test	Special modifications to the code under test to capture information not normally retained in the course of operations. Manual testing verifies conformance to requirements by exercising observable functional operations in a manual fashion. Testing is generally more extensive than the exercises performed using the demonstration method and is appropriate for requirements fulfilled by developmental items.
Automated Test	Automated testing verifies conformance to requirements by exercising observable functional operations in an automated fashion.
Certification	Certification verifies conformance to requirements by examination of vendor (or supplier) documentation attesting that the product was developed and tested in accordance with the vendor's internal standards.

6.2.7 Test Requirements Definition

Recall that in previous chapters, the importance of testable system requirements or use cases was emphasized. Now these systems requirements need to be analyzed and specified in terms of test requirements. (Test requirements analysis and test design are described in detail in Chapter 7.) The test requirements analysis discussion addresses what to look for when identifying test requirements for the target application, how to decompose the application design or system requirements or use cases into testable test requirements, and how to analyze application documentation so as to identify test requirements. Test requirements provide a detailed outline of what is to be tested.

The development of test requirements, as noted in Table 6.2, requires the test team to complete several preliminary steps, including gaining an understanding of customer needs. These steps also include a test team review of system requirements or use case requirements and/or the system mission description to better comprehend the purpose and direction of the system. Another step includes the identification of critical and high-risk system functions. Test requirements analysis is performed to develop test goals, objectives, and strategies. The particular test tools being applied to the project are identified. Several test program parameters are then defined, such as assumptions, prerequisites, system acceptance criteria, and risks. Finally, test requirements need to be defined.

Test requirements can be derived from business requirements, functional system requirements, and use case requirements. This strategy for developing test requirements is referred to as a *requirements-based* or *behavioral* approach. Test requirements can also be derived based on the logic of the system design, which is referred to as a *structural* approach. The approach taken may depend on the timeframe within the development life cycle in which test requirements are defined. It can also vary according to the contractual and safety critical requirements. For example, decision coverage is often required in avionics and other safety-critical software. Various test requirements definition approaches are further outlined in Chapter 7.

When developing test requirements from system requirements or use cases, the test team can expect to develop at least one test requirement for each system requirement. The ratio of system requirements to system-level test requirements varies and can be either one-to-one or one-to-many, depending on the risk assigned to each functionality and the granularity of the requirement. The ratio of use case requirements to system-level test requirements also varies, depending on the risk and use case scenarios to be tested. System requirements or use cases that have been decomposed to a software specification or design level are often tested at the unit and integration test levels. The test team should be cognizant of the fact that a customer for an application development effort may wish to have some lower-level (derived or decomposed) software requirements addressed during system test and user acceptance test.

The mechanism for obtaining concurrence with a particular customer on the scope and depth of test requirements is the test plan. The customer reviews and eventually approves the test plan, which outlines test requirements and contains a requirements traceability matrix. The requirements traceability matrix specifies requirements information, as well as mappings between requirements and other project products. For example, the requirements traceability matrix usually identifies the test procedures that pertain to the project and maps test procedures to test requirements; and it also maps test requirements to system requirements or use cases. A requirements management tool such as DOORS allows for automatic mapping of these matrices (see Section 6.3 for more detail).

The traceability matrix explicitly identifies every requirement that will undergo examination by the test team, thereby ensuring that all requirements will be successfully implemented before the project goes forward. The term "examination" in this context means that the test team will perform a verification (or qualification) of the system implementation. Verification methods are summarized in Table 6.3.

The customer signifies his or her approval for the scope of requirements, which will be examined by the test team, by approving the test plan. To obtain early feedback on the scope of test coverage of requirements, the test team might submit a draft copy of the traceability matrix to the customer. (The traceability matrix may also be referred to as a test compliance matrix, verification cross–reference matrix, or requirements traceability matrix.) Early feedback on the traceability matrix from the customer gives the test team more time to respond to requests for changes in the test plan.

Another important benefit of early feedback on the traceability matrix is the mutual agreement reached on the verification method to be employed to support verification or qualification of each requirement. Some verification methods are easier to implement and less time-intensive than other methods. For example, the test for the various COTS products implemented for a system usually involves far more of an effort than simply qualifying the COTS products via the certification verification method.

6.3 | Test Requirements Management

Test planning involves both the definition of test requirements and the development of an approach for managing test requirements. Test requirements management includes the storage of requirements, maintenance of traceability links, test requirements risk assessment, test requirements sequencing (prioritization), and identification of test verification methods. Traceability links include the mapping of test procedures to test requirements and of defects to test procedures.

In the test plan, the test team needs to outline the way in which the test requirements will be managed. Will test requirements be kept in a word-processing document, spreadsheet, or requirements management tool? Key considerations with regard to the storage of test requirements include the ease and flexibility of requirement sorting and reporting, the ease and speed of requirement entry, and the efficiency of requirements maintenance. Another consideration is whether a large number of project personnel will be able to access the requirements information simultaneously. Also important is the ability of the storage mechanism to accommodate various test requirements management data needs and to maintain the integrity and security of the requirements information.

Many organizations use word-processing documents and spreadsheets to maintain requirements information. There are many disadvantages of maintaining requirements in a word-processing document. For example, limitations exist regarding the ways that requirements can be sorted and filtered. Likewise, it is not easy to maintain a history of changes that indicates what changes were made, when, and by whom. Often people get so frustrated with the burden of maintaining requirements within these kinds of tools that the activity of maintaining requirements information is abandoned.

Commercial requirements management tools are available to handle these requirements management concerns. These tools are especially beneficial in maintaining traceability links. Traceability between system requirements or use cases and various project products can become complicated very quickly. Not only is this mapping difficult to maintain when done manually, but changes to requirements and the various project products also make the mapping highly tedious and even more difficult to maintain.

6.3.1 Requirements Management Tools

Special automated tools are particularly useful when applied to tedious or otherwise time-consuming tasks. The task of test requirements management fits this description. The test team needs to verify whether the organization has established a standard tool to support requirements management. Next, it needs to determine whether the tool is being applied to the current project or whether it can be installed in the system's engineering environment to specifically support test requirements management for the project. When no standard tool has been established or planned for the project, the test team may need to present this absence as an issue to management or take the lead in evaluating and selecting a tool. Noteworthy tools on the market include Requisite Pro by Rational, DOORS by QSS, and RTM by Integrated Chipware.

Many advantages can be realized by using a requirements management (RM) tool. For example, all requirements pertinent to the project can be maintained within the tool's database. The RM tool uses a central database repository to hold all related data. Requirements can include contractual, system, and test requirements. Adding test requirements to the RM tool database allows for easy management of testing coverage and mapping test requirements to business requirements or functional requirements.

As most RM tools support multiuser access, test team personnel need not worry that they are modifying a test requirement or procedure that is currently being modified elsewhere. These tools also offer a great benefit for test management. The test manager or lead can simply assign test procedures to the various test engineers, and then monitor test procedure development progress using the RM tool. With the DOORS tool, for example, simple filters can be set up to view the inputs provided by the various test engineers working on the project. Most RM tools also automatically maintain a history of any requirements changes (that is, the what, when, and how of the change).

Test teams can also benefit from the RM tool's automatic capability for linking test requirements to test procedures, or linking defects to test procedures. Most RM tools provide an automated mapping of the test requirements to business requirements as well, based on the use of database object identification numbers. For example, DOORS uses the dxl language (a proprietary DOORS language); running a simple .dxl script allows for automatic linking of each test requirement to the applicable business requirement or detailed design component. With this linkage, the test team can obtain reports from the RM tool outlining the status of test requirement coverage. Additionally, test engineers can verify that a test requirement has been written for each business requirement with the execution of a simple script. Once the test team has completed the test procedures, a modified .dxl script can be run that automatically maps or links each test procedure to all of its respective test requirements, thus creating a requirements traceability matrix. More information on the requirements traceability matrix is provided in Section 6.3.4.

When test procedure information is stored within the RM tool, the test engineer needs to update the status of only the test procedure, which includes test pass/fail information and indicates whether the procedure has been executed yet. In DOORS, a simple filter on the status of test procedure execution permits the generation of an overall test execution status report, thereby providing percentage completion status for the project.

The fact that the requirements information can be continuously updated with relative ease is another benefit of using a RM tool. Columns can be moved around as necessary, and new columns can be added, while maintaining the integrity of the data. When requirements change, the test engineer can easily and quickly identify any test procedures that are affected (linked to the requirements) by the change. The test manager or lead can also readily identify the test engineers who are responsible for the affected test procedures.

Most seasoned test professionals have likely worked on a project where requirement changes occurred in midstream, but where each requirements change was not translated into a modified test requirement or test procedure. In other situations, requirements may be deleted or moved to the next delivery of an incremental build program without changes being made to an existing requirements traceability matrix. A RM tool can quickly make the changes to the requirements field that keeps track of the release version. The tool can then reproduce an updated requirements traceability matrix by running a simple script using defined parameters.

The first step is to add all test procedures into the RM tool (keep all test procedures in one place). Don't go through the trouble of keeping the manual test procedures in one place and the automated test procedures in another place. If all test procedures are in one place and the test team decides to automate 50% of them, most RM tools will allow the test procedures to be exported into a .csv file, which can then be imported into any test management tool that can handle .csv or .txt files.

6.3.2   Assessing the Test Requirements Risk

Once the test requirements have been identified, the test team should assess the risks inherent in the various test requirements, by evaluating the requirements in terms of the following factors:

- Impact. Assess the value of the requirement. Suppose that the particular test requirement was not incorporated in the scope of the test effort and that the applicable performance area of the system eventually failed following system deployment. What impact would this failure have on system operations and on end users' ability to perform their jobs? Does the failure represent a potential liability for the company?

- Probability. Assess the likelihood of a failure occurring if the particular test requirement is not incorporated into the scope of the test effort. Analyze the frequency with which the applicable performance area of the system would be exercised by the end user. Gauge the experience of the user within the particular performance area.

- Complexity. Determine which functionality is most complex and then focus test team resources on that functionality.

- Source of failure. Assess the failure possibilities and identify the test requirements that are most likely to cause these failures.

6.3.3   Prioritization of Tests

The test team needs to prioritize test requirements, while assessing the risk inherent in each test requirement. It should also review the critical functions and high-risk factors identified for the system, and use this information as input for determining the order in which to group the test requirements. The best idea is to group test requirements into those with the most critical functionality and those with the least critical functionality. Remember to include input from end users when determining which functionality is most critical and which is least critical. Another benefit of structuring and organizing the test requirements in this way is that it will make it easier to assign the test tasks to the various test engineers.

The criteria outlined here for determining the order in which to group test requirements represents the recommendation of Rational Corporation, as outlined within its test methodology literature [2].

- Risk level. Based upon the risk assessment, test requirements are organized so as to mitigate a high risk to system performance or the potential exposure of the company to liability. Examples of high risks include functions that prohibit data entry and business rules that could corrupt data or violate regulations.

- Operational characteristics. Some test requirements will rank high on the priority list due to the frequency of usage or the lack of end-user knowledge in the area. Functions pertaining to technical resources and internal users, and infrequently used functions, are ranked lower in priority.

- User requirements. Some test requirements are vital to user acceptance. If the test approach does not emphasize these requirements, the test program may possibly violate contractual obligations or expose the company to financial loss. It is important that the impact to the end user of the potential problem be assessed.

- Available resources. As usual, the test program will have constraints in the areas of staff availability, hardware availability, and conflicting project requirements. Here is where the painful process of weighing trade-offs is managed. A factor in the prioritization of test requirements is the availability of resources.

- Exposure. Exposure is defined as the risk (probability) multiplied by the cost of failure. For example, a highly probable defect with a high cost of failure has a high exposure.

6.3.4 Requirements Traceability Matrix

System requirements or use cases are usually maintained within an RM tool. Once identified during test planning or design, test procedures are documented within the RM tool and linked to the corresponding system requirements or use cases. Later, when tests are observed, their results are recorded and linked to corresponding test procedures.

The requirements traceability matrix represents an automated output of the RM tool, helping to track system requirements or use cases and test procedure coverage of requirements. It may take any of several forms based upon the particular mapping of interest. The requirements traceability matrix identifies every requirement that

Table 6.4   Requirements Traceability Matrix*

Para ID	Text	Key	Verification Method	PRI	D1	D2	D3	Test Procedure
3.2.1a	System shall perform software installation and upgrades	178	Test	NN	D1	—	—	SM2012
3.2.1b	System shall perform software system load balancing for WFTS system servers	179	Test	NN	—	D2	—	SM2013
3.2.1c	System shall perform a recovery of the system and data in the event of a system failure	180	Test	HR	—	D2	—	SM2014
3.2.1d	System shall manage disk and file structure and allocation to include the ability to determine the amount of disk space used and available	181	Test	NN	—	D2	—	SM2015
3.2.1e	System shall be able to configure electronic mail and manage directory service capabilities	182	Test	NN	D1	—	—	SM2016
3.2.1f	System shall monitor the software configuration of critical system components and workstations to include checks for outdated versions	183	Test	NN	—	D2	—	SM2017
3.2.5a	System shall meet certification criteria as specified by Federal Reserve Bank	190	Certification	NN	—	—	D3	CT001–CT100
.	.	.	.	.	.	.	.	.
.	.	.	.	.	.	.	.	.
.	.	.	.	.	.	.	.	.

*Refer to Appendix D.B for a description of this matrix and the terminology used.

will undergo examination by the test team and specifies a verification method for each system requirement. Most importantly, the matrix maps test procedures to system requirements or use cases, which helps to ensure that system requirements or use cases requiring test verification have been successfully implemented.

It is important that the test team obtain early feedback on the requirements traceability matrix from end users or system customers, as a means to reach agreement on the verification method to be employed to support verification or qualification of each requirement. This decision is especially significant because some verification methods are easier to implement and less time-intensive than other methods. Early feedback on the matrix from the customer helps provide more time for the test team to respond to potential changes.

As the requirements traceability matrix identifies the test procedures that will be performed, approval of this matrix by the customer also signifies customer satisfaction with the scope of test coverage for system requirements or use cases. When user acceptance test (UAT) is performed later, the customer will review the requirements traceability matrix to verify test coverage of system requirements or use cases. Table 6.4 provides a sample requirements traceability matrix.

The requirements traceability matrix in Table 6.4 includes a system requirements specification paragraph identifier, requirement statement text, unique requirement identifier generated by the RM tool, qualification method, risk/priority classification of the requirement, and test procedure associated with the requirement. It also identifies the system delivery (D1, D2, or D3) in which the solution to the requirement has been implemented.

6.4 | Test Program Events, Activities, and Documentation

Key elements of test planning include the planning associated with project milestone events, test program activities, and test-program-related documentation. The technical approach for these key elements is developed, personnel are assigned, and performance timelines are defined in the test program schedule.

6.4.1 Events

The major events for the test team should be reflected in the test schedule. These events include requirements and design reviews, test readiness reviews, system configuration audits, technical interchange meetings, and formal test-related working group meetings. Other limited-timeframe activities may include the conduct of special tests, such as security testing, and the performance of acceptance tests.

To bolster the life-cycle performance of the test program, a test and integration work group (TIWG) may be defined. TIWG provides a forum to facilitate iterative interchange between test engineers, development staff, and customer representatives. TIWGs are held on a periodic basis, and TIWG meetings should be incorporated in the test schedule. The goals of the TIWG include the following:

- Ensure that planned testing activities support the verification of functional, performance, and technical requirements for the system.

- Ensure that testing addresses human engineering aspects of system operability.

- Identify and monitor major test program risks to ensure that test prerequisite activities are performed correctly and are proceeding according to the project schedule.

- Obtain early and informal customer feedback on draft test plans and traceabilty matrices so as to finalize the scope and depth of the test effort and to expedite approval of test documentation.

- Enhance the customer's familiarity with and understanding of the detailed aspects of the test program so as to bring about a more efficient acceptance test effort.

Test readiness reviews (TRR) may be conducted as part of a project to ensure that the test program is ready to support a UAT. On large development projects, a TRR may involve comprehensive reviews that examine requirements specification and design document changes, unit- and integration-level test status, test environment readiness, and test procedure development. Test environment readiness may need to address the availability status of test data requirements, as well as the availability status of hardware and software required to support the test system configuration.

6.4.2   Activities

The test plan must identify the scope of test activities to be performed. Typically, a work breakdown structure (WBS) is developed to identify the categories of test activities that may be carried out (see Chapter 5).

One important activity that needs to be defined is the review of project documentation. Although documentation review by the test team is an effective defect removal strategy, the test team needs to be careful about leaving the scope of this activity open-ended. As noted previously, test resources are limited but expectations of test team support may be greater than the budget allows. It is important to clearly define which project documents will be reviewed. The test team should list the title of each project document to be reviewed within the test plan.

6.4.3   Documentation

In addition to reviewing project-generated documents, the test team will produce test documentation. It should develop a list containing the title of each test document type, indicate whether the document will be delivered outside the organization (deliverable), and list the scheduled due date or timeframe in which the document will be created. When the document is produced on a monthly (periodic) basis, the due date column can simply read *monthly*. Table 6.5 contains a sample listing of test documentation.

Table 6.5   Test Documentation

Test Program Document	Description	Due Date/ Timeframe
Test Plan	Test planning document	(date)
Requirements Traceability Matrix	A matrix that maps test procedure coverage of requirements and specifies a test qualification method for each system requirement	(date)
Test Procedures/ Cases	Scripts to be used to perform/execute testing	(timeframe)
Test and Integration Work Group Meeting Minutes	Meeting minutes from TIWG meetings	Periodic
Test Development Progress Reports	Reports that outline the progress status of the test procedure development effort	Biweekly
Test Readiness Report or Presentation Slides	Report or presentation that outlines the readiness of the test program to conduct user acceptance test	(date)
Test Execution Progress Reports	Reports that outline the progress status of test execution	Biweekly
Defect Tracking Reports	Reports that outline the number and severity of outstanding defects (trouble reports)	Biweekly
TPM Status Reports	Reports that outline the progress of the system toward meeting defined technical performance measures	Biweekly
Test Report	Report documenting the outcome of the test	(date)

6.5 | The Test Environment

Test planning must outline the resources and activities that are required to support the timely setup of the test environment. The test team should identify the hardware, software, and network and facility requirements needed to create and sustain the support of the test environment. The procurement, installation, and setup activities for various test environment components need to be planned and scheduled. Such test environment plans should identify the number and types of individuals who will access and use the test environment and ensure that a sufficient number of computers is planned to accommodate these individuals. Consideration should be given to the number and kinds of environment setup scripts and testbed scripts that will be required.

6.5.1   Test Environment Preparations

Early in the test planning exercise, the test team must review project plans so as to become familiar with the systems engineering (development) environment planned for the project. Project plans, which should be reviewed when available, include the software development plan, system evolution plan, migration plans, systems engineering management plan, and project management plan. While such plans are still under development, the test team should review the draft plans and identify questions and potential concerns related to the development environment or the migration of the development environment to an operational (production) environment.

The test team needs to review project planning documents specifically with regard to the plans for a separate test lab that mimics an operational environment. While unit- and integration-level (developmental) tests are usually performed within the development environment, system and user acceptance tests are ideally performed within a separate test lab setting; this lab should represent an identical configuration of the production environment or, at the minimum, a scaled-down version of the operational (production) environment. The test environment configuration needs to be representative of the production environment because it must replicate the baseline performance and relative improvement measures. Simulators and emulators can be used in situations where the production environment cannot be reproduced; such tools can prove vital in testing the environment and measure performance.

Next, the test team needs to document the results of its fact gathering. It then performs the following preparation activities, which support the development of a test environment design:

- Obtain information about the customer's technical environment architecture (when applicable), including a listing of computer hardware and operating systems. Hardware descriptions should include such items as video resolution, hard disk space, processing speed, and memory characteristics. Printer characteristics include type, capacity, and whether the printer operates as a stand-alone unit or is connected to a network server.

- Identify network characteristics of the customer's technical environment, such as use of leased lines, circuits, modems, Internet connections, and use of protocols such as Ethernet, or TCP/IP.

- Obtain a listing of COTS products to be integrated into the system solution.

- Count how many automated test tool licenses will be used by the test team.

- Identify development environment software that must reside on each computer desktop within the test environment.

- Identify hardware equipment required to support backup and recovery exercises within the test environment.

- Ensure that the test environment can accommodate all test team personnel.

- Review system performance test requirements to identify elements of the test environment that may be required to support applicable tests.

- Identify security requirements for the test environment.

After completing these preparation activities, the test team develops a test environment design consisting of a graphic layout of the test environment architecture plus a list of the components required to support the test environment architecture. The list of components should be reviewed to determine which components are already in place, which can be shifted from other locations within the organization, and which need to be procured. The list of components to be procured constitutes a test equipment purchase list. This list needs to include quantities required, unit price information, and maintenance and support costs. A sample test equipment purchase list is provided in Table 6.6.

Next, the test team needs to identify and track adherence to the timeline for equipment receipt, installation, and setup activities. Although these activities may be performed by a network support staff from another department within the organization or from another project, the test team will need to ensure that these activities are kept on track to meet test program requirements. Where possible, it is beneficial for the test team to have at least one individual who has network, database, and system administration and integration skills. Such skills are particularly valuable during test environment setup and during the performance of manual hardware-related tests on the project.

The test team will need to monitor the purchase and receipt of test environment components carefully to ensure that hardware and software procurement delays do not affect the test program schedule. It may want to include in the test equipment

Table 6.6   Test Equipment Purchase List

Site	Product Requirement	Product Description	Vendor	Quan- tity	Unit Cost	Annual Mainte- nance
Site 1	Application Server	Compaq ProLiant 6500	Compaq	1	(cost)	(cost)
Site 1	Communication Server	Compaq ProLiant 1600	Compaq	1	(cost)	(cost)
Site 1	Database Server	Sun Workstation	Sun	1	(cost)	(cost)
Site 1	Server Operating System	Windows NT	Microsoft	2	(cost)	(cost)
Site 1	Server Operating System	Sun Solaris	Sun	1	(cost)	(cost)
Site 1	Database Management System (DBMS)	Sybase Server	Sybase	1	(cost)	(cost)
Site 1	CORBA Server	Iona ORBIX	IONA	1	(cost)	(cost)

order a few backup components to mitigate the risk of testing coming to a halt due to a hardware failure. The test team might consider an alternative risk mitigation option as well—the identification of hardware within the organization that can be substituted within the test environment in the event of a hardware failure.

One requirement of the system might be that it should remain operational 24 hours per day and never shut down. The test team may need to become involved in finding software/hardware that meets these high availability requirements. All such special test environment considerations should be documented by the test team.

6.5.2   Test Environment Integration and Setup

At least one member of the test team should have some network, database, and system administration skills. This person can then assist in the installation and integration of hardware components on behalf of the test team. She would also be responsible for installing and configuring software, including automated test tools and any necessary development environment software. The test environment configuration would need to be created, and scripts would need to be developed and used to refresh the test environment configuration. Chapter 8 describes the use of environment setup scripts.

Besides hardware and software receipt, installation, and integration, administration activities must be carried out to enable test activities within the test environment. These activities ensure that the test team personnel will have access to the necessary systems, software, networks, databases, and tools.

Plans must be defined for obtaining or developing the data and file types, which must be loaded into the test environment for use in test procedure development and test execution. Test data creation and management are further discussed in Chapter 7.

6.6 | The Test Plan

The test plan should comprehensively document test program plans, and test team personnel must become very familiar with the content of this plan. The effort to build a test plan is an iterative process, requiring feedback and agreement between the various project participants on the defined approaches, test strategies, and timelines for performance.

When the development effort will support a particular customer, the test team needs to obtain end-user or customer buy-in on the test plan. This buy-in includes acceptance of the test strategy as well as the detailed test procedures, which define the actual tests planned. That is, the end user must concur that the test plan and associated test scripts will adequately verify satisfactory coverage of system requirements or use cases. What better way to ensure success of the test effort and obtain end-user acceptance of the application than to involve the end user throughout test planning and execution?

Many test strategies could potentially be implemented on the project, but there is never enough money in the test program budget to support all possible kinds of tests. A successful, cost-effective test program therefore requires a clear vision of the goals and an explicit understanding of the various test program parameters outlined in Section 6.2, which define the boundary of the test effort. A thorough understanding of the system and system requirements or use cases, coupled with careful definition of test program parameters and test requirements, is necessary to effectively tailor the test program solution to the particular project. Communication and analysis are key to selecting the right mix of test strategies to support the accomplishment of test goals and objectives.

The purpose of the test plan can be summarized as follows:

- It provides guidance for the management and technical effort necessary to support the test program.

- It establishes the nature and the extent of tests deemed necessary to achieve test goals and objectives.

- It outlines an orderly schedule of events and activities that use resources efficiently.

- It provides assurance of the highest level of test coverage possible through the creation of a requirements traceability matrix.

- It outlines the detailed contents of test procedure scripts and describes how the test procedure scripts will be executed.

- It outlines the personnel, financial, equipment, and facility resources required to support the test program.

Once the test team is satisfied that the test plan incorporates all pertinent details of the test program, an approval authority should review the plan. In some cases, a particular customer may need to approve the test plan before execution of the test program can begin. In other situations, the manager responsible for the project will review and approve the test plan. In any event, it is important that the development staff also reviews and endorses the test plan.

The test team may wish to organize and conduct a test plan walkthrough, which would involve the principal personnel responsible for test program execution and test plan approval. Prior to the walkthrough, the test team should solicit reviews of the test plan and ask for comments. The significant comments can then be addressed at the walkthrough and resolved in a single setting.

It is important to remember that test planning is not a single event, but rather a process. The test plan is a living document that guides test execution through to conclusion, and it must be updated to reflect any changes. The test team should refer to the test plan often during the performance of test on the project. Table 6.7 provides a sample outline for a test plan.

Table 6.7   Test Plan Outline

Test Plan Section	Title	Contents	Textbook Section
1.0	**Introduction**		
1.1	Purpose	Purpose of test plan	6.6
1.2	Background	Project background information	6.1
1.3	System Overview	System description, critical/high-risk functions	6.2, 4.2
1.4	Applicable Documents	Documentation pertinent to test program	6.1
1.5	Test Program Master Schedule	Events, activities, deliverable documents	6.4, 8.1

continued

continued from page 218

Test Plan Section	Title	Contents	Textbook Section
2.0	**Roles and Responsibilities**		
2.1	Project Organization	Project organization chart	6.1, 4.2, 5.1
2.2	Project Roles and Responsibilities	Roles and responsibilities	5.5
2.3	Test Task Structure	Test activities and work breakdown structure	5.2
2.4	Test Team Resources	Test team profile, training requirements	5.4, 4.2
3.0	**Test Program**		
3.1	Scope	Top-level description of test coverage	6.2
3.2	Test Approach	Goals, objectives, and process methodology; test program parameters	4.1, 6.2
3.3	Test Strategies	Test strategies	4.1
3.4	Automated Tools	Tool descriptions, decision to automate test, test tool selection, test tool compatibility check	2, 3, 4.2
3.5	Verification Methods	Verification methods	6.2
3.6	Test Requirements	Test requirements	6.2, 6.3, 7.1
3.7	Test Design	Test design, procedure naming convention	7.2, 7.3
3.8	Test Development	Development architecture	8.2
4.0	**Test Environment**		
4.1	Test Environment Configuration	Technical environment design, procurement, installation, setup, and administration	6.5
4.2	Test Data	Test data creation and management	7.3
5.0	**Test Execution**		
5.1	Test Program Reporting	Progress status reporting, metrics, sequence list	9.3
5.2	Defect Tracking	Defect tracking	9.2
5.3	Configuration Management	Configuration management	8.1
6.0	**Detailed Test Schedule**	**Detailed test schedule**	**8.1**
A	**Test Procedures**	**Acceptance test procedures**	**7.3**

6.6.1   Test Completion/Acceptance Criteria

Before the target application goes into production, test results analysis can help to identify any defects that need to be fixed and those whose correction can be deferred. For example, corrections of some defects may be reclassified as enhancements and addressed as part of a later software release. The project or software development manager who heads the engineering review board will likely determine whether to fix a defect or risk shipping a software product with the uncorrected defect. Several questions are commonly asked in this situation. What is the rate of regressions? How often are defect corrections failing? If the rate of regressions is high for a particular subsystem and that subsystem has light test coverage, then the risk impact of a defect correction is high.

With or without tools, there comes a day when testing must be halted and the product must be actually deployed. Perhaps the most difficult question in software testing is deciding when to stop. Humphrey notes that as the number of *detected* defects in a piece of software increases, the probability of the existence of more *undetected* defects also increases:

> The question is not whether all the defects have been found but whether the program is sufficiently good to stop testing. This trade-off should consider the probability of finding more defects in test, the marginal cost of doing so, the probability of the users encountering the remaining defects, and the resulting impact of these defects on the users. [3]

It is important that the test team establish quality guidelines (criteria) for the completion and release of software. It should answer several questions. What type of testing and improvements need to be implemented, and when will they be finished? What type of resources will be needed to perform testing? A simple acceptance criteria statement could indicate that the application-under-test will be accepted provided that no problem reports with an associated priority level of 1 (fatal), 2 (high), or 3 (medium) are outstanding. Acceptance criteria might state that the existence of level 4 or 5 (low) outstanding problem reports is acceptable.

6.6.2   Sample Test Plan

The sample test plan given in Appendix D indicates the test planning carried out for a fictitious company called Automation Services Incorporated (AMSI), which is testing a system called the WallStreet Financial Trading System (WFTS). The content of this sample test plan has been developed for the sole purpose of illustrating the kinds of information and the ways of presenting relevant information within a test plan. For reasons of illustration, the information contained within the sample test plan may not necessarily be consistent from one section to another.

Chapter Summary

- The test planning element of the Automated Test Life-Cycle Methodology (ATLM) incorporates the review of all activities required in the test program. It is intended to ensure that testing processes, methodologies, techniques, people, tools, schedule, and equipment are organized and applied in an efficient way.

- The test team should begin its test plan development effort by locating or creating a test plan template, and then tailoring the test plan outline as necessary. Once a test plan has been constructed and refined to fully document the intended approach, it will become the guiding instrument for the subsequent test program.

- The scope of the test program is provided in the test plan as a top-level description of test coverage. The scope is further refined through the definition of test goals, objectives, and strategies, as well as test requirements. These definitions can be recorded once the test team has a clear understanding of the system, chooses the automated tools for the test program, and documents several test program parameters.

- Test planning involves both the definition of test requirements and the development of an approach for managing those requirements. Test requirements management encompasses the storage and maintenance of requirements, maintenance of traceability links, test requirements risk assessment, test requirements sequencing (prioritization), and identification of a test verification method for each system requirement.

- The requirements traceability matrix explicitly identifies every requirement that will undergo examination by the test team, and an associated verification (qualification) method for each system requirement. The traceability matrix maps test procedures to system requirements or use cases, allowing team members to readily confirm that system requirements or use cases requiring test verification have been fully and successfully implemented.

- Key elements of test planning include the planning associated with project milestone events, test program activities, and test program-related documentation. The technical approach for these key elements is developed, personnel are assigned, and performance timelines are specified in the test program schedule.

- Test planning efforts must outline the resources and activities that are necessary to support the timely setup of the test environment. The test team must identify the hardware, software, network, and facility requirements needed to create and sustain the test environment. The procurement, installation, and setup activities for various test environment components need to be planned and scheduled.

○ The test team needs to comprehensively document test program plans, and team members need to become very familiar with the content of this plan. The effort to build a test plan is an iterative process, requiring feedback and agreement between the various project participants on the defined approaches, test strategies, and timelines for performance.

○ The test team needs to obtain end-user or customer buy-in on the test plan. This buy-in includes the customer's acceptance of both the test strategy and the detailed test procedures, which define the actual tests planned. As part of this buy-in, the end user concurs that the test plan and associated test scripts adequately verify satisfactory coverage of system requirements or use cases.

○ A successful, cost-effective test program requires a clear vision of goals and an explicit understanding of the various test program parameters that define the boundary of the test effort. A thorough understanding of the system requirements or use cases, coupled with careful definition of test program parameters and test requirements, is necessary to effectively tailor the test program solution to the particular project. Communication and analysis are key to selecting the right mix of test strategies to support the accomplishment of test goals and objectives.

○ Test planning is not a single event, but rather a process. The test plan is the document that guides test execution through to conclusion, and it needs to be updated frequently to reflect any changes. The test team should refer to the test plan often during the performance of testing for the project.

References

1. Adapted from ANSI/IEEE Std 1008–1987.

2. Rational Unified Process 5.0. Jacobson, I., Booch, G., Rumbaugh, J. *The Unified Software Development Process.* Reading, MA: Addison-Wesley, 1998.

3. Humphrey, W.S. *Managing the Software Process.* Reading, MA: Addison-Wesley, 1989.

Test Analysis and Design

Automated testing involves a mini-development life cycle.

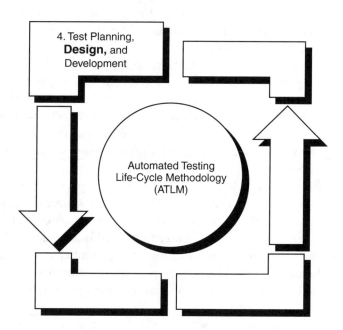

An effective test program that incorporates the automation of software testing has a development life cycle of its own. This development effort comes complete with its own strategy and goal planning, test requirement definition, analysis, design, and coding. Like software application development, the test development effort requires careful analysis and design.

With respect to the overall test program, the test effort can be classified into two primary categories: static and dynamic testing. Test strategies supporting the static test category were described in Chapter 4 and include various reviews, inspections, and walkthroughs. This chapter focuses on dynamic tests—its definition and the associated requirements and/or use case analysis and design required. Dynamic testing consists of the implementation of test techniques that involve the development and execution of test procedures designed to validate requirements; various *verification methods* are employed in the requirements validation process.

This chapter describes several approaches to test requirements analysis, including various techniques to derive test requirements from the various application requirements (that is, business requirements, functional requirements, design requirements, sequence diagrams) and/or use case specifications. Test requirements statements should clearly outline test conditions that will provide the highest probability of finding errors. Test requirements analysis also involves the review of the system's most critical success functions and high-risk functionality, as part of risk management. Test requirements statements should specify attributes of the most critical success functions and high-risk functionality, and testing should then verify that those requirements have been met.

In this chapter, methods for modeling the design of the (dynamic) test program are depicted. The approach to test design should ensure that the test effort verifies system requirements or use cases, increasing the probability that the system will actually succeed at what it is supposed to do. White-box and black-box test techniques that can be used in the test program design are outlined. White-box testing addresses the verification of software application internals, while black-box testing applies to the verification of application externals.

Test procedure definition is addressed along with parts of the requirements traceability matrix, which maps test procedures to test requirements (see Table 6.4 on page 210). The test engineer is reminded that these matrices can be automatically generated using a requirements management (RM) tool, such as DOORS. Test procedure definition involves the specification of the number and kinds of test procedures that will be carried out. During test procedure definition, it is important to identify the various test procedures that will exercise the test conditions mandated in the test requirements statements.

This chapter also addresses the need to analyze whether a test procedure should be performed manually or via an automated test tool, as well as the need to associate test data requirements with test procedures. Other topics considered include test procedure standardization and test procedure management. To facilitate test procedure development, test procedure design standards need to be established and then followed. Such standards promote the development of reusable, modular, maintainable, robust, and uniform test procedures.

All of these activities and issues pertain to the test analysis and design process. The progressive steps inherent in this process are outlined in Table 7.1.

Table 7.1   Test Analysis and Design Process

Step	Description
	Analysis
1	Goals and objectives. The test team reviews the test goals, objectives, and strategies.
2	Verification methods. Verification methods are assigned to system requirements or use cases and documented within a requirements traceability matrix.
3	Test requirement analysis. Test requirements statement definition is performed. Test requirements are derived from various system requirements of the application-under-test (AUT).
4	Test requirements matrix. Test requirements statements are mapped to system requirements or use cases and/or to system design (architecture) components.
5	Test technique mapping. A preliminary association of test requirements statements to test techniques is made. The test requirements matrix is modified to reflect this mapping.
	Design
6	Test program model definition. Various test techniques are reviewed for their applicability to the test program, and the test team ensures that the test techniques are justified by associated test requirements. The test requirements matrix is updated accordingly. The test program model is defined to identify the test techniques that apply to the test program.
7	Test architecture definition. This activity involves the selection of a test architecture model and population of model attributes.
8	Test procedure definition. Logical groups of test procedures are defined. A naming convention for the suite of test procedures is defined. The test procedure format is defined.
9	Test procedure mapping. An association between test procedures and test requirements statements is made. The test procedure matrix is created, reflecting this mapping.
10	Automated/manual test mapping (decision what to automate). The test procedure matrix is modified. This matrix specifies whether an automated tool will support the test procedure execution, or whether the procedure will be performed manually. An additional column in the matrix identifies potential automated test script reuse assets.
11	Test data mapping. The test procedure matrix is modified to reflect test data requirements for each test procedure.

7.1 | Test Requirements Analysis

Similar to the process followed in software application development, test requirements must be specified before test design is constructed. Such test requirements need to be clearly defined and documented, so that all project personnel will understand the basis of the test effort. They are derived from requirements statements as an outcome of test requirements analysis. This analysis, which is aimed at identifying the different kinds of tests needed to verify the system, can be undertaken by studying the system from several perspectives, depending on the testing phase.

As already mentioned in Chapter 6, one perspective includes the study of the system design or the functional process flow inherent in user operations, also known as the *structural* approach. It relies on unit and integration tests, also referred to as white-box tests. Test requirements analysis at the development test level is primarily based upon review of design specifications.

Other perspectives involve a review of system requirements or use cases, also referred to as the *requirements* or *behavioral* approach. This test requirements analysis pertains to testing performed in support of the system as a whole. This level, referred to as the system test level, most often involves black-box testing. The system test level consists of system and acceptance tests. Analysis at the system test level is geared primarily toward system (or business) requirements.

An alternative way of studying the system is to review critical success and highest-risk functions. The extra effort made to review these important functions can result in important insights that facilitate the creation of test requirements statements. Such thorough test requirements ensure that the test team will adequately exercise these functions in ways that guarantee proper operation when the system is eventually deployed.

Note, however, that the scope of test requirements that apply to the particular system needs to be limited. The test requirements definition is bounded by several parameters, including the description of the system and the system requirements definition. Other parameters include the defined scope of the test program and the test goals and objectives. Test requirements statements become the blueprint that enables the test team to design the next progressive step in the test analysis and design process by specifying a detailed outline of what is to be tested. A preliminary association of test requirements statements to test techniques is developed, and a test program model is created depicting the scope of test techniques that apply on the project.

The remainder of the section considers the test requirements analysis effort, as well as the two test levels (development and system levels).

7.1.1   Development-Level Test Analysis (Structural Approach)

An analysis should be performed to identify the test requirements that pertain to the development test effort. This analysis at the unit and integration testing level is also known as structural analysis.

The design-based structural analysis method requires the review of the detailed design and/or the software code. It emphasizes software module input and output.

The resulting test requirements statements are based on examination of the logic of the design or the implementation of the software code, where a detailed design is not available. The design-based analysis method addresses test requirements from a white-box-based view, which is concerned with actual processing activities such as control, logic, and data flows. Design-based analysis may also be referred to as structural coverage, reflecting its focus on the inherent structure of the software code.

DO-178B, an international avionics standard produced by RTCA, defines three different approaches for design-based test requirements analysis: statement coverage, decision coverage, and modified condition decision coverage (MC/DC). The statement coverage approach invokes every statement in a program at least once. In decision coverage, every point of entry and exit in the program is invoked at least once and every decision in the program takes on all possible outcomes at least once. MC/DC is a structural coverage criterion that requires each condition (term) within a decision (expression) to be demonstrated by execution, ensuring that it independently and correctly affects the outcome of the decision (a process called Boolean instrumentation).

The strength of these test requirements development approaches lies in the fact that the resulting test procedures will provide step-by-step instructions that are detailed down to keystroke entry; quite often, these instructions eventually become the structure for the system operation and user manuals. Such design-based requirements analysis investigates whether test procedures need to be developed for both source and object code, in an effort to find errors introduced during design, coding, compiling, linking, and loading operations.

A potential weakness of this kind of test requirements development approach relates to the fact that, because the design is being exercised, the test engineer is not viewing test requirements from a system-high level. This method requires that all entries and exits of the software units be tested. This level of activity can require a large number of test procedures, consume a great deal of time, and require the work of a larger number of personnel.

If the test team does plan testing at the development level, it is worthwhile to analyze test requirements that specify the need for exercising software under abnormal conditions. The test team needs to phrase test requirements statements so as to call for attempts to drive arrays out of bounds, drive loops through too many iterations, and drive input data out of range. The goal of these test requirements is to uncover errors by forcing the software to operate under unintended or abnormal conditions.

When analyzing development-level test requirements, the test team might also derive test requirements by analyzing the program logic pertaining to decision trees. The test engineer can examine the code entry and exit conditions and derive test requirements intended to ensure that every point of entry and exit in the program is invoked at least once. Test requirements can include statements pertaining to testing every condition for a decision within a software program.

7.1.1.1   Development Test Requirements Matrix

The test requirements for development-level testing should be defined and entered into a requirements traceability database or matrix. Table 7.2 outlines parts of such a matrix. Within this database or matrix, each test requirement should be associated with a system architecture component or a design component identification number. The architecture component is then traced to detailed software requirements (SWR ID) and to system requirements (SR ID) or use cases. Where no detailed software requirements have been defined, the architecture component is traced to system requirements or use cases. Requirements management allows the test engineer to maintain these traceability matrices in an automated fashion.

In Table 7.2, each test requirement (TR) is linked to a requirement statement, and each requirement statement is assigned a test requirement identification (TR ID) number. Once test requirements have been defined, the test team should make a preliminary decision about the test technique that can best handle each requirement.

Some test requirements may be derived as a result of analysis, and thus may not specifically relate to a software or system-level requirement. In this case, the entries for SR ID and SWR ID in Table 7.2 are cited as "various." The derived test requirement may also pertain to a number of system architecture components; in this case, the entry in the "Architecture Component" column is also "various." The test team may also wish to note in this column that the test requirement was derived as a result of test analysis.

7.1.2   System-Level Test Analysis (Behavioral Approach)

Test analysis also needs to be performed to identify the test requirements pertaining to the system test effort. Test requirements analysis at the system test level is also known as the behavioral approach.

The requirements-based analysis method requires the review of system/software requirement specifications. The emphasis with this analysis method is on test input and expected output. The resulting test requirements statements are based on examination of the system/software requirements specifications. The requirements-based analysis method approaches test requirements from a black-box-based perspective. It is aimed at deriving test requirements that will generate test procedures intended to show that the software performs its specified functions under normal operating conditions.

Table 7.2   Development Test Requirements Matrix

SR ID	SWR ID	Architecture Component	TR ID	TR Statement	Test Technique
3.2.1a	SM001	Systems Management	1001	System connectivity checks shall be selectable within a range of 1 to 60, and shall not accept values outside of this range	Fault Insertion
3.2.1a	SM002	Systems Management	1002	System shall provide appropriate error message for value selections outside of range	Error Handling
3.2.1b	SM003	Systems Management	1003	System shall perform system load checks between established servers and automatically adjust loads between servers, as necessary	String Test
3.2.1c	SM004	Systems Management	1004	System shall maintain a 50% memory reserve capacity for routine load levels	Memory Usage
3.2.1d	SM005	Systems Management	1005	System shall perform daily checks to monitor user authentication/passwords	String Test
3.2.1d	SM006	Systems Management	1006	System shall note authentication/password violations	Error Handling
3.2.1d	SM007	Systems Management	1007	Users must verify new passwords twice before the new passwords will be accepted; when an error occurs in the password entry, the user shall receive an error message	Error Handling
Various	Various	Various (derived from analysis)	1008	All statements in this module should be executed at least once	Statement Coverage
Various	Various	Various (derived from analysis)	1009	Test the number of times the logical branches have been exercised for both true and false conditions	Branch Coverage
.	.	.	.	.	.
.	.	.	.	.	.
.	.	.	.	.	.

Another approach for deriving test requirements includes the use of functional threads. Test requirements created via this method result from analysis of the functional thread of the high-level business requirements. The test engineer reviews the high-level business process by examining the results of enterprise business process reengineering or by employing use case analysis.

Business process reengineering (BPR) is a structured method for analyzing the procedures that a business entity uses to accomplish its goals and redesigning the business's processes with a focus on the end user of its products. Consequently, rather than simply providing computer systems to support the business practices as they currently exist, BPR examines the entire scope of the processes, determining the flow of information through components of the business and suggesting major improvements. Frequently, the reengineering process incorporates an infusion of new technologies and automated information systems.

Use case analysis, on the other hand, is a way of modeling requirements and a requirements analysis methodology that involves the development and subsequent analysis of a number of mini-scenarios, which themselves exercise combinations of the system-level requirements. Each use case has a defined starting point, set of discrete steps, and defined exit criteria. The use case construct defines the behavior of a system or other semantic entity without revealing its internal structure. Each use case specifies a sequence of actions, including variants, that the entity can perform by interacting with actors of the entity.

Derived requirements elicitation and the identification of system capabilities to be developed are accomplished by analyzing each step in the use case. This analysis includes the identification of what the user does, what the software does, what the user interface does, and what the database needs to do to support the step. The accumulation of the various user actions facilitates the development of training and user documentation as well as the design of test procedures.

An auxiliary approach for deriving test requirements at the system test level involves the review of critical success and high-risk functions of the system. While it is important to outline test conditions that provide the highest probability of finding errors, it is also crucial to find errors in critical and high-risk functionality. Table 7.3 provides an example of a listing of critical and high-risk functionality that might be included in a test plan. Each defined risk is ranked, from the most critical risk to the least critical risk. The test engineer would analyze these functions in more detail and outline test requirements that would later result in test procedures intended to verify the comprehensive operation of the functionality.

As noted, it is important that test requirements statements also outline test conditions that provide the highest probability of finding errors. Test requirements statements should specify input values so that the test team can generate tests that

Table 7.3   Critical/High-Risk Functions

Rank	Function	Software Component	Indicator
1	Verify identification of trading partner account prior to any automated exchange of asset trading information	SG-07	High Risk
2	Sort through asset trade opportunities and identify the best-value trade and close deal on best-value trade	AT-12	Critical
3	Provide communications and flow of information between software components operating at different levels of security classification	SG-07	High Risk
4	Monitor exchange rates and primary economic indicators for changes in the securities market and the worldwide economy	DS-13	High Risk
5	Monitor securities and the most significant securities movement	TV-10	Critical
6	Create simulation modeling producing extended forecasts, analyze future of evolving trends, and provide long-term executive decision support	DS-13	Critical

utilize out-of-range input data. The goal of these test requirements is to uncover errors by forcing the software to exercise unintended or abnormal conditions.

7.1.2.1   System Test Requirements Matrix

The test requirements supporting system-level testing need to be defined and reflected in a matrix like that depicted in Table 7.4. Each test requirement is correlated with a system requirement. System requirements are reflected in the first column of Table 7.4, through the entry of the associated system requirement identification (SR ID) number. Test requirements may also be referenced to the associated system architecture component.

Each test requirement (TR) is linked to a requirement statement, and each requirement statement is assigned a test requirement identification (TR ID) number. Once test requirements have been defined, the test team should make a preliminary decision about the test technique that will best meet the test requirement. Even though this effort may look like a lot of time spent cross-referencing different numbers, an RM tool, such as DOORS, can provide automated maintenance.

Table 7.4   **System Test Requirements Matrix**

SR ID	Architecture Component	TR ID	Test Requirement Statement	Test Technique
3.2.1a	Systems Management	2001	System shall verify the connectivity with external data sources at least once per minute	Functional Test
	Systems Management	2002	System connectivity checks verifying external data sources shall be selectable within a range of 1 to 60 seconds	Functional Test
	Systems Management	2003	System connectivity checks shall be selectable within a range of 1 to 60 seconds and must not accept values outside of this range; system shall provide an appropriate error message for value selections outside of range	Boundary Value
3.2.1b	Systems Management	2004	System shall perform system load checks between established servers and automatically adjust loads between servers	Functional Test
3.2.1c	Systems Management	2005	Performance measures need to be assessed at 4-, 16-, 24- and 48-hour intervals	Performance Test
3.2.1d	Systems Management	2006	System shall perform checks of user authentication password values against dictionaries and tables of easily guessed passwords	Functional Test
3.2.1d	Systems Management	2007	Where authentication password violations are detected, system shall prompt user to change password at the time of the next system logon	Functional Test
3.2.1d	Systems Management	2008	Users must verify their new passwords twice before they will be accepted; when error occurs in password entry, the user shall receive an error message	Functional Test

7.2 | Test Program Design

Much as in any software development effort, the test program must be mapped out and consciously designed to ensure that the test activities performed represent the most efficient and effective tests for the system. Test program resources are limited, yet ways of testing the system are endless. This section addresses ways of graphically portraying the test program design so as to give project and test personnel a mental framework on the boundary and scope of the test program.

7.2.1 Test Program Design Models

Test program design activities follow test analysis exercises. The results of test analysis include definition of test goals and objectives, the selection of verification methods and their mapping to system requirements or use cases, and creation of test requirements statements. The test requirements are then mapped to system requirements or use cases and/or system design components, depending upon the relevant test life-cycle phase. After this mapping is complete, a preliminary association of test requirements to test techniques is developed.

Armed with a definition of test requirements and an understanding of the test techniques that may be suited to the particular project, the test team is then ready to develop the test program design models. The first of these design models consists of a test program model. The test program model consists of a graphic illustration that depicts the scope of the test program. At a minimum, it includes test techniques that will be employed at the development test and system test levels. The model may also outline static test strategies that are utilized throughout the application development life cycle. In addition, it may explicitly identify verification methods other than testing that will be employed during development- and system-level tests.

Figure 7.1 depicts a sample test program model. This figure defines the various test techniques, some of which will be implemented on a particular test program, depending on the test requirements. The test engineers on a project would develop this model by documenting the test techniques identified during the test analysis effort. The test team would start with a template model that included a laundry list of test techniques that could be applied to any given test program and then pare the list down to match the results of the test analysis. Working from a template saves the test team time and effort.

Having defined a test program model, the test team's next task is to construct a test architecture for the particular project. The test architecture consists of a graphic illustration depicting the structure of the test program. The objective is to define the way that test procedures will be organized within the test effort.

Static Test Strategies		*Other Verification Methods*	
• Requirements Review		• Demonstration	• Manual Test
• Use of Process Standards		• Analysis	• Automated Test
• Design Review Participation		• Inspection	
• Inspections and Walkthroughs		• Certification	

Development-Level Techniques		*System-Level Techniques*	
• Condition Coverage	• Equivalence Partitioning	• Configuration Testing
• Path Coverage	• Boundary Value Analysis	• Performance Testing
• Fault Insertion	• Cause-Effect Graphing	• Functional Testing
• Memory Leak	• Random Testing	• Security Testing
• Error Handling	• Error Guessing	• Operational Readiness
• String Test	• Regression Testing	• User Acceptance
• Statement Coverage	• Stress Testing	• Compatibility/Conversion
• Decision Coverage	• Replication Testing	• Benchmark Testing
• Cyclomatic Complexity	• Data Integrity Testing	• Usability Testing
• Data Flow Coverage	• Backup and Recoverability	• Alpha/Beta Testing

Figure 7.1   Test Program Model

The structure of the test program is commonly portrayed in two different ways. One test procedure organization method involves the logical grouping of test procedures with the system application design components; it is referred to as a design-based test architecture. The second method associates test procedures with the various kinds of test techniques represented within the test program model; it is referred to as a technique-based test architecture.

In both architecture models, a distinction is made between the architecture that applies to the development test level and the architecture that applies to the system test level. The test architecture for a test program may, however, be represented by a combination of design- and technique-based approaches. For example, the architecture that applies to the development test level might be design-based, while the architecture that applies to the system test level might be technique-based. Refer to Section 7.3.1 or Appendix D for an example of a *hybrid* test architecture that reflects both the design-based and technique-based approaches.

7.2.1.1 Design-Based Test Architecture

The design-based test architecture associates test procedures with the hardware and software design components of the system application. The logic of this model stems from the understanding that the hardware and software design components can be traced to system and software requirements specifications. Additionally, test requirements statements can be traced to design components, as well as to system and software requirements specifications. Therefore, the test team can refer to a requirements traceability matrix to ascertain the test techniques that correlate to each of the various design components, as portrayed by the design-based test architecture depicted in Figure 7.2.

The test architecture in Figure 7.2 provides the test team with a roadmap for identifying the different test procedures needed to support each design component. The various design components are represented by their associated design identification numbers. The identifier SM-06, for example, stands for a design component called system management; this design component is the sixth component within the project's software architecture diagram. Only four design components are included in Figure 7.2. The right-hand column is entitled "Others," signifying that

Development Test Level

SM-06	SG-07	SA-08	TV-10	Others . . .
Error Handling	Error Handling	Cyclomatic Complexity	Cyclomatic Complexity	. . .
Memory Leak	Memory Leak	Path Coverage	Path Coverage	. . .
		Fault Insertion	Fault Insertion	. . .
		Decision Coverage	Decision Coverage	. . .
		Data Flow Coverage	Data Flow Coverage	. . .

System Test Level

SM-06	SG-07	SA-08	TV-10	Others . . .
Functional	Functional	Functional	Functional	. . .
Security	Security	Stress/ Volume	Stress/ Volume	. . .
		Boundary	Boundary	. . .
		Performance	Performance	. . .

Figure 7.2 Design-Based Test Architecture

other design components depicted within the project's software architecture diagram would be represented in a column of the test architecture diagram.

With the construction of the design-based test architecture, the test team gains a clear picture of the techniques that will be employed in testing each design component. The test team can now readily define all corresponding test procedures for the design component by referring to the requirements traceability matrix.

7.2.1.2   Technique-Based Test Architecture

The technique-based test architecture associates the requirement for test procedures with the test techniques defined within the test program model. The rationale for this model stems from the understanding that the test procedures supporting a particular test technique are logically coupled. Additionally, test techniques have already been traced to test requirements statements within a requirements traceability matrix.

Only four test techniques are included in the technique-based test architecture depicted in Figure 7.3. The right-hand column is entitled "Others," signifying that other test techniques that apply to the test effort should be listed within a column of the test architecture diagram.

The technique-based test architecture provides the test team with a clear picture of the test techniques to be employed. The test team can then identify the test requirements associated with each test technique by referring to the requirements traceability matrix. They can also readily define the test procedures that correspond to the applicable test techniques and the associated test requirements.

7.2.1.3   Effective Test Program Design

The overall test program design involves both dynamic and static test activities, as shown in Figure 7.1. Effective use of test engineers' time to support static test activities can greatly improve system application design and development. The development of a quality system application design can streamline the test effort, as can an effective test design. An effective test design enables the test team to focus its efforts where they are most clearly needed.

The test architecture serves as a roadmap for the dynamic test effort. The dynamic test effort, in turn, facilitates the development- and system-level test efforts. These two test efforts are primarily based on the use of white-box and black-box approaches to testing. The white-box approach focuses on application "internals," while the black-box approach concentrates on "externals." Testing performed at the development and system levels may employ one of these approaches or a combination of both approaches.

Development Test Level

Error Handling	Path Coverage	Fault Insertion	Memory Leak	Others . . .
List Modules/ Units	List Modules/ Units	List Modules/ Units	List Modules/ Units	List Modules/ Units
. . .	. . .	. . .	. . .	. . .
. . .	. . .	. . .	. . .	. . .
. . .	. . .	. . .	. . .	. . .
. . .	. . .	. . .	. . .	. . .

System Test Level

Functional	Security	Stress/ Volume	Performance	Others . . .
Identify Test Procedure Series or Design Components	Identify Test Procedure Series or Design Components	Identify Test Procedure Series or Design Components	Identify Test Procedure Series or Design Components	Identify Test Procedure Series or Design Components
. . .	. . .	. . .	. . .	. . .
. . .	. . .	. . .	. . .	. . .
. . .	. . .	. . .	. . .	. . .
. . .	. . .	. . .	. . .	. . .

Figure 7.3   Technique-Based Test Architecture

To develop the test program design models described here, test personnel need to be familiar with the test techniques associated with the white-box and black-box testing approaches. Table 7.5 provides an overview of these two test approaches.

7.2.2   White-Box Techniques (Development-Level Tests)

Many books have been written about the various white-box and black-box testing techniques [1]. This book does not offer a full review of all such test techniques, but instead focuses on automated testing. It is important to note that an understanding of the most widely used test techniques is necessary when developing the test design. This section covers several widely used development-level test techniques, and Section 7.2.3 discusses system-level test techniques.

Table 7.5   White Box/Black Box Overview

White-Box Approach	Black-Box Approach	
Test Approach	**Test Approach**	
Structural testing approach focuses on application internals. Program-based.	Functional testing approach focuses on application externals. Requirements- or specification-based.	
Characteristics	**Characteristics**	
Module design	Functionality	
Implementation	Requirements, use, standards	
Do modules/functions meet functional and design specifications?	Correctness	
Do program structures meet functional and design specifications?	Business forms, documents	
How does the program work?	Does system meet business requirements?	
Type of Test	**Type of Test**	
Unit testing	System testing	
Integration testing	User acceptance testing	
Techniques	**Techniques**	
• Fault Insertion	• Boundary Value Analysis	• Performance Testing
• String Test	• Cause-Effect Graphing	• Functional Testing
• Error Handling	• Random Testing	• Security Testing
• Statement Coverage	• Error Guessing	• Equivalence Partitioning
• Decision Coverage	• Regression Testing	• Operational Readiness Testing
• Condition Coverage	• Stress (Volume) Testing	• User Acceptance Testing
• Path Coverage	• Replication Testing	• Compatibility/Conversion Testing
• Data Flow Coverage	• Data Integrity Testing	• Benchmark Testing
• Memory Leak	• Backup and Recoverability	• Usability Testing
• Cyclomatic Complexity	• Configuration Testing	• Alpha/Beta Testing
Personnel Involved	**Personnel Involved**	
Developers and/or Test Engineers	Developers, Test Engineers, and End Users	

White-box testing techniques are aimed at exercising internal facets of the target software program. These techniques do not focus on identifying syntax errors, as a compiler usually uncovers these types of defects. Instead, the white-box techniques perform tests that seek to locate errors that are more difficult to detect, find, and fix. That is, they attempt to identify logical errors and verify test coverage.

Test procedures associated with the white-box approach make use of the control structure of the procedural design. They provide several services, including the following:

1. They guarantee that all independent paths within a module have been exercised at least once.

2. They exercise all logical decisions on their true and false sides.

3. They execute all loops at their boundaries and within their operational bounds.

4. They exercise internal data structures to ensure their validity.

White-box testing usually includes the unit test strategy, which involves testing at the module or function level in a program, where testing focuses on the internal paths of the module. This type of testing is also called unit testing, clear-box, or translucent testing because the individual performing the test has insight into the operation of the program code and can see the program's internal workings. This approach to testing is referred to as a structural approach as well.

This level of testing examines the control flow (each path) performed at the unit level. Test drivers are used to guarantee that all paths within a module have been exercised at least once, all logical decisions have been exercised with all possible conditions, loops have been exercised on upper and lower boundaries, and internal data structures have been exercised.

7.2.2.1 Descriptions of White-Box Techniques

The white-box techniques discussed here are described in only brief detail. Most of these techniques can be automatically executed using the applicable testing tools. For a more complete description of white-box testing techniques, refer to books that focus on software test techniques.

Fault Insertion.   Fault insertion involves forcing return codes to indicate errors and seeing how the code behaves. It represents a good way to simulate certain events, such as disk full, out of memory, and so on. A popular method involves replacing `alloc( )` with a function that returns a NULL value 10% of the time to see how many crashes result, an approach also called erroneous input testing. This testing checks the processing of both valid and invalid inputs. Testers may also select values that exercise the range of input/output (I/O) parameters as well as values outside the boundary range of the parameters.

Fault insertion offers a way to measure the effectiveness of false tests being performed. In general, a defect is purposely inserted into the application being tested at a particular point, which is intended to cause a single test to fail. Following the insertion of the defect, the entire suite of tests is rerun. Results of the test are reviewed.

Unit Testing.   To verify that software code performs adequately and correctly implements detailed design, unit tests are conducted while the code is being generated for each software unit. Unit testing verifies that the new code matches the detailed design; checks paths through the code; verifies that screens, pull-down menus, and messages are formatted properly; checks inputs for range and type; and verifies that each block of code generates exceptions or error returns when appropriate. Each software unit is tested to ensure that the algorithms and logic are correct and that the software unit satisfies the requirements and functionality assigned to it. Errors documented as a result of unit testing can include logic, overload or overflow of range, timing, and memory leakage detection errors.

Error Handling Testing.   This technique acknowledges the fact that it is nearly impossible to test for every possible error condition. For this reason, an error handler can smooth the transition when an unexpected error occurs. The test engineer needs to ensure that the application returns error messages properly. For example, an application that returns a message indicating a system error generated by middleware (for example, a "Common Object Request Broker Architecture [CORBA] user exception error") has little value to the end user or the test engineer.

Error handling tests seek to uncover instances where the system application does not return a descriptive error message, but instead crashes and reports a runtime error. This testing ensures that errors are presented and dealt with properly in the target application. An efficient error handler will act at the function or module level. The error handling functionality therefore needs to be tested at the development test level. Of course, such tests cannot uncover all possible errors, but some invalid values can be passed to the function to test the performance of error handling routines.

Memory Leak.   The memory leak test technique focuses on the execution of the application, attempting to find instances where the application is not releasing or freeing up allocated memory and, as a result, experiences performance degradation or a deadlock condition. The application of this test technique is valuable in program debugging as well as in testing a complete software release. Tools are available to facilitate the execution of the memory leak test technique, which may track the application's memory usage over a period of hours or days to see whether memory consumption continues to increase. These tools may also be able to identify the program statements where allocated memory is not released following use of the memory space.

Integration Testing. The purpose of integration testing is to verify that each software unit interfaces correctly to other software units. Integration testing may utilize a top-down or bottom-up structured technique, where the leaf modules are integrated with the next lower- or higher-level modules until the entire software tree has been constructed. This testing technique examines not only the parameters passed between two components, but also the global parameters and, in the case of object-oriented applications, all high-level classes.

Each integration test procedure consists of a high-level test script that simulates a user performing a defined task by invoking the lower-level unit tests with the requisite parameters to exercise the interface. Units are incrementally integrated and tested together based upon control flow, after all unit test problem reports have been resolved. Because units may consist of other units, some integration testing may take place during unit testing. When unit test scripts have been developed using an automated test tool, these scripts may be combined and new scripts added to test module interconnectivity.

Integration test procedures are executed and refined as necessary, and trouble reports are documented and tracked. Trouble reports are generally classified in a range of 1 to 4, based on their degree of severity (1 being the most critical and 4 being the least). After handling these trouble reports, test engineers perform regression testing to verify that problems have been completely resolved.

String Testing. String testing involves the examination of a related group of modules that constitute a software function. Also known as module testing, it ensures sufficient testing of a system's components. It determines whether modules work successfully to form a cohesive unit and whether the software unit produces accurate and consistent results.

A module consists of one or more functions. String testing concentrates on the interactions of the functions. The parameters passed from function to function within the module are tested for correctness in terms of data type and data validity. This type of testing assesses the soundness of the programmer's assumptions, as each function in the module is examined for errors and completeness. The coding standards that apply to the development effort can be verified at this time.

During module/function-level testing, the test team verifies that each program statement executes at least once. This program statement execution takes into account all loops and conditional statements. Each conditional relationship is tested for all resulting conditions—that is, it is tested for all possible valid and invalid values. Each boundary condition is considered to either pass or fail. State changes are predicted, and the test ensures that the appropriate trigger is fired. In addition, the team determines whether individual edits are working by testing with valid and invalid values.

Coverage Analysis.   When selecting a coverage analysis tool, it is important that the test team analyze the type of coverage required for the application. Coverage analysis can be obtained using many different techniques, some of which are described here.

Statement Coverage.   The statement coverage technique is often referred to as *C1,* which also denotes node coverage. This measure reports whether each executable statement is encountered. It verifies coverage at a high level, rather than decision execution or Boolean expressions. It offers an advantage in that this measure can be applied directly to object code and does not require processing source code. Performance profilers commonly implement this testing technique.

The statement coverage technique requires that every statement in the program be invoked at least once. A weakness of this technique is that it does not verify decisions (paths/results) but is affected by computational statements [2]. Another weakness involves the fact that the technique does not test Boolean expressions thoroughly and source code coverage does not assure object code coverage [3]. Decisions need to be tested to validate the design—checking, for example, to ensure that the logical operator is correct. Logical operator checks include whether the *and* operator should actually be an *or.* Likewise, the technique could check whether the operator should read *greater than or equal* instead of *greater than.*

Inputs necessary to support the design of test procedures include design documents and source code listings. It is important that enough test procedures be developed to execute every statement at least once [4].

Decision Coverage.   The decision coverage test technique seeks to identify the percentage of all possible decision outcomes that have been exercised by a suite of test procedures. The decision coverage technique is sometimes referred to as branch coverage and is denoted as *C2.* It requires that every point of entry and exit in the software program be invoked at least once. It also requires that all possible conditions for a decision in the program be exercised at least once. The technique further requires that each decision in the program be tested using all possible outcomes at least once [5].

A weakness of the decision coverage test technique pertains to the fact that the tests performed are inadequate for high-integrity applications, because they do not ensure decision coverage of the object code. Additionally, an incorrect evaluation of a condition can be masked by other conditions. For example, logic errors are not necessarily visible.

Condition Coverage. Condition coverage is similar to decision coverage. It seeks to verify the accuracy of the true or false outcome of each Boolean subexpression. This technique employs tests that measure the subexpressions independently of each other. The results of these measures are similar to those obtained with decision coverage except that the former show greater sensitivity to the control flow.

Path Coverage. The path coverage technique seeks to verify whether each of the possible paths in each function has executed properly. A path is a set of branches of logic flow. Because loops introduce an unbounded number of paths, the path coverage technique employs tests that consider only a limited number of looping possibilities. Boundary-interior path testing considers two possibilities for loops: zero repetitions and more than zero repetitions [6].

The path coverage technique provides very thorough testing, but has two significant drawbacks. First, the number of possible paths that need to be supported by test procedures may be exceedingly exhaustive and beyond the scope of most test programs. This drawback arises because the number of paths is exponential to the number of branches. Second, path coverage is very time-consuming. It should therefore be used for critical success functions only.

Data Flow Coverage. The data flow coverage test technique is a variation of path coverage. It seeks to incorporate the flow of data into the selection of test procedures. Such techniques are based on the selection of test path segments that satisfy some characteristic of the data flow for all possible types of data objects [7]. Test procedures derived from data flow analysis examine interactions involving definitions to program variables and subsequent references that are affected by these definitions [8].

Branch Coverage. Branch coverage measures the number of times that logical branches have been exercised for both true and false conditions. This analysis is used most often for detailed unit testing of systems.

7.2.2.2 Automated Tools Supporting White-Box Testing

When selecting white-box test techniques to include as part of the overall test program design, it is helpful to be familiar with the kinds of test tools that are available to support the development and performance of related test procedures. Table 7.6

Table 7.6   White-Box Test Techniques and Corresponding Automated Test Tools

White-Box Test Techniques	Automated Test Tools
• Fault Insertion	• Coding Tools
• String Testing	• GUI and Server Test Tools
• Error Handling	• Error Handling Tools
• Statement Coverage	• Static and Dynamic Analyzers
• Decision Coverage	• Static and Dynamic Analyzers, Coverage Analysis Tools
• Condition Coverage	• Static and Dynamic Analyzers, Coverage Analysis Tools
• Path Coverage	• Static and Dynamic Analyzers, Coverage Analysis Tools
• Test Data Flow Coverage	• Data Modeling Tools, Flow Diagram Editors
• Memory Usage	• Memory Usage Tools
• General Resource Usage	• General Resource Usage Tools
• Code Complexity	• Static and Dynamic Analyzers, Source Code Analyzers
• Cyclomatic Complexity	• Cyclomatic Complexity Analyzers, other Software Metrics Tools

matches white-box test techniques with various types of automated test tools. When selecting white-box test techniques and making commitments to use pertinent automated test tools, the test team should keep in mind the fact that the test tools may not be compatible with each other.

7.2.3   Black-Box Techniques (System-Level Tests)

Black-box testing is testing only via established, public interfaces such as the user interface or the published application programming interface (API). While white-box testing concerns itself with the program's internal workings, black-box testing compares the application's behavior against requirements. Additionally, the latter techniques typically seek to investigate three basic types of errors: those associated with the functional paths supported by the software, the computations performed by the software, or the range or domain of possible data values that can be executed by the software. At this level, the testers do not primarily concern themselves with the inner workings of the software components, though the inner components of the software are nevertheless exercised by default. Instead, the test team is concerned about the inputs and outputs of the software. In the context of this discussion, black-box testing is considered to be synonymous with system testing, although black-box testing can also occur during unit or integration testing.

User participation is important to black-box testing, as users are the people who are most familiar with the results that can be expected from the business functions. The correctness of data is key in successfully completing the system testing. Therefore, during the data generation phase, it is imperative that the end users give as much input as possible. Section 7.3.6.2 discusses black-box data definition.

Black-box testing attempts to derive sets of inputs that will fully exercise all functional requirements of a system. It is not an alternative to white-box testing. This type of testing attempts to find errors in many categories, including the following:

- Incorrect or missing functionality

- Interface errors

- Usability problems

- Errors in data structures or external database access

- Performance degradation problems and other performance errors

- Loading errors

- Multiuser access errors

- Initialization and termination errors

- Backup and recoverability problems

- Security problems

7.2.3.1   Black-Box Technique Descriptions

The black-box techniques outlined in this section are the most commonly used approaches.

Equivalence Partitioning.   As noted in Chapter 4, exhaustive input testing typically is not possible. Instead, testing must be performed using a subset of all possible inputs.

Three basic types of equivalence classes apply when testing for range and domain errors: *in-bound, out-of-bound,* and *on-bound* situations. It is a good practice to develop test procedures that examine boundary cases plus/minus one to avoid missing the "one too many" or "one too few" error. In addition to developing test procedures that utilize highly structured equivalence classes, the test team should perform exploratory testing. Test procedures that are developed and later execute as expected are called positive cases. Test procedures that should result in an error when executed are referred to as negative cases.

One advantage of the equivalence partitioning technique is that it reduces the scope of exhaustive testing to a well-defined set of test procedures, as opposed to an ad hoc definition of test procedures. One disadvantage relates to the fact that the resulting test procedures do not include other types of tests that have a high probability of finding an error.

Boundary Value Analysis. [9]   Boundary value analysis can be applied to both structural and functional testing levels. Boundaries define three classes of data: good, bad, and on the border. Boundary testing uses values that lie in or on the boundary (such as endpoints), and maximum/minimum values (such as field lengths). The analysis should always include plus/minus one boundary values. Outside boundary testing uses a representative sample of data from outside the boundary of values—that is, invalid values. For example, data type tests should check for numeric and alphabetic values. Does the field accept numeric values only as specified or does it accept alphanumeric values?

It is a judgment call to select the *representative sample* so that it truly represents the intended range of values. This task is sometimes very difficult when numerous interrelationships exist among values. Consider using random samples of possible cases. When the number of possibilities is very large and possible results are very close in value, choose input values that give largest variances in output—that is, perform *sensitivity analysis.*

Cause/Effect Graphing. [10]   Cause-effect graphing is a technique that provides a concise representation of logical conditions and corresponding actions. Four steps are involved in this technique. The first step involves the listing of causes (input conditions) and effects (actions) for a module and the assignment of an identifier to each module. In the second step, a cause-effect graph is developed. The graph is converted to a decision table in the third step. The fourth step involves the identification of causes and effects by reading the functional specifications. Each cause and effect is assigned a unique identifier. The causes are listed vertically on the left-hand side of a paper and the effects are listed on the right-hand side. After the lists are complete, part of the semantic content between the causes and effects is illustrated by directly and indirectly linking the causes to the effects with lines. The graph is then annotated with symbols representing Boolean expressions, which combine two or more causes associated with an effect. Decision table rules are then converted to test procedures.

System Testing.   "System testing" is often used as a synonym for "black-box testing," because during system testing the test team concerns itself mostly with the application's "externals." System testing encompasses several testing subtypes, such as functional, regression, security, stress, performance, usability, random, data integrity, conversion, backup and recoverability, configuration, operational readiness, user acceptance, and alpha/beta testing.

Functional Testing.   A functional test exercises a system application with regard to functional requirements with the intent of discovering nonconformance with end-user requirements. This test technique is central to most software test programs. Its primary objective is to assess whether the application does what it is supposed to do in accordance with specified requirements.

Test development considerations for functional tests include concentrating on test procedures that execute the functionality of the system based upon the project's requirements. One significant test development consideration arises when several test engineers will be performing test development and execution simultaneously. When these test engineers are working independently and sharing the same data or database, a method needs to be identified to ensure that test engineer A does not modify or affect the data being manipulated by test engineer B, potentially invalidating the test results produced by test engineer B. Chapter 9 discusses ways to structure the test procedure execution schedule so as to avoid these issues.

Another test development consideration pertains to the organization of tests into groups related to a business function. Automated test procedures should be organized in such a way that effort is not duplicated. The test team should review the test plan and the test design to perform the following analyses:

- Determine the order or sequence in which specific transactions must be tested, either to accommodate database issues or as a result of control or workflow

- Identify any patterns of similar actions or events that are used by multiple transactions

- Review critical and high-risk functions so as to place a greater priority on tests of this functionality and to address associated test procedures early in the development schedule

- Create a modularity-relationship matrix (see Chapter 8)

These analyses will help the test team organize the proper sequence of test development, ensuring that test procedures can be properly linked together and played back in a specific order to permit contiguous flow of playback and operation of the target application.

Another consideration when formulating functional tests pertains to the creation of certain test procedures with the sole purpose of supporting screen navigation. Such test procedures are not intended to validate specific functional requirements, but reflect user interface actions. For example, the test team may record a procedure that navigates the application through several windows and concludes at the particular window under test. The test engineer may then record a separate procedure to validate the destination window. Such navigation test procedures may be shared and reused several times during the test development effort.

Regression Testing.   The whole notion of conducting tests is aimed at finding and documenting defects and tracking them to closure. The test engineer needs to be sure that the action performed to fix the software does not, in turn, create a new error in another area of the software system. Regression testing determines whether any errors have been introduced during the error-fixing process. It is in the area of regression testing that automated test tools offer the largest return on investment. All scripts developed prior can be executed in progression to verify that no new errors have been introduced through changes made to fix another error. This goal can be easily achieved because the scripts can be run with no manual intervention and therefore can be executed as many times as deemed necessary to detect errors.

Test engineers often feel that once they have tested something manually and the software checks out, that no further testing is required. In this instance, the test engineer does not take into consideration that a module change might have introduced a bug that affects a different module. Therefore, once the application is somewhat stable, the test team should focus on automating some or all regression tests, especially those involving high-risk functionality, repetitive tasks, and reusable modules. Regression tests may be reused many times during the development life cycle, including for the various new releases of the application-under-test. Some regression tests can also be reused for stress, volume, and performance testing.

Security Testing.   Security tests involve checks to verify the proper performance of system access and data access mechanisms. Test procedures are devised that attempt to subvert the program's security checks. The test engineer uses security tests to validate security levels and access limits and thereby verify compliance with specified security requirements and any applicable security regulations.

Test development considerations for security tests include the creation of test procedures based upon security specifications. Depending upon the particular application, security testing might involve tests of a COTS product that is integrated into the application to support security.

Stress Testing.   Stress testing involves the exercise of a system without regard to design constraints, with the intent to discover the as-built limitations of the system. These tests are performed when processing of transactions reaches its peak and steady loads of high-volume data are encountered. Stress testing measures the capacity and resiliency of the system on each hardware platform. In this technique, multiple users exercise specific functions concurrently and some use values outside of the norm. The system is asked to process a huge amount of data or perform many function calls within a short period of time. A typical example could be to perform the same function from all workstations simultaneously accessing the database.

Tools are available to support stress tests intended to ensure that an application performs successfully under various operating conditions. For example, tools can exercise the system by creating virtual users and allowing for an incremental increase of the number of end-user workstations that are concurrently exercising the application. Response times can be captured and logged by the tool throughout the progressive increase in user load on the system to track any performance degradation.

Automated tools can be applied to exercise the application system under high-stress scenarios, such as system operations involving complex queries, large query responses, and large data object retrievals. Other high-stress scenarios include an application being exercised for many hours and the concurrent operation of a large number of test procedures. Stress test tools typically monitor resource usage, including usage of global memory, DOS memory, free file handles, and disk space, and can identify trends in resource usage so as to detect problem areas, such as memory leaks and excess consumption of system resources and disk space.

Several types of stress testing exist. Unit stress tests generate stress on a single interface. Module stress testing verifies that business functions are processed in a common area. System stress testing involves loading the system using high-volume transactions. It can include data volume tests, where the test engineer verifies that the application can support the volume of data and the number of transactions required. Also included are concurrency tests, where the test engineer verifies that the application can support multiple users accessing the same data without lockouts or multiuser access problems. The test team will also want to conduct some scalability tests, verifying that the system can support planned and unplanned growth in the user community or in the volume of data that the system is required to handle.

Test development considerations for stress tests include planning to determine the number of transactions that are required to be run by the test script, the number of iterations, the number of virtual users, the kinds of transactions, and the length of time to run the test script. The test team will need to identify the system limitations and perform tests to discover what happens when the system is pushed to the border and beyond these limitations.

The test team should understand and define the transaction performance monitoring considered necessary in terms of database time, response time, and central processing unit (CPU) time. Test outcome information can include minimum transaction response time, maximum transaction response time, mean transaction response time, number of parsed transactions, and number of failed transactions.

The test team needs to develop a benchmark plan to support stress testing. Benchmarks should include month, day, and week values based upon functional requirements. The test team also needs to determine occurrence rates and probabilities. It uses the benchmark plan and applicable values to perform stress testing on the software baseline. Benefits of stress testing include the identification of threshold failures, such as limitations involving not enough memory, SWAP or TEMP space, maximum number of concurrent open files, maximum number of concurrent users, maximum concurrent data, and DBMS page locking during updating.

Performance Testing.   Performance tests verify that the system application meets specific performance efficiency objectives. Performance testing can measure and report on such data as input/output (I/O) rates, total number of I/O actions, average database query response time, and CPU utilization rates. The same tools used in stress testing can generally be used in performance testing to allow for automatic checks of performance efficiency.

To conduct performance testing, the following performance objectives need to be defined:

- How many transactions per second need to be processed?
- How is a transaction defined?
- How many concurrent users and total users are possible?
- Which protocols are supported?
- With which external data sources or systems does the application interact?

Usability Testing.   Usability tests verify that the system is easy to use and that the user interface appearance is appealing. Such tests consider the human element in system operation. That is, the test engineer needs to evaluate the application from the prospective of the end user. Table 7.7 outlines the various kinds of tests to consider as part of usability testing.

Test development considerations for usability tests include approaches where the user executes a prototype of the actual application that lacks the real functionality. By running a capture/playback tool in capture mode while the user executes the prototype, recorded mouse movements and keystrokes can track where the user moves and how he would exercise the system. Reading such captured scripts can help the designers understand the approach of the usability of the application design.

Random Testing.   Random tests consist of spontaneous tests identified by the test engineer during test development or execution. These types of tests are also referred to as *monkey* tests, reflecting the spontaneous nature of their creation. With these

Table 7.7   Usability Test Considerations

General On-Line/Screen Testing

Mode and commands
Confirmation required for deletions
Layout conforms to standards
Screen field names conform to standards
Positive/negative/null responses to entries
Menu flows
Backout of possible end-user errors
Lockout keys that could alert the end user
Spelling grammar, accepted terms
Same name for same fields
Data obscured by system messages
Logical flow of screens
Standard hotkey usage
Ability to save user's work
Memory allocations
Meaningful system messages
Type ahead runaway
GUI considerations
    Icons (de)selection
    Graphic reflects data
    Backout/cancel options
    Horizontal/sidebar functions
Colors

Cursor

At first field requiring data
Skip right fields during edits
Behavior in locked on noneditable fields
Movement from one field to the next
Edit order of fields

Lists

Garbage/blanks
Too many/too few entries
Omitted/invalid delimiters
Too much /too little visible

Error Messages

User-oriented, easy to understand
Appropriate messages
Standardized messages
Account for known errors

Edits—Numeric

Valid values
Maximum/minimum or table
Leading zeroes, decimals
Proper sign
Field conforms to requirements
Defaults
Integer versus floating

Edits—Dates

Format
Display back after fill-in
Range checks, leap year, year 2000, and so on
Blank, spaces, nulls
Field conforms to requirements
Defaults

Edits—Character

Format
Range, domain
Display back after fill-in
Field conforms to requirements
Defaults
Leading/trailing blanks

Reports

Sort order
Display order
Date printed/page numbers
Data truncation versus wrapping in columns
Consistency in reports

tests, there is no formal design, nor are the tests commonly rerun as part of regression testing. The most important consideration with this type of testing is that it be documented, so that the developer will understand what test sequence was executed during random testing when a defect was discovered.

Random testing—one of the more common test strategies—does not assume any knowledge of the system under test, its specifications, or its internal design. This technique is insufficient for validating complex, safety-critical, or mission-critical software. Instead, it is best applied as a complementary test strategy with the use of other more specific and structured test strategies. Random testing can be applied throughout all test phases.

Data Integrity Testing.   The data integrity test technique verifies that data are being stored by the system in a manner where the data is not compromised by updating, restoration, or retrieval processing. Validation to be performed can include checking data fields for alphabetic and numeric characters, for information that is too long, and for correct date format (with regard to year 2000 compliance verification). Data consistency checks include both internal and external validations of essential data fields. Internal checks involve data type checking and ensure that columns are of the correct data types; external checks involve the validation of relational integrity to determine whether duplicate data are being loaded from different files. Additionally, this type of test is intended to uncover design flaws that may result in data corruption, unauthorized data access, lack of data integrity across multiple tables, and lack of adequate transaction performance.

Conversion Testing.   Conversion testing measures and reports the capability of the software to convert existing application data to new formats. Conversion accuracy is measured by comparing the test data file dump with the new database. Conversion testing will be done separately as part of the initial database load software test.

Backup and Recoverability Testing.   The backup and recoverability test technique verifies that the system meets specified backup and recoverability requirements. These tests help to prove that the database and software can recover from partial or full catastrophic failures of system hardware or software. They are conducted to determine the durability and recoverability levels of the software on each hardware platform. The aim of recovery testing is to discover the extent to which data can be recovered after a system breakdown. Does the system provide possibilities to recover all of the data or just part of it? How much can be recovered and how? Are the recovered data still correct and consistent? This type of test technique is especially appropriate for applications that must meet high reliability standards.

Configuration Testing.   Configuration testing verifies that an application operates properly on machines with different hardware and software configurations. Such tests check for compatibility issues and help to determine the optimal configuration of hardware and software to support an application.

Operational Readiness Testing.   This test technique helps determine whether a system is ready for normal production operations. All valid and invalid values are defined and applied during these tests. Each value is passed to the AUT, and the resulting behavior of the software is observed. It is very important to test all possible invalid values to verify that the AUT will meet the project's specifications.

Operational readiness tests also verify that the AUT can be installed on its targeted hardware platforms using the documentation provided by the development/test group and determine whether the application runs as expected. Uninstall instructions are tested for their impact on the environment.

Apart from general usability-related aspects, procedures supporting operational readiness tests are particularly useful for assessing the interoperability of the software system. This test technique verifies that the different software components making up the system can function correctly and communicate with one another once integrated. It also involves checks to determine whether all components that make up the AUT (such as .dll and .vbx libraries and .exe files) have been included as part of the installation package or have been installed correctly when the installed or actual production environment is tested.

User Acceptance Testing.   Getting the user involved early in the testing process pays off at this stage. This way, the users will be familiar with the software at this point rather than experiencing a rude awakening when seeing the software for the first time. The acceptance test phase includes testing performed for or by end users of the software product. Its purpose is to ensure that end users are satisfied with the functionality and performance of the software system. Commercial software products don't generally undergo customer acceptance testing, but do often allow a large number of users to receive an early copy of the software so that they can provide feedback as part of a beta test.

In a controlled environment, where a customer or end user is required to evaluate a system and make a determination of whether to accept the system, the acceptance test may be composed of test scripts performed during system testing. In an uncontrolled environment, where end users may be free to exercise a beta version of a software product at will, the purpose of the test may be to solicit end-user feedback. This feedback would then be evaluated and changes to the software product would be contemplated prior to formal release of the software.

The acceptance test phase begins only after the successful conclusion of system testing and the successful setup of a hardware and software configuration to support acceptance testing, when this configuration differs from the system test environment.

Alpha/Beta Testing.   Most software vendors use alpha and beta testing to uncover errors through testing by the end user. Customers at the developer's site, with the developer present, usually conduct alpha testing. Beta testing is usually conducted at one or more customer sites with the developers not present.

7.2.3.2   Automated Tools Supporting Black-Box Testing

When selecting black-box test techniques as part of developing the overall test program design, it is beneficial to be familiar with the various kinds of test tools available. Table 7.8 maps the black-box test techniques to various types of automated test tools. When choosing the desired black-box test techniques and making commitments to use pertinent automated test tools, the test team should keep in mind that some test tools may not be compatible with each other. Data from one tool might not be accessible from another tool, for example, if there is no import/export facility. The tools might use different databases, different database setups, and so on. Refer to Appendix B for more details on various test tools.

Table 7.8   Black-Box Techniques and Corresponding Automated Test Tools

Black-Box Test Techniques	Automated Test Tools
• Equivalence Partitioning	• Develop program code to perform tests
• Boundary Value Analysis	• Develop program code to perform tests
• Cause-effect Graphing	• Flow Graphing Tools
• Random Testing	• GUI Test Tools
• Error Guessing	• GUI Test Tools
• Regression Testing	• GUI/Server Test Tools
• Stress Testing	• Load Test Tools
• Replication Testing	• Load Test Tools
• Data Integrity Testing	• Data Analysis Tools
• Backup and Recoverability Testing	• Load Test Tools/GUI Test Tools/Server Test Tools
• Configuration Testing	• Multiplatform Test Tools
• Performance Testing	• Load Test Tools
• Functional Testing	• Load Test Tools/GUI Test Tools/Server Test Tools
• Security Testing	• Security Test Tools
• Operational Readiness Testing	• Load Test Tools/GUI Test Tools/Server Test Tools
• User Acceptance Testing	• GUI Test Tools
• Compatibility/Conversion Testing	• Load Test Tools/GUI Test Tools/Server Test Tools
• Benchmark Testing	• Benchmarking Tools
• Usability Testing	• Usability Measurement Tools
• Alpha/Beta Testing	• Load Test Tools/GUI Test Tools/Server Test Tools

7.2.4   Test Design Documentation

Test design is a complex task that should be documented in the test plan. Various documents and information that support test design activities are outlined in Table 7.9.

Table 7.9   Documents Supporting Test Design

Document	Function
Verification method as part of the requirements traceability matrix (RTM)	The proper implementation of system and software requirements can be verified in several ways. When the verification method for a requirement consists of a "test," then the associated test requirement needs to be factored into test design. Verification methods may be identified in a requirements traceability matrix developed using a spreadsheet or in an automated fashion using a requirements management (RM) tool.
Test requirements	Test requirements maintained in a document or in an automated fashion using a RM tool are essential in supporting test design.
Test procedure template	A test procedure template is used as a baseline when designing a test procedure format for a particular project.
Software application critical path diagram	This information aids in the prioritization of test procedures.
Risk analysis documentation	This information aids in the prioritization of test procedures.
Decision logic table	This table helps to understand conditional and logic flow within software modules.
Detailed test schedule	This schedule provides information on the kinds of tests that need to be performed, the planned duration of such tests, and the duration of test phases within the test life cycle. This information aids the prioritization of test procedure development.
Manual versus automated test considerations	The test team should perform and document analysis to determine the tests that will be automated and those that will be performed manually.
Test procedure design standards	The test team should refer to standard guidance on test procedure design.
Input data file requirements	The test team should perform and document analysis to determine the necessary white-box and black-box data sources. The outcome of this analysis is beneficial when designing test procedures.
Data flow diagram/ data dictionary	This information aids in the identification of test data sources.

continued

continued from page 255

Document	Function
Use case analysis	Use case scenario information is beneficial when designing test procedures. Some CASE/RM tools have mechanisms to automatically generate test procedures.
Environment	The test team should document dependencies between test procedures and the applicable technical environment. It needs to identify any differences in the technical environment for each test life cycle phase (unit, integration, system, acceptance).
Outputs	Reports, graphs, data, and test logs may serve to document test runs. They are helpful in redesigning test procedures.
Documentation of build (version) of the software	While designing test procedures, it is important to have documentation of the version of the software, including information about the functionality that the version of software contains, the fixes included in the new version of software, and so on.
Benchmarks with review and approvals	Benchmarks are the expected level of software quality that has been reviewed by management and approved. They lay the foundation for expectations of test procedures and quality of the software.
Test procedure modularity-relationship matrix	See Section 8.1 for details.

7.3 | Test Procedure Design

After test requirements have been derived, test procedure design can begin. Test procedure definition consists of the definition of logical groups of test procedures and a naming convention for the suite of test procedures. With a test procedure definition in place, each test procedure is then identified as either an automated or a manual test. The test team now has an understanding of the number of test techniques being employed, an estimate for the total number of test procedures that will be required, and estimates of the number of test procedures that will be performed manually as well as those that will be performed with an automated test tool.

The next step in the test procedure design process, as depicted in Table 7.10, is to identify the more sophisticated test procedures that must be defined further as part of detailed test design. These test procedures are flagged, and a detailed design document is prepared in support of the more sophisticated test procedures. Next, test data requirements are mapped to the defined test procedures. To create a repeatable, reusable process for producing test procedures, the test team needs to create a document that outlines test procedure design standards. Only when these standards are followed can the automated test program achieve real efficiency and success by being repeatable and maintainable.

Table 7.10   Test Procedure Design Process

Step	Description
1	**Test architecture review.** The test team reviews the test architecture to identify the relevant test techniques.
2	**Test procedure definition (development level).** A test procedure definition is constructed at the development test level that identifies the test procedure series relevant to the different design components and test techniques.
3	**Test procedure definition (system level).** A test procedure definition is constructed at the system test level that identifies the test procedure series relevant to the different test techniques.
4	**Test procedure design standards.** Design standards are adopted, and a naming convention is created that uniquely distinguishes the test procedures on the project from test procedures developed in the past or on other projects.
5	**Manual versus automated tests.** Test procedures will be depicted as being performed either manually or as part of an automated test.
6	**Test procedures flagged for detailed design.** Test procedures that stand out as more sophisticated are flagged. These test procedures are further defined as part of detailed test design.
7	**Detailed design.** Those test procedures flagged in step 6 are designed in further detail within a detailed test design file or document. This detailed design may consist of pseudocode of algorithms, preliminary test step definition, or pseudocode of test automation programs.
8	**Test data mapping.** The test procedure matrix is modified to reflect test data requirements for each test procedure.

7.3.1   Test Procedure Definition

Test procedures address preconditions for a test, data inputs necessary for the test, actions to be taken, expected results, and verification methods. Because the goal of the test effort is to find defects in the application under test while verifying that the system meets the test requirements, an effective test procedure design will consist of tests that have a high probability of finding previously undiscovered errors. A good test procedure design should not only cover expected inputs and outputs, but also attempt to account for unexpected input and output values. An effective suite of test procedures, therefore, should account for what the system should do and include tests for unexpected conditions.

Unfortunately, the scope of the test effort can be infinite, as noted in Chapter 4. As a result, the scope of the test program needs to be bounded. The exercise of developing the test procedure definition not only aids in test development, but also helps to quantify or bound the test effort. The development of the test procedure definition involves the identification of a suite of test procedures that will need to be created and executed in support of the test effort. The design exercise involves the organization of test procedures into logical groups and the definition of a naming convention for the suite of test procedures.

To construct the test procedure definition, the test must review the test architecture. Figure 7.4 depicts the test architecture of a project for which development-level tests are design-based and system-level tests are technique-based. In this example, the design components referenced were retrieved by the test team from the project's software architecture. Five components are being tested at the development level: System Management (SM-06), Security Guard (SG-07), Distributed Computing (DC-08), Support Applications (SA-09), and Active Trade Visibility (TV-10). For each of these design components, the test techniques that will be applied are noted.

At the system test level, Figure 7.4 identifies the test techniques that are being applied. For each test technique, the scope of each technique test area is defined in

Development Test Level				
SM-06	**SG-07**	**DC-08**	**SA-09**	**TV-10**
Error Handling	Error Handling	Error Handling	Error Handling	Error Handling
Memory Leak	Memory Leak	Memory Leak	Memory Leak	Memory Leak
		Path Coverage	Path Coverage	Path Coverage
		Fault Insertion	Fault Insertion	Fault Insertion
		Decision Coverage	Decision Coverage	Decision Coverage

System Test Level				
Functional	**Security**	**Stress/ Volume**	**Performance**	**Usability**
SM-06	SM-06	TV-10	TV-10	SM-06
SG-07	SG-07			SG-07
DC-08	and			DC-08
SA-09	Security Plan			SA-09
TV-10	Requirements			TV-10

Figure 7.4   Sample Test Architecture

terms of the design components involved and extraneous system requirement sources, such as security requirements outlined within a security plan.

The test architecture provides the test team with a clear picture of the test techniques that need to be employed. The test team can further identify the test requirements associated with each test technique by referring to the requirements traceability matrix. Test personnel can now readily define the test procedures that correspond to the applicable test techniques and the associated test requirements.

Table 7.11 gives a sample test procedure definition for development-level tests. Column 1 of this table identifies the series of test procedures allotted to test the

Table 7.11   Test Procedure Definition (Development Test Level)

TP Numbering Allocation	Design Component ID	Test Technique	Number of Test Procedures
100–150	SM601–SM634	Error Handling	35
151–199		Memory Leak	35
200–250	SG701–SG728	Error Handling	30
251–299		Memory Leak	30
300–350	DC801–DC848	Error Handling	50
351–399		Memory Leak	50
400–599		Path Coverage	200
600–650		Fault Insertion	50
651–849		Decision Coverage	200
850–899	SA901–SA932	Error Handling	35
900–950		Memory Leak	35
951–1150		Path Coverage	200
1151–1199		Fault Insertion	35
1200–1399		Decision Coverage	200
1400–1450	TV1001–TV1044	Error Handling	45
1451–1499		Memory Leak	45
1500–1699		Path Coverage	200
1700–1750		Fault Insertion	45
1751–1949		Decision Coverage	200
1950–1999		Integration Test	25

Total = 1,745

particular design component using the particular test technique. Column 2 identifies the software or hardware design components that need to be tested.

In the example given in Table 7.11, the design components referenced were retrieved from the test architecture. As depicted in Table 7.10, the SA component has been allocated test procedures numbering from 850 to 1399. The SA component has 32 software units (901–932) associated with it, as indicated in column 2. The test technique is listed in column 3, and the number of test procedures involved in each set of tests (row) is estimated in column 4.

Table 7.12 gives a sample test procedure definition for system-level tests. Column 1 of this table identifies the series of test procedures allotted to support each particular test technique. Column 2 identifies the test technique, which is derived from the test architecture. Although Table 7.12 includes only software tests, hardware tests could be represented as well.

Columns 3 through 5 provide information to identify the number of test procedures that will be involved at the system test level. The number of design units or functional threads that will be involved in the tests appears in column 3. A functional thread represents a useful or logical way for an end user to navigate (follow a functional path) through an application. If process flow documentation or user interface design information is available, the test team may include numbers in column 3 pertaining to threads to be used. In the example in Table 7.12, four functional threads are planned to support stress and performance testing. Usability tests will be conducted as part of functional testing, and, as a result, no additional test procedures are developed for this test technique.

The number of system requirements or use cases that are involved in the tests appears in column 4, and the number of test requirements that apply is noted in col-

Table 7.12   Test Procedure Definition (System Test Level)

TP Numbering Allocation	Test Technique	Number of Units or Threads	Number of System Requirements	Number of Test Requirements	Number of Test Procedures
2000–2399	Functional	186	220	360	360
2400–2499	Security	62	70	74	74
2500–2599	Stress	4	12	24	96
2600–2699	Performance	4	14	14	56
—	Usability	186	4	4	—
					586

umn 5. The value in the test requirements column reflects the need to have at least one test requirement per each system requirement. Note that test requirements may specify different conditions to be applied against a number of system requirements or use cases. Testing against some system requirements or use cases might necessitate that two or three different conditions be exercised. As a result, the total number of test requirements may exceed the number of system requirements or use cases for any row.

The last column in Table 7.12 gives the estimated number of test procedures that will be required for each test technique listed. For functional and security tests, there may be one test procedure for every test requirement. For stress and performance testing, four threads will be altered for each test procedure so as to examine 12 or 14 different system requirements or use cases. Additionally, the test team may choose to examine two different levels of system load for each stress and performance test—expected usage and double expected usage. By using the two levels and capturing two different measurements, the test team would be able to examine the performance degradation between the two levels.

With the test procedure definition in place for both the development and system levels, it is now time to adopt a test procedure naming convention that will uniquely distinguish the test procedures on the project from test procedures developed in the past or on other projects. Table 7.13 provides the test procedure naming scheme for a fictitious project called the WallStreet Financial Trading System (WFTS). The test procedure numbering scheme used in the previous test procedure definitions has been augmented by attaching the prefix *WF*.

Table 7.13 Test Procedure Naming Convention

Naming Convention	Design Component/ Test Technique	Test Level	Test Procedure Estimate
WF100–WF199	System Management (SM)	Development	70
WF200–WF299	Security Guard (SG)	Development	60
WF300–WF849	Distributed Computing (DC)	Development	550
WF850–WF1399	Support Applications (SA)	Development	505
WF1400–WF1949	Active Trade Visibility (TV)	Development	535
WF1950–WF1999	Integration Test	Development	25
WF2000–WF2399	Functional/Usability Tests	System	360
WF2400–WF2499	Security	System	74
WF2500–WF2599	Stress	System	96
WF2600–WF2699	Performance	System	56
WF2700	System Test Shell	System	1

7.3.2   Automated Versus Manual Test Analysis

Tests at the white-box or developmental level comprise primarily automated tests. Tests at the system level generally represent a combination of automated and manual tests. At the system level, the test team needs to review all test procedure requirements to determine which test procedures can be automated and which should be performed manually.

This section will describe an approach for deciding when to automate and when to test manually. Not everything should be automated immediately; instead, the test team should take the automation approach step by step. It is wise to base the automation effort on the test procedure execution schedule. While conducting the automated versus manual test analysis, keep in mind that it can take as much effort to create an automated test script for a complex functionality as it took to develop the code. The team should therefore analyze the automation effort. If it takes too much effort and time, a better approach might be to manually test the functionality. Remember that one of the test automation goals is to avoid duplicating the development effort.

If an automated test cannot be reused, the associated test automation effort may represent an inefficient use of test team resources. The test team needs to focus the automation effort on repetitive tasks, which can save on manual testing time and enable test engineers to focus on other, more pressing test issues and concerns.

Part of test procedure definition involves determining whether a test will be executed manually or whether the test lends itself for automation. During unit testing, it is a relatively simple task to use an automated testing tool for a variety of different kinds of tests. For example, a code coverage test tool or a memory leakage test tool may be used without much concern for identifying the various parts of the application amenable to automation. During system testing, the task of deciding what to automate is a bit more complex when using a capture/playback tool or a server test tool. Analyzing what to automate is one of the most crucial aspects of the automated testing life cycle. Several guidelines for performing the automation versus manual test analysis are outlined in this section.

7.3.2.1   Step by Step—Don't Try to Automate Everything at Once

If the test team is not experienced with the use of automated test tools across a number of different projects, it is best to take a more cautious approach for introducing automation. Avoid trying to automate everything at once. Take a step-by-step approach by automating the more obvious applications of test tools first and postponing the automation of other tests until more experience is gained with test automation.

Consider the example test team, which decided to add *all* of its test requirements into the test management tool in support of system-level testing. The test team was eager to automate every possible test. It identified 1,900 test procedures amenable to automation. When the time came to develop these test procedures, however, the test team discovered that the automated test tool was not as easy to use as had been thought. The test team also learned that the test requirements had to be loaded. It eventually called in consultants to help with the test automation effort in an attempt to stay on schedule. The test team had not fully appreciated the magnitude of the automation effort. The lesson learned in this example was that a test team should not try to automate every test without experience with the kinds of tests planned and the particular test tools purchased. It is better to apply an incremental approach toward increasing the depth and breadth of test automation.

7.3.2.2   Not Everything Can Be Tested or Automated

As noted in Chapter 2, not everything can be tested, so consequently not everything can be automated. Now that the test engineer is trying to figure out which test procedures to automate, it is important to remember this fact. For example, it's not possible to automate the verification of a print output. The test engineer must manually retrieve the output at the printer and inspect the output against the expected result. In this case, the application might have indicated a printer error when the printer was simply out of paper. In addition, it is not feasible to automate every required test given schedule and budget constraints.

7.3.2.3   Don't Lose Sight of Testing Goals

When determining what to automate, the test engineer should not lose sight of the testing goal. A test engineer could feverishly be creating fancy automated scripts that take weeks to develop and along the way lose sight of the overall testing goal: to find defects early. While developing the most eloquent automated test scripts, he might forget about executing manual tests, which could discover defects immediately. The automation effort might postpone the immediate discovery of the defects because the test engineer is too involved in creating complex automated test scripts.

7.3.2.4   Don't Duplicate Automation of the AUT's Program Logic

When analyzing what to automate, keep in mind that the test program should not duplicate the AUT's program logic. One rule of thumb to consider is that if it takes as much or more effort to automate a test script for a specific test requirement as it did to code the function, a new testing approach is required. Also, if the AUT's program logic is duplicated by the automated test tool but a problem exists with the AUT's program logic, then the automated script would not be able to determine the logic error of the AUT.

7.3.2.5   Analyze the Automation Effort

The suggestion that the initial automation effort should be based on the highest-risk functionality has one caveat. Experience shows that the highest-risk functionality is most often the most complex and thus the most difficult to automate. The test team should therefore analyze the automation effort at first. Also, whenever reviewing the effort required to automate test procedures pertaining to a functionality, it is important to be sensitive to the test schedule. If only two weeks are allotted for test development and execution, the schedule may not permit the creation of elaborate automated test scripts. In such a situation, it may be desirable not to use an automated test tool at all.

7.3.2.6   Analyze the Reuse Potential of Automated Modules

When determining which test procedures to automate, keep reuse in mind. Suppose that the test team decided to automate the highest-risk functionality of the application, but did not contemplate the level of effort required to automate the test procedures or consider the extent to which test scripts could be reused. If the scripts cannot be reused, automation efforts are wasted. Instead, the test team should examine the ability to reuse the test scripts in a subsequent software application release.

Another question to pose is whether and how much the baseline functionality would be expected to change. The test team should investigate whether the initial software baseline represents a one-time complex functionality that could change significantly with the next release. If so, automation is unlikely to produce labor-hour savings during test development. Automation may still permit test execution and regression test schedule savings, which may be more important for the particular project than overall test budget considerations.

7.3.2.7   Focus Automation on Repetitive Tasks—
Reduce the Manual Test Effort

In addition to focusing the initial test automation efforts on the high-risk functionality of a stable module, it is beneficial to consider automation of repetitive tasks. If repetitive tasks are automated, test engineers can be freed up to test more complex functionality.

Consider a test engineer who must test a requirement that states "the system should allow for adding 1 million account numbers." This task lends itself perfectly to automation. The test engineer would record the activity of adding one account number once, then modify the tool-generated program code to replace the hard-coded values with variables. A program loop could increment and test the account number, with iterations up to a specified level. This kind of script could be developed in less than 30 minutes, while it would take the test engineer weeks to test this specific requirement by manually keying in 1 million account numbers and their descriptions.

7.3.2.8 Focus Automation on Data-Driven Tasks— Reduce the Manual Test Effort

An example of automating repetitive tasks is the performance of century date testing by entering year 2000 data values. The test team should write a script that allows for reading such values from a file to perform add, delete, and update activities associated with various tests. Drawing values from such a file enables the test engineer to spend more time conducting complex and important test activities. Still another consideration when choosing to perform repetitive test tasks manually is the fact that such manual efforts are prone to errors. Individual test engineers do not perform as well on such repetitive tasks as do computers and software programs.

7.3.2.9 Consider the Test Tool's Capabilities

When evaluating which test procedures to automate, the test engineer needs to keep in mind the test tool's capabilities. What parts of the application can be automated, using what tool? The test engineer should view client-side GUI tests as different from server-side tests, because more than one test tool may be required for each environment. When deciding which parts of the GUI or server function tests to automate, the test engineer should review the capabilities of the GUI or server test tool.

7.3.2.10 Automate Test Requirements Based on Risk

One way that the test team can select which test procedures to automate relies on risk analysis. Chapter 6 discussed how the test requirements can be ordered by risk and by most critical functionality. When reviewing the defined test procedures to determine which are amenable to automation, take a look at the highest-risk functionality and its related test requirements, and analyze whether those requirements warrant priority attention with regard to the application of automation. The test team should also review the test procedure execution schedule when selecting test procedures to automate because the schedule sequence is generally based on risk, among other issues.

By applying these guidelines, the test team should be able to decide which test procedures warrant automation and which can be performed most efficiently using manual methods. Table 7.14 gives a portion of a traceability matrix that breaks down each test procedure required in system-level testing. Such tables can be updated and automatically generated using an RM tool.

RM tools such as DOORS allow the test engineer to cross-reference each test procedure (as in Table 7.14) to several other elements, such as design components

Table 7.14   Automated Versus Manual Tests

TP Number	Design Component	Test Technique	SR ID	SWR ID	TR ID	Verification Method
2330	TV1016	Functional	3.2.3c	TV029	2220	A
2331	TV1016	Functional	3.2.3c	TV030	2221	A
2332	TV1016	Functional	3.2.3c	TV031	2412	M
2333	TV1017	Functional	3.2.3d	TV032	2222	A
2334	TV1017	Functional	3.2.3d	TV033	2412	A
2335	TV1018	Functional	3.2.3e	TV034	2223	A
2336	TV1018	Functional	3.2.3e	TV035	2412	M
2337	TV1019	Functional	3.2.3f	TV036	2224	A
2338	TV1019	Functional	3.2.3g	TV037	2412	A
2339	TV1019	Functional	3.2.3g	TV038	2225	A

and test techniques, and automatically generate a report. The last column in Table 7.14 indicates whether the test will be performed using an automated test tool (A) or whether it will be performed manually (M). Note that the matrix depicted in Table 7.14 has two columns for requirement identifiers. The "SR ID" column lists the associated system requirement, while the "SWR ID" column identifies a more detailed software requirement. When detailed software requirements have not been defined for a project, the "SWR ID" column would be left blank.

7.3.3   Automated Test Design Standards

To develop a repeatable and reusable process, a document needs to be created that lists the test procedure design standards that everyone involved in the test design effort should follow. Enforcing compliance with these standards is important to achieving a successful automated test program. Test procedure design standards will promote consistency and will facilitate the integration of various test procedures into the testing framework discussed in Chapter 8. Test design for automated test procedures should seek to minimize the script development effort, minimize maintenance, and promote reusability and flexibility of scripts so as to accommodate later changes to the AUT. It should also lead to more robust test procedures.

7.3.3.1   When to Design

As mentioned throughout this book, test development and particularly test design are most efficiently performed in parallel with the application development effort. Test requirements and test design can be initially addressed during the application requirements-gathering phase. At this time, the test engineer can begin to evaluate whether each requirement can be tested or decide on another verification method to verify that a requirement has been met. During the application design phase, he or she can provide input with regard to whether an application design is testable and influence the *testability* of the resulting application code. During the unit and integration development phase, test requirements can be gathered and test design can be initiated. Note that the test design effort should not interrupt application development work, but should be integrated smoothly into the application development life cycle.

7.3.3.2   What to Design

The previous sections in this chapter described how test requirements are derived from the various system requirements, depending on the current testing phase. Now it is time to design the test procedures, based on these test requirements. As the goal of testing is to find defects in the AUT while verifying that the system application meets test requirements, well-designed test procedures should have a high probability of finding previously undiscovered errors. A good test design needs to cover expected inputs and outputs and attempt to account for unexpected input and output. Good test procedures, therefore, should not only account for what the system should do, but also include test exercises to verify performance for unexpected conditions.

Test procedures are created to verify test requirements. Tests are therefore designed to answer several questions, including the following

Has an automated versus manual test analysis been conducted and documented?

What is the sequence of actions necessary to satisfy the test requirements?

What are the inputs and expected outputs for each test procedure?

What data are required for each test procedure used?

How is the function's validity verified?

What classes of input will make for good test procedures?

Is the system particularly sensitive to certain input values?

How are the boundaries of a data class isolated?

What data rates and data volume can the system tolerate?

What effect will specific combinations of data have on system operation?

7.3.3.3   How to Design

Tests should be developed that cover the important aspects of the application. The test design needs to comply with design standards, which mandate such things as use of templates and naming conventions and define the specific elements of each test procedure. Before designing tests, the test engineer needs to employ the test design techniques discussed so far to derive test requirements. She can then use these test requirements as a baseline for test procedure design. A robust test design should make the automated test reusable and repeatable as well as helpful in identifying errors or defects in the target software. It should also tackle the high-priority tasks first. If test engineers solicit customer and end-user involvement early in test design, they may avoid surprises during test implementation.

7.3.3.4   Test Procedure Modularity

Test procedure design standards or guidelines need to address the size of a test. For example, the standard may stipulate the maximum number of steps allowed in a single test procedure. It is beneficial to limit the scope of a test procedure to a single function, so it will remain manageable and maintainable. Chapter 8 gives suggestions on how to develop *maintainable test procedures*.

7.3.3.5   Test Procedure Independence

When designing test procedures, it is a good idea to avoid data dependency between test procedures, whenever feasible. Execution of data-dependent test procedures can result in a domino effect, where the failure of one test procedure affects the next test procedure. Whenever a data dependency exists, make sure to document it in the modularity-relationship matrix, discussed in Chapter 8.

It is also important to avoid creating test procedures in a context-dependent fashion, such that where one test procedure ends, the other one begins. Whenever possible, test procedures should start and end at the same place. This approach is not always feasible, but it remains useful as a rule of thumb. Otherwise, if one test procedure doesn't complete execution and the next test procedure depends on the outcome of this test procedure to start running, testing may stall. Make sure to document any test procedure context dependency in the modularity-relationship matrix.

7.3.3.6   Scripting Language

Some automated test tools come with multiple scripting languages. The test organization will need to document within its test design standards which scripting language has been adopted. For example, SQA Suite, an automated test tool, supports both SQA Basic and Visual Basic scripting languages. The test team needs to adopt a standard language for its test procedures. This choice eliminates any dependencies and allows any member of the team to read and interpret the test procedure code that is generated.

7.3.3.7   Test Tool Database

Some automated test tools also come with a variety of databases. Test Studio, for example, allows the use of either an MS Access or SQL Anywhere database. The test team must evaluate the benefits and drawbacks to each particular database. It should consider the rate of database corruption problems encountered, any database record size limitations, requirements for ODBC connections, and the use of SQL statements. If a large test database is expected and many test engineers will require access to the database simultaneously, a more robust database, such as SQL Anywhere, should be selected. When the test effort involves only a handful of test engineers, an Access database may be sufficient.

7.3.3.8   Test Procedure Template

A test procedure design template provides a structure for the individual test. It facilitates the design of the test and promotes consistency among the automated tests. Table 7.15 provides an example of a test procedure design template. A test procedure design template should be adopted by the test team and included within the test procedure design standard. The team should use the test procedure template in conjunction with the test execution schedule and the test modularity model.

7.3.3.9   Naming Conventions

A fairly complex AUT will have a large number of test procedures associated with it. When creating these test procedures, it is very important to follow a naming convention that ensures the names of the different test procedures follow a standard format. Such conventions also help to prevent duplication of test procedure IDs and, more importantly, help avoid duplications of test procedures.

Standard naming conventions also enable the entire test team to quickly ascertain the kind of test being performed, making the entire test suite more maintainable. For example, a standard test procedure ID of ACCADD1 would be understood to mean account add test procedure 1. The naming convention may address issues such as whether positive and negative test data are tested within the same test procedure or whether the test for positive data will be separate from the test for negative data.

Test procedure naming conventions make procedures manageable and readable. Test procedures that test a particular functionality of an application should therefore have similar names. Identify the file naming limitations of the particular automated test tool being used, if any.

Table 7.15   Automated Test Procedure Template

Template Example (Automated Tests)

Test Procedure ID	ACC002
Name of Module	Monthly statement generation
Name of Function	Calculate the monthly payment
Name of Programmer	Michael Montgomery
Functional Cross-Reference	2.2.1. Create monthly statements
	Detail: Input and output from each function is tested by verifying the interactions with other functions in the module. Each function is tested for integration and all the assumptions are verified.

Function	Description	Expected Result	Date Executed	Actual Result
ID of environment setup script to be run	Env001 setup script needs to be run to play back this test procedure	Environment is in the expected state		
Starting location/ end location	Main application window			
ID or name of test procedure that must be executed prior to the start of this test procedure	ACC001 adds the new account 001	ACC001 run successfully		
Scope	Calculates interest rate of account 001			
Input	Inputs an amount and compares it to make sure the amount entered is greater than 0	Amount > 0	10/10/98	Amount > 0; pass
Action taken	Checks whether the valid interest rate is calculated and retrieved	Interest rate = expected result	10/10/98	Fails intermit- tently
Test requirement	ACC143			
External data file (or the data or state of the data that should already exist in the database being used for testing)	Test procedure ACC001 will put data in the correct state			
Name of specification file	Functional specs B			

Case Study
Naming Conventions

The best approach to making the point about the naming convention is to illustrate one through an example. A test engineer named Debbie was involved in testing a human resource information management system developed to track employee personal, leave, pay, and benefit information. The software requirements for the application were divided evenly into these four categories. There were ten developers and three test engineers on the project. The system was developed in six months and permitted two months of acceptance testing.

Debbie came up with a test procedure naming convention in an effort to communicate to the test team which approach to take when establishing the name of each test procedure. Debbie documented her assumptions, such as the notion that the AUT would use a single test database repository. Her naming conventions, which Debbie shared with both the test team and the application developers, are outlined below. Note that the seventh and eighth letters in the naming convention specify the sequence number of the test scripts.

First letter in the file naming convention:

Module to Be Tested	Letter Denoting the Module
Employee personal information	E
Employee leave information	L
Employee pay information	P
Employee benefit information	B

Second letter in the file naming convention:

Source of Test Script	Letter Denoting Source
Functional requirement	F
Detail requirement	D
System integration	S
Design verification	V

Third and fourth letters in the file naming convention:

Functionality	Letters Denoting Functionality
Add	AD
Edit	ED

continued

continued from page 271

Functionality	Letters Denoting Functionality
Security	**SE**
Menu	**MN**
Help	**HE**
Delete	**DE**
Graphs	**GR**
Report	**RE**

Fifth and sixth letters in the file naming convention:

Name of the Test Script Developer	Letters Denoting Test Engineer
Debbie Trekker	**DT**
Jack Burner	**JB**
Rick Black	**RB**

Some examples of the test procedures defined by Debbie and the test team utilizing the naming convention guideline are provided here:

Name of Test Procedure	Interpretation
EFADDT07	Employee personal information, to meet a functional requirement, for add capability, developed by Debbie Trekker and seventh in the sequence.
PVSERB13	Employee pay information, verification of development, security module, developed by Rick Black and thirteenth in the sequence

7.3.4 Manual Test Design Guidelines

Standards for test procedure design need to be enforced so that everyone involved will conform to the design guidelines. Test procedure creation standards or guidelines are necessary whether the test team is developing manual test procedures or automated test procedures.

7.3.4.1 Naming Convention

Like automated test procedures, manual test procedures should follow a naming convention.

7.3.4.2 Test Procedure Detail

The standards for manual test procedures should include an example indicating how much detail a test procedure should contain. The level of detail may be as simple as step 1—click on the File menu selection, step 2—select Open, step 3—select directory, and so on. Depending on the size of the AUT, there might not be time to write extensive test procedure descriptions, in which case the test procedure would only contain a high-level test procedure description. Also, if a test procedure is written using very low-level detail, the test procedure maintenance can become very difficult. For example, every time a button or control on the AUT changes, the test procedure would need to reflect the change.

Test Procedure ID. Use naming convention when filling in the test procedure ID.

Test Procedure Name. This field provides a longer description of the test procedure.

Test Author. Identify the author of the test procedure.

Verification Method. The method of verification can be certification, automated test, manual test, inspection, and analysis.

Action. The clear definition of goals and expectations within a test procedure helps ensure its success. Document the steps needed to create a test procedure, much as you might write pseudocode in software development. This effort forces the test engineer to clarify and document his thoughts and intentions.

Criteria/Prerequisites. Test engineers need to fill in criteria or prerequisite information that must be satisfied before the test procedure can be run, such as specific data setup requirements.

Dependency. This field is completed when the test procedure depends on a second test procedure—for example, where the second test procedure needs to be performed before the first test procedure can be carried out. This field is also completed in instances where two test procedures would conflict with one another when both are performed at the same time.

Requirement Number. This field needs to identify the requirement identification number that the test procedure is validating.

Expected Results. This field defines the expected results associated with the execution of the particular test procedure.

Actual Results. The automated test tool may have a default value for *actual result* field, which may read "Same as Expected Result." The value for the field would change if the test procedure fails.

Status. Status may include the following possibilities: testable/passed, testable/failed, not testable, partially not testable/passed, or partially not testable/failed. A test requirement could not be testable, for example, because the functionality has not been implemented yet or has been only partially implemented. The status field is updated by the test engineer following test execution. Using the status field, a database management system or RM tool (such as DOORS) automatically calculates the percentage of test procedures executed and passed versus the percentage that executed and failed. It then creates a progress report.

7.3.4.3   Expected Output

Test procedure standards can include guidelines on how the expected results are documented. The standard should address several questions. Will tests require screen prints? Will tests require sign-off by a second test engineer who observes the execution of the test?

7.3.4.4   Manual Test Procedure Example

An example of a manual test procedure created in DOORS is provided below. In this example, the details of the test procedure are either generated by the system or completed by a test engineer.

Object Level (system-generated)—Shows the hierarchy and relationships of test procedures.

Object Number (system-generated)

Object Identifier (system-generated)—Links defects to each test procedure.

Absolute Number (system-generated)

Created by (system-generated)—Gives the name of the test engineer generating the test procedure.

Created on (system-generated)—Gives a date.

Created Thru (system-generated)

Criteria/Prerequisites—Includes criteria or prerequisite information completed by the test engineer before the test procedure could be run (such as specific data setup necessary).

Expected Results—Explains the expected results of executing the test procedure.

Actual Result—Lists "Same as Expected Result" as the default, but is changed if the test procedure fails.

Last Modified by (system-generated)

Last Modified on (system-generated)

Object Heading (system-generated)

Object Short Text

Object Text

Precondition/Dependency—Filled in if the test procedure has a dependency on another test procedure or when two test procedures would conflict with each other if run at the same time.

Requirement Number—Gives the number of the system or software requirement that applies.

Status—Identifies the status of the executed test.

Step—Documents the steps needed to create a test procedure. It is equivalent of pseudocode in software development.

Test Procedure ID—Defines the naming convention used to document the test procedure ID.

Test Procedure Name—Provides a full description of the test procedure.

Verification Method—Automated or manual test, inspection, analysis, demonstration, or certification.

7.3.5 Detailed Test Design

When testing at the system level, it may be worthwhile to develop a detailed test design for sophisticated tests. These tests might involve test procedures that perform complex algorithms, consisting of both manual and automated steps, and test programming scripts that are modified for use in multiple test procedures.

The first step in the detailed design process is to review the test procedure definition at the system test level so as to flag or identify those test procedures that may warrant detailed design. The test team could begin this exercise by printing out a list of all planned system-level test procedures, including a blank column as shown in Table 7.16. This blank column can be filled in depending on whether each test procedure should be further defined as part of a detailed design effort.

With Table 7.16 in hand, the test team now has a clear picture of how many test procedures will benefit from further definition as part of a detailed design effort. The test team should next create a detailed design document, as shown in Table 7.17. The detailed design document is intended to be an aid to the test engineers while

**Table 7.16   Detailed Design Designation
                for System Test Approach**

TP Number	Design Component	Test Technique	SR ID	TR ID	A/M	Detailed Design
2330	TV1016	Functional	3.2.3c	2220	A	—
2331	TV1016	Functional	3.2.3c	2221	A	—
2332	TV1016	Functional	3.2.3c	2412	M	—
2333	TV1017	Functional	3.2.3d	2222	A	DD
2334	TV1017	Functional	3.2.3d	2412	A	—
2335	TV1018	Functional	3.2.3e	2223	A	DD
2336	TV1018	Functional	3.2.3e	2412	M	—
2337	TV1019	Functional	3.2.3f	2224	A	—
2338	TV1019	Functional	3.2.3g	2412	A	DD
2339	TV1019	Functional	3.2.3g	2225	A	—
.	.	.	.	.	.	.
.	.	.	.	.	.	.
.	.	.	.	.	.	.

Table 7.17   Detailed Design Document Outline

Section	Description
1. Introduction	Describes the purpose of the document and the parameters by which the particular test procedures were selected to be included as part of the detailed design effort.
2. Test Procedure List	Lists test procedures for which the detailed design applies. The rationale for requiring a detailed design of the test procedure should be provided.
3. Detailed Design	Includes a detailed design for each test procedure. The detailed designs should be provided in order by test procedure (alphanumeric) number.
4. Summary	Summarizes key points and notes pertaining to the design and subsequent development of the test procedures.

they develop the test procedures. As a result of the detailed design effort, test procedures should be more consistent and include all of the tests required.

The detailed design may take the form of program pseudocode when test programming is required. That is, it may be represented simply as a sequence of steps that need to be performed during testing. When programming variables and multiple data values are involved, the detailed design may include a loop to indicate an iterative series of tests involving different values plus a list or table identifying the kinds or ranges of data required for these tests.

7.3.6 Test Data Requirements

After the creation of the detailed test design, test data requirements need to be mapped against the defined test procedures. Once test data requirements are outlined, the test team should plan the means for obtaining, generating, or developing the test data. The mechanism for refreshing the test database to an original baseline state—a necessity in regression testing—also needs to be documented within the project test plan. In addition, the project test plan needs to identify the names and locations of the applicable test databases and repositories necessary to exercise software applications.

The data flow coverage testing technique described earlier in this chapter seeks to incorporate the flow of data into the selection of test procedures. Using this technique will help the test team to identify those test path segments that exhibit certain characteristics of data flows for all possible types of data objects. The following sections address test data requirements for both the white-box and black-box testing approaches.

7.3.6.1 White-Box Test Data Definition

Most testing techniques require that test data be defined and developed for the resulting test procedures. The identification of test data requirements is an important step in the definition of any test design. Test engineers should define the test data needed for activities such as executing every program statement at least once, assuring that each condition is tested, and verifying that the expected results include as many variations and combinations as possible and feasible. Test data are also required for exercising every boundary condition.

When available, data dictionary and detailed design documentation can be very helpful in identifying sample data for use in test procedures. In addition to providing data element names, definitions, and structures, the data dictionary may provide data models, edits, cardinality, formats, usage rules, ranges, data types, and domains. As part of the process of identifying test data requirements, it is beneficial to develop a matrix listing the various test procedures in one column and the test data requirements in another column. Table 7.18 presents such a matrix.

In addition to defining the requirements for test data, the test team should identify a means of developing or obtaining the necessary test data. When identifying white-box test data sources, it is worthwhile to keep in mind design-related issues, such as the use of arrays, pointers, memory allocations, and decision endpoints. When reviewing white-box (system-level) data concerns, it is also beneficial to be cognizant of possible sources of sample data. Such source documents may clarify issues and questions pertaining to the kind of test data required. Such source documentation may consist of the following items:

- Flow graphs (cyclomatic complexity)
- Data models
- Program analyzers
- Design documents, such as structure charts, decision tables, and action diagrams
- Detail function and system specifications
- Data flow diagrams
- Data dictionaries, which include data structures, data models, edit criteria, ranges, and domains
- Detailed designs, which specify arrays, networking, memory allocation, data/program structure, and decision endpoints

Table 7.18   White-Box (Development-Level) Test Data Definition

TP Number	Design Component	Data Requirement	Description
1530	TV1016	Database tables	Screen inputs
1531	TV1016	Variable input	Range of data values (see test requirement)
1532	TV1016	Variable input	Range of data values (see test requirement)
1533	TV1017	Data object	Requires a bitmapped data object
1534	TV1017	Variable input	Range of data values (see test requirement)
1535	TV1018	Database tables	Screen inputs
1536	TV1018	—	Printer output test using existing data
1537	TV1019	Database tables	Screen inputs
1538	TV1019	Data object	Requires a bitmapped data object
1539	TV1019	Variable input	Range of data values (see test requirement)
.	.	.	.
.	.	.	.
.	.	.	.

7.3.6.2 Black-Box Test Data Definition

In black-box testing, test data are required that will ensure that each system-level requirement is adequately tested and verified. A review of test data requirements should address several data concerns [11].

- Depth—volume or size of databases
- Breadth—variation of data values and data value categories
- Scope—the accuracy and completeness of the data
- Test execution data integrity—the ability to maintain data integrity
- Conditions—the ability to store particular data conditions

Depth. The test team must consider the volume or size of the database records needed for testing. It should identify whether 10 records within a database or particular table are sufficient or whether 10,000 records are necessary. Early life-cycle tests, such as unit or build verification tests, should use small, hand-crafted databases that offer maximum control and minimal disturbance. As the test effort progresses through the different phases and types of tests, the size of the database should increase to a size that is appropriate for the particular tests. For example, performance and volume tests are not meaningful if the production environment database contains 1,000,000 records but the tests are performed against a database containing only 100 records.

Breadth. Test engineers need to investigate the variation of the data values (for example, 10,000 different accounts and a number of different types of accounts). A well-designed test should incorporate variations of test data, as tests for which all data are similar will produce limited results. For example, tests may need to consider the fact that some accounts may have negative balances while others have balances in the low range (hundreds of dollars), moderate range (thousands of dollars), high range (hundreds of thousands of dollars), and very high range (tens of millions of dollars). Test must also utilize data that represent an average range.

In the case of a bank, customer accounts might be classified in several ways, such as savings, checking, loans, student, joint, and business.

Scope. The relevance of the data values must be investigated by the test team. The scope of test data includes considerations of the accuracy, relevance, and completeness of the data. For example, when testing the queries used to identify the various different kinds of accounts at a bank that have a balance due amounts greater than 100, not only should there be numerous accounts meeting this criteria, but the tests need to employ data such as reason codes, contact histories, and account owner demographic data. The inclusion of a complete set of test data enables the test team to fully validate and exercise the system and provides better results. The test engineer would also need to verify that the return of a record as a result of this query indicates a specific condition (more than 90 days due), rather than a missing value or inappropriate value.

Test Execution Data Integrity.   Another test data consideration involves the need for the test team to maintain data integrity while performing tests. The test team should be able to segregate data, modify selected data, and return the database to its initial state throughout test operations. Chapter 8, in its discussion of the test execution schedule, addresses these test data management concerns. The test team also needs to make certain that when several test engineers are performing tests at the same time, one test will not adversely affect other tests.

Another data integrity concern relates to data used in testing that cannot be accessed through the user interface. This information might include a date value that is updated from another server. These types of values and elements should be identified and a method or resource identified when data are only readable and not writeable. Following test execution, the test team needs to be able to reset the test data set to an initial (baseline) state. Chapter 8 provides more information on this type of activity.

Conditions.   Another concern pertains to the management of test data intended to reflect specific conditions. For example, health information systems commonly perform a year-end closeout. Storing data in the year-end condition enables the year-end closeout to be tested without actually entering the data for the entire year. When the test team is testing a health information system application for which the year-end closeout function has not yet been implemented as part of an operational system, it would create a set of test data to stand in for the entire year.

As part of the process of identifying test data requirements, it is beneficial to develop a matrix listing the various test procedures in one column and test data requirements in another column. When developing the list of test data requirements, the test team needs to review the black-box (system-level) data concerns mentioned earlier. Table 7.19 depicts such a matrix that cross-references test data requirements to individual test procedures.

When reviewing black-box data concerns, the test team will need to be cognizant of possible sources of sample data. Such source documents may also clarify issues and questions pertaining to the kind of test data required. Such source documents may include the following items:

- System concept documents (business proposals, mission statements, concept of operations documents)

**Table 7.19   Black-Box (System-Level)
                Test Data Definition**

TP Number	Design Component	Data Requirement	Description
2330	TV1016	Database tables	Screen inputs
2331	TV1016	Variable input	Range of data values (see test requirement)
2332	TV1016	Variable input	Range of data values (see test requirement)
2333	TV1017	Data object	Requires a bitmapped data object
2334	TV1017	Variable input	Range of data values (see test requirement)
2335	TV1018	Database tables	Screen inputs
2336	TV1018	—	Printer output test using existing data
2337	TV1019	Data object	Requires a bitmapped data object
2338	TV1019	Variable input	Range of data values (see test requirement)
2339	TV1019	Database tables	Screen inputs
.	.	.	.
.	.	.	.
.	.	.	.

- System requirements documentation (customer requirements definition, system/software specifications)

- Business rules (functional/business rule documentation)

- Entity relationship diagrams (and other system design documentation)

- Use case scenarios and data flow diagrams (and other business process documentation)

- Event partitioning (and state transition diagrams)

- Data dictionaries (and data element and interface standards, application programming interface documentation)

- Help desk logs (pertaining to existing operational systems)

- User expertise (end-user input)

- Regulations and standards (industry and corporate standards)

- White-box data definition documentation (developed by test team)

Test Data Generators.   The test team may wish to look into the use of test data generator tools, which automatically generate data for an application based on a set of rules. These rules may be derived from specifications or database documentation, or they can be manually modified by the test team to fit its particular requirements. Test data generators can quickly produce test data, if needed, for example, for the simulation of load testing. For more information on test data generators and other test performance and support tools, see Appendix B.

Test Procedure (Case) Generators.   Some test procedures may be generated automatically through the use of a test procedure generator. Some test procedure generators, such as StP/T, are highly integrated with analysis and design products and enable developers to test code functionality against system design specifications. Other test procedure generators take documented requirement information from a common repository and create test procedures automatically. Because this generation is automatic, test procedures can be created as soon as application requirements are recorded. For more information, see Appendix B.

Chapter Summary

- An effective test program incorporating the automation of software testing involves a mini-development life cycle of its own, complete with strategy and goal planning, test requirements definition, analysis, design, and coding.

- Similar to the process followed in software application development, test requirements must be specified before a test design is constructed. Test requirements need to be clearly defined and documented, so that all project personnel will understand the basis of the test effort. Test requirements are defined within requirements statements as an outcome of test requirements analysis.

- Much as in a software development effort, the test program must be mapped out and consciously designed to ensure that the test activities performed represent the most efficient and effective tests for the target system. Test program resources are limited, yet ways of testing the system are endless. A test design that graphically portrays the test effort will give project and test personnel a mental framework for the boundary and scope of the test program.

- Following test analysis, the test team develops the test program design models. The first of these design models, the test program model, consists of a graphic illustration that depicts the scope of the test program. This model typically shows the test techniques required for the dynamic test effort and outlines static test strategies.

- Having defined a test program model, the test team constructs a test architecture, which depicts the structure of the test program and defines the organization of test procedures.

- The structure of the test program (test architecture) is commonly portrayed in two different ways. One test procedure organization method, known as a design-based test architecture, logically groups test procedures with the system application design components. A second method, known as a technique-based test architecture, associates test procedures with the various kinds of test techniques represented within the test program model.

○ An understanding of test techniques is necessary when developing test designs and test program design models. Test personnel need to be familiar with the test techniques associated with the white-box and black-box test approach methods. White-box test techniques are aimed at exercising the software program's internal workings, while black-box techniques generally compare the application's behavior with requirements via established, public interfaces.

○ When selecting white-box and black-box test techniques as part of the development of the overall test program design, it is beneficial to be familiar with the kinds of test tools that are available to support the development and performance of related test procedures.

○ The exercise of developing the test procedure definition not only aids in test development, but also helps to quantify or bound the test effort. The development of the test procedure definition involves the identification of the suite of test procedures that will ultimately need to be created and executed. The design exercise involves the organization of test procedures into logical groups and the definition of a naming convention for the suite of test procedures.

○ At the system level, it may be worthwhile to develop a detailed test design for sophisticated tests. These tests might include test procedures that perform complex algorithms, procedures that consist of both manual and automated steps, and test programming scripts that are modified for use in multiple test procedures. The first step in the detailed design process is to review the test procedure definition at the system test level. This review enables the test team to identify those test procedures that stand out as being more sophisticated and should therefore be defined further as part of detailed test design.

○ Detailed test design may take the form of test program pseudocode, when test programming is required. The detailed design may be represented simply as a sequence of steps that need to be performed during testing. When programming variables and multiple data values are involved, the detailed design may include a loop to carry out an iterative series of tests involving different values plus a list or table identifying the kinds of data or ranges of data required for the test.

○ After the detailed test design is complete, test data requirements need to be mapped against the defined test procedures. Once test data requirements are outlined, the test team needs to plan the means for obtaining, generating, or developing the test data.

References

1. Book examples include Boris Beizer's *Software Testing Techniques* and John Joseph Chilenski's *Applicability of Modified Condition/Decision Coverage to Software Testing,* to mention only a few.

2. *Software Considerations in Airborne Systems and Equipment Certification.* RTCA SC-167, EUROCAE WG-12, Washington, DC: RTCA, 1992.

3. Myers, G.J. *The Art of Software Testing.* New York: John Wiley and Sons, 1979.

4. Ibid.

5. Ibid.

6. Ntafos, S. "A Comparison of Some Structural Testing Strategies." *IEEE Transactions on Software Engineering* 1988; 14:868–874.

7. Beizer, B. *Software Testing Techniques,* 2nd ed. New York: Van Nostrand Reinhold, 1990.

8. See note 7.

9. Adapted from Myers, G.J. *The Art of Software Testing.* New York: John Wiley and Sons, 1979.

10. Adapted from Myers, G.J. *The Art of Software Testing.* New York: John Wiley and Sons, 1979.

11. Adapted from SQA Suite Process, January 1996. (See www.rational.com.)

Chapter 8

Test Development

Continuing the mini-development life cycle.

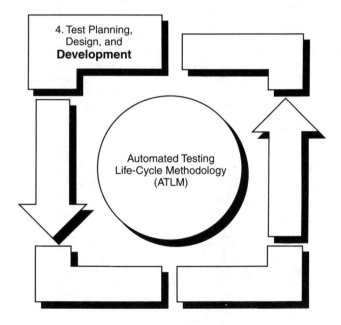

Chapter 7 outlined the approach for performing test analysis and design. The test team is now ready to perform test development. Table 8.1 correlates the development process phases to the test process phases. In the table, the testing processes and steps are strategically aligned with the development process. The execution of these steps results in the refinement of test procedures at the same time that developers are creating the software modules. Automated and/or manual test procedures

Table 8.1   Development–Test Relationship

Phase	Development Process	Test Process
Module (Unit) Development	Design module from requirements.	Perform test planning and test environment setup.
	Code module.	Create test design and develop test data.
	Debug module.	Write test scripts or record test scenario using module.
	Unit test module.	Debug automated test script by running against module. Use tools that support unit testing.
	Correct defects.	Rerun automated test script to perform regression testing as defects are corrected.
Integration	Build system by connecting modules. Perform integration testing connected modules. Review trouble reports.	Combine unit test scripts and add new scripts that demonstrate module interconnectivity. Use a test tool to support automated integration testing.
	Correct defects and update defect status.	Rerun automated test scripts as part of regression testing as defects are corrected.
System Test	Review trouble reports.	Integrate automated test scripts into system-level test procedures, where possible, and develop additional system-level test procedures. Execute system test and record test results.
	Correct defects and update defect status.	Rerun automated test scripts as part of regression testing as defects are corrected.
Acceptance Test	Review incident reports.	Perform a subset of system tests as part of user acceptance testing.
	Correct defects.	Rerun automated test scripts as part of regression testing as defects are corrected.

are developed during the integration test phase with the intention of reusing them during the system test phase.

Many preparation activities need to take place before test development can begin. The test development architecture (Figure 8.1) provides the test team with a clear picture of the test development preparation activities or building blocks necessary for the efficient creation of test procedures. As described in Section 8.1, the test team will need to modify and tailor this sample test development architecture to reflect the priorities of their particular project. These setup and preparation activities include tracking and management of test environment setup activities, where material procurements may have long lead times. This preparation activity was described in detail within Chapter 6. Prior to the commencement of test development, the test team also needs to identify the potential for reuse of already-existing test procedures and scripts within the automation infrastructure (reuse library).

The test team should develop test procedures to meet the test procedure development/execution schedule. This schedule allocates personnel resources and reflects development due dates, among other things. The test team needs to monitor development progress and produce progress status reports. Prior to the creation of a complete suite of test procedures, it performs a modularity relationship analysis. The results of this analysis help to define data dependencies, plan for workflow dependencies between tests, and identify common scripts that can be repeatedly applied to the test effort. As test procedures are being developed, the test team should perform configuration control for the entire testbed, including the test design, test scripts, and test data, as well as for each individual test procedure. The testbed needs to be baselined using a configuration management tool.

Test development involves the creation of test procedures that are maintainable, reusable, simple, and robust, which in itself can prove as challenging as the development of the application-under-test (AUT). Test procedure development standards need to be in place, supporting structured and consistent development of automated tests. Such standards can be based on the scripting language standards of a particular test tool. For example, Rational's Robot uses SQABasic, a Visual Basic-like scripting language; the script development standards could therefore be based on the Visual Basic development standards.

Usually internal development standards exist that can be followed if the organization chooses to work in a language similar to the tool's scripting language. The adoption or slight modification of existing development standards generally represents a better approach than creating a standard from scratch. If no development standards exist within the organization for the particular tool scripting language, then the test team must develop script development guidelines. Section 8.2 provides an example of test development standards and guidelines. Such guidelines can include directions on *context independence,* which specifies the particular place where a test procedure should start and where it should end. Additionally, modularity and reusability guidelines need to be addressed.

By developing test procedures based on the development guidelines described in Section 8.2, the test team creates the initial building blocks for an automation infrastructure. The automation infrastructure, described in detail in Section 8.3, will eventually contain a library of common, reusable scripts. Throughout the test effort and in future releases, the test engineer can use the automation infrastructure to support reuse of archived test procedures, minimize duplication, and thus enhance the entire automation effort.

8.1 | Test Development Architecture

Test team members responsible for test development need to be prepared with the proper materials. These personnel should follow a test development architecture that, for example, lists the test procedures assigned and the outcomes of automated versus manual test analysis. Additionally, the test engineers should adhere to the test procedure development and execution schedule, test design information, automated test tool user manuals, and test procedure development guidelines. Armed with the proper instructions, documentation, and guidelines, they will have a foundation of information that allows them to develop a more cohesive and structured set of test procedures. Note that the test team's ability to repeat a process and repeatedly demonstrate the strength of a test program depends on the availability of documented processes and standard guidelines such as the test development architecture.

Figure 8.1 illustrates the major activities to be performed as part of one such test development architecture. Test development starts with test environment setup and preparation activities. Once they are concluded, the test team needs to ensure that information necessary to support development has been documented or gathered. It will need to modify and tailor the sample test development architecture depicted in Figure 8.1 to better reflect the priorities of its particular project.

8.1.1 Technical Environment

Several setup activities precede the actual test procedure development. The test development activity needs to be supported by a technical environment that facilitates the development of test procedures. This test environment must be set up and ready to go before such development begins. It represents the technical environment, which may include facility resources as well as the hardware and software necessary to support test development and execution. The test team needs to ensure that enough workstations are available to support the entire team. The various elements of the test environment need to be outlined within the test plan, as discussed in Chapter 6.

Environment setup activities can also include the use of an environment setup script, as described in Section 8.3, as well as the calibration of the test tool to match the specific environment. When test tool compatibility problems arise with the AUT, work-around solutions must be identified. When developing test procedures,

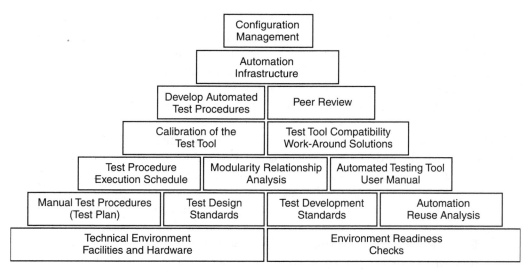

Figure 8.1   Building Blocks of the Test Development Architecture

the schedule for developing test procedures should be consistent with the test execution schedule. It is also important that the test team follow test procedure development guidelines.

The test team will need to ensure that the proper test room or laboratory facilities are reserved and set up. Once the physical environment is established, the test team must verify that all necessary equipment is installed and operational. Recall that in Chapter 6, the test plan defined the required technical environment and addressed test environment planning. Also within the test environment section of the test plan, the test team should have already identified operational support required to install and check out the operational readiness of the technical environment. These staff members must likewise ensure that operational support activities have been properly scheduled and must monitor progress of these tasks.

Specific tasks and potential issues outlined in the test plan should have been addressed and resolved at this point. Such issues could include network installation, network server configuration and allocated disk space, network access privileges, required desktop computer processing speed and memory, number and types of desktop computers (clients), video resolution requirements, and any additional software required to support the application, such as browser software. Automated test tools should have been scheduled for installation and assessment. These tools now should be configured to support the test team and operate within the specific test environment.

As part of the test environment setup activity, the test team tracks and manages test environment setup activities, where material procurements may have long lead times. These activities include the scheduling and tracking environment setup activities; the installation of test environment hardware, software, and network resources; the integration and validation of test environment resources; the procurement and refinement of test databases; and the development of environment setup scripts and testbed scripts.

The hardware supporting the test environment must be able to ensure complete functionality of the production application and to support performance analysis. In cases where the test environment uses hardware resources that also support other development or management activities, special arrangements may be necessary during actual performance testing. The hardware configuration supporting the test environment needs to be designed to support processing, storage, and retrieval activities, which may be performed across a local or wide area network, reflecting the target environment. During system testing, the software configuration loaded within the test environment must be a complete, fully integrated release with no patches and no disabled sections.

The test environment design also must account for stress testing requirements. Stress and load tests may require the use of multiple workstations to run multiple test procedures simultaneously. Some automated test tools include a virtual user simulation functionality that eliminates or greatly minimizes the need for multiple workstations under these circumstances.

Test data will need to be obtained with enough lead time to allow their refinement and manipulation so as to better satisfy testing requirements. Data preparation activities include the identification of conversion data requirements, preprocessing of raw data files, loading of temporary tables (possibly in a relational database management system format), and performance of consistency checks. Identifying conversion data requirements involves performing in-depth analysis on data elements, which includes defining data mapping criteria, clarifying data element definitions, confirming primary keys, and defining data-acceptable parameters.

During test planning, the test team defined and scheduled the test environment activities. Now it tracks the test environment setup activities. That is, it identifies the resources required to install hardware, software, and network resources into the test environment and integrate the test environment resources. The test environment materials and the AUT need to be baselined within a configuration management tool. Other test environment materials may include test data and test processes.

The test team will need to obtain and modify any test databases necessary to exercise software applications, and develop environment setup scripts and testbed scripts. In addition, it should perform product reviews and validate all test source materials. The location of the test environment for each project or task should be specified in the test plan for each project. Early identification of the test site is critical to cost-effective test environment planning and development.

8.1.2 Environment Readiness Checks

Once the environment setup and tracking activities have been performed, the test team is then ready to perform some final environment readiness checks. These checks include a review of the organization's automation infrastructure (reuse library) to ascertain whether existing test program code can be applied to the project.

The test team should check the status of any software functionality that pertains to its test development assignment and ascertain the stability of the AUT. When an application is constantly changing—for example, in the case of GUI test automation development—automation efforts might prove futile. Experience shows that it is best to start automating when parts of the AUT are somewhat stable, meaning that functionality does not change constantly with each release. Ideally, a prototype of the application will exist and the test engineer can develop the object table layout for table-driven scripts. (See Section 8.3 for more detail on the use of table-driven scripts.)

The ATLM supports the iterative development approach, where a system development life cycle contains multiple iterative builds. This iterative methodology, which involves a "design a little, code a little, test a little" approach [1], is applied to each build. Before starting to execute test procedures, the test team must verify that the correct version of AUT is installed. In a GUI application, the version is usually updated in the *About* selection of the opening GUI menu.

8.1.3 Automation Framework Reuse Analysis

Prior to the commencement of test development, the test team needs to analyze the potential for reusing existing test procedures and scripts within the automation infrastructure (reuse library) that might already exist (if this project is not a first-time automation effort). In Chapter 7, the test design effort identified which test procedures were to be performed manually and which were to be automated. For each test procedure that will be supported by an automated test tool, the test team now needs to research the automation infrastructure (reuse library) to determine the extent to which existing test procedures can be reused. The test team will find it beneficial to modify the matrix that was already created during test design (see Table 7.15) and add a column listing existing test script library assets (see Table 8.2) that potentially can support the current test development. The outcome of this analysis provides input into the test modularity matrix.

Table 8.2   Automation Reuse Analysis

TP Number	Design Component	Test Technique	SR ID	SWR ID	TR ID	A/M	Reuse Asset
2330	TV1016	Functional	3.2.3c	TV029	2220	A	—
2331	TV1016	Functional	3.2.3c	TV030	2221	A	MMS2079
2332	TV1016	Functional	3.2.3c	TV031	2412	M	—
2333	TV1017	Functional	3.2.3d	TV032	2222	A	—
2334	TV1017	Functional	3.2.3d	TV033	2412	A	—
2335	TV1018	Functional	3.2.3e	TV034	2223	A	LW2862
2336	TV1018	Functional	3.2.3e	TV035	2412	M	—
2337	TV1019	Functional	3.2.3f	TV036	2224	A	—
2338	TV1019	Functional	3.2.3g	TV037	2412	A	ST2091
2339	TV1019	Functional	3.2.3g	TV038	2225	A	ST2092

Table 8.2 gives a sample matrix depicting the results of a reuse analysis performed by one test team. In this example, the test team identified four test scripts available within the automation infrastructure that might be reusable as part of the current project. These test procedures were originally defined within the test procedure definition that was developed as part of the test design effort.

To enhance the usefulness of test script library assets within the automation infrastructure, the test team should be careful to adhere to test procedure creation standards, which are discussed in Section 8.3.

8.1.4   Test Procedure Development/Execution Schedule

The test procedure development/execution schedule is prepared by the test team as a means to identify the timeframe for developing and executing the various tests. The schedule takes into account various factors, such as the following:

- The individuals responsible for each particular test activity are identified.
- Setup activities are documented.
- Sequence and dependencies are included.
- Testing will accommodate the various processing cycles that pertain to the application.
- Test procedures that could potentially conflict with one another are documented.
- Test engineers are allowed to work independently.

- Test procedures can be grouped according to specific business functions.

- Test procedures will be organized in such a way that effort is not duplicated.

- The test procedures' organization considers priorities and risks assigned to tests.

- A plan for various testing phases and each activity in a particular phase exists.

The schedule aids in *identifying the individual(s) responsible* for each particular test activity. By defining a detailed test procedure development/execution schedule, the test team can help prevent duplication of test effort by personnel. The test procedure modularity-relationship model (described later in this chapter) is essential to developing this schedule.

The test procedure development/execution schedule needs to include test setup activities, test procedure sequences, and cleanup activities. *Setup activities need to be documented* to ensure that they adhere to configuration management standards, as it is essential that testing be performed within a controlled environment. For example, the test engineer needs to be able to return the environment to its original state after executing a particular test.

Test procedure *sequence and dependencies* need to be documented, because for many application test efforts, a particular function cannot be executed until a previous function has produced the necessary data setup. For example, a security access control cannot be verified until the security access privilege has been established. For a financial management application, a financial securities instrument cannot be transferred to a bank until the securities instrument has first been posted to an account and verified. Additionally, the financial management application might require a transaction summary or end-of-day report produced at the conclusion of business, which identifies the number of securities or funds delivered to the Federal Reserve for a particular day. Such an end-of-day summary report cannot be constructed and verified until the prerequisite was met—that is, until an entire day's transactions has been properly recorded.

The test procedure development/execution schedule must *accommodate testing that examines the various processing cycles pertaining to the application*. For example, a health information management system may need to perform daily, weekly, quarterly, and annual claim report transaction summaries. The setup activities required to produce and test a yearly claim summary report need to be included in the test procedure development and execution schedule.

The test procedure development/execution schedule will also need to *document all test procedures that could potentially create conflicts*, thereby allowing test engineers to execute functionality and workflow without running into unknown dependencies or wrongfully affecting one another's outcome. It is beneficial to determine the order or sequence in which specific transactions must be tested so as to better accommodate control or workflow.

Test engineers will need to be able to work independently and must be able to share the same data or database. A test procedure development/execution schedule helps ensure that one test engineer does not modify or affect the data being manipulated by another test engineer. Such interference could potentially invalidate the test results produced by one or both of these team members. As noted earlier, the schedule also identifies the individuals who will be developing and performing the various test procedures and the sequence for when particular test procedures are executed; the goal is to avoid execution mishaps and to clarify roles and responsibilities.

One of the primary tasks to be undertaken when developing the test procedure development and execution schedule pertains to organizing tests into groups. For example, *tests may be grouped according to the specific business function*. By scheduling separate groups of tests, business functionality A, for example, can be assigned to test engineer Cordula. Business functionality B, on the other hand, can be assigned to test engineer Thomas. A third business functionality, C, could be assigned to test engineer Karl. By assigning specific functionality to a separate test engineer, the test manager will be better able to monitor progress and check status by setting due dates for the completion of each test procedure.

It is important that *automated test procedures be organized in such a way that effort is not duplicated*. The test team should review the test plan and the test design to verify that the results of test analysis and design are incorporated into the test schedule. When developing the test procedure execution schedule, the test team should be aware of the test schedule considerations discussed below.

The test procedure development/execution schedule must take into consideration *the priorities and risks* assigned to the various tests. The test schedule should place greater emphasis on execution of mission-critical and high-risk functionality. These tests should be performed early in the schedule, giving more time for this functionality to be tested and regression-tested as necessary. The test procedure execution schedule will need to document the breakdown of the *various testing phases and discuss the activities in each phase* (that is, functional, regression, or performance testing).

When defining the test procedure execution schedule, the test team must allow time *to accommodate multiple iterations of test execution*, time to correct documented discrepancies, and time to carry out the regression testing required to verify the proper implementation of software fixes. It is also important to plan for the release of multiple application builds that incorporate software fixes. As a result, the test procedure execution schedule must reflect the planned delivery for each new build, which may be daily or weekly, and may be defined with a detailed development schedule.

Inevitably, changes will occur within the project schedule or within the detailed development schedule. The test team must monitor these changes and *alter the test schedule* accordingly. The project schedule may slip in one place or the timeframe for system test activities may be shortened in another situation. Other modifications to the test schedule arise when functionality that was supposed to be implemented in a particular release is omitted instead. Additionally, personnel who had been assigned to support test activities may be reassigned.

Given the variety of changes that require adjustments to the test schedule, it is beneficial to baseline the original test schedule and each subsequent major change to the schedule. Each schedule change needs to be documented, using schedule-tracking systems such as the earned value management system discussed in Chapter 9. The original test schedule and subsequent baselined changes to it should be reviewed with the proper authority to obtain approval for each version of the schedule. Formal approval of each test schedule baseline helps to keep performance expectations in line with test program implementation.

The test procedure execution schedule can be created using a project scheduling tool or developed within a spreadsheet or a table using a word-processing package, as noted in Table 8.3. Test procedure execution is initiated after the execution of the environment setup scripts, which are also noted on this schedule. These scripts perform a variety of functions, such as setting up video resolution, shutting down screen savers, and checking and setting the date format.

8.1.5 Modularity-Relationship Analysis

Prior to the creation of a complete suite of test procedures, it is very important to create a layout or logic flow that shows the interrelationship of the various scripts. This logic flow should reflect the test plan and the test team's goals. It consists of the high-level design of the scripts and takes their integration into account. It can be based on a use case model or a system sequence diagram among other workflow artifacts. An important reason for performing this modularity-relationship analysis is to identify any data dependencies or workflow dependencies between automated test procedures. The test engineer needs to be aware of the state of the data when performing tests. For example, a record must exist before it can be updated or deleted. Thus the test team must determine which scripts need to be run together in a particular sequence using the modularity-relationship matrix.

The modularity-relationship analysis also enables the test team to plan for dependencies between tests and to avoid scenarios where failure of one test procedure affects a subsequent test procedure. In addition, it allows test engineers to identify common scripts that can be repeatedly applied to the test effort.

Table 8.3   Test Procedure Execution Schedule—System Test Phase

Build 1.5: System Test Procedure Execution Schedule

Test Procedure	Test Engineer	Test Procedure Dependency	Test Data File
Setup001	Thomas	N/A	N/A
ACC0001–ACC0005	Thomas	Setup001 has to execute successfully	addacc.txt
ACC0006–ACC0020	Perpetua	ACC0001 has to execute successfully	modacc.txt
ACC0020–ACC0030	Karl	ACC0001–ACC0005 have to execute successfully	delacc.txt
PRIVSEC01	Cordula	N/A	privsec.txt
SEC0001	Cordula	PRIVSEC has to execute successfully	read modsec.txt wrtversec.txt
SEC0002	Felicitas	SEC0001 has to execute successfully	versec.txt
SEC0003	Felicitas	SEC0002 has to execute successfully	versec.txt
EndofDay01	Perpetua	ACC0001–ACC0030, SEC0001–SEC0003, and PRIVSEC all have to execute successfully	eod.txt
.	.	.	.
.	.	.	.
.	.	.	.

The first step in creating the modularity-relationship matrix involves the creation of a visual flow using boxes for each section of the application under test. Next, the test engineer breaks down each box into smaller boxes or lists each component or screen for each section of the AUT. This process will bring to light dependencies (preconditions and post-conditions) that are key to developing, debugging, and maintaining the scripts.

Status of Test Data after Execution	Environment Setup Activity	Estimated Execution Time	Execution Date/Time
Test data are populated	Data is baselined; see test procedure Setup001 for more detail	0.25 hr	10/11 7:30 A.M.
Additional accounts	Access privileges to environment; baselined test data	1 hr	10/11 8 A.M.
Modified accounts	No new activity necessary	1 hr	10/11 9 A.M.
Deleted accounts	No new activity necessary	1 hr	10/11 10 A.M.
Adds security; modify privileges for various test engineers	Access privileges to environment; baselined test data	0.5 hr	10/11 8 A.M.
Additional securities	No new activity necessary	1 hr	10/11 9 A.M.
Verified securities	No new activity necessary	1 hr	10/11 10 A.M.
Deliver securities	No new activity necessary	1 hr	10/11 11 A.M.
Run end-of-day audit report	No new activity necessary	2 hr	10/11 5 P.M.
.	. .	.	.
.	.	.	.
.	.	.	.

The relationships between test scripts are reflected within a modularity-relationship matrix, as depicted in Table 8.4. Such a matrix graphically represents how test scripts will interact with one another and how they are related to one another, either by script modularity or via functional hierarchy. This graphical representation allows test engineers to identify opportunities for script reuse, thereby minimizing the effort required to build and maintain test scripts.

Table 8.4   Sample Modularity-Relationship Matrix

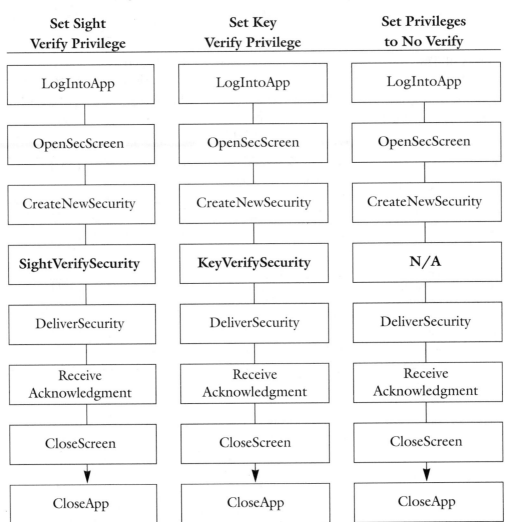

Set Sight Verify Privilege	Set Key Verify Privilege	Set Privileges to No Verify
LogIntoApp	LogIntoApp	LogIntoApp
OpenSecScreen	OpenSecScreen	OpenSecScreen
CreateNewSecurity	CreateNewSecurity	CreateNewSecurity
SightVerifySecurity	**KeyVerifySecurity**	**N/A**
DeliverSecurity	DeliverSecurity	DeliverSecurity
Receive Acknowledgment	Receive Acknowledgment	Receive Acknowledgment
CloseScreen	CloseScreen	CloseScreen
CloseApp	CloseApp	CloseApp

The test procedure modularity-relationship analysis will also help the test team organize the proper sequence of test execution, so that test procedures can be correctly linked together and played back in specific order to ensure continuous flow of playback and maximum benefit. Modularity definition helps the team associate test procedures to the application design by using naming conventions and following the design hierarchy.

The modularity-relationship matrix shows how the various test procedures fit together and indicates how test procedures may be reused or modified. This matrix includes information such as the test procedure ID or names of the test procedures that must be executed prior to the start of a particular test procedure, as well as the data (or state of the data) that should already exist in the database being used for testing. It therefore helps to identify patterns of similar actions or events that are used by one or more transactions.

8.1.6 Explanation of the Sample Modularity-Relationship Matrix

In the modularity-relationship matrix portrayed in Table 8.4, the Shell Procedure (Wrapper) Name column identifies the name of the parent procedure that calls subordinate procedures. In this case, the parent procedures are called "Set Sight Verify Privilege," "Set Key Verify Privilege," and "Set Privilege to No Verify." The parent shell procedure consists of a single main procedure that calls many procedures. The three shell procedures identified in Table 8.4—Set Sight Verify Privilege, Set Key Verify Privilege, and Set Privileges to No Verify—call multiple test procedures from within each shell procedure. Even though the shell procedures primarily invoke the same test procedures (with the exception of a single test procedure), they are accomplishing different tests and support different requirements or use case scenarios. This example shows how shell procedures can prove very effective in testing various requirements by simply adding or deleting a specific test procedure.

Each of the first three shell procedures logs into the application under test and opens a screen that contains information about a financial instrument called a security. The three shell procedures differ in that each tests different privileges that are required to verify a security (financial instrument). The first shell procedure tests system security using a *sight verify* function, where the privilege has been set up so that a user must verify the correctness of a security by visual examination. For example, the script conducts object property comparisons. The second shell script tests the *key verify* privilege, where a user (the script) has to reenter some values to verify the security. The third shell script tests the delivery of the security where no privilege has been established, which could apply when a particular user has special access authority. The detailed descriptions below outline the functions of the first three shell procedures depicted in Table 8.4.

```
Shell Procedure called Set Sight Verify Privilege, as created using
Rational's TestStudio.
********
Sub Main
 Dim Result As Integer

CallProcedure "LogIntoApp"
CallProcedure "OpenSecScreen"
CallProcedure "SetSightVerifyPrivilege"
CallProcedure "CreateNewSecurity"
```

```
CallProcedure "SightVerifySecurity"
CallProcedure "DeliverSecurity"
CallProcedure "ReceiveAcknowledgment"
CallProcedure "CloseScreen"
CallProcedures "CloseApp"

End Sub
********
```

Shell Procedure called *Set Key Verify Privilege*, as created using Rational's TestStudio.

```
********
Sub Main
   Dim Result As Integer

CallProcedure "LogIntoApp"
CallProcedure "OpenSecScreen"
CallProcedure "SetKeyVerifyPrivilege"
CallProcedure "CreateNewSecurity"
CallProcedure "KeyVerifySecurity"
CallProcedure "DeliverSecurity"
CallProcedure "ReceiveAcknowledgment"
CallProcedure "CloseScreen"
CallProcedures "CloseApp"

End Sub
********
```

Shell Procedure called *Set No Verify Privilege,* as created using Rational's TestStudio.

```
********
Sub Main
   Dim Result As Integer

CallProcedure "LogIntoApp"
CallProcedure "OpenSecScreen"
CallProcedure "SetNoPrivilege"
CallProcedure "CreateNewSecurity"
CallProcedure "DeliverSecurity"
CallProcedure "ReceiveAcknowledgment"
CallProcedure "CloseScreen"
CallProcedures "CloseApp"

End Sub
********
```

Although these shell procedures appear very similar, they accomplish different tests simply by adding or deleting one subordinate procedure. They also provide a good example of the reuse of test procedures. The purpose of each test procedure called by the three shell procedures is described below.

- `LogIntoApp` logs the user into the application and verifies that the password is correct. Error checking is built in.

- `OpenSecScreen` opens the security (financial instrument) screen, verifies the menu, and verifies that the correct screen is open and the security screen hasn't changed from the previous build. Error checking is built in.

- `SetSightVerifyPrivilege` sets the security (financial instrument) verify privilege to "sight verify," meaning that sight verification is necessary before a security can be delivered to the Federal Reserve Bank. Error checking is built in.

- `KeyVerifySecurity` sets the security (financial instrument) verify privilege to "key verify," meaning that a specific data field has to be verified by rekeying specific information before a security can be delivered to the Federal Reserve Bank. Error checking is built in.

- `SetNoPrivilege` resets the security (financial instrument) verify privilege to none, meaning that no verification is necessary before a security can be delivered to the Federal Reserve Bank. Error checking is built in.

- `CreateNewSecurity` creates a new security. Error checking is built in.

- `SightVerifySecurity` uses the sight verify method by checking the object properties of the security to be delivered. If the object properties test passes, it goes on to next procedure; if it fails, it sends the user an error message and the procedure ends. Other error checking is built in.

- `KeyVerifySecurity` uses the "key verify" method by automatically rekeying the information and then checking the object properties of the security to be delivered. If the object properties test passes, it goes on to the next procedure; if it fails, it sends the user an error message and the procedure ends. Other error checking is built in.

- `DeliverSecurity` delivers the security to the Federal Reserve Bank.

- `ReceiveAcknowledgment` receives acknowledgment of receipt from the Federal Reserve Bank. Error checking is built in.

- `CloseScreen` closes the security screen. Error checking is built in.

- `CloseApp` closes the application. Error checking is built in.

Student Question 8.1

The test procedures in the sample modularity-relationship matrix could be sequenced in other ways. Give examples.

8.1.7   Calibration of the Test Tool

At this stage, the test team has established the required test environment and, during the test design effort, has defined test data requirements and specified the scripting language. Poised to begin test development, the test team first needs to calibrate the test tool.

In Chapter 4, the test team worked out tool-related third-party custom control (widget) issues. Now, when calibrating the automated test tool to match the environment, it will have to decide upon the tool *playback speed*, even though the playback speed can change from one test procedure to the next. Many tools allow for modification of the playback speed. This capability is important, because the test engineer might want to slow down the playback speed when playing back the script for an end user or to allow for synchronization.

The test team needs to make other decisions, such as what to do when an unexpected active window is observed, and then adjust the automated test tool accordingly. A common problem for unattended testing involves failures that have the domino effect. For example, following the failure of one test, an unexpected active window might appear displaying an error message and leaving the application in an unexpected state. Some tools, such as Test Studio, can handle these unexpected active windows by allowing the test engineer to set a parameter that instructs the test tool to automatically shut down unexpected windows during playback. As a result, the subsequent test scripts continue to execute even though an unexpected window has been encountered.

When the automated test tool does not have a provision for overcoming such failures, then the domino effect is often observed. When the product is left in an unexpected state, subsequent script logic cannot execute because the error message continues to be displayed. To run the test suite, the product must be reset and the test suite must be restarted following the test failure. Successive failures will require the tests to be restarted repeatedly. Therefore, it is beneficial if the chosen test tool provides for automatic handling of unexpected active windows and other unexpected application states.

8.1.8   Compatibility Work-Around Solutions

As previously mentioned, associated with the effort to verify whether an automated test tool is compatible with the AUT, the test team may wish to consider work-around solutions for any incompatibility problems that arise. When a previous version of the application already exists (or a prototype), the test engineer needs to analyze the application to determine which particular parts of the application should and can be supported by automated tests. He or she can install the test tool on the workstation where the application resides and conduct a preliminary compatibility analysis. A good understanding of the AUT is beneficial when contemplating a work-around solution to an incompatibility problem.

A particular test tool might work well under one operating system, but behave differently on another. It is very important to test for compatibility between the automated tools and the third-party controls or widgets that are in use for the particular AUT. The automated test tool might not recognize some third-party objects; therefore the test engineer may need to develop extensive work-around solutions for it. Some of these fixes might take time to develop, so it is worthwhile to work on these solutions concurrently with application development.

Case Study
Incompatibility Work-Around Solution

Brett, a test engineer, was responsible for testing an application that used a third-party control made by a company called ABX. Brett learned that the company had stopped supporting the ABX Grid (a data grid displayed on the screen) and that the automated test tool did not have built-in support for the outdated grid and could not recognize the ABX Grid. Brett and the other test engineers on his team therefore developed a work-around solution.

The team added a flag to the source code similar to the following algorithm:

Tool Incompatibility Work-Around Solution Example

```
If flag= true then   (test mode is set)
 write  data to a file
else   (not in test mode)
write  data to the Agility Grid on the screen
```

When the team was in a test mode, the flag was set to be true and the program was instructed to dump the output to a file. A test script could therefore perform a file comparison between the baseline data file and the new data file and identify any discrepancies. When the team was not in a test mode, the flag was set to be false and the data were displayed to the application's ABX Grid. This solution was not particularly elegant, as values were being hard-coded and had to be changed repeatedly. Nevertheless, it worked for this small testing effort.

The solution was one of many work-around possibilities that could have been implemented. For example, the team could have used an SQL query in a script and had the script compare the data output of the SQL query with the expected result.

8.1.9   Manual Execution of Test Procedures

Another test development readiness activity that can be performed by the test engineer is the manual execution of the test procedure prior to automated test procedure development. In this activity, the test engineer steps through the test procedures associated with a particular segment/functionality of the system once manually and then decides whether to automate the test procedures associated with it based on the outcome. This step verifies that all intended/designed functionality is inherent in the system or contained within a particular segment of the system. When functionality is missing within the application, test automation of test procedures can be inefficient and unproductive. In this verification, a test engineer executes each step in a test procedure. By executing the manual tests, the test team can ensure that test engineers do not begin to automate a test procedure, only to find halfway through the effort that the test procedure cannot be automated.

The test engineer may be able to streamline the overall test effort by investing some time in this manual verification process. After executing all of the steps in the test procedure without any problems, he or she can start automating the test script for later reuse. Even if the steps in the test procedure didn't pass, the test engineer can automate this script by manipulating it to record the "expected result." Some automated test tools, such as Rational's TestStudio, allow for manipulation of the recorded baseline data. For example, if a test engineer records an edit box called *Las Name* (typo) that should really be called *Last Name,* the baseline data can be corrected to the expected data result. Afterward, when the script is played back against a new software build and the script performs successfully (passes), the test engineer knows that the fix has been properly implemented. If the script fails, then the defect remains unresolved.

8.1.10   Test Procedure Inspections—Peer Reviews

When test procedures are being developed for the various phased test components, the test team may find it worthwhile to conduct peer review inspections of the test procedures being developed by the individual test engineers. Test procedure inspections are intended to detect defects, incorrect use of business rules, violations of development standards, and test coverage issues, as well as review test programming code and ensure that test procedure development is consistent with test design.

Test procedure inspections represent an excellent way to uncover any discrepancies with the test procedures, test requirements, or system requirements. Functional requirements can serve as a resource for developing test requirements and subsequent test procedures. As every test requirement will be tested, the peer review process can clear any questions that arise during the development of test procedures. In this review, the test team examines design information, such as computer-aided software engineering (CASE) tool information (if a CASE tool is used), to clarify the use of system paths and business functions. Test procedure design walkthroughs are therefore a helpful technique for discovering problems with the test requirements, errors in the system requirements, or flawed test procedure design.

8.1.11   Test Procedure Configuration Management

During the development of test procedures, the test team needs to ensure that configuration control is performed for test design, test scripts, and test data, as well as for each individual test procedure. Automated test scripts need to be baselined using a configuration management (CM) tool. Groups of reusable test procedures and scripts are usually maintained in a catalog or library of test data comprising a *testbed*.

Testbeds have many uses—for example, during regression testing that seeks to verify the integrity of an application following software updates implemented to correct defects. It is especially important to baseline automated test procedures, so as to maintain a basket of reusable scripts that apply to one application version and can be implemented again in a subsequent version of the application. The reuse of the scripts helps to verify that the new software in the subsequent application release has not adversely affected software that should have remained unchanged from the previous release.

CM tools, such as Source Safe or CCC Harvest, can provide this function (for more CM tools, see Appendix B). Numerous CM tools are on the market, and one will undoubtedly be compatible with the specific automated test tool being used. In the case where a project does not have a budget to purchase a configuration management tool, the test team needs to make sure that backups are performed daily for test program files, test databases, and everything else that is part of the test repositories. In some cases, twice-daily backups may be warranted.

When the test team uses a requirement management tool, such as DOORS, to maintain test requirements and test procedures, baseline control of test procedures is provided automatically. A tool such as DOORS also keeps a history of each test procedure modification or any other modification. This history typically includes the name of the person making the change, the date of the change, the reason for the change, and a description of the change.

When the test team creates test procedures in a simple word-processing document, it needs to ensure that the documents are baselined. Scripts can be destroyed if they are saved in a database, that later becomes corrupt—a not uncommon occurrence. Therefore the database should be backed up regularly.

A test procedure script could be lost, if not baselined, if safeguards are not in place and an individual simply modifies the script or—even worse—accidentally overwrites an existing script or deletes it. Similarly, a test procedure script could be destroyed, if not baselined in a CM tool, when a server or the network goes down and a particular script is in the middle of playback and subsequently becomes corrupted.

Another concern for the test team pertains to the maintenance of the testbed. After test procedures have been executed, these personnel should perform cleanup activities. Team members can use SQL scripts or play back automated scripts that will automatically clean up anything necessary to restore the application to its original state.

Testbed management also includes management of changes to software code, control of the new-build process, test procedures, test documentation, project documentation, and all other test-related data and information. In most organizations, a separate CM group is responsible for testbed management and other CM tasks. This group typically uses a CM tool to support these efforts.

It is important that testbed management include configuration control. As multiple versions of the AUT exist, multiple versions of the test procedure library will exist as well. Testbed management should ensure that the correct test procedure library is used with the corresponding and current AUT version and baselined test environment.

CM tools also facilitate coordination between project team members with regard to changes. The test team needs to keep abreast of any changes that can affect the test environment integrity, such as changes to the test lab, testbed, and AUT. Specific changes that may alter the test environment include a change to a network connection, modification of disk space, or the implementation of a faster processor or other AUT upgrades.

Poor CM can cause many problems. For example, a script that previously incorporated programmed code may now incorporate only tool-generated code. A defect that had been fixed at a great expense may reappear or a fully tested program may no longer work. Good CM can help avoid these problems. If common test procedures are modified, for example, the modification should be communicated to all test engineers. Without test procedure management, all test engineers affected might not be notified of these changes.

8.2 | Test Development Guidelines

Once the test team has performed test development setup, including the setup of the test development architecture, it has a clear picture of the test procedures that must be created for the various testing phases. The team next needs to identify the test procedure development guidelines that will apply on the project's various test development activities. Figure 8.2 provides an overview of test development activities, including the input and output of each activity.

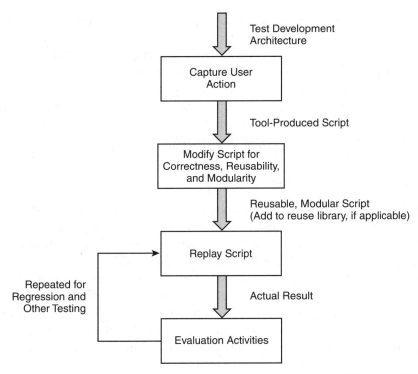

Figure 8.2 Test Development Activities Using a Capture/Playback Tool

The automated test developer needs to follow the development standards of the scripting language that applies to the particular tool in use. For example, the test tool Test Studio uses SQA Basic, a Visual Basic-like language. In this particular case, it is recommended that the test engineer follow a published Visual Basic development standard. In the case of the test tools offered by Mercury, which use a C-like language, the test engineer should follow one of the many published C development standards. This section addresses some of the important programming considerations in test procedure script development, including those related to the scripting language used in the respective testing tool.

For the entire team of test engineers to be able to simultaneously develop test procedures that are consistent, reusable, and maintainable, the test team should consolidate all development guidelines into a single document. Where an organization-level test development standard exists, the team can adopt or modify those guidelines as necessary to support a particular project. Once a test development standard has been adopted, all test team personnel should receive this document. A means for ensuring that test development guidelines are implemented needs to be applied, such as test procedure walkthroughs.

Test procedure development guidelines should be available to support the development of both manual and automated test procedures, as outlined in Table 8.5. Reusability is one of the most important test procedure creation factors. If a test procedure is not reusable, the test engineer has wasted much of his effort; the test procedure has to be recreated and frustration sets in. Additionally, the test procedure should be maintainable, simple, and robust.

8.2.1 Design-to-Development Transition

Provided that design standards are in place, the test team needs to ensure that test development represents a natural transition from test design. It is important that tests be properly designed before test development begins. Test design, which is the baseline for test development, is discussed in detail in Chapter 7. The test design baseline consists of several elements, including the test program model, test architecture, and test procedure definition. Futhermore, this baseline consists of several test procedure matrices, such as mappings of test procedures to test requirements, the automated/manual test mapping, and the mapping of test procedures to test data. It should provide the test team with a clear picture of how test development needs to be structured and organized.

With the test design baseline in place, the test team needs to perform the setup activities. Once test development setup activities have concluded, the test team then defines a test development architecture, which itself defines the overall test development approach. Such a diagram graphically illustrates the major components of the test development and execution activity to be performed. The test procedure design and development are closely intertwined. For example, the test team needs to be aware of any dependencies between test procedures. It should identify any test procedures that must be developed before other test procedures as well as procedures that must be executed before others. The test procedure execution schedule discussed in this chapter further addresses these issues.

The test development architecture, which was depicted in Figure 8.1, should be the foundation from which the test development and execution schedules are developed. The test team needs to create test procedures according to a test development schedule that allocates personnel resources and specifies development due dates. In addition, it needs to monitor development progress and produce progress status reports. The test team should hold a meeting to discuss the specific way in which test design, development setup, and the test development architecture will be translated into test development action. The results of this meeting should be recorded within a test development guideline document and promulgated to all test personnel.

Table 8.5   Test Development Guidelines

Development Guideline Topics	Description
Design-to-Development Transition	Specify how design and setup activities will be translated into test development action
Reusable Test Procedures	Test procedures need to be reusable for highest test program return on investment
Data	Avoid hard-coding data values into scripts, rendering them not reusable
Application Navigation	Standard navigation method needs to be deployed for reusable test scripts
Bitmap Image Recording	Addresses the use of a bitmap image recording method for test procedure development
Automation Wildcards	Development guidelines supporting reusable test procedures
Capture/Playback	Outlines on how to apply the use of capture/playback recording
Maintainable Test Procedures	A test procedure whose defects are easy to remove and can easily be adapted to meet new requirements
Cosmetic Standards	Standards defined to promote test program code that is easy to read and comprehend
Test Script Comments	Specifies where and how comments are used within procedures and scripts
Test Script Documentation	Specifies that test script documentation is important for test procedure maintainability
Test/Application Synchronization	How to synchronize the server/GUI/AUT with the test script
Test Procedure Index	Guidelines supporting the maintenance of an index to find test procedures of interest
Error Handling	Guidelines for how test procedures will handle errors
Naming Standards	Defines the standard naming convention for test procedures
Modularity	Guidelines for creating modular test scripts
Looping Constructs	Looping constructs support script modularity
Branching Constructs	Branching constructs support script modularity
Context Independence	Directs development of test procedures given test procedure relationships
Global Files	Globally declared functions are available to any procedure and support maintainability
Constants	Guidelines addressing use of constants to support maintainable test procedures
Other Guidelines	Other test development guidelines
Output Format	Users need to define what the test procedure results output format should look like
Test Procedures/Verification Points	Guidelines can specify which verification points to use most often and which ones to avoid
User-Defined Verification	Addresses the use of script programming for user-defined verification
API Calls, Dynamic Link Libraries (.dll), and Other Programming Constructs	Addresses test automation using application programming interfaces and .dll files as part of the user-defined verification methods

8.2.2   Reusable Test Procedures

Automated test procedure scripts can be extended through the use of custom code. For example, as noted in Section 8.2.2.5, a test script that is created using the recording feature of an automated test tool is not very reusable. This method records every mouse click and every screen; as soon as the test procedure encounters a changed location for a button or a missing screen, however, the test procedure script fails. Test scripts can be easily extended for continued reusability through the use of procedural control and conditional logic.

The most important issue when developing or modifying a test procedure is reusability. The test team may find it beneficial to establish a separate test creation standard that addresses the development of reusable test procedures. Reusability of the test procedures is important in improving test team efficiency. For example, when the user interface for an application changes, the test team will not want to spend the time and energy updating each test script so that it accurately reflects and tests the application. Instead, the test team would be better off if it built in flexibility from the start.

To create a library of reusable functions, the best practice calls for the separation of functionality such as data read/write/validation, navigation, logic, and error checking. This section provides guidelines on several topics related to practices that help to build in test procedure reusability. These guidelines are based on the same principles that underlie good software development practices.

Reusable Test Procedures

Read data from file

Practice smart application navigation

Avoid bitmap image recording

Avoid straight capture/playback

8.2.2.1   Data

One way to design reusable test procedures is to use a data-driven approach to test development, where data values are either read in from data files, instead of having the values hard-coded within the test procedure script, or written to data files. In this case, the test engineer identifies the data elements and data value names or data variable names that can be used by each test procedure. This information enables the test engineer to assess the benefit of using a particular data file.

When recording a test procedure script using an automated test tool, the tool automatically embeds hard-coded values. The action of simply recording test procedures that rely on hard-coded values limits the reuse of the test procedure. For example, a date field recorded today as a constant will prevent the script from functioning properly tomorrow. Also, consider the need to add a series of account numbers into an application. If account numbers represent a key data element, the account numbers added each time need to be unique; otherwise, an error message may be displayed, such as *Duplicate Account Number.*

Generally, it is recommended that the test engineer not hard-code data values into a test procedure. To avoid execution failure, the test engineer needs to replace such hard-coded values with variables and, whenever possible and feasible, read data from a .csv or ASCII file, spreadsheet, or word-processing software.

As part of the test development effort, the test team identifies the data elements, data value names, or data variable names used by the various test procedures. The key pieces of data added to the test procedure script are the variable definitions and the definition of the data source (that is, the location of the data file).

Another reason for using this technique of externalizing the input data is to facilitate maintenance of the data being entered and to make the scripts more efficient. Whenever the test procedure should be played back with a different set of data, the data file simply can be updated.

The following sample test script reads data from an input file.

Data Read from a File (using Rational Robot's SQA Basic)

```
-   This is a sample script using SQA Basic
-   Create a data-driven script that reads a .CSV file to read in the data
and associated test procedure(s)
-   Separate sample input file (input.txt):
"01/02/1998","VB16-01A"
"12/31/1998","VB16-01B"
"09/09/1999","VB16-01C"
"12/31/1999","VB16-01D"
"12/31/2000","VB16-01E"
...
...
"10/10/2000","VB16-01Z"
Sample Code:
hInput = FreeFile
Open "input.txt" For Input Shared As # hInput
Do While Not Eof( hInput )
    Input # hInput , sDateIn , sTCName
    Window SetContext, "Name=fDateFuncTest", ""
    InputKeys sDateIn
    PushButton Click, "Name=cmdRun"
    Result = WindowTC (CompareProperties, "Name=fDateFuncTest", __
            "CaseID=" & sTCName & "")
```

```
Loop
Close # hInput
```

The pseudocode for this sample test script follows:

```
Open Input File
For Each Record in the Input File Do the Following Steps:
 Read Input Date, Test Procedure Name
 Enter Input Date into Date Field
 Click on Run Command
 Verify Results in the Date Field
Close Input File
```

8.2.2.2   Application Navigation

Test procedure development standards should address the ways that automated test procedures navigate application screens. To achieve higher reusability of the test scripts, a test engineer needs to select the navigation method that is least susceptible to changes in the AUT. Navigation functionality should reside in a separate module in the test library. The standards should specify whether test procedure development using a test tool recorder moves through the application by use of *tabs,* keyboard *accelerator keys* (hotkeys), or *mouse clicks,* capturing the *x, y* coordinates or the object names assigned to a particular object. For example, within environments that do not use object names (such as C, Visual C, and Uniface), the "caption," or window title, is used to identify a window.

All of these choices may potentially be affected by design changes. For example, if test procedure scripts use the tab method to navigate between objects, the resulting scripts are tab-order-dependent. When the tab order changes, all scripts must be corrected, which can pose a monumental challenge. If accelerator keys are employed as a navigation method and new accelerator keys are later assigned, the recording again will become useless. If the mouse is used, a field could change and the mouse click might occur on a nonexistent field; once again, the script would need to be recreated. The best way to navigate through an application is to identify each field by its object name as assigned by the particular development tool—for example, Visual Basic, PowerBuilder, or Centura. The field can then be moved to any position on the screen, but the script would not be affected by this change. In this way, a recorded script would not be as susceptible to code changes and will become more reusable. Whenever possible, the test procedure needs to retrieve a window's object name, which is most likely to stay static, instead of identifying a window by caption.

Case Study
Navigation Using Tabs or Mouse Clicks

A test engineer named Byron found that tabs were easier to use than mouse clicks. With each new version of a particular application, however, he encountered problems with the execution of the test procedures. In particular, problems arose when new tabs were added or deleted from an existing screen.

Byron decided to implement the use of mouse clicks on the test development effort, which involved 50 test procedure scripts. In an effort to minimize test procedure modifications, Byron attempted to perform the mouse click near the upper-left corner of the object so that the coordinates would not be a problem in the future. The major difficulty he encountered with this approach related to the fact that the application was relatively keyboard-intensive, meaning that each user generally entered a significant amount of data, and that all users preferred to tab between objects rather than use the mouse.

Confronted with this problem, Byron approached the application developers and requested that they enable application navigation via a *Field ID*. Each field of a given form (screen) typically has a corresponding unique ID value. The developers use this Field ID value to reference the screen within their code. In response to Byron's request, the developers enabled a control-shift function that did two things. First, the function made visible the ID values for all displayed fields. Second, the function displayed a dialog box that allows an individual to go to any displayed field by entering its ID value. Byron exercised the function and found it to work well. He no longer needed to ensure that the tab order remained consistent from one application build to another.

Student Question 8.2
In this case study, which solution would you propose? Describe a solution.

8.2.2.3   Bitmap Image Recording

Test development guidelines should address the application of the bitmap image recording method for developing reusable test procedures. Guidelines should stress that the use of test tools to perform bitmap image recording does not represent efficient test automation and that the use of this method of test procedure recording should be minimized.

Most automated GUI testing tools allow the test engineer to record bitmap images, which are also known as *screen shot* recordings. This method for developing

314 Chapter 8 Test Development

a test procedure may prove valuable when trying to determine whether one or more pixels in the application's screen display has changed. It allows a test procedure to compare a screen or an edit box with a baseline recording of the screen or edit box. Matching up pixel information, which is synonymous with the x, y coordinates, performs the comparison. The resulting test is overly sensitive to any change, including those that are appropriate. Test procedure maintenance using this method can prove too burdensome, given the significant amount of effort required.

Another drawback to the use of bitmap image recording pertains to the fact that when test procedures are played back on a system that uses a different video resolution or different color setting for screen display, the procedures will fail. For example, test procedures recorded using a system with a screen display of 1024×768 cannot be applied to a screen display with a resolution of 640×480.

Yet another concern for bitmap image recording involves the fact that test procedures that record screen capture take up a big chunk of storage space. In the case of a 1024×768 screen resolution at 24 bits per pixel (16 million colors), or 3 bytes per pixel, the result of $1024 \times 768 \times 3$ is 2,359,296 bytes, or 2.3 megabytes, for a single snapshot.

Case Study
Testing Bitmaps Using a Capture/Playback Tool [2]

In this AUT, using the graphical editor developed in the baseline project, it is possible to equip and configure electrical switch gear cabinets of different types with various modules. Switch gear components are displayed in the GUI editor as bitmaps. Double-clicking the mouse on certain positions within the bitmaps will either call a context menu in which modules can be selected as equipment or, when the position can be equipped with multiple modules at a time, call *another bitmap* that can be used in the same way as the first one. As many as three bitmap levels can be supported.

The test script depicted in this case study is designed to test the correct navigation through these bitmap levels, the decision to select either a menu or a new window, and the contents and functions of the menus. Because the great number of monotonous navigation steps would quickly exhaust the most committed test engineer, this task seems an ideal candidate for automation.

Upon closer examination, however, automating this test proves difficult, as the bitmaps are problematic to address. For example, the coordinates must be introduced to the test program beforehand in a teach-in-step approach. Another obstacle is the realization of the context menus as pop-ups, which appear to be a major problem for the test tool. Access is not possible via standard methods, so special routines must be developed.

Menu Item Test Script (Created Using WinRunner)

```
# Click every menu item
for (i=1; i <= number, i++)           # Loop all menu items
{
        if (find InArray(mlist,liste[i],   # Checks if item is in list of
        1)==1)                             valid items
        {
        win_activate (thewin);             # Activate current window
        set_window (thewin,10);            # Set context to current window
        move_locator_abs(ox,oy);           # Move mouse pointer to proper
                                           location
        dbl_click("Left");                 # Double click left mouse button
        selectPopupValue(100,              # Function call selects item in
        200,list[i]);                      popup
        }
        if (list[i] == "Set Standard")     # If item equals "Set Standard",
        stdPos=i;                          store position
}
```

8.2.2.4 Automation Wildcards

Some automated testing tools permit the use of "wildcards." Standards need to be developed for the use of wildcards within test program code. Wildcards, such as the use of the asterisk "*", enable a line in the test program to seek a match of a certain value or to identify when conditions meet certain criteria.

When using an automated test tool to record test procedures, a wildcard can be employed to look for a caption of a window so as to identify the window. For example, when using the Test Studio test tool, the *Window Set Context* command identifies the window in which subsequent actions should occur. Within environments that do not use object names (such as C, Visual C, and Uniface), the "caption," or window title, is used to identify the window.

The test engineer can edit the test procedure script, remove the caption, and then insert standard wildcard expressions so that when the test script runs, it will place focus on a window; that is, a specific window is selected, even when the window title changes. This consideration is especially important when window titles change and the application's window titles contain the current date or a customer number. In some testing tools, such as SQA Suite, the caption terminator technique can allow the test procedure to use a single character to designate the end of a window caption string. Note that the caption itself must be enclosed in braces ({ }), as reflected in the following code:

Test Studio Example

```
Window SetContext, "Caption={Customer No: 145}"
Window SetContext, "Caption={Customer No: *}" OR
Window SetContext, "Caption={Customer No: 1}"
```

8.2.2.5   Capture/Playback

Reusable test development guidelines should address the use of capture/playback methods of test procedure recording. Guidelines should stress that the out-of-the-box use of GUI test tools does not provide the most efficient test automation and that the use of the capture/playback method of test procedure recording should be minimized. As explained in Appendix B, in capture/playback an automated test tool records the keystrokes of user interactions that execute the functionality of an application. These keystrokes are recorded as part of test procedure development and then played back as part of test execution. Test procedures created using this simplified method have significant limitations and drawbacks.

A major drawback for the capture/playback method for test procedure development pertains to the fact that values are hard-coded within the underlying script language code that the test tool automatically produces during recording. For example, input values, window coordinates, window captions, and other values are all fixed within the code generated during recording. These fixed values represent a potential problem during test execution when any number of these values has changed within the product being tested. Because of the changed values in the AUT, the test procedure will fail during script playback. Because a particular window may appear in a number of test procedures, a single change to a single window can ripple throughout a significant number of test procedures and render them unusable. Another example of the capture and recording of a fixed value within a test procedure involves the capture of the current date stamp during test development. When the test engineer attempts to exercise the test procedure the following day or any day thereafter, the test procedure will fail because the hard-coded date value doesn't equal the new date.

Clearly, test procedures created using the capture/playback method are not reusable and, as a result, are not maintainable. Basic scripts are useful in a few situations, but most often test engineers developing test procedures under this method will need to re-record the test procedures many times during the test execution process to accommodate any changes in the AUT. The potential advantages of using a test tool are negated by this need to continually recreate the test procedures. The use of this test procedure development method will result in a high level of frustration among test personnel, and the automated tool in use is likely to be shelved in favor of manual test development methods.

Instead of simply using the capture/playback capability of an automated testing tool, the test team should take advantage of the scripting language by modifying the code automatically generated by the capture/playback tool to make the resulting test scripts reusable, maintainable, and robust.

8.2.3 Maintainable Test Procedures

In addition to creating reusable test procedures, it is important that the test team follow guidelines that support the creation of maintainable test procedures. Developing test procedures with the standards described in this section can result in more easily maintained test procedures.

By carefully designing and developing modular procedures, the team can simplify the maintenance of the test scripts. The time spent actually building and maintaining tests can be minimized by designing carefully and by understanding the interdependence of the test procedures.

Maintainable Test Procedures

Follow cosmetic standards
Document test scripts
Allow for synchronization
Use test procedure index
Allow for error handling
Use naming standards
Create modularity scripts
Use looping constructs
Use branching constructs
Allow for context independence
Use global files

8.2.3.1 Cosmetic Standards

The test team should establish and adopt standards that promote the development of test program code that is easy to read, understand, and maintain. These standards stipulate the cosmetic appearance of test program code. Cosmetic coding standards would specify how to represent *if/then/else* statements and *case* statements within code, for example. They would also stipulate how to align the indentation of the first and last statements of each individual routine (loop) within the code. Ideally, the alignment for the first and last statements should be the same.

Cosmetic coding standards might articulate rules for code development that specify that program code not exceed the length of the screen, so that the individual does not have to scroll up and down (or back and forth) to follow the code logic. Rules for the use of continuation characters, such as "_" in Visual Basic, should be promulgated. These characters serve as a "carriage return" for each line of code, thereby minimizing the length of each line of code so that test procedure scripts become more readable.

When using an automated test tool that records test procedures in an object mode, it is easy to read the resulting code. The object mode makes scripts readable by clarifying the context of each command or action. That is, it recognizes context, such as field controls and labels. If the test tool records in analog mode, then the resulting test procedure script is incomprehensible with regard to where row-column and pixel coordinates are recorded. The first sample program code in this section illustrates code that is difficult to read, while the second example shows code that follows cosmetic coding standards.

Sample Test Script Using No Layout Standard

```
Sub Main
Dim sInput As String
Dim word, numeric
Dim Counter As Integer
'Initially Recorded: 12/01/97  23:52:43
Open "C:\temp\wordflat.txt" For Input As #1
Counter = 1
Do While Counter < 5000
Input #1, sInput
word = Trim(Left$(sInput,Instr(sInput," ")))
numeric = Trim(Mid$(sInput,Instr(sInput," ")))
Window SetContext, "Caption=Microsoft Word - Document1", ""
MenuSelect "Tools->AutoCorrect..."
Window SetContext, "Caption=AutoCorrect", ""
inputKeys word &"{TAB}" &numeric
Window Click, "", "Coords=358,204"
Counter = Counter +1
Loop
Close #1

End Sub
```

Sample Test Script Using Layout Standard

```
Sub Main

    Dim sInput As String
    Dim word, numeric
```

```
Dim Counter As Integer

'Initially Recorded: 12/01/97  23:52:43
Open "C:\temp\wordflat.txt" For Input As #1

Counter = 1
Do While Counter < 5000

    Input #1, sInput
    word = Trim(Left$(sInput,Instr(sInput," ")))
    numeric = Trim(Mid$(sInput,Instr(sInput," ")))

    'Window SetContext, "Caption=Microsoft Word - Document1", ""
    'MenuSelect "Tools->AutoCorrect..."

    Window SetContext, "Caption=AutoCorrect", ""
    InputKeys word &"{TAB}" &numeric
    Window Click, "", "Coords=358,204"
    Counter = Counter +1

Loop
Close #1

End Sub
```

The structure of the script layout does not enhance performance, but it does facilitate debugging and the review of the test scripts. A tremendous payback is realized when trying to make sense of the different program constructs, such as loops.

8.2.3.2 Test Script Comments

Another guideline that helps to create maintainable test scripts relates to the use of comments within a test procedure. Such comments are meant to clarify the scope of the test. They represent test engineers' notes and logical thoughts that enable other individuals to more easily understand the purpose and structure of the test scripts. This embedded documentation has no effect on script performance, but it offers a tremendous return on investment with regard to the maintenance of the scripts in the long term.

Comments should be used liberally in both manual and automated test procedures. As a standard practice, each test procedure should be prefaced with comments outlining the nature of test. Additionally, the steps making up the procedure should be clearly explained in complete sentences.

Guidelines should specify how comments are to be incorporated when using an automated test tool to develop test procedures. Most automated test tools allow the test engineer to add comments to the test procedure while recording the test. In instances where the automated test tool does not permit the addition of comments during recording, guidelines should specify that the test engineer add comments after test procedure recording ends.

The practice of outlining comments within automated test scripts helps to avoid confusion when the test team develops test automation scripts or attempts to reuse scripts from an existing automation infrastructure (reuse library). Detailed comments within the test procedure make it easier for test engineers to complete accompanying test scripts, revise existing test scripts, and allow archived test scripts to be reused on other projects. Such comments also facilitate the conduct of test procedure peer reviews and the audit of test scripts by outside teams, such as the quality assurance group or an independent verification and validation team.

Another potential benefit of documenting comments within each test procedure arises from the automatic extraction of comments from within test scripts so as to create a special report outlining the scope of the entire suite of test scripts. For example, a test engineer could create a simple program that parses all comments from within the test scripts to create an output that details the scope and purpose of the various tests being performed [3]. Functional analysts, application end users, and other project personnel can later review this report to obtain a more complete understanding of the test program's scope.

8.2.3.3 Test Script Documentation

Along with commenting scripts to enhance their maintainability, it is very important that the test team document the test scripts. Such documentation is beneficial for any individual reviewing the test script who must understand the test script, yet doesn't have the programming background to be able to read the scripting language. Additionally, this documentation supports the greater use of the script within a reuse library or automation infrastructure, as described in Section 8.3.

Case Study
Automating Documentation

A test engineer named Woody [4] developed a Form Generator (FG) that takes the automated SQA Basic test scripts generated by an automated test tool and translates them into readable documents. The FG converts SQA Basic code into standard English statements and includes a user-defined translation dictionary. It allows Woody to specify the SQA scripts (.rec files) to translate, and then generates a .txt file for each .rec file (recorded script) selected. All common SQABasic statements are automatically converted. Woody can then create his own user-defined .map file, which allows him to map the object names (such as w_fltrops) to a specified output such as a filter options window. There are many user-definable preferences and conversion options that Woody can set to control his output.

8.2.3.4 Test Procedure Header

Another guideline that needs to be in place pertains to the use of the test procedure introduction. A test procedure header is used as an introduction that defines the purpose of the test procedure. Guidelines need to specify the contents of this header. Information to be documented may include the test procedure ID, test procedure name, preconditions, data criteria, input arguments, test conditions, expected results, status, and related requirements (system, software, test) that are being verified by the test procedure.

At a minimum, each header should contain the test procedure name, test procedure ID, author of test procedure, date test procedure created. It should also define the prerequisites for running the test procedure, the functionality of the test procedure, the window or screen in which the test procedure must start, and the window or screen where it concludes. The range of information to be documented can be ascertained from the test procedure design matrix depicted in Chapter 7.

Automated test management tools, such as TeamTest, provide a built-in test procedure template that can be modified to accommodate the particular needs of the test team. Once modified, the new template serves as the standard for test procedure development. During development, each test engineer would operate with the same test procedure format and the required header information would be predefined. As a result, all test scripts will have the same look and feel. Figure 8.3 provides an example of a test procedure developed using a template managed by an automated test tool. When the automated test tool does not come with a built-in template, each test engineer should be instructed to use the same test procedure format, including the same style of test procedure introduction.

The use of a standard test procedure template together with test procedure introduction guidance allows test engineers and project personnel to share the same interpretation of test documentation. Such standardized information helps to create a common look and feel for each test procedure that makes all such procedures easy to read and understand.

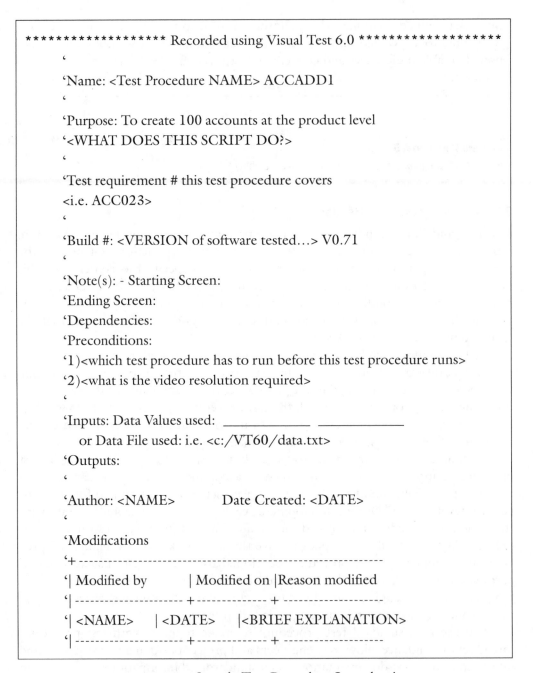

```
****************** Recorded using Visual Test 6.0 ******************
    '
    'Name: <Test Procedure NAME> ACCADD1
    '
    'Purpose: To create 100 accounts at the product level
    '<WHAT DOES THIS SCRIPT DO?>
    '
    'Test requirement # this test procedure covers
    <i.e. ACC023>
    '
    'Build #: <VERSION of software tested...> V0.71
    '
    'Note(s): - Starting Screen:
    'Ending Screen:
    'Dependencies:
    'Preconditions:
    '1)<which test procedure has to run before this test procedure runs>
    '2)<what is the video resolution required>
    '
    'Inputs: Data Values used:  _____   _____
       or Data File used: i.e. <c:/VT60/data.txt>
    'Outputs:
    '
    'Author: <NAME>          Date Created: <DATE>
    '
    'Modifications
    '+ -----------------------------------------------------------
    '| Modified by       | Modified on |Reason modified
    '| ------------------- + ------------- + -------------------
    '| <NAME>    | <DATE>    |<BRIEF EXPLANATION>
    '| ------------------- + ------------- + -------------------
```

Figure 8.3   Sample Test Procedure Introduction

8.2.3.5   Synchronization

Guidelines should be documented that address the synchronization between test procedure execution and application execution. A problem potentially exists with regard to the response time to information requests, which can include the server response plus the network response. The response time to information requests may not stay aligned with recorded test procedures.

A major factor in synchronization is the communications protocol employed. Such protocols provide the means for communication between the workstation computer and the server or host computer. This communication may consist of dial-up, network, or Internet access. Programs interact when one program requests something from another program, sends a message, or provides data to another program.

In test procedure script execution, wait times need to be incorporated into the script that allow for synchronization (that is, the script should wait until a specific response occurs). For example, the test engineer might add a wait state to pause the program while an hourglass changes back to its normal state. Note that this technique may not always work, because the hourglass might flicker. Alternatively, test engineers could record a message that appears at the bottom of a window and add a wait state until the message changes. Also, a wait state could last until a specific window appears—for example, a window that displays a message indicating that some task is complete. Similarly, test personnel can add a wait state to wait for the focus to change.

When designing test procedure scripts, the test team should ensure that the test procedure scripts remain synchronized with the AUT. For example, when a test procedure script performs a complex query to a database, it might take several extra milliseconds for the query to produce results. To account for this wait time, the test engineer will need to synchronize the test procedure script with the application response; otherwise, the script will fail.

A standard guideline needs to be in place that promulgates synchronization methods so that test procedure scripts can be reused. A particular synchronization method might direct test engineers on how to implement synchronization. For example, the guideline could identify a preference for a *WaitState* approach instead of a *DelayFor* approach when using the test tool TeamTest. The *WaitState* method (wait for window to pop up) is generally preferable, because the *DelayFor* method is hard-coded within the test script and may add unnecessary overhead to test procedure execution. For example, a function called `DelayFor 6` will make the script wait 6 seconds, even if the desired state is reached within 4 seconds.

8.2.3.6   Test Procedure Index

With test programs that involve hundreds of test procedures, it quickly becomes difficult for the test team to readily ascertain the purpose and scope of every test procedure. Maintainability therefore becomes a problem. Sometimes the test team may need to pinpoint tests for certain application functionality or certain type of testing for reuse analysis, as described in Section 8.1.3, Automation Reuse Analysis. Therefore a guideline should document how the test team can quickly locate test procedures supporting a particular kind of test or a particular functionality. Essentially, the test team needs to maintain some type of index to find applicable test procedures.

When the test team has followed development guidelines that specify the inclusion of comments in the test procedures, it can generate a special report outlining the scope and purpose of the various tests performed in the parsing program discussed in Section 8.2.3.2. One way to find relevant test procedures is to carry out an electronic search within the special report file.

The test team could also develop and maintain a test dictionary. The test dictionary contains information associated with test procedures, test scripts, and pass/fail results. Additionally, it can include information such as document names, windows/screen names, fields/objects, vocabulary for tests, and cross references.

8.2.3.7   Error Handling

Test procedure development standards should account for the fact that error checking needs to be coded into the script, where errors are most likely to occur. Errors need to be reported from the test procedure that detects the error and knows what the error is. Incorporating an error-handling capability to take care of the most likely errors will increase the maintainability and stability of the test procedures.

Many test procedures are designed without considering the possible errors that a test might encounter. This omission can cause problems, for example, when the tests are played back unattended and one test fails; a subsequent test then cannot execute because error recovery is not built in. The entire test suite will therefore fail. To make a suite of tests truly automated, error recovery must be built in and must take into consideration the various types of errors that the test script could encounter.

Logic within a test script can be implemented to allow for branching to a different script or calling a script that cleans up the error condition. The error message generated should be self-explanatory to the test engineer. This approach facilitates debugging of a test procedure, because the error message should pinpoint the problem immediately. Guidelines need to be documented to specify how test procedures should handle these errors and to provide examples on how a script should handle errors. The test code given here, which was developed using SQA Basic, checks for a Test Station Name; when it doesn't find this name, it exits the procedure. The test engineer can then code the script to allow it to start the next procedure.

Test Station Check

```
DataSource = SQAGetTestStationName()

    'Check for valid test station name
    If DataSource = "" Then
        MsgBox "No Test Station Name Found"
        Exit Sub
    End If
```

The following test script, which was also developed using SQA Basic, checks for the existence of a file. When the test script does not find the file, the test script returns an error message stating that the file could not be found and then exits the procedure. When the test script does find the file, a message box pops up on the screen to inform the user (that is, to write a message to the log) that the file was found and the script continues to execute.

File Check

```
'Make sure files exist
        DataSource = SQAGetDir(SQA_DIR_PROCEDURES) & "CUSTPOOL.CSV"
        If Dir(DataSource) = "" Then
            MsgBox "Cannot run this test.  File not found: " & DataSource
            Result = 0
            Exit Sub
        End If
    Else
        WriteLogMessage "Found " & DataSource
    End If
```

When designing modules, the test engineer should pay special attention to pre- and post-execution condition requirements. Each module should provide for this type of error checking to verify that pre-conditions are met. For example, the post-conditions for one test procedure may invoke the steps to clean up and set up the environment necessary for another test procedure to execute, thus fulfilling the pre-conditions for that test procedure.

8.2.3.8 Naming Standards

Naming standards improve script maintainability. The benefits of using naming standards include those listed here:

- They help test engineers standardize and decode the structure and logic of scripts.
- Variables are self-documenting as to the data they represent.

- Variables are consistent within and across applications.

- The resulting script is precise, complete, readable, memorable, and unambiguous.

- The standards ensure that scripts are consistent with programming language conventions.

- They aid in being efficient from a string size and labor standpoint, thus allowing a greater opportunity for longer or fuller variable names, procedure names, function names, and so on.

The test team should follow the Hungarian Notation or another naming standard that is agreeable to the team. Briefly, the Hungarian Notation is

> a naming convention that (in theory) allows the programmer to determine the type and use of an identifier (variable, function, constant). It was originally developed by Charles Simonyi of Microsoft and has become an industry standard in programming. [5]

Variable names need to be standardized with automated test scripts. In Hungarian Notation, a variable name consists of three parts: the prefix (or constructor), base type (or tag), and qualifier. The qualifier is the part that gives the most meaning to a variable name or a function name. Ideally, the name should describe the function being performed. It is important to be aware of the limitations of variable names when creating such a standard.

- Examples of bad variable naming conventions include `Dim Var1`, `Counter1`, and `Test1 As Integer`.

- Examples of good variable naming conventions include `Dim nCustomerCounter As Integer`, `Dim sCustomerName As String`, and `Dim nMnuCounter as Integer`.

- Some prefixes for commonly used variable types are listed here.

Variable Type	Prefix
double	d
short	s
long	l
int	n
date	dt
string	str
char	c

- Some examples of tags are listed below.

Tag Description	Tag
Menu	mnu
Text boxes	txt
List box	lst

To make test scripts efficient, it is very important to understand the scope of the variables. The larger the scope of a variable, the more the variable tends to use the valuable memory that could be available to the AUT. A good scripting practice is to limit the number of variables that have global scope. Of course, some variables must have global scope to maintain continuity in running test scripts.

8.2.3.9 Modularity

A modular script increases maintainability. A smaller test script is easier to understand and debug. Dividing the script into logical modules would therefore be one way to handle complex scripting tasks. If the test team sets up the logical flow correctly in the planning stage, each box in the diagram will be changed into a module. Additionally, through the use of modularity, the scripting tasks can be divided among test engineers in the group. If a test procedure is designed and developed in a modular fashion and part of the AUT changes, then the test team needs to alter only the affected modular test script components. As a result, changes usually must be made in only a single place.

Each module can consist of several small functions. A function comprises several lines of script that perform a task. For example, the `Login( )` function will perform the following actions:

1. Start the AUT.
2. Input the login user ID.
3. Verify the login user ID (error checking).
4. Input the login password.
5. Verify the login password (error checking).
6. Hit OK.

Rather than including a long sequence of actions in the same test procedure, test procedures should be short and modular. They should focus on a specific area of testing, such as a single dialog box, or on a related set of recurring actions, such as navigation and error checking. For more comprehensive testing, modular test procedures can easily be called from or copied into other test procedures. In addition, they can be grouped into a combination of procedures (wrappers or *shell* procedures) that represent top-level, ordered groups of test procedures. Modular test procedures offer several benefits:

- Modular test procedures can be called, copied, or combined into umbrella-level shell procedures.
- They can be easily modified if the developers make intentional changes to the AUT.
- Modular test procedures are easier to debug.
- Changes have to be made only in one place, thereby avoiding the cascading effect.
- Maintenance of modular test procedures becomes easier.

While recording a test procedure, most automated test tools allow the test engineer to call previously recorded test procedures. By reusing existing test procedure functionality, the test engineer can avoid having to create repetitive actions within a test procedure.

Automated tests should be designed to operate as stand-alone tests, meaning that the output for one test does not serve as the input to the next test. Under such a strategy, common scripts can be used in any test procedure in any order. A *database reset* script is one such common script that is designed to restore the database to a known baseline. This script can be used to "reset" the database after a test has altered its contents, allowing the next test to start with the contents of the database being a known entity. The reset script would be called only by those tests that alter the database's contents. Structuring tests in this fashion allows tests to be randomly executed, which more closely simulates real-life use of the system.

The random sequencing of all tests may not be possible where the results of the various tests do not have an effect on other tests. These particular instances would represent an exception to the overall design strategy. Such test scripts could be annotated with a unique descriptive extension to ensure that they execute properly.

8.2.3.10 Looping Constructs

Test engineers need to use looping constructs just as application developers do. Looping constructs support modularity and thus maintainability. Almost all test tool scripting languages support two kinds of loops. The *counted* loop acts as a *FOR* loop, while the *continuous* loop performs as a *WHILE* loop. In instances where application requirements specify a specific number or when the test engineer can determine a specific number of times that a task needs to be performed, then it is best to utilize the FOR loop.

FOR Loop Examples. Suppose that the requirement specifies that the application must be able to add five account numbers to a database:

```
FOR nLoopCounter=1 to 5
    Add account_number
END FOR LOOP
```

Giving the test script some more thought, the test engineer may consider enhancing the script further by using a variable for the endpoint of the loop, so that the loop can be further reused by the passing of a variable. Passing in a variable for the FOR loop in this manner gives the following script:

```
FOR nLoopCounter = 1 to nEndLoop
    Add account_number
END FOR LOOP
```

Looping constructs are an essential part of any program code. When a test procedure should read data from a file, the looping construct might contain statements such as "read the data until end of file is reached." In the preceding example, all records would be located in a file and the test procedure script would read the records from the file until it reached the end of the file.

Looping constructs are useful in other situations. Consider a test procedure that records the contents of a third-party data grid after data are added. The approach taken to develop the test procedure would require repeated recording of the state of the data grid so as to capture changes to its content. This approach is cumbersome, and the resulting test script would not be reusable should the data grid contents change in any unexpected way. A better approach involves the modification of the test procedure script to programmatically parse the data grid information and compare it with a baseline data file. The resulting test script can be repeated much more easily.

In addition, looping constructs could be applied to a test procedure that must handle expected changes to the state of a record. For example, the status of a record might be expected to change from *edit pending* to *edit complete*. To capture the time required for a record to make this change, the specific status could be included in a loop and timed until the status of the record changed from pending to complete. Such a change to the test procedure allows for unattended playback of the script, timing of the functionality, and repeatability of the script.

8.2.3.11 Branching Constructs

Another good test procedure coding practice involves the use of branching constructs. As with looping constructs, branching constructs support modularity and thus maintainability of a test procedure. Branching involves the exercise of an application by taking a different path through an application, based upon the value of a variable. A parameter used within the test script can have a value of either true or false. Depending on the value, the test script may exercise a different path through the application.

Many reasons exist for using branching constructs. Test engineers can use branching constructs such as *If..then..else, case,* or *GOTO* statements in order to make automated test procedures reusable. If..then..else statements are most often used for error checking and other conditional checking. For example, they can be incorporated in a test procedure that checks whether a window exists.

As already described in Section 8.2.3.7, branching constructs can be used to branch from one test script to another if the test encounters a specific error. When an application could possibly be left in several different states, the test procedure should be able to gracefully exit the application. Instead of hard-coding steps to exit the application within the test procedure, the test procedure can call a cleanup script that uses conditional steps to exit the AUT, given the state of the application at the time. Consider the following cleanup script sample:

```
if windowA is active then
 do this
 and this
else if windowB is active then
 do this
else exception error
endif
```

The use of GOTO routines often inspires debate within programming circles. It can create *spaghetti code,* meaning unstructured code that is hard to follow. Only in very rare circumstances is the use of GOTOs warranted. For scripting purposes, occasional use of GOTOs could prove advantageous to the test engineer, especially when testing complex applications. To save time, the test engineer could skip certain sections of the application so as to expedite testing. In case of SQA Basic scripting, for example, the GOTO statements can aid in the development of scripts. The test engineer can use GOTOs to skip already-working lines of scripts and go to the point where debugging needs to begin. Using a GOTO statement will also avoid script failure, because the script can go directly to the part that fails, allowing the test engineer to debug that section of the code rather than going through all input fields.

Another reason for using branching constructs is to verify whether a particular file exists. Before a test procedure opens a file to retrieve data, for example, it needs to verify the existence of the file. When the file doesn't exist, the user needs to be prompted with an error message. This error message can also be written to the test result log and the script might end, depending on the logic setup of the built-in error-checking routine.

A branching construct can also prove valuable when a test script must operate with a specific video resolution. A test procedure can include a statement that says "if video resolution is 640×480," then execute this script; else "when video resolution is some other value, update to 640×480;" otherwise, provide an error message and/or exit the program.

8.2.3.12   Context Independence

Another guideline for a test team that is trying to create maintainable scripts pertains to the development of context-independent test procedures. These guidelines should define where test procedures begin and end; they can be adapted from the test procedure design matrix given in Chapter 7. Context independence is facilitated by the implementation of the modularity principles already described in this chapter. Given the highly interdependent nature of test procedures and the interest in executing a sequential string of tests, a suite of test procedures are often incorporated into a test script shell or wrapper function. In this case, the test procedures are incorporated into a file in a specified sequence and can then be executed as a single test script or procedure.

In instances when a test script shell or wrapper function is not used, the test team must manually ensure that the AUT is at the correct starting point and that the test procedures are played back in the correct order. The required sequencing for test procedure execution could be documented within each test procedure as a precondition for execution. This manual approach to performing context-independent test procedures minimizes the benefits of automation. In any event, the test team needs to ensure that the guidelines are in place to direct the development and documentation of test procedures, given the relationship between test procedures that may exist.

Guidelines could specify that all test procedures pertaining to a GUI application must start at the same initial screen and end at that same window or that the application must be in the same state. This approach represents the ideal way of implementing modularity, because the scripts are independent and therefore result-independent, meaning that the expected result of one test will not affect the outcome of others and that data and context are not affected. This guideline would simplify interchangeability of test procedures, allowing for the creation of shell procedures. (See the modularity model depicted in Table 8.4.) It is not always feasible, however, especially when the test procedure must step through many lower-level windows to reach the final functionality. In such a case, it would not be practical to require that the test procedure trace back repeatedly through all windows.

A work-around solution for this situation could create test procedures in a modular fashion—that is, where one test procedure ends, another test procedure could begin. With this model, a series of test procedures can be linked together as part of a higher-level script and played back in a specific order to ensure continuous flow of test script playback as well as ongoing operation of the AUT. When using this strategy, however, test failure can cause domino effects. That is, the test sequence outcome of one test procedure affects the outcome of another procedure. Error recovery can easily become complex.

Case Study
Automated Random Testing

A test engineer named Jackie was responsible for creating an automated random test capability that could stress-test the AUT. She came up with the following script pseudocode:

1. Create various modular test procedures that are result-independent, meaning that the outcome of one script doesn't affect the outcome of another script.

2. Make sure that each test procedure starts at the same initial state, meaning that one test procedure doesn't begin where the other one ends.

3. Allow for checks to verify that each test procedure produces results as expected and add error checking that provides for the restoration or recovery of a test procedure.

4. Add a random number generator into the overall script to allow for execution of the various test procedures in a random fashion.

Student Question 8.4

Produce a script based on the pseudocode described in the "Automated Random Testing" case study.

8.2.3.13   Global Files

Automated test procedures can be maintained more easily by adding global files. For example, the scripting language used by an automated test tool will prompt the test engineer to declare and define the program code for each test procedure. Test engineers need to take advantage of .sbl (Visual Basic) files when developing test automation. For example, in the case of the TeamTest tool, the basic header files have .sbh extensions and contain the procedure declarations and global variables referred to in the test procedure script files. Source code files have .sbl extensions and contain the procedure definitions that are used in the test script files.

Global files offer a benefit because the globally declared procedures are available for any test procedure. If a globally declared procedure must be modified the change must be made in only one place—not in all of the procedures that use the global test procedure. The test team can develop these global files parallel with application development or later when software modules have become stable enough to support test procedure scripting.

A prime candidate for inclusion within a global file would be test procedures related to the login screen. Each time that the AUT test needs to display the login script, the test script can pass the required user Id and password values to the application.

To take advantage of the .sbh or header file in SQA Basic code, the test engineer must place an *include* statement in the main body of the test script. This statement simply pulls in the source code to be included as part of the procedure during compilation time. An include file allows the test engineer to maintain one central copy of common code instead of repeating the same code in many test procedures. The .sbh files are normally restricted to holding the declarations for external functions as well as some information about where to find those functions (that is, BasicLib "Global").

The external functions themselves (sbl/sbx) are similar to .dll files. The .sbl contains the code that is compiled to create the executable, which is stored in a .sbx file. If the source code .sbl file changes, then the .sbx file remains the same until it is recompiled. The .sbx file executes but is not included in the source code, because they are linked dynamically at run time. The .sbx file is therefore used to call the external functions. The .sbl files must be compiled and the parameters must exactly match the function declarations that are included in the .sbh file.

8.2.3.14 Constants

Use of constants enhances the maintainability of test procedures. The test team should store constants in one or more global files, so that they can easily be maintained. For example, the *DelayFor* command in SQA Suite permits synchronization of an application and accepts a time given in milliseconds. For example, the script might include a statement that would read `DelayFor (60,000)`, meaning "hold the next step for 1 minute." Whenever the test engineer wishes to use milliseconds, then some calculations must be performed. To make life simpler, the test engineer could put the time in a constant. The following SQA Basic script uses a constant in this way:

Test Station Check

```
* * * * * * * * * * * * * * * * *
Sub Main
Const
MILLI_SEC = 1000
MILLI_MIN = 60000
MILLI_HOUR = 360000

DelayFor ((2 * MILLI_SEC) + (2 * MILLI_MIN)

StartApplication "C:\notepad"
......
```

8.2.4   Other Guidelines

8.2.4.1   Output Format

During the test planning phase, the test team should identify the test result output format, which is based on end-user input. When developing test procedures, it is necessary to know the desired test procedure output format. For example, the test engineer can add the output format into the automated test script via *Write to Log* statements or other output statements.

For one project, the test engineer developed an elaborate output format that relied on an automated script. The output information was embedded in the test script and written to the test log. The end users for the application did not like this solution, however. They believed that the test engineer could programmatically manipulate the results output to their liking. Instead, they wanted to see screen prints of each resulting output, as they had in the past. To satisfy this request, the test engineer created an automated script to perform this function and used an automated testing tool. From this experience, the test engineer learned how important it is to obtain customer or end-user approval for the planned test results output format.

8.2.4.2   Test Procedures/Verification Points

As part of test procedure design standards, the test team needs to clarify which test procedures/verification points to use and when to use them. Testing tools come with various test procedures, also called verification points. Test procedures can examine the object properties of the various controls on a GUI screen. They can verify the existence of a window, test the menu, and test the OCX and VBX files of an application. For example, Test Studio allows for recording and insertion of 20 verification points: object properties, data window, OCX/VBX data, alphanumeric, list, menu, notepad, window existence, region image, window image, wait state test procedure, start application, start timer, end timer, call test procedure, write to test log, insert comment, object data, and Web site.

The test engineers might have a preference as to which verification points they use most often and which ones they avoid. For example, when working with Test Studio, some test engineers avoid the region image and window image verification points, because these tests are sensitive to every x, y coordinate (pixel) change.

8.2.4.3   User-Defined Verification Methods

Another place to incorporate variability is in the definition of the data that the test procedure requires to determine whether a test has passed or failed. When using standard test procedures and verification methods, the test team defines the exact string that should appear in order to pass a test. In contrast, instead of expecting a specific date when using the Test Studio tool, the test script can simply check that the data appear in a date form; in this example, any date is acceptable.

To allow for variation (beyond that offered by built-in verification methods, such as a numeric range), the test may incorporate a custom-built verification method. Test automation, involving code development, is necessary to create such a verification method. The test engineer can also take advantage of application programming interfaces (API) calls and dynamic link library (.dll) files.

8.2.4.4   API Calls and .dll Files

The use of API calls can drastically enhance test scripts. API calls represent a (rather large) set of functions built into Windows that can be used within a test script to enhance the script's capabilities.

The test team needs to verify whether its chosen test tool supports the use of API calls. Usually, it can consult the test tool vendor to identify the various APIs that are compatible with the tool. To create an API call, the test engineer declares the API function within the test procedure code, usually in the declarations section of the program module. The program then calls the function as it would any other function.

There are many ways to use APIs in support of the test effort and many books have been published that address the use of APIs. A few examples of API calls employing the WinRunner test tool are outlined below.

Example 1: Determine Available Free Memory

Declaration: Declare Function GetFreeSpace& Lib "Kernel" (ByVal flag%)

API call: x& = GetFreeSpace(0)

Example 2: Identify System Resources in Use

Declaration: Declare Function GetFreeSystemResources& Lib "User" (ByValflags%)

API call: x& = GetFreeSystemResources(0)

The use of .dll files allows the test engineer to extend the usefulness of the script. Like API calls, they can be used in many ways.

Example 1 [6]: Sort the array contents by means of a .dll function.

Syntax: array_sort_C(array[ ], property1, property2);

array[ ]: Field to be output.

property1: Primary sorting criteria (object property).

property2: Secondary sorting criteria (object property) – optional.

This code sorts a field that consists of object names. The new order is determined by comparing object properties. The new index begins with 1. As many as two sorting criteria can be specified; multistep sorting is thus possible.

Example 2: Sort a field according to class and x-position

```
# init sample
win_get_objects(window,all,M_NO_MENUS);
# sort array
array_sort_C(all, "class", "x");
```

8.3 | Automation Infrastructure

The application of test automation to a project, including the development of test scripts (programs) or the manipulation of automated test tool-generated test programs, is best supported by the use of a library of reusable functions. This library is known as an automation infrastructure or automation framework.

The creation and maintenance of an automation infrastructure is a key component to any long-term test automation program. Its implementation generally requires a test team organization structure that supports the cohesiveness of the test team across multiple projects.

By following the development guidelines described in Section 8.2, the test team will start building reusable functions that become the building blocks of its automation infrastructure. An automation infrastructure represents a library of reusable functions that may have been created for test efforts on different projects or to test multiple or incremental versions of a particular application. These functions may be used to minimize the duplication of the test procedure development effort and to enhance the reusability of test procedures.

Typically, a minimal set of functionality becomes incorporated into a single test procedure. For example, a test procedure might activate a menu item by initiating a *call* to that test procedure from within another test procedure. If the application menu item changes, the test team must make the change in only a single place—the test procedure where the menu item is called—and then reexecute the test procedure. An automation infrastructure is augmented and developed over time, as test personnel create reusable functions (subprocedures) to support test procedures for a multitude of application development and maintenance projects.

It is important to document the contents and functionality of the automation infrastructure in support of reuse analysis efforts, as discussed in Section 8.1. The following functional scripts might prove especially valuable within an automation infrastructure:

- Table-driven test automation
- PC environment setup script
- Automated recording options
- Login function
- Exit function
- Navigation function
- Verifying GUI standards function
- Smoke test
- Error-logging routines
- Help function verification script
- Timed message boxes function
- Advanced math functions

8.3.1 Table-Driven Test Automation

A table-driven approach to testing [7] is similar to the use of a data template, as discussed in Section 8.2. This approach makes further use of input files. Not only is data input from a file or spreadsheet, but controls, commands, and expected results are incorporated in testing as well. Test script code is therefore separated from data, which minimizes the script modification and maintenance effort. When using this approach, it is important to distinguish between the action of determining "what requirements to test" and the effort of determining "how to test the requirements." The functionality of the AUT is documented within a table as well as step-by-step instructions for each test. An example is provided in Table 8.6.

Once this table has been created, a simple parsing program can read the steps from the table, determine how to execute each step, and perform error checking based on the error codes returned. This parser extracts information from the table for the purpose of developing one or multiple test procedure(s). Table 8.6 data are derived from the following SQA Basic code:

Script From Which Table 8.6 Is Derived

```
Window SetContext, "VBName=StartScreen;VisualText=XYZ Savings Bank", ""

    PushButton Click, "VBName=PrequalifyButton;VisualText=Prequalifying"

    Window SetContext, "VBName=frmMain;VisualText=Mortgage Prequalifier", ""
        MenuSelect "File->New Customer"

        ComboListBox Click, "ObjectIndex=" & TestCustomer.Title ,
        "Text=Mr.           "
        InputKeys TestCustomer.FirstName & "{TAB}" & TestCustomer.LastName &
        "{TAB}" & TestCustomer.Address & "{TAB}" & TestCustomer.City
        InputKeys "{TAB}" & TestCustomer.State & "{TAB}" &
        TestCustomer.Zip

    PushButton Click, "VBName=UpdateButton;VisualText=Update"
        .
        .
        .

'End of recorded code
```

The test team could create a GUI map containing entries for every type of GUI control that would require testing. Controls would include every push button, pull-down menu, drop-down box, and scroll button. Each entry in the GUI map would contain information on the type of control, the control item's parent window, and the size and location of the control in the window. Each entry would contain a unique identifier similar in concept to control IDs. The test engineer uses these

Table 8.6   Table Driven Automated Testing

Table Used to Generate Automated Testing Script

Window (VB Name)	Window (Visual Text)	Control	Action	Arguments
StartScreen	XYZ Savings Bank	—	SetContext	—
PrequalifyButton	Prequalifying	PushButton	Click	—
frmMain	Mortgage Prequalifier	—	SetContext	—
FrmMain	File	—	MenuSelect	New Customer

unique identifiers within test scripts much in the same way that object recognition strings are used.

The GUI map serves as an index to the various objects within the GUI and the corresponding test scripts that perform tests on the objects. It can be implemented in several ways, including via constants or global variables. That is, every GUI object is replaced with a constant or global variable. The GUI map can also take advantage of a data file, such as a spreadsheet. The map information can then be read into a global array. By placing the information into a global array, the test engineer makes the map information available to every test script in the system; the same data can be reused and called repeatedly.

In addition to reading GUI data from a file or spreadsheet, expected result data can be placed into a file or spreadsheet and retrieved. An automated test tool can then compare the actual result produced by the test with the expected result maintained within a file.

The test team should continually add reusable and common test procedures and scripts to the electronic test program library. This library can offer a high return on investment, regardless whether the test engineer wants to create a common function that sets up the PC environment or develop a common script to log all errors. A key to the usefulness of the program library is the ease with which test engineers can search for and find functions within the library. The naming convention adopted should enable them to readily locate desired functions, as outlined in the discussion of test development guidelines in Chapter 7. A naming convention is also helpful in supporting reuse analysis. For example, the creation of a table like Table 8.2 on page 292, only without the column "Reuse Asset" filled in, would aid in this endeavor.

8.3.2 PC Environment Automated Setup Script

As mentioned throughout this book, a PC environment setup script is a useful addition to the reuse library. The state of the PC environment should exactly match the state during the recording stage to permit a script to be played back successfully. Otherwise playback problems can occur because of environment problems.

To prevent such playback problems from happening, the test team should develop a common and often reused test environment setup script. This setup script should prepare the environment for test execution by verifying the PC configuration. It can ensure, for example, that all desktop computers (PCs) allocated to the test environment are configured in the same way. It could check that the computer drive mapping is the same for all pertinent PCs and verify all network connections. One subsection of the script can check that the video resolutions for all PCs are the same, while another could ensure that the screen saver for each computer has been turned off. Still another script might synchronize the date and time for each desktop computer. The setup script can also verify that the correct version of the AUT is in place. It can provide data initialization, restore the state of the data to its original state after add, delete, or update functions are executed, and provide file backups.

This test environment setup script can also include functionality that checks the installation of all dynamic link libraries (.dll) and verifies registry entries. It could turn on or off the operation of system messages that might interfere with the development or playback of the scripts. This script can verify available disk space and memory, sending an appropriate warning message if either is too low.

Because the setup script can incorporate significant functionality, the test engineer must take care to keep modularity in mind. It is best to restruct the major functionality to a single script and to consolidate a number of separate scripts into one setup shell procedure (or wrapper).

Student Question 8.5
What other functionality could a PC environment setup script contain? Give examples.

8.3.3   Automated Recording Options

Another useful script in a test library repertoire might automate all recording options. Most automated test tools allow the test engineer to set up script recording options in various ways. So that members of the test team will use a consistent approach, a script can be created that automates this setup. This function will provide instructions on how to select a number of parameters, such as mouse drags, certain objects, window settings, and an object window.

In some automated test tools, such as Robot, the test engineer can specify how the tool should identify list and menu contents and unsupported mouse drags. Test personnel can specify which prefix to use in script auto-naming, whether to record think time, and whether Robot should save and restore the sizes and positions of active windows [8]. These sorts of setup activities can be automated to ensure that they remain consistent for each PC setup.

Additionally, most automated test tools will provide the capability to set up script playback options. For the playback option in Robot, the test engineer can specify how much of a delay should separate commands and keystrokes, whether to use the recorded think time and typing delays, whether to skip verification points, whether to display an acknowledge results box, and what happens to the Robot window during playback. Test personnel can specify which results to save in a log and whether the log should appear after playback. Other selections in Robot include the ability to specify "Caption Matching," "Wait State," "Unexpected Active Window" handling, "Error Recovery" handling, and "Trap" handling [9]. Again, this setup should remain consistent among all PCs within the test environment—perfect justification for automating the test environment setup.

8.3.4 Login Function

Another important part of a reuse library is a login script. This script can start and end at a specific point. It can start the AUT and verifies the login ID and password. In addition, it can verify the available memory before and after the application starts, among other things. This script can be called at the beginning of all procedures.

8.3.5 Exit Function

An endless number and variety of scripts can be added to the automation infrastructure (reuse library). The automation infrastructure includes common functions found within the test environment that can be called by a test procedure or incorporated within a new test procedure. Scripts can be created that select the various ways of opening, closing, deleting, cutting, and pasting records. For example, a test procedure script that randomly selects the method to exit an application could be called when needed from another test procedure script. The actions necessary for exiting an application might include the selection of an Exit button, selection of the Exit value from the File pull-down menu, selection of the Close value under the File pull-down menu, and double-clicking on the Window Control menu box, just to name a few. The single test procedure step (exit application) would be performed differently each time the script executed, thereby fully exercising the system.

8.3.6 Navigation

As already explained in the test development guidelines in Section 8.2, the navigation of an application requires its own script. The test team needs to add test procedures for navigation purposes only to the automation infrastructure. These test procedures are not designed to validate specific functional requirements, but rather to support user interface actions. For example, a test engineer may record a procedure that navigates the application through several windows and then exits at a particular window. A separate test procedure may then validate the destination window. Navigation procedures may be shared and reused throughout the design and development effort.

8.3.7 Verifying GUI Standards

Another script that could be added to the library of reusable scripts might verify the GUI standards. The test team can consider developing specific test procedures for performing checks against GUI standards (such as those examining font, color, and tab order choices) that could be run as part of a regression test, rather than as part of the system test. Team members might create a script that verifies GUI standards based on a set of rules that appear in a .csv file. The script then could read the rules from the .csv file and compare them with the actual GUI implementation.

8.3.8 Smoke Test

A very important addition to the library of reusable scripts consists of a build verification test, otherwise known as a *smoke test*. This test, which was described in Chapter 2, focuses on automating the critical high-level functionality of the application. Instead of repeatedly retesting everything manually whenever a new software build is received, a test engineer plays back the smoke test, verifying that the major functionality of the system still exists. An automated test tool allows the test engineer to record the manual test steps that would usually be taken in this software build verification.

The test team first determines which parts of the AUT test account for the high-level functionality. It then develops automated test procedures targeting this major functionality. This smoke test can be replayed by the test engineers or developers whenever a new software release is received to verify that the build process did not create a new problem and to prove that the configuration management checkout process was not faulty.

When the test effort is targeted at the first release of an application, smoke tests may consist of a series of tests that verify that the database points to the correct environment, the correct (expected) version of the database is employed, sessions can be launched, all screens and menu selections are accessible, and data can be entered, selected, and edited. One to two days of test team time may be required to perform a smoke test involving the creation and execution of automated scripts for that software release and the analysis of results. When testing the first release of an application, the test team may want to perform a smoke test on each segment of the system so as to be able to initiate test development as soon as possible without waiting for the entire system to become stable.

If the results meet expectations, meaning that the smoke tests passed, then the software is formally moved into the test environment. If the results do not meet expectations and the failures do not result from setup/configuration, script or test engineer error, or software fixes, then the test team should reject the software as not ready for test.

Case Study
Smoke Test Application

The potential application of smoke testing was first introduced in Chapter 2. Instead of blindly initiating test activities, only to find that the software application build is not correct, the smoke test can verify that the major functionality found in previous AUT builds is still in proper working condition.

A test engineer named Carla worked on a project involving the introduction of a new configuration management tool. The CM personnel administering the tool were not familiar with its full capabilities and had received only preliminary training on the tool. Carla and the other test team members chose to run a smoke test each time that a new software build was received.

In the majority of cases, the smoke tests failed because the build process had been faulty. The CM personnel either forgot to check in the correct component or forgot to check out the correct version of another component. In the first few months following the acquisition of the CM tool, the project depended on the smoke test to verify that the build process had been performed correctly.

Student Question 8.6
Create a sample smoke test for an existing application.

8.3.9   Error-Logging Routine

As mentioned in the development guidelines, error-logging routines should be part of a reuse library. The test engineer can create an error-checking routine by recording any error information that the tool might not already collect. For example, it might gather such information as "actual versus expected result," application status, and environment information at time of error.

8.3.10   Help Function Verification Script

A help verification script can verify that the help functionality is accessible, that the content is correct, and that correct navigation is occurring. What follows are some examples of reusable script libraries implemented by various test engineers.

A group of test engineers using WinRunner, a test tool from Mercury Interactive, created a library of reusable scripts and made the scripts available to all test engineers by making them accessible via the Web [10]. This library contains templates for test scripts, extensions of the test script language, and standardized test

Table 8.7 Reusable Functions of WinRunner Scripts

Module	Description	Initali-zation Script	Function Generator Category
array	Functions for associative arrays	init/ini_arr	imbus: Array
file	Functions for file access	init/ini_file	imbus: File
general	Miscellaneous universal functions	init/ini_gen	imbus: General
geo	Functions for checking the geometric alignment of objects	init/ini_geo	imbus: Geometrics
list	Functions for simplified access to list objects	init/ini_list	imbus: List
menu	Functions for handling menus	init/ini_menu	imbus: Menu
standard	Standard tests	init/ini_std	imbus: Standard Tests
stdClass	Standard tests for object classes, such as radio buttons	init/ini_stdC	imbus: Standard Tests (class)
string	Functions for handling character strings	init/ini_str	imbus: String
tab	Functions for accessing tab-card controls	init/ini_tab	imbus: Tab
tooltips	Functions for accessing tool tips and toolbars	init/ini_tt	imbus: Tooltips

procedures for GUI testing using WinRunner. Table 8.7 provides examples of reusable functions written to support this project.

The library consists of three basic components: script templates, functions, and GUI checks. All three components are designed to simplify the work of the test developer and to standardize the test results. The script templates enable the test engineers to write their own scripts. The script can be copied and developed into complete test scripts or function sets. GUI checks are integrated into the WinRunner environment by starting the corresponding installation script. They work much like built-in GUI checks.

8.3.11 Timed Message Boxes Function

Another example of a reusable script is the timed message boxes function. This function allows message boxes to be displayed and then disappear after a specified amount of time, so as to avoid script failure.

8.3.12 Advanced Math Functions

Advanced math functions, once created, can be reused whenever applicable for any AUT.

Chapter Summary

- Test development involves the creation of test procedures that are maintainable, reusable, simple, and robust, which in itself can be as challenging as the development of the AUT. To maximize the benefit derived from test automation, test engineers need to conduct test procedure development, like test design, in parallel with development of the target application.

- The test development architecture provides the test team with a clear picture of the test development preparation activities (building blocks) necessary to create test procedures. This architecture graphically depicts the major activities to be performed as part of test development. The test team must modify and tailor the test development architecture to reflect the priorities of the particular project.

- Test procedure development needs to be preceded by several setup activities, such as tracking and managing test environment setup activities, where material procurements may have long lead times.

- Prior to the commencement of test development, the test team needs to perform an analysis to identify the potential for reuse of existing test procedures and scripts within the automation infrastructure (reuse library).

- The test procedure development/execution schedule is prepared by the test team as a means to identify the timeframe for developing and executing the various tests. This schedule identifies dependencies between tests and includes test setup activities, test procedure sequences, and cleanup activities.

- Prior to the creation of a complete suite of test procedures, the test team should perform modularity-relationship analysis. The results of this analysis help to clarify data independence, plan for dependencies between tests, and identify common scripts that can be repeatedly applied to the test effort. A modularity-relationship matrix is created that specifies the interrelationship of the various test scripts. This graphical representation allows test engineers to identify opportunities for script reuse in various combinations using the wrapper format, thereby minimizing the effort required to build and maintain test scripts.

- As test procedures are being developed, the test team needs to peform configuration control for the test design, test scripts, and test data, as well as for each individual test procedure. Groups of reusable test procedures and scripts are usually maintained in a catalog or library of test data called a testbed. The testbed needs to be baselined using a configuration management tool.

- The team next needs to identify the test procedure development guidelines that will apply on the project to support the various test development activities.

These guidelines should apply to the development of both manual and automated test procedures that are reusable and maintainable.

○   An automation infrastructure (or automation framework) is a library of reusable functions that may have been originally created for test efforts on different projects or to test multiple or incremental versions of a particular application. The key to these functions is their potential for reuse, which minimizes the duplication of the test procedure development effort and enhances the reusability of the resulting test procedures.

References

1. "Analyze a little, design a little, code a little, test a little" has been attributed to Grady Booch.

2. Linz, T., Daigl, M. GUI Testing Made Painless, Implementation and Results of the ESSI Project Number 24306. Moehrendorf, Germany, 1998. www.imbus.de

3. http://www3.sympatico.ca/michael.woodall/sqa.htm.

4. http://www3.sympatico.ca/michael.woodall.

5. VB Flavor Hungarian Notation: www.strangecreations.com/library/c/naming.txt for. Also see http://support.microsoft.com/support/kb/articles/Q110/2/64.asp.

6. Linz, T., Daigl, M. How to Automate Testing of Graphical User Interfaces, Implementation and Results of the ESSI Project Number 24306. Moehrendorf, Germany, 1998. www.imbus.de.

7. Pettichord, B. Success with Test Automation. (Web page.) 1995. www.io.com/~wazmo/qa.html.

8. Jacobson, I., Booch, G., Rumbaugh, J. *The Unified Software Development Process.* Reading, MA: Addison-Wesley, 1999.

9. Ibid.

10. See note 2.

Part IV

Test Execution and Review

Things which matter most must never be at
the mercy of things which matter least.

—Johann Wolfgang von Goethe

Test Execution

Executing the test plan.

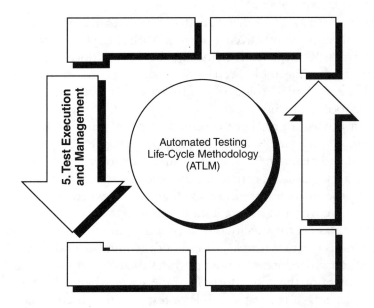

At this stage, the test team has addressed test design (Chapter 7) and test development (Chapter 8). Test procedures are now ready to be executed so as to exercise the application-under-test (AUT). Also, as discussed in Chapter 8, test environment setup planning and implementation was addressed consistent with the test requirements and guidelines provided within the test plan.

With the test plan in hand and the test environment now operational, it is time to execute the tests defined for the test program. When carrying out these test procedures, the test team will need to comply with a test procedure execution schedule, as discussed in Chapter 8. The test procedure execution schedule implements the strategy defined within the test plan. Plans for unit, integration, system, and user acceptance testing are executed. Together, these testing phases make up the steps that test the system as a whole.

After test execution ends, the test results need to be evaluated. Section 9.1 covers test outcome evaluation procedures and their documentation. These procedures describe the steps that should be completed after a test has been executed. For example, the actual result (outcome) of execution will be compared to the expected result. Commonly, during any test phase, many discrepancies between expected and actual results are identified. All discrepancies, however, do not necessarily indicate a problem with the AUT. Instead, a problem could relate to the test data or other items unrelated to the AUT. Section 9.1 therefore, outlines the things to look for so as to avoid these false negatives.

Once the test team has determined that a discrepancy between the expected result and actual result derives from a problem with the AUT, a defect or software problem report (SPR) is generated. Ideally, the SPR is documented and tracked within a defect tracking tool. Section 9.2 addresses defect tracking and also describes the characteristics to look for within a defect tracking tool and how the defect tracking tool can be used.

After a test procedure has been executed, the test team must undertake additional administrative activity. For example, test procedure execution status needs to be documented and maintained. The test team needs to be able to identify the status of test progress. Status reporting includes the ability to determine whether any particular test procedure has been executed, and if so, whether the test passed or failed. Section 9.3 covers test program status reporting.

To be able to assess the quality of test progress, the test team needs to collect and analyze various measurements. The ratio of the number of defects identified to the number of test procedures executed provides the test team with a measurement of the effectiveness of the test effort. In some cases when a high defect rate is observed, adjustments to the test schedule or test plan may become necessary.

As discussed in Section 9.3, the collection and evaluation of metrics is an activity associated with test program execution and status reporting. The metrics that receive extra attention during the test execution phase include test acceptance criteria, earned value/progress measurements, quality of application, and quality of the test life-cycle process. In addition to tracking test execution status, the test team must clarify when test execution should begin and when test execution has been completed. Test execution generally concludes when the test team verifies that the defined acceptance criteria have been satisfied, as outlined within the test plan.

Implementation of the ATLM constitutes the adoption of a set of best practices. Appendix E summarizes recommendations and suggestions that constitute a set of best practices for the development and execution of automated test procedures. These best practices are aimed at helping the test team avoid the kind of test program missteps that consume test engineer time and increase test program effort.

9.1 | Executing and Evaluating Test Phases

At this stage, the test team is ready to execute and evaluate the test procedures, as defined in the test plan for each of the various test phases. It therefore implements and analyzes the results of integration, system, and user acceptance testing. The primary input for each test phase is the associated suite of test procedures. The output of each test phase consists of the achieved or modified acceptance criteria, as defined in the test plan. Software problem reports are documented throughout each test phase, fixes are implemented and documented, and automated test scripts are baselined in the integration test phase and later reused in the system test phase. Figure 9.1 depicts a detailed test execution flow that incorporates the tracking of software problem reports.

The level of formality required for each test phase depends on the particular organization of the test team or the specifications detailed in customer or end-user requirements. The test team needs to clearly identify all required test program documentation within the test plan and then ensure that the documentation is produced according to schedule. Test program documentation may need to comply with specific industry or regulatory standards. These standards, when imposed, specify the level of detail for which the documentation must be produced.

9.1.1 Unit Test Execution and Evaluation

Unit tests should be performed in accordance with the test plan and should remain consistent with the detailed development schedule, as discussed in Chapter 8. Test procedures should consist of input and expected results to facilitate an automated results checkout process. At the white-box testing level, test procedures focus on the smallest collection of code that can be usefully tested. Because unit testing requires a detailed understanding of the code, it is generally more efficient to have application developers execute the unit tests than to have independent test engineers perform these tests. During unit testing, test engineers formally assigned to perform system-level testing can help by documenting and witnessing unit tests. This involvement allows developers to focus their attention on developing the utilities or the respective tools needed to automate and execute the unit tests.

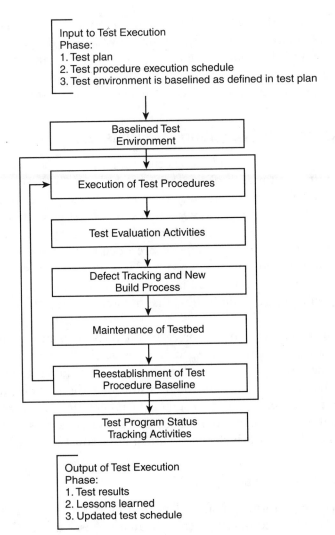

Figure 9.1   Test Execution Flow

Where possible, an individual other than the developer responsible for a unit of code should execute tests on the particular unit of code. Such a person will perform testing more objectively because the code will be new to him or her and because developers (and people in general) are often blind to their own mistakes. It is also best to execute unit tests shortly after the code has been created and before any code integration has occurred. This approach will allow software defects to be found early and will help prevent such errors from being carried forward.

Also during unit testing, static analysis can be performed. For example, when the development team creates applications in C++, tools such as PC Lint can perform static analysis of the code to look for anything suspect. For more information on the various tools described in this section, refer to Appendix B.

During the unit testing phase, code profiling can be performed. Many profiling tools are available, including a tool called Visual Quantify that carries out runtime profiling. Traditionally, profiling is a tuning process that determines, for example, whether an algorithm is inefficient or a function is being called too frequently. Profiling can discover improper scaling of algorithms, instantiations, and resource utilization. For instance, code profiling activities may identify the need to change from a bubble sort to a quick sort. In other cases, it can highlight a slow search routine in a third-party library or redundant API calls that can cause performance delays. These problems may remain invisible during initial implementation but can cause catastrophic disaster during production.

Most code development test tools come with their own debuggers. Yet, these debuggers offer little help during unit testing when the individual does not have access to the source code. Several development test tools, such as Purify and Quantify, may pinpoint problems in object files and libraries while providing good stack tracebacks. Purify, for example, can identify memory leaks in the application as well as in third-party components. Quantify may identify resource leaks. The various types of tools that can be employed in support of unit and integration-level testing are noted in Chapter 3.

When unit testing uncovers problems, such defects need to be documented and tracked. Test documentation is more the exception than the rule when it comes to the performance of unit testing. Commonly, an application developer executes a test, notes any defects, and then immediately proceeds with troubleshooting activities to fix the defect, without documenting it. For metric collection and process improvement purposes, development teams may find it worthwhile to record and track defects observed during unit testing. Code and unit test scripts need to be refined to permit this activity. Unit test activities can be documented within a software development folder (SDF) associated with the particular software unit, depending on the required level of formality. Selected unit testing evaluation criteria follow.

Unit Testing Evaluation Criteria List

UT1 Does the code meet the design specifications?

UT2 For each conditional statement, does the condition execute correctly?

UT3 Have the tests exercised the unit over the full range of operational conditions that the unit of software is expected to address?

UT4 Do all exceptions work correctly?

UT5   Are errors firing correctly?

UT6   Code coverage: Have all statements been covered at least once?

UT7   Code coverage: Has each conditional statement been exercised at least once by the tests?

UT8   Code coverage: Have all boundary cases been exercised?

UT9   Were any design assumptions made about the operation of this unit? Did the tests demonstrate these assumptions?

UT10   Did the code pass the memory leakage test?

UT11   Did it pass the code profiling test?

UT12   Have all control paths of critical units been exercised successfully by the test data?

Once the unit test phase is complete, the software application code is baselined and the test team evaluates test results and prepares a test report that summarizes test activities. Table 9.1 gives a sample unit test evaluation report. Test results need to satisfy unit completion criteria, and the test team may need to obtain sign-off from management, end users, and the QA department after each phase before initiating the next test phase.

9.1.2   Integration Test Execution and Evaluation

Integration testing can be conducted either by developers or by the test group, depending upon the decision made during test planning with regard to the allocation of funding for test activities. Integration testing resembles system testing, but concentrates on the application internals more than system testing does. During integration testing, units are incrementally integrated and tested together based upon control flow. Because units may consist of other units, some integration testing (also called module testing) may take place during unit testing.

Integration test procedures are based on an integration test design addressed in Chapter 7. After tests have been executed, the test team performs a careful analysis (see Section 9.1.3 for further discussion of the detailed evaluation activities). For process improvement purposes, defect reports (that is, SPRs) need to be documented and tracked. Section 9.2 provides further detail on software problem reporting and defect tracking.

The development team must generate software fixes to resolve problem reports, and integration test procedures subsequently need to be refined. When the test team takes responsibility for executing integration tests, the test engineers can enhance developer's understanding of system and software problems and help replicate a problem when necessary. Each defect report will be classified in a range of 1

Table 9.1 Unit Test Evaluation Report

Unit Test ID	Evaluation Criteria	Results	Automated Tool
AccAdd	UT1	✓	Code Coverage Tool
	UT2	✓	Static Analyzer
	UT3	See SPR 51	Code Coverage Tool
	UT4	✓	Exception Handler
	UT5	✓	Exception Handler
	UT6	See SPR 52	Code Coverage Tool
	UT7	TBD	Code Coverage Tool
	UT8	TBD	Code Coverage Tool
	UT9	TBD	N/A
	UT10	TBD	Memory Leak Detector
	UT11	TBD	Code Profiler
	UT12	TBD	Code Coverage Tool
DelAdd	UT1	✓	Code Coverage Tool
	UT2	✓	Static Analyzer
	UT3	✓	Code Coverage Tool
	UT4	✓	Exception Handler
	UT5	✓	Exception Handler
	UT6	TBD	Code Coverage Tool
	UT7	TBD	Code Coverage Tool
	UT8	TBD	Code Coverage Tool
	UT9	TBD	N/A
	UT10	TBD	Memory Leak Detector
	UT11	TBD	Code Profiler
	UT12	TBD	Code Coverage Tool

to 4, based upon the degree of priority. Section 9.2 addresses the classification of defects in further detail.

Test engineers may participate in engineering review boards, as applicable, to review and discuss outstanding defect reports. Following the development effort intended to mitigate defect reports, test engineers perform regression tests to verify closure of the problems. During integration testing, some test scripts can be automated successfully for reuse during system testing. Given this reuse opportunity, the automated scripts employed in integration testing need to be baselined following their successful execution. After integration testing ends, the test team prepares a report that summarizes test activities and evaluates test results. End-user approval of the test report constitutes the conclusion of unit and integration testing.

9.1.3   System Test Execution and Evaluation

System testing is another form of integration testing, albeit one conducted at a higher level. During system testing, the test engineer examines the integration of parts, which make up the entire system. System-level tests are usually performed by a separate test team that implements the test procedure execution schedule and the system test plan. They may require a large number of individual test procedures to verify all necessary combinations of input, process rules, and output associated with a program function.

9.1.3.1   False Negatives

Once test procedures supporting system test have been executed, the test team compares the expected result for each test procedure with the actual result. If the actual result differs from the expected result, the delta (that is, the discrepancy) must be further diagnosed. A failed test procedure does not necessarily indicate a problem with the AUT. The problem could be a *false negative,* meaning that the test failed even though no problem exists with the AUT. Incidents of false-negative outcomes can be caused by a necessary change in the application, test setup errors, test procedure errors, user errors, automated test script logic errors, or test environment setup errors. Test environment setup problems, for example, may stem from the installation of the wrong version of the application software.

The test team needs to be able to replicate the problem and must ensure that the problem did not result from a user error. For example, a test engineer might expect a specific data outcome after a test procedure has executed; in reality this data outcome might not be possible unless specific data setup activities have occurred. To prevent this type of user error, the test procedure description should contain the level of detail necessary and test procedures must be properly verified. See Section 8.1.10 for further information on test procedure reviews.

Additionally, test engineers, when investigating a failure of an automated test script, must ensure that the problem does not result from a procedural error. For example, a screen menu item may have been changed based upon user input, but the automated script, which was created during a previous software version, may not properly reflect the change. The automated script will indicate a failure when executed, but this failure does not reflect a problem with the AUT.

To document the various failures that occur, a table such as Table 9.2 can be generated to facilitate the evaluation of test outcomes. This table outlines the various test outcome evaluation activities that can be conducted and documented for test metric collection purposes.

The results depicted in Table 9.2 can be used to collectively analyze reported problems. For example, when a number of false negatives point to a fault in the test procedure development, an improvement in the test procedure creation process is warranted. Table 9.3 comprises a legend that delineates the reason codes, troubleshooting activity codes, and solution codes possible when developing a table like Table 9.2.

9.1.3.2 False Positives

Even when test execution results match the expected results, the test team must ensure that the results are not based upon *false positives*, where a test procedure appears to have executed successfully but a problem actually exists with the AUT. The test team needs to stay alert for false positives caused by automated test tools that are not sensitive enough to the nuances of the AUT. Given the possibility of this kind of condition, it is important that test procedure walkthroughs be con-

Table 9.2   Test Outcome Evaluation Activities

Test Pro- cedure ID	Actual Test Result of Test Procedure Execution	Potential Reason for Failure	Trouble- shooting Activities	Proposed Solution
ACC0001	Incorrect delivery dates	R3: test records are using expired dates, so securities are invalid	TA3	S3
ACC0002	As expected	N/A	N/A	N/A
ACC0003	Interest calculation incorrect	R6: interest calculation algorithm incorrect	TA6, TA7	S6 (SPR# VIS346)
ACC0004	Securities verification screen is missing	R2: securities verification screen existed in the last build (Build 5.3)	TA2	S6 (SPR# VIS347)
DEL0001	Not able to deliver security	R6: Deliver button is not enabled	TA6, R6	S6 (SPR# VIS348)
DEL0002	Not able to verify security	R7: securities server is down	TA8, bring securities server up	S6 (SPR# VIS349)
DEL0003	Test script fails in the middle of playback	R5	TA6, TA5	S5

Table 9.3   Test Outcome Report Legend

Potential Reason for Failure	Troubleshooting Activities	Proposed Solution
R1 Environment Setup	TA1 Verify Environment Setup	S1 Correct Environment Setup (Hardware, Software)
R2 Build Problems	TA2 Verify Build	S2 Correct Build
R3 Test Data	TA3 Verify Test Data	S3 Correct Test Data
R4 Test Procedure Error	TA4 Verify Test Procedure Error	S4 Correct Test Procedure Error
R5 Test Script Error	TA5 Verify Test Script Error	S5 Correct Test Script Error
R6 Application Problem	TA6 Repeat Test Procedure Execution	S6 SPR
R7 User Error	TA7 Rework User Error Issues	
R8 Other, please describe	TA8 Generate SPR	
	TA8 Verify "Other," please describe	

ducted prior to test execution. In addition to conducting test procedure walk-throughs or peer reviews, the test team should evaluate and spot-check the correctness of the test result, even if the script has passed the first time. If the expected test result does not match the actual test result, because of a problem in the AUT rather than because of a false positive or a false negative, the test team needs to create a software problem report to document the defect.

9.1.4   Test Results Analysis of Regression Tests

When the test group receives a new application baseline, build release notes should accompany the new build. These release notes should address all new functionality additions and defects that were fixed in the revision. Additionally, once the test team receives the new build, a smoke test should be executed to verify that the major functionality from the previous build still functions properly in the new build. When the smoke test flags discrepancies, then the new build should not be accepted for system testing. When a smoke test passes, the new build is accepted for system testing and incremental regression testing is performed.

Regression testing can consist of running a specific selection of automated tests that reexercise high-risk and potentially affected areas of code after defects have been fixed. Regression test result analysis ensures that previously working system functionality has not been affected as a result of software modifications implemented to correct defects. The test team therefore needs to perform regression tests against both modified code as well as code which was not changed, but potentially could have been affected by the change. When the test engineer encounters a large number of errors associated with functionality that previously worked, it can be inferred that the application developers may have been careless in implementing changes. These findings should be documented as part of the metrics collection process, discussed in Section 9.3.2.

When errors are observed for a system functionality that previously worked, the test team needs to identify other functional areas that are most likely to have an effect on the functionality where the error occurred. Based on the results of such analysis, a greater regression testing emphasis can be placed on the selected functionality. Regression testing is further performed on the problem functionality area to verify closure of the open defects, once the development team has implemented its fixes.

The test team also performs analysis to identify particular components or functionality that are experiencing a greater relative number of problem reports. This analysis may reveal that additional test procedures and test effort need to be assigned to the components. If developers indicate that a particular functional area is now fixed, but regression testing uncovers problems for the particular software, then the test engineer needs to ascertain whether an environment issue is the culprit or whether poor implementation of the software correction is at fault.

Analysis of test results can also confirm whether executed test procedures are adept at identifying errors. This analysis also helps to identify the functionality where most defects have been uncovered and suggests where further test and repair efforts require further focus. The test team may therefore need to consider reallocation of test engineer effort and reassessment of application risk allocation.

System testing is completed once the system acceptance criteria have been met. For more information, see the acceptance criteria metric described in Section 9.3.2.

9.1.5 User Acceptance Test Execution and Evaluation

The test team may need to perform a user acceptance test (UAT) that involves end-user participation. The UAT commonly consists of a subset of the suite of tests performed at the system test level. The specific suite tests planned must be defined and communicated to the customer or end user for approval. Acceptance testing will be performed in a defined test environment.

Defects observed during UAT are documented via a SPR and assigned a priority rating. SPRs, which cannot be readily fixed during the scheduled UAT timeframe, may be referred to an engineering review board (ERB) for further evaluation and engineering review. Depending on the user acceptance criteria, system acceptance could be achieved, for example, following resolution of all level 1 and level 2 problem reports.

Following the performance of UAT or any other testing phase, the test team prepares a report that provides a summary of test activities and includes an evaluation of test results. The satisfactory resolution of all level 1 and level 2 SPRs and approval of the test report generally constitutes the conclusion of UAT testing.

Site acceptance tests may be warranted for some tasks and projects, when required by a customer and specified within approved test plans. These tests usually consist of the same set of test procedures and scripts used during UAT, minus any tests that may not apply for a specific site. The same process for resolving software problem reports applies. Following the performance of site testing, the test team may prepare another test report.

9.2 | Defect Tracking and New Build Process

Test engineers will need to help developers understand and replicate system and software problems, when necessary. Each defect is commonly classified in a range of 1 to 4 based upon degree of priority. Test engineers will need to participate in ERBs, as applicable, to review and discuss outstanding defect reports. Following development effort to correct identified defects, test engineers perform regression testing on the applicable software to verify closure of problem reports.

Each test team needs to perform problem reporting operations in compliance with a defined process. Typically, the test engineer creates the SPR within a defect tracking system. Following the creation of the SPR, an automatic e-mail notification is forwarded to cognizant members of the configuration management (CM) group and application development team to advise them that a SPR has been generated. Once the SPR has been corrected and unit testing has been carried out to the satisfaction of the software development team, the new software code is checked via a software CM tool. Once a number of software problem reports have been corrected, the development team issues a new software build and software updates are made to the test environment.

One action required during defect tracking is the assignment of a level of priority for the defect. The test engineer must assess the importance of the solution to the successful operation of the system. The most critical defects cause the software to fail and prevent the continuation of the test activity. In contrast, high-priority defects need to be fixed soon but generally do not prevent the test activity from continuing. A common classification of defect priority levels follows.

1. Fatal. Operation of the application is interrupted, and testing cannot be continued.

2. High priority. A significant problem, but the application is still operational.

3. Medium priority. The problem has little impact on operation of the application.

4. Low priority. The problem has no impact on the operation of the application.

Defects that cannot be readily fixed are referred to an ERB for further evaluation and disposition. The ERB may confirm that the SPR is valid and possibly adjust the priority level of a SPR. In other cases, the ERB may confirm that the SPR is not valid and cancel the SPR. An SPR that represents an enhancement, will be reclassified as a change request. Figure 9.2 provides an example of a typical defect tracking procedure.

The documentation and tracking of defects are greatly facilitated by an automated tool. An automated defect tracking tool helps to ensure that reported defects receive the proper attention. Without such a tool, some problem reports may not be assigned to a developer for proper corrective action. In other cases, application developers may inadvertently close defect reports without proper verification by test personnel. Automated defect tracking tools generally support the maintenance of a central defect tracking repository; this repository is accessible by all project team members.

Several basic characteristics can be assessed to determine the value of a defect tracking tool (see Table 9.4 for more details). For example, the tool should be able to perform the following tasks:

- Identify the priority of a defect
- Assign a unique identifier to each defect
- Link each defect to the applicable test procedure as well as to a particular application build
- Log the date on which the defect was reported
- Log the date on which the defect was assigned to an application developer
- Log the date on which the defect was updated
- Identify the developer assigned to the defect
- Identify the test engineer who reported the defect
- Log and track the status of the defect, including values such as new, open, assigned, fixed, retest, and closed

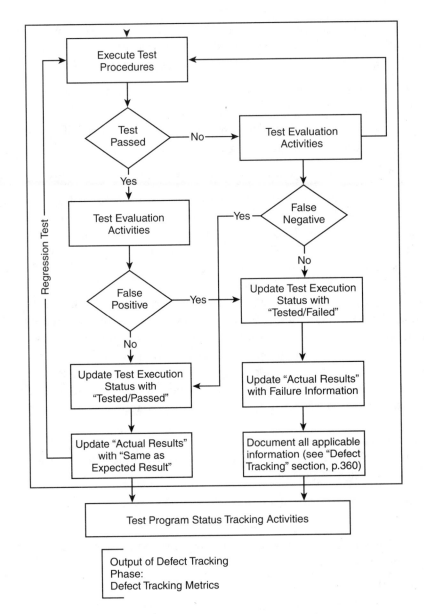

Figure 9.2 Defect Tracking Procedure

Table 9.4 Defect Tracking Tool Evaluation Criteria

Criterion	Weight (1–5)	Score (1–5)	Value
Can interface with automated testing tool	5	5	25
Allows for automatic generation of defects from within automated testing tool	5	4	20
Advanced reporting facility: generates defect reports, both predefined and modifiable/customizable, that support progress measurements and trend analysis	5	3	15
Allows for querying and sorting of data	5	3	15
Provides simultaneous access by multiple users	5	4	20
Supports access of various users via the World Wide Web	4	5	20
Allows for setup of various defect tracking tool users, with different access rights; security features control the data made available to each user	5	5	25
Allows for adding project-specific attributes; tool is customizable	5	4	20
Provides defect life-cycle model for tracking defects from initial discovery to final resolution; statuses and substatus are customizable; easy configuration of data collection/workflow on a project-by-project basis	5	3	15
Allows files to be attached to defect reports	5	3	15
Provides automatic notification to the responsible party when a new defect is generated	5	4	20
Allows user selection of a particular database type	4	5	20
Supports multiplatform development environment	5	5	25
Integrates with requirements management tool	4	4	16
Integrates with configuration management tool	4	4	16
Integrates with test management tool	4	4	16

The test management tool should permit the automatic validation of as many of the test results as possible. Some test tools, such as Rational's TestStudio, allow the anticipated results of a test to be hard-coded within the test procedure when a specific response is expected. As a result, when a test script fails, the test engineer can be confident that the actual result does not meet the specific result expected from the test. A specific result cannot always be programmed into the tool, however, especially when numerous transactions are performed against the application's database and results are very dynamic. The sequential order of the transactions may vary, and the transactions occurring prior to the test may affect the results. In this situation, the test results could be evaluated by querying the database directly using SQL statements and then comparing the query results and the application generated results to the expected results.

Most automated test tools maintain test results and permit for the automatic generation of test results (that is, the test log). The test log will maintain information such as pass or fail status, the name of each test procedure executed, and the start and end times for each test execution. Test tools vary in terms of the level of sophistication that they provide with regard to test result analysis. The more test result attributes that can be documented by a test tool, the more information that the test engineer can use to analyze results. Some tools, for example, may identify the state of the application and the state of the system.

As with any tool to be applied on a project, the selection of a defect tracking tool involves the consideration of a number of characteristics. With a defect tracking tool, the responsible person should go through the various steps described in Chapter 3 to make a decision about the tool (or any other tool). First, the responsible person comes up with a table of tool characteristics to be considered, like that depicted in Table 9.4. Next, he or she assigns a weight to each characteristic.

Defects may be discovered throughout the entire testing life cycle. Therefore, it is recommended that the test team generate and classify SPRs according to the life-cycle phase or product in which the defect emerged. Table 9.5 provides an example of the possible categories for software problem reports.

Table 9.5 SPR Categories

Category	Apply if a Problem Has Been Found in:	System	Software	Hardware
A	System development plan	✓		
B	Operational concept	✓		
C	System or software requirements		✓	✓
D	Design of the system or software		✓	✓
E	Coded software (of AUT)		✓	
F	Test plans, cases, and procedures or the test report		✓	✓
G	User or support manuals		✓	✓
H	Process being followed on the project		✓	✓
I	Hardware, firmware, communications equipment			✓
J	Any other aspect of the project	✓	✓	✓

9.2.1   Defect Life-Cycle Model

When using a defect tracking tool, the test team will need to define and document the defect life-cycle model, also called the defect workflow. In some organizations, the configuration management group takes responsibility for the defect life cycle; in other organizations, it is a test team responsibility. Figure 9.3 provides an example of a defect life-cycle model.

9.3 | Test Program Status Tracking

The test team manager is responsible for ensuring that tests are executed according to schedule, and that test personnel are allocated and redirected when necessary to handle problems that arise during the test effort. To perform this oversight function effectively, the test manager must conduct test program status tracking and management reporting.

Throughout the testing phase, the test engineer will need to provide meaningful reports based on the measures and metrics defined within the test plan and outlined in this section. As part of this effort, the test engineer produces test logs and test coverage reports (see Section 9.3.2). Test logs can be used to verify that all SPRs have been documented and corrected (by checking the status of the SPR). The test engineer reviews the test coverage report to ascertain whether complete (100%) test procedure execution coverage has been achieved. In addition, he determines whether test coverage criteria have been met or whether these criteria should be modified. The test team further needs to decide whether additional test requirements and test procedures are needed to satisfy test coverage or test completion criteria. Several reports produced by the test team will prove especially valuable, including software problem report summaries (or individual problem reports) as well as defect density and defect trend analysis reports. This section will discuss the various metrics that the test engineer can produce and report to management.

To effectively monitor testing progress and report to senior management, the test manager needs to implement an earned value approach to test progress status effort. Implementing an *earned value management system* (EVMS) is one of the best ways of tracking the test program status [1]; this section provides examples of how to implement an EVMS. Similarly, the test manager needs to collect other measurements of test performance, such as those related to test coverage, predictions of time to release AUT, and quality of the software at time of release. Although an abundant number of test metrics can be collected, time limitations often restrict the test team's ability to collect, track, and analyze such measurements.

1. When a defect is generated initially, the status is set to "New." (Note: How to document the defect, what fields need to be filled in, and so on also need to be specified.)

2. The tester selects the type of defect:
   - Bug
   - Cosmetic
   - Enhancement
   - Omission

3. The tester then selects the priority of the defect:
   - Critical—fatal error
   - High—needs immediate attention
   - Medium—needs to be resolved as soon as possible, but not a showstopper
   - Low—cosmetic error

4. A designated person (in some companies, the software manager; in other companies, a special board) evaluates the defect and assigns a status and makes modifications of type of defect and/or priority if applicable.

   The status "Open" is assigned if it is a valid defect.

   The status "Close" is assigned if it is a duplicate defect or user error. The reason for "closing" the defect needs to be documented.

   The status "Deferred" is assigned if the defect will be addressed in a later release.

   The status "Enhancement" is assigned if the defect is an enhancement requirement.

5. If the status is determined to be "Open," the software manager (or other designated person) assigns the defect to the responsible person (developer) and sets the status to "Assigned."

6. Once the developer is working on the defect, the status can be set to "Work in Progress."

7. After the defect has been fixed, the developer documents the fix in the defect tracking tool and sets the status to "Fixed," if it was fixed, or "Duplicate," if the defect is a duplication (specifying the duplicated defect). The status can also be set to "As Designed," if the function executes correctly. At the same time, the developer reassigns the defect to the originator.

8. Once a new build is received with the implemented fix, the test engineer retests the fix and other possible affected code. If the defect has been corrected with the fix, the test engineer sets the status to "Close." If the defect has not been corrected with the fix, the test engineer sets the status to "Reopen."

Figure 9.3 Defect Life-Cycle Model

9.3.1   Earned Value Management System

This section outlines an approach for using earned value calculations as a test program status tracking method, and presents a case study of a high-level implementation of an EVMS. Earned value analysis involves tracking the value of completed work and comparing it to planned costs and actual costs so as to provide a true measure of schedule and cost status and to enable the creation of effective corrective actions. The earned value process includes four steps:

1. Identify short tasks (functional test phase).
2. Schedule each task (task start date and end date).
3. Assign a budget to each task (task will require 3,100 hours using four test engineers).
4. Measure the progress of each task, enabling the engineer to calculate schedule and cost variance.

The use of earned value calculations requires the collection of performance measurements—for example, assessments of test program progress relative to predetermined goals or objectives. This approach also helps to recast quantified objectives in terms of technical, schedule, resource, or cost/profit parameters. Two key earned value calculations pertain to the assessment of cost and schedule variance:

Earned value for work completed – planned budget = schedule variance
Earned value for work completed – actual cost = cost variance

---

Case Study
System Test Status Tracking

A test manager named Laura determines that a test effort will require a budget of 4,440 hours to conduct system test activities over a period of four and a half months. To carry out test scheduling and cost allocation, she uses the test program work breakdown structure provided in Table 5.3 on pages 158–163. Laura allocates the test effort for each specific task in terms of hours as shown in Table 9.6.

Note that the allocation of hours pertains only to test personnel on the test team and does not define the hours, for example, that would apply to an application developer who is modifying application software in response to SPRs. Tasks that fall to the development team in this case study have been scheduled and budgeted and are being tracked separately in another control account by a software development manager.

Once the high-level breakdown of budgeted hours for work scheduled is completed, Laura breaks down the various tasks into further detail. For example, she decomposes task 842 from Table 9.6 into the subtasks given in Table 9.7.

Table 9.6   Test Effort Allocation by Task

WBS	Task Number	Schedule	Weeks	Hours	People	Task Description
9.1	840	February	4	400	2.5	Environment setup. Develop environment setup scripts.
9.2	841	February	4	400	2.5	Testbed environment. Develop testbed scripts and perform Testbed development logistics.
9.3	842	March–May	13	3,120	6	Test phase execution. Execute the various test strategies—strategic execution of automated testing.
9.4	843	June	1.5	360	6	Test reporting. Prepare test reports.
9.5	844	February	4	160	1	Issue resolution. Resolve daily issues regarding automated test tool problems. If necessary, contact the test tool vendor for support.

Table 9.7   Test Phase Execution Subtasks

Subtask Number	Weeks	Hours	Spend Plan	People	Subtask Description
842.1	8	1,920	50/50	6	First-time execution of functional test procedures, such as test execution, prioritization of defects, and providing status updates
842.2	5	600	50/50	3	Execution of functional regression tests
842.3	5	100	50/50	0.5	Performance testing
842.4	5	100	50/50	0.5	Stress testing
842.5	5	100	50/50	0.5	Backup and recoverability testing
842.6	5	100	50/50	0.5	Security testing
842.7	5	100	50/50	0.5	Usability testing
842.8	5	100	50/50	0.5	System test evaluation activities

In this case study, Laura is primarily interested in tracking progress of subtask 842.1. She notes that 600 functional test procedures must be executed. In addition, she reviews the test schedule and notes that the first-time execution of 50% of the test procedures (300) is slated for March, while the remaining 50% (300) are scheduled to be performed in April.

Laura previously allocated 50% of the hours for task 842.1 to the month of March (960 hours), so she jots down on a piece of paper that she has 960 *planned hours* for March. In other words, the test team is expected to expend 960 hours in March to accomplish the 50% test procedure execution planned and to expend an additional 960 hours in April to accomplish the first-time execution of the remaining 50% of the functional test procedures.

Next, Laura reviews the amount of work that was actually accomplished in March. For example, the test team finished only 80% (240 procedures) of the 300 test procedures that had been planned for execution. She also notes that the test team spent only 740 of the 960 planned hours for March and that the actual cost rate was $40/hour. Subtask 842.1 was budgeted to cost $76,800, with an even expenditure occurring across the scheduled eight-week period. As a result, the spend plan for 960 hours at $40/hour for March totaled $38,400. As Laura observed, only $30,720 (80% of 38,400) worth of work was actually completed in March.

Laura performed the following cost and schedule variance calculations for subtask 842.1 for the month of March:

Schedule Variance Calculation

$30,720	Earned value for work completed
$38,400	Planned budget for March
–$7,680	Schedule variance
EV status:	Earned value < spend plan
Result:	Task is behind schedule

Cost Variance Calculation

$30,720	Earned value for work completed
$29,600	Actual cost of the work performed for March
+$1,120	Cost variance
EV status:	Earned value > actual cost
Result:	Test team is underrunning the cost estimate and producing more per hour than originally planned

Laura next had to prepare a report to her boss outlining the status of subtask 842.1 and specifying any corrective actions necessary. She reported that work was behind schedule, but also that the test engineers had been productive. In addition, she indicated that the test effort had fallen behind schedule by approximately 200 hours, as a result of one of the test engineers being reassigned during March to help with a new contract proposal effort. She added that the test engineer had returned to the team and that the team would try to get back on schedule.

When reviewing her report with her boss, Laura realized that she needed to estimate when the test team would complete the required work at the end of April by working overtime. She therefore computed a new estimate at completion (EAC), which involved taking the actual cost to date and adding the effort necessary to complete the remaining work. The EAC total amounted to 1,180 hours, with 960 hours planned for the next four weeks. She calculated that continuing with the original spending plan would mean that the test team would be about 220 hours short of completion at the end of April.

Laura understood that she had at least two options with regard to completing the task. If the test team pressed on under the current plan, subtask 842.1 would be completed approximately one week late, meaning the project schedule would be delayed by a week. Another option would require that the six test team personnel work overtime about nine hours per week during the next four weeks to make up time. In her report to her boss, Laura indicated that the test team would work the extra hours to keep the overall project on schedule and that the cost of overtime would offset the cost underrun to date by the exact amount. Therefore, the EAC would be equal to the budget at completion (BAC).

Student Question 9.1

In this case study, the management decision to pull a person off the test team had a significant effect on test operations. Asking test team personnel to work 9 hours extra each week may affect employee moral and contribute to employee turnover. What is another solution that Laura could have suggested?

9.3.2 Test Metrics Collection and Analysis

Test metrics can provide the test manager with key indicators of the test coverage, progress, and the quality of the test effort. Many test metrics can be collected to monitor test program progress, so the test team needs to be careful to choose that set of metrics that best serves its performance concerns. Gathering and analyzing too many test metrics can become time-consuming and reduce the number of hours that are spent actually performing actual test activities. For example, Ivar Jacobsen [2] has noted that the most important measurement during system development is "the rate of change." The team should take care to measure whether the rate of change in one particular area (such as in requirements, components, or modules) is much larger than that observed in other areas. Improvement activities then focus on those areas with the highest rate of change.

This section identifies some of the more important metrics to collect when the test engineer does not have an elaborate metrics management system in place and has minimal time to collect data. Just as the test design effort was broken down in Chapter 7 into white-box and black-box test design techniques, the effort to manage metrics can be separated into white-box and black-box testing efforts. Before discussing this breakdown, however, it is beneficial to address the scope of the metric collection and analysis process. Basic elements and prerequisites of a software metric process are structured as follows [3]:

- Goals and objectives are set relative to the product and software (test) management process.

- Measurements are defined and selected to ascertain the degree to which the goals and objectives are being met.

- The data collection process and recording mechanism are defined and used.

- Measurements and reports are part of a closed-loop system that provides current (operational) and historical information to technical staff and management.

- Data on post-software product life measurement are retained for analysis that could lead to improvements for future product and process management.

9.3.2.1 White-Box Testing Metrics

White-box testing techniques target the application's internal workings; similarly, white-box metrics collection has the same focus. During white-box testing, the test engineer measures the *depth of testing* by collecting data related to path coverage and test coverage. This white-box testing metric is called *coverage analysis,* which is described in detail in Section 7.2.2.1.

Source code analysis and code profiling help discern the code quality. As already mentioned, code profiling is a tuning process that determines whether an algorithm works inefficiently or whether a function is being called too frequently. Many tools are available to accomplish this task by identifying coding and development errors, such as out-of-range indices, unused code (dead code), and unreachable code. These tools help focus the efforts on those parts of the code that have the greatest potential for defects. An example of such a tool is Rational Quantify.

The objective of source code complexity analysis is to identify complex areas of the source code. High-complexity areas of source code can be sources of high risk. Unnecessary code complexity can decrease code reusability and increase code maintenance. Consequently, testing efforts need to focus on high-complexity code. McCabe's Cyclomatic Complexity measurement helps determine high complexity code, thus identifying error prone software [4].

Another white-box test metric of interest is *fault density* [5]. The test team can predict the remaining faults by comparing the measured fault density with the expected fault density and thereby determine whether the amount of testing is sufficient. Fault density is calculated per thousand source lines of code (KSLOC) using the equation *Fd = Nd/KSLOC,* where *Nd* is the number of defects, and *KSLOC* is the number of noncomment lines of source code.

Design complexity metrics measure the number of ways that a module can call other modules. They can serve as an indicator of the integration testing effort required for a set of modules.

9.3.2.2   Black-Box Testing Metrics

During black-box testing, metrics collection focuses on the breadth of testing, such as the amount of demonstrated functionality and the amount of testing that has been performed. Black-box testing techniques are based on the application's external considerations. As a result, test procedures are based upon system requirements or use cases as described in Chapter 7.

Table 9.8 and the remainder of this section describe the various testing metrics to be collected during the black-box testing phase and their purposes. Each metric is assigned to one of three categories: coverage, progress, or quality.

Coverage Metrics

Test Coverage.   This measurement divides the total number of test procedures developed by the total number of defined test requirements. It provides the test team with a barometer with which to gauge the depth of test coverage. The depth of test coverage is usually based on the defined acceptance criteria. When testing a mission-critical system, such as an operational medical system, the test coverage indicator would need to be high relative to the depth of test coverage for nonmission-critical systems. The depth of test coverage for a commercial software product that will be used by millions of end users may also be high relative to a government information system that will serve a few hundred end users.

System Coverage Analysis.   System coverage analysis measures the amount of coverage at the system interface level. This measurement is collected automatically by SRI's TCAT tool. It expresses test coverage as the percentage of function call pairs

Table 9.8   Sample Black-Box Test Metrics

Metric Name	Description	Classi-fication
Test Coverage	Total number of test procedures/total number of test requirements. The *test coverage* metric indicates planned test coverage.	Coverage
System Coverage Analysis	The *system coverage analysis* measures the amount of coverage at the system interface level.	Coverage
Test Procedure Execution Status	Executed number of test procedures/total number of test procedures. This *test procedure execution* metric indicates the extent of the testing effort still outstanding.	Progress
Error Discovery Rate	Number of total defects found/number of test procedures executed. The *error discovery rate* metric uses the same calculation as the defect density metric. It is used to analyze and support a rational product release decision.	Progress
Defect Aging	Date defect was opened versus date defect was fixed. The *defect aging* metric provides an indication of turnaround of the defect.	Progress
Defect Fix Retest	Date defect was fixed and released in new build versus date defect was retested. The *defect fix retest* metric provides an idea about whether the test team is retesting the fixes fast enough so as to get an accurate progress metric.	Progress
Defect Trend Analysis	Number of total defects found versus number of test procedures executed over time. *Defect trend analysis* can help determine the trend of defects found. Is the trend improving as the testing phase winds down?	Progress
Current Quality Ratio	Number of test procedures successfully executed (without defects) versus the number of test procedures. The *current quality ratio* metric provides indications about the amount of functionality that has successfully been demonstrated.	Quality
Quality of Fixes	Number of total defects reopened/total number of defects fixed. This *quality of fixes* metric will provide indications of development issues.	Quality
	Ratio of previously working functionality versus new errors introduced. This *quality of fixes* metric will keep track of how often previously working functionality was adversely affected by software fixes.	Quality
Defect Density	Number of total defects found/number of test procedures executed per functionality (that is, per use case or test requirement). *Defect density* can help determine if a specific high amount of defects appear in one part of functionality tested.	Quality
Problem Reports	Number of software problem reports broken down by priority. The *problem reports* measure counts the number of software problems reported, listed by priority.	Quality
Test Effectiveness	*Test effectiveness* needs to be assessed statistically to determine how well the test data have exposed defects contained in the product.	Quality

that the tests exercise in relation to the total number of function calls in the system. Appendix B contains more information on the TCAT tool.

Functional Test Coverage. This metric can measure test coverage prior to software delivery. It indicates the percentage of the software tested at any point during the test effort [6]. The functional test coverage metric is calculated by dividing the number of test requirements that were supported by test procedures by the total number of test requirements.

Progress Metrics. During black-box testing, test engineers collect data that help identify test progress, so that the test team can predict the release date for the AUT. Progress metrics are collected iteratively during various stages of the test life cycle, such as weekly or monthly. Several progress metrics are described below.

Test Procedure Execution Status. This execution status measurement divides the number of test procedures already executed by the total number of test procedures planned. By reviewing this metric value, the test team can ascertain the number of test procedures remaining to be executed. This metric, by itself, does not provide an indication of the quality of the application. Instead, it provides information about the depth of the test effort rather than an indication of its success.

Some test management tools, such as Rational's Test Manager, allow test engineers to automatically keep track of test procedure execution status. In Test Manager, test engineers can enter test requirements and then link these requirements to the automated tests that have been created with the SQA Robot test tool. The test tool identifies which test procedures have executed successfully, which were unsuccessful, and which were not executed.

Error Discovery Rate. This measurement divides the total number of documented defects by the number of test procedures executed. Test team review of the error discovery rate metric supports trend analysis and helps forecast product release dates.

Defect Aging. Another important metric in determining progress status is the measure reflecting the turnaround time for a defect fix—that is, the time from when the defect was identified to the resolution of the defect. Defect aging pertains to the turnaround time required for an SPR to be corrected. Using defect aging data, the test team can conduct trend analysis. For example, 100 defects may be recorded on a project. When documented past experience indicates that the development team can fix as many as 20 defects per day, then the turnaround time for these problem reports may be only one work week. In this case, the defect aging statistic would be an average of 5 days. When the defect aging measure equals 10 to 15 days, the slower response time by the developers to make corrections may affect the ability of the test team to meet scheduled deadlines.

When evaluating the defect aging measure, the test team also needs to take the priority of the SPRs into consideration. A defect aging measure of 2 to 3 days may be appropriate for level 1 SPRs, while 5 to 10 days may be appropriate for level 3 SPRs. Under this type of rule of thumb, defect aging measurement is not always appropriate and needs to be modified to take into account the complexity of the AUT, among other criteria.

Defect Fix Retest. This metric provides a measure of whether the test team is retesting the corrections at an adequate rate. It is calculated by measuring the time between when the defect was fixed in a new build and when the defect was retested.

Defect Trend Analysis. Defect trend analysis can help to determine the trend of defects found. Is the trend improving as the system testing phase winds down or is the trend worsening? This metric compares the total number of defects found with the number of test procedures executed over time.

Quality Metrics

Test Success Index. This measurement, which is also known as the current quality ratio, is computed by taking the total number of test procedures executed and passed divided by the total number of test procedures executed. It provides the test team with further insight into the amount of functionality that has been successfully demonstrated.

Quality of Fixes1 = Number Total Defects Reopened/Number of Total Defects Fixed. The value obtained from this calculation provides a measure of the quality of the software corrections implemented in response to software problem reports. When this value is high, then the test team may need to notify the developers of this problem.

Quality of Fixes2 = Previously Working Functionality versus New Errors Introduced. This metric aids the test team in determining the degree to which previously working functionality has been adversely affected by software corrections.

Defect Density. The defect density metric is calculated by taking the total number of defects found and dividing this value by the number of test procedures executed for a specific functionality or use case. For example, if a high defect density appears in a specific functionality, a causal analysis should be conducted. Is this functionality very complex and therefore it would be expected that the defect density is high? Is there a problem with the design/implementation of the functionality? Were the wrong (or not enough) resources assigned to the functionality, because an inaccurate risk had been assigned to it? It also could be inferred that the developer responsible for this specific functionality needs more training.

Additionally, when evaluating defect density, the test team should consider the priority of the SPRs. For example, one application requirement may have as many as 50 low-priority SPRs, while the acceptance criteria have been satisfied. Another requirement might have one open high-priority SPR that prevents the acceptance criteria from being satisfied.

Defect Trend Analysis. Defect trend analysis is calculated by dividing the total number of defects found by the number of test procedures executed. For example, if a high amount of defects was found at the beginning of test execution and the number of defects generated decreases after all test procedures have been executed once, then the test engineer can see an improving trend.

Test Effectiveness. Test effectiveness needs to be assessed statistically to determine how well the test data have exposed defects contained in the product. In some cases, test results may have received inadequate analysis. The test team should solicit the assistance of personnel who are experienced in the use of the application, so as to review test results and determine their correctness.

Problem Report—Acceptance Criteria Metric. The acceptance criteria metric (that is, the number of SPRs classified by priority level) needs to be defined during the test planning phase, before test execution begins. The acceptance criteria will stipulate the conditions under which the system is ready to be shipped or implemented at a customer location. The test engineer must ascertain whether an AUT satisfies these criteria, which are stipulated by the customer and defined in the test plan. For example, the acceptance criteria for a simple application might include one of the following statements:

- The system is acceptable providing that all level 1, 2, and 3 (fatal, high, and medium) SPRs documented as a result of testing have been resolved.

- The system is acceptable providing that all level 1 and 2 (fatal and high) SPRs documented as a result of testing have been resolved.

- The system is acceptable providing that all level 1 and 2 (fatal and high) SPRs documented as a result of testing have been resolved, and that 90% of level 3 problem reports have been resolved.

Test Automation Metric. It is important to generate a metric that calculates the value of automation, especially the first time that the project uses an automated testing approach. The test team will need to measure the time spent developing and executing test scripts and compare it with the results that the scripts produced. For example, the test team could compare the number of hours required to develop and execute test procedures with the number of defects documented that would not likely have been revealed during manual testing.

Sometimes it is difficult to quantify or measure the automation benefits. For example, automated test tools may reveal defects that manual test execution could not have discovered. For example, during stress testing, 1,000 virtual users execute a specific functionality and the system crashes. It would be very difficult to discover this problem manually, using 1,000 test engineers. An automated test tool can also be applied to data entry or record setup. In this case, the metric measures the time required to manually set up the needed records versus the time required to set up the records using an automated tool.

Consider the test effort associated with the following system requirement: "The system shall allow the addition of 10,000 new accounts." Imagine having to manually enter 10,000 accounts into a system to test this requirement! An automated test script can easily handle this requirement by reading account information from a file through the use of a looping construct. The data file can quickly be generated via a data generator. The effort to verify this system requirement using automation tools requires far fewer number of man-hours than performing such a test using manual methods.

In another case, once the test script has entered the 10,000 accounts, it may be desirable to delete all of these records from the test database and reset the database to its original condition. A simple SQL script can quickly and easily manage the deletion of these records. Now imagine that the test team wants to delete only those specific accounts added by the original script. The test team would simply create an automated script that accesses the existing data file, queries for the matching record in the AUT database, and then deletes each corresponding record. Once again, automation of this activity involves a significantly lower number of man-hours than manual testing.

Chapter Summary

❍ When executing test procedures, the test team will need to comply with a test procedure execution schedule. Following test execution, test outcome evaluations are performed and test result documentation is prepared.

❍ Plans for unit, integration, system, and user acceptance testing together make up the steps that are required to test the system as a whole. During the unit testing phase, code profiling can be performed. Traditionally, profiling is a tuning process that determines whether an algorithm is inefficient or a function is called too frequently. It can uncover improper scaling of algorithms, instantiations, and resource utilization.

❍ Integration testing focuses on the application's internal workings. During integration testing, units are incrementally integrated and tested together based on control flow. Because units may consist of other units, some integration testing (also called module testing) may take place during unit testing.

○ During system testing, the test engineer examines the integration of the parts that make up the entire system. System-level tests are usually performed by a separate test team. The test team implements the test procedure execution schedule and the system test plan.

○ The test team must perform analysis to identify particular components or functionality that are generating a greater relative number of problem reports. As a result of this analysis, additional test procedures and test effort may need to be assigned to the components. Test results analysis can also confirm whether executed test procedures are worthwhile in terms of identifying errors.

○ Each test team must perform problem reporting operations in compliance with a defined process. The documentation and tracking of software problem reports are greatly facilitated by an automated defect tracking tool.

○ The test team manager is responsible for ensuring that tests are executed according to schedule and that test personnel are allocated and redirected when necessary to handle problems that arise during the test effort. To perform this oversight function effectively, the test manager needs to perform test program status tracking and management reporting.

○ Test metrics provide the test manager with key indicators of the test coverage, progress, and the quality of the test effort. During white-box testing the test engineer measures the depth of testing by collecting data about path coverage and test coverage. During black-box testing, metrics collection focuses on the breadth of testing, including the amount of demonstrated functionality and the amount of testing that has been performed.

References

1. *Software Program Management*. Laguna Hills, CA: Humphreys and Associates, 1998.

2. Jacobson, I. "Proven Best Practices of Software Development." Rational '99 Worldwide Software Symposium, Washington, DC, January 26, 1999.

3. Florac, W.A., et al. *Software Quality Measurement: A Framework for Counting Problems and Defects*. Technical Report, CMU/SEI-92-TR-22, ESC-TR-92-022. Software Engineering Institute, Pittsburgh, PA, September 1992.

4. McCabe, T.J. *Structured Testing: A Software Testing Methodology Using the Cyclomatic Complexity Metric*. NBS Special Publication 500-99. Washington, DC: U.S. Department of Commerce/National Institute of Standards and Technology, 1982.

5. ANSI/IEEE Standard 982.2-1988.

6. See note 5.

Chapter 10

Test Program Review and Assessment

Improvements in quality always and automatically result in reductions in schedules and costs, increases in productivity, increases in market share, and consequently increases in profits.

—W. Edwards Deming

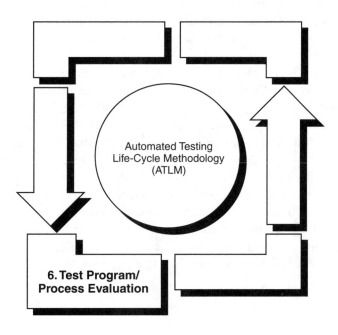

Automated Testing
Life-Cycle Methodology
(ATLM)

6. Test Program/
Process Evaluation

Following test execution, the test team needs to review the performance of the test program to determine where enhancements can be implemented during the next testing phase or on the next project. This test program review represents the final phase of the ATLM. The ATLM is cyclical and implemented incrementally. Parts of the ATLM are repeated within a project or when the test team moves on to a new release or another project.

Throughout the test program, the test team collects various test metrics, including many during the test execution phase (see Chapter 9). The focus of the test program review includes an evaluation of earned value progress measurements and other metrics collected. The evaluation of the test metrics should examine how well the original test program cost and sizing measurements compared with the actual number of labor hours expended and test procedures developed to accomplish the test effort. If applicable, the review of test metrics should conclude with suggested adjustments and improvement recommendations.

Just as important, the test team should document those activities that it performed well and those done correctly, so that it can repeat these successful processes. This chapter addresses the test program review activities related to test metrics analysis, lessons learned, corrective actions, and the test program's return on investment for test automation.

The test team should record lessons learned throughout each phase of the test program life cycle. It is not beneficial to wait until the end of the system development life cycle to document insights about improving specific procedures. Where possible, the test team needs to alter the detailed procedures during the test program, when it becomes apparent that such changes might improve the efficiency of an ongoing activity.

Once the project is complete, proposed corrective actions will surely prove beneficial to the next project. Corrective actions applied during the test program, however, can be significant enough to improve the final results of the current AUT testing program. For example, the incorporation of a modular test script may save several hours of test development and execution effort that might make the difference between the test program concluding within budget versus exceeding the number of hours allocated.

The test team needs to adopt, as part of its culture, an ongoing iterative process focusing on lessons learned. Such a program would encourage test engineers to raise corrective action proposals immediately, when such actions could potentially have a significant effect on test program performance. Test managers, meanwhile, need to promote such leadership behavior from each test engineer.

10.1 | Test Program Lessons Learned—Corrective Actions and Improvement Activity

Although a separate quality assurance (QA) department commonly assumes responsibility for conducting audits to verify that the appropriate processes and procedures are implemented and followed, the test team can nevertheless conduct its own test program analysis. Test personnel should continuously review the QA audit findings and follow suggested corrective actions. Additionally, throughout the entire test life cycle, it is good practice to document and begin to evaluate lessons learned at each milestone. The metrics that are collected throughout the test life cycle and especially during the test execution phase will help pinpoint problems that need to be addressed. Consequently, the test team should periodically "take a pulse" on the quality of the test effort with the objective of improving test results, whenever necessary, by altering the specific ways that the test team performs its business. Not only should the test team concentrate on lessons learned for the test life cycle, but it should also point out issues pertaining to the development life cycle.

When lessons learned and metrics evaluation sessions take place only at the end of a system development life cycle, it is too late to implement any corrective action for the current project. Nevertheless, lessons learned that are recorded at this stage may benefit subsequent test efforts. Therefore the team should document lessons learned at this late stage, rather than not at all.

Lessons learned, metrics evaluations, and any corresponding improvement activity or corrective action need to be documented throughout the entire test process in an easily assessible central repository. A test team intranet site can prove very effective in maintaining such documentation. For example, lessons learned could be documented using a requirements management tool database. Keeping an up-to-date database of important issues and lessons learned gives all individuals on the project the ability to monitor the progress and status of issues until closure.

The test manager needs to ensure that lessons learned records are viewed as improvement opportunities. The records, for example, should not list the names of the individuals involved in the particular activity. Each record should include at least one corrective action that suggests how the process or process output can be improved. (Tables 10.2 through 10.5 provide examples of lessons learned records together with such corrective actions.) Suggested corrective actions must undergo much analysis and scrutiny. For example, for some projects, personnel might conduct a lessons learned review for each life-cycle phase and document the results. For each lesson learned, a measure showing the potential range of gain (hours saved) if the particular improvement activity were to be implemented could be specified. Sometimes a corrective action initially sounds like the perfect solution to a problem, but further analysis can show no specific gain. As a result, the test team must also be careful when coming up with improvements to testing lessons learned. It is often beneficial to construct a small prototype or pilot project to implement the suggested changes so as to gather a valid estimate of suggested corrective action/improvement gains.

Table 10.1 gives an example of a simplified improvement table that represents the outcome of a prototype implementation of improvement opportunities. Gain estimates are expressed as a percentage of hours saved. This table shows, for example, how many hours could be saved by implementing a new process or tool.

When reviewing the test program events, recall that test program goals, strategies, and objectives were defined and documented within the test plan. Test processes were adopted or defined as required. Test design, development, and execution were performed. Following test execution, the test team must match the actual implementation of the test program to the initially planned criteria. Several questions need to be addressed by the test team, with the QA department sharing insight. Was the documented test process entirely followed? If not, which parts were not implemented? Why? What was the effect of not following the process? Have the test program goals been met? Were strategies implemented as planned? If not, why not? Have objectives been accomplished? If not, why not? Were the defect prevention activities successfully implemented? If not, which defect prevention activity step was omitted and why? Were the risks made clear and documented in advance? Ideally, any deviations from the process and/or test plan, such as strategy changes, have been adequately documented, including the rationale for the change. Were lessons learned activities conducted throughout the life cycle and corrective actions taken, when appropriate?

Process improvement is an iterative endeavor. Test program analysis represents an important aspect of this improvement effort. For example, where applicable, the lessons learned from previous projects and insights gained from pursuing industry articles and reports should have been incorporated into the organization's test life-cycle process. At the conclusion of a test program, test personnel should evaluate the effectiveness of the defined processes. The test team should find out whether the same mistakes were repeated and confirm whether any suggested improvement opportunities were bypassed.

This sort of test program analysis can identify problem areas and potential corrective actions, as well as review the effectiveness of implemented corrective action changes. Examples of test program analysis activities are provided in Tables 10.2 through 10.5. For instance, test engineers might want to conduct schedule slippage analysis, process analysis, tool usage analysis, environment problem analysis, and more. Additionally, they might perform the test outcome evaluation activities given in Table 9.2 on page 357. Likewise, software problem report analysis can help narrow down the cause of many problems. The test engineer would create a table like Table 10.2, which was taken from real-world experiences, at the conclusion of each phase of the development life cycle. It is important not only to determine the corrective

Table 10.1   Test Program Improvements

Testing Activity	Current Method	Gain	Use of New Process and Tool A	Gain	Use of Tool B	Gain
Integration of testing tool with a requirements management tool	Excel spread-sheet	0%	Integration allows for traceability between test requirements and business requirements	30%	Tool is integrated with requirements management tool	30%
Integration of testing tool with a configuration management tool	Manual (using XYZ CM tool)	0%	Tool is not integrated with CM tool	0%	Tool is integrated with CM tool	5%
Preparation of test procedures	Manual	0%	Tool allows for automated test procedure generation	20%	Tool does not allow for automated test procedure generation	0%
Test execution	Manual	0%	Tool allows for recording and playback of test scripts, including automatic success/ failure reporting with traceability to test requirements	60%	Tool allows for recording and playback of test scripts, including automatic success/failure reporting (no traceability to test requirements)	50%
Preparation of test data	Manual	0%	Tool can generate test data	10%	Tool cannot generate test data	0%
Stress/load testing	Manual	0%	Tool allows for virtual user stress/ load testing	30%	Tool allows for virtual user stress/load testing	20%
Defect tracking	Home-grown Access database	0%	Tool is integrated with defect tracking tool	20%	Tool is not integrated with defect tracking tool	0%

Table 10.2   Examples of Schedule-Related Problems and Corrective Actions

Problem	Effect	Corrective Action
Code development was two months late.	The testing schedule was moved out two months because of development dependencies, resulting in a negative schedule variance and negative cost variance.	Add buffer to schedule, if necessary. (Note that there could be many reasons why the code was late. The development group will have to analyze this corrective action. Try to get resolution from development department and insert here.)
Time constraints. Code development was late. The system testing phase was shortened because the implementation deadline had to be met.	Tests were executed incrementally. Not all tests could be executed as planned in the test execution schedule because of test sequence dependencies on missing functionality. Much system testing time was spent on retesting and regression testing, due to incremental addition of functionality that should have existed before system testing began. System testing time was spent doing integration testing. Incomplete and inadequate testing was done. Testers worked many hours of overtime. Tester morale is low. The test engineer turnover rate has increased. The entire effect is not known at this time. Many post-release defects and high maintenance costs are expected.	Add a buffer to the schedule, and don't allow the testing phase to be shortened. Shortening the testing phase requires overtime, which in turn lowers employee morale. Moreover, it increases the risk that the application will be shipped or implemented with an expensive production failure.
Many high-priority defects were found during system testing (late in the system life cycle), instead of early on in the system development process.	Many more build and test iterations were necessary than were planned, resulting in negative schedule and cost variance (cost and schedule overrun).	Revisit and analyze the entire life-cycle process. Was it followed? Were defect prevention activities conducted? Review corrective action requests. Discover where corrective actions were implemented as suggested.

continued

continued from page 384

Problem	Effect	Corrective Action
Metrics weren't used appropriately to recalculate the projected release date.	The project release date was recalculated, but the modified projected release date was inaccurate and wasn't met.	Use metrics to reevaluate a projected release date, such as total numbers of tests to be executed, number of tests executed so far, numbers of tests passed/failed, including historical trends such as the number of test procedures per test cycle (ratio of errors to total test procedures) and the number of defects versus fixed data. Use earned value management system.
Fixed software problem reports were not retested within a specified timeframe.	Fixes weren't retested fast enough by test team for development to know whether the fixes were acceptable. Progress measurements were therefore inaccurate. If a fix affected other areas, the developer found out too late.	Verify that the test team retests the fix within the specified time-frame.
Software defects took a long time to be fixed.	Retests couldn't take place, because development took too long to fix defects. Due to test dependencies on fixes testers were idle until fix was put in place.	Verify that developers fix the software problem reports within the specified timeframe.
Not enough resources were available.	The use of an automated test suite requires additional time and resources. Neither time nor resources were available. Tool eventually became shelfware, because test engineers had to focus on issues at hand.	Allow additional time and resources when using an automating testing tool. Also allow for a learning curve. Allow for the services of a tool mentor.
Most defects were found in one specific, critical module.	Most time was spent retesting the critical module.	Risk management needs to reapply staff to critical path activity. The risk management process needs improvement.

Table 10.3   Examples of Test Program/Process-Related Problems and Corrective Actions

Problem	Effect	Corrective Action
Testers lacked business knowledge.	Much handholding was necessary. Not all application functionality errors may have been addressed.	Testers need to be involved from the beginning of the system development life cycle to gather information on customer needs and to gain business knowledge (starting at the business analysis and requirements gathering phase).
Some of the requirements weren't testable (for example, one requirement stated that the system should allow addition of an unlimited amount of accounts—this requirement is not testable, because the scope of the word "unlimited" is unclear).	Some of the requirements couldn't be tested.	Testers need to be involved during the requirements gathering phase, so they can verify the testability of requirements.
Test procedures were written too detailed (for example, click on save button, click on edit button, and so on).	A significant amount of time was required to develop test procedures and the procedures had to be modified or rewritten to accommodate minor application changes.	Write high-level test procedures to allow for application changes (for example, "Save record, edit record," instead of "Click on Save button, click on Edit button").
Too many test procedures were created for the timeframe allocated.	Testers didn't know which test procedures to give the highest priority.	Risk management needs to be improved. Priorities need to be assigned to test procedures. Use OATS (statistical techniques) to narrow the testing scope. Use better test design techniques. Manage expectations. Remember, not everything can be tested.

continued

continued from page 386

Problem	Effect	Corrective Action
No process training.	Process was scarcely followed.	Verify that the process is being documented, followed, and measured. Allow process training to be built in early in the project schedule as part of the test program implementation.
Requirements changed constantly.	Negative cost and schedule variance occurred. Test procedures had to be rewritten to account for changing requirements.	Improve user involvement and improve requirements and risk management procedures. Baseline requirements.
Test procedures weren't useful.	System testing test procedure execution didn't discover any major problems with the AUT. User discovered major problems during user acceptance testing.	Evaluate user acceptance test procedures and compare them to system test procedures. What aspects were missed during system testing? Conduct test procedure walkthroughs that include the development and user communities. Test engineers need to be properly trained and involved throughout the entire development life cycle.
Roles and responsibilities were unclear.	Development expected test team support for integration testing, but no time had been scheduled for this task.	Document and communicate the roles and responsibilities of test team members. Get approval or sign-off from management and everyone else involved.
A lack of communication occurred between developers and test team.	The test team wasn't aware of what changes were implemented between builds.	Verify that each new build is accompanied by a description of the fixes implemented and any new functionality that was added.
A defect tracking tool wasn't used.	Some defects discovered during testing were not captured and corrected.	Have everyone follow a defect tracking process and use a defect-tracking tool.

continued

continued from page 387

Problem	Effect	Corrective Action
Developers closed defects before correction was implemented.	One developer closed a defect just because the developer didn't have the time to correct the problem.	A defect tracking workflow process has to be in place and under configuration management control (don't give developers authority or privilege to close a defect).
Problems occurred with the new build process and configuration management process. Functionality that worked in a previous build didn't work in the new build.	Much time was spent figuring out the configuration management process and the build process.	A build and configuration management process needs to be documented, followed, and automated. A smoke test should be run before the new build is passed to the test group to ensure that previously working functionality has not been adversely affected. Revisit the CM process and provide CM training.
Lessons learned analysis was not conducted until the end of the life cycle.	Lessons learned are not relevant to the next test program life cycle because it often comprises an entirely new project. Corrective action wasn't taken at the time when it would have been beneficial.	Conduct lessons learned activities throughout the test program life cycle, so corrective actions can be implemented when most beneficial.

Table 10.4   Examples of Tool-Related Problems and Corrective Actions

Problem	Effect	Corrective Action for Future Phase
Many tools were used, but the tools could not be integrated.	Much time was spent trying to move information from one tool set to another, using elaborate programming efforts, resulting in extra work. The code generated was not reusable because a new upgrade to the various tools was anticipated.	Conduct feasibility study to measure the need to purchase easily integrated tools.

continued

continued from page 388

Problem	Effect	Corrective Action for Future Phase
The tool drove the testing effort. The focus was on automating test procedures, instead of performing testing.	More time was spent automating test procedures than on testing.	Keep in mind: automating test scripts is part of the testing effort. Evaluate which tests lend themselves to automation. Not everything can or should be automated.
Elaborate and extensive test scripts were developed.	Test script development resulted in near duplication of the development effort using the tool's programming language. Too much time was spent on automating scripts, without much additional value gained.	Avoid duplication of the development effort, which results when developing elaborate test scripts. Conduct automation analysis and determine the best approach to automation by estimating the highest return.
Training was too late in the process and therefore testers lacked tool knowledge.	Tools were not used correctly. Scripts had to be created over and over, causing much frustration.	Allow training to be built in early in the project schedule as part of the test program implementation. Have a test tool expert on staff. Create reusable and maintainable test scripts.
A lack of test development guidelines was noted.	Each test engineer used a different style for creating test procedures. Maintaining the scripts will be difficult.	Create test development guidelines for test engineers to follow, so as to increase script maintainability.
The tool was not used.	No scripts were automated because the tool wasn't used. Testers felt that the manual process worked fine.	Use a personal tool mentor, someone who is an advocate of the tool. Show the benefits of using tools.
The tool had problems recognizing third-party controls (widgets).	The tool could not be used for some parts of the application.	Verify with developers that third-party controls (widgets) used are compatible with the automated testing tool, before software architecture is approved (if possible). Give developers a list of third-party controls supported by test tool vendor. If developers have a need to use an incompatible third-party control, require that developers formally document the reason.

continued

continued from page 389

Problem	Effect	Corrective Action for Future Phase
Automated test script creation was cumbersome.	Creation of automated scripts took longer than expected. Work-around solutions had to be found to some incompatibility problems.	Conduct initial compatibility tests to manage expectations. The tool will not always be compatible with all parts of applications.
Tool expectations were not met.	Expectations were that the tool would narrow down testing scope, but instead it increased the testing scope.	Manage expectations. An automated testing tool does not replace manual testing, nor does it replace the test engineer. Initially, the test effort will increase, but it will decrease on subsequent builds.
Reports produced by the tool were useless.	Reports were set up, but necessary data were not accumulated to produce meaningful reports.	Set up only reports specific to the data that will be generated. Produce reports as requested by users.
The tool was intrusive but the development staff wasn't informed of this problem until late in the testing life cycle.	Developers were reluctant to use the tool because it required additions to the code.	Let developers know well in advance that the tool requires code additions, if applicable (not all tools are intrusive). Assure developers that the tool will not cause any problems by giving them feedback from other companies that have experience with the tool.
Tools were selected and purchased before a system engineering environment was defined.	There were many compatibility issues and work-around solutions had to be found while trying to match the system engineering environment to the requirements of the tools already purchased.	The system-engineering environment needs to be defined before tools are selected. Tools need to be selected to be compatible with the system-engineering environment, not vice versa.
Various tool versions were in use.	Procedures created in one version of the tool were not compatible in another version, causing many compatibility problems and requiring many work-around solutions.	Everyone involved in the testing life cycle needs to use the same version of the tool. Tool upgrades need to be centralized.

Table 10.5   Examples of Environment-Related Problems and Corrective Actions

Problem	Effect	Corrective Action for Future Phase
Lack of stable and isolated test environment.	Test environment could not be rolled back to the original state. Other project members, besides test team, were affected by the test data. Test results were often unpredictable.	An isolated, baselined test environment is necessary to conduct successful testing. Review CM procedures to verify that hardware and software controls are being implemented within the test environment.
PC constraints. PCs experienced memory constraints when loading the tools.	Tools could not be loaded on all testing PCs.	Verify that test PCs meet all configuration requirements for tools installation, all other software necessary to conduct testing activities, and the AUT. New PC hardware may need to be acquired.
Not enough testing PCs available (PCs were on backorder).	Testers could not execute as many test procedures as planned. A schedule had to be developed giving a specific time period when a specific tester could use a PC; which contributed to negative schedule variance.	Order PCs and all other testing environment hardware early enough in the testing schedule to allow for delivery delays.
Irrelevant test data.	The test data used could not verify that a test procedure produced correct results.	Relevant test data (of sufficient breadth and depth) are necessary to verify that test results are accurate.
Smaller test database than target environment database.	Performance issues weren't discovered until the target environment database was run, which contributed to negative schedule variance.	Performance testing needs to be conducted using the same size database as in the target environment.

actions for each problem encountered, but also to monitor corrective actions to ensure that they are being implemented effectively, so that problems do not recur.

10.2 | Test Program Return on Investment

After collecting lessons learned and other metrics, and defining the corrective actions, the test engineers also need to assess the effectiveness of the test program, including the test program's return on investment. For example, test engineers capture measures of the benefits of automation realized throughout the test life cycle. One benefit might include the fact that the various new tools used throughout the life cycle boosted productivity due to the increased speed of automating test activities in a repeatable fashion while contributing an element of maintainability. Test engineers could therefore focus on more complex, nonrepeatable tests.

One method of collecting the benefits of automated testing relies on the test engineer's comparison of the execution time of a manual test to the execution time of an automated test (see Chapter 2). Another method of collecting benefits is by collecting metrics throughout the test life cycle and evaluating them to determine which other benefits the test program reaped. An additional option is to use a survey (see Figure 10.1) that is distributed to the various groups involved throughout the test life cycle. Often the success of a test program depends on everyone involved working together and correctly following the processes and outputs. Unlike reviews of lessons learned, which involve coming up with corrective actions so as to avoid the same mistakes in future cycles/projects, the return on investment exercise is aimed at identifying and repeating those activities that have proven to be effective.

Case Study
Test Program Return on Investment

A test engineer named Paula collected several lessons learned from a just-concluded project. Paula worked with other test team members to develop a corrective action (improvement recommendations) for each of the documented lessons learned. She then remembered that senior management within her organization had expressed optimism that the automated tools implemented on the project would improve test operations. Paula realized that management would expect her to quantify the value of test automation by comparing it with the additional costs associated with test automation. She set out to define the positive aspects of the testing process utilized on the project, including the benefits realized through the use of automated tools. She documented the benefits gained as they occurred throughout the test life cycle. As with lessons learned, often if one waits to the end to determine the benefits gained throughout the testing life cycle, they will have already been forgotten.

One way of ascertaining the benefits (return on investment) of the test program is to document these findings as depicted in Table 10.6, which outlines sample automated test program benefits observed by test engineers. It is not easy to quantify all of these benefits in terms of man-hours saved, yet the items listed in Table 10.6 undoubtedly are benefits gained throughout the test life cycle.

Table 10.6 Test Program Return on Investment

Return on Investment	Estimated Hours Saved or Process Improvement
Using the requirements management tool DOORS allowed for simultaneous access of multiple test engineers, who were able to create test procedures for their specific business area. This access allowed simple management of the test procedure creation progress. Development of test procedures took two months, using eight test personnel. Test procedure documents didn't need to be merged, as would be required if team had used word-processing software.	Approximately 8 hours (time saved, as no documentation merges were necessary)
The automated test tool automatically and continuously calculated and produced reports on the percentage of testing completed.	Approximately 10 hours—the time it would have taken to do the percentage calculations manually
The requirements management tool allowed for automatic traceability by running a simple script (.dxl file) within the tool of 5,000 test procedures to 3,000 test requirements.	Approximately 80 hours—the time it would have taken to come up with and maintain a traceability matrix of this size
More test-cycle iterations were possible in a shorter timeframe (at the push of a button). More tests were performed, and 60 automated test procedures were played back on 10 builds taking on average 1 minute per test procedure. Test procedures would have taken on average 10 minutes to execute manually. Automated scripts were kicked off automatically and ran unattended.	Approximately 99 hours (60 automated test procedures times 10 builds times 1 minute, versus 60 manual test procedures times 10 builds times 10 minutes)
Improved regression testing. Regression testing had to be done all over again, because a defect fix that affected many areas was implemented. Luckily, the initial regression test had been scripted/automated and therefore the test engineer was able to run those tests back (instead of having to manually redo all testing efforts).	40 hours—the time it would have taken to conduct the entire regression test manually
Defect prevention activities were performed that resulted in a smaller amount of high-priority defects during test execution than during the first release, even though complexity and size of both releases were comparable. The first release had 50 high-priority defects, while the later release had only 25 high-priority defects.	Approximately 100 hours (on average) to fix 25 high-priority defects

continued

continued from page 393

Return on Investment	Estimated Hours Saved or Process Improvement
The test tool improved configuration testing. The same scripts were played back using various hardware configurations. If the automated configuration script had not existed, the test would have had to be repeated on the various configurations using a manual process.	50 hours (baseline script was created on one configuration; five additional configurations were tested with 10 hours of manual testing)
The test engineer gained additional insight into the business by playing back test scripts that had been created by other business area test experts. Even though test engineer A wasn't familiar with functionality B of the system, she was able to play back the recorded scripts that test engineer B had created while he was on vacation. Test engineer A was able to point out errors on functionality B, because the recorded scripts failed against the baseline. Test engineer A was able to discuss with the programmer what the outcome should have been, based on the automated baseline.	Approximately 5 hours—the time it would have taken to train another person on the business aspects of the functionality
Simplified performance testing resulted in tests that couldn't have been done without the automated performance testing tool, such as simulating 1,000 users.	Didn't require 1,000 users, but difficult to quantify; also process improvement
Simplified stress testing resulted, and the test team could determine the thresholds of the system and identify a multiuser access problem.	Didn't require 1,000 users, but difficult to quantify; also process improvement
The tool was used to populate a database simulating user input.	20 hours—the time used to populate database
A requirement was added, consisting of a high number of accounts that system needed to be able to add. This task couldn't have been done without the automated tool, which added and deleted accounts.	80+ hours—the time it would have taken to manually test and regression test
Test tool and Y2K: The project used the test tool to perform Y2K tests for the initial release. By developing a script and populating some of the date fields with 35 date "cases," the team was able to automate the entry, storage, and retrieval of the dates for verification. The test tool was useful for testing the front-end GUI for Y2K compliance for most of the application. The reports developed proved useful in documenting the Y2K test procedures.	50 hours—the time it would have taken to manually execute these scripts (this calculation is based on a manual test execution iteration)
Repetitive steps that were error-prone were automated. Tests became repeatable.	Process improvement

continued

continued from page 394

Return on Investment	Estimated Hours Saved or Process Improvement
Automating mundane testing tasks allows test engineers to spend more time performing analysis work and concentrating their effort on the more difficult test problems. Also, test engineers could develop better manual test procedures.	Process improvement
The project schedule and milestones were met because the automated test tools helped produce a higher-quality product in a shorter timeframe, by allowing repetition of test scripts at no additional cost. The automated test effort produced an increase in defect detection. Automated tests discovered problems that manual testing had not discovered in previous releases of the AUT.	Process improvement
Automated tests exercise the application using a great variety and number of input values. Errors were discovered by using automated testing tools that could not have been discovered via manual testing. For example, the tool delivered a financial instrument—a security—over and over again in a loop until funding ran out, to see how the system reacted. The system actually crashed once funding was down to zero.	Process improvement
Issues were kept in the DOORS tool, allowing for simple maintenance of this central repository and maintenance of lessons learned and subsequent corrective actions.	Process improvement
Automated testing improved the way UAT was conducted: During one specific application test, a critical success function (CSF) script was developed that was played back to verify each new application build. As one project member put it: "This script saved us from having to call the users down to the test room and have them start testing, only to find out that the build was missing major functionality." With the CSF script, before the users were called into the test room, the script (a smoke test) was played back to verify the new build. The users weren't called in for testing until the build was accepted, thus saving the users a lot of time and frustration.	Process improvement
Automated testing was beneficial for subsequent releases. Many project team members observed that the test tool was particularly useful when there were many phased releases before a final project release. Once a baseline of reusable scripts had been created, these scripts could be consistently played back. This step took out the monotony and frustration of having to manually test the same functionality repeatedly.	Process improvement

continued

continued from page 395

Return on Investment	Estimated Hours Saved or Process Improvement
The central repository allowed for easier metrics collection.	Process improvement
The tools improved defect tracking. On previous releases, no defect tracking tool was used and defect maintenance became a nightmare.	Process improvement
Increased reporting and testing status availability: The test tool requirements hierarchy allowed for detailed planning of the test requirements and was very helpful for checking testing status and other reporting purposes.	Process improvement
Improved communication between testers and developers: The test tool improved the communication between the testers and developers. The testing group worked with the project teams to develop a software module hierarchy in conjunction with the test tool defect tracking system so that it could be used to link the defect to its corresponding software module. Developers and test engineers communicated via the test tool defect tracker's status workflow, and the project leads felt that communication between the test engineers and developers improved.	Process improvement

In Section 2.2, the benefits of automated testing were laid out; these benefits were evident in Paula's experience. Please remember that these benefits were produced by following a defined process such as the ATLM and by using documented test design and development standards. The use of an automated tool without a defined process will not produce the same benefits.

Student Questions 10.1
- When comparing the manual testing effort with the automated testing effort, which criteria need to be considered if the comparison is to be valuable?
- What other approaches could be implemented to measure the test program return on investment?

Case Study
Quantify Tool Return on Investment [1]

The information for this case study was obtained through a survey conducted by an independent consultant. The goal of the survey was to measure and document actual experiences using Rational tools. Forty-three companies participated, including manufacturers (automobiles and components, computers and components, aircraft, medical equipment), software companies (CAD, CASE, database, systems software, medical imaging), service companies (banking, finance, insurance, hospitals), and universities. Most respondents were employees of large organizations (having more than 500 employees, with revenues exceeding $100 million annually). Most were from North America. The majority of the respondents had titles such as "technical lead," "project leader," or "senior software engineer."

Table 10.7 summarizes the survey results. It shows the calculated return on investment from organizations implementing the various Rational test tools. This table also shows the average payback period in terms of months, as realized by the various organizations contributing to the survey.

Table 10.7   Test Tool Return on Investment

Product	Average Payback Period (months)	Average Return on Investment (3 years)
Purify	2.69	403%
Quantify	3.63	295%
PureCoverage	1.88	580%
PureLink	2.53	429%

Rational's Quantify Tool's User Results:

- The average programmer spends 4% to 8% of his or her time optimizing or improving performance. The calculation uses 5%.

- Quantify 5× productivity factor (range 5×–25×)

Time spent addressing performance issues without Quantify (weeks)

$$0.05 \times 48 \text{ weeks per year} = 2.4 \text{ weeks/year}$$

continued

continued from page 397

Time spent addressing performance issues with Quantify (weeks)

   2.4 weeks/year × 1/5 (Quantify productivity factor) = 0.48 week/year

Quantify saves 2.4 - 0.48 = 1.92 hours/month per developer

Additional Considerations:

- Organizations that list performance as a critical product differentiation feature spent roughly 9.4 person-weeks per year addressing performance issues in addition to the 5% spent by the average developer. The additional savings calculated for dedicated performance individuals were 7.84 weeks. These additional savings are not included in the ROI calculations.

- Quantify reduced setup 15× to 20× with respect to current tools.

- Several users reported that Quantify allowed them to collect data from their complex applications that were previously unattainable.

Quantify Tool's Return on Investment

Item	Average Amount in U.S. Dollars
Annual Programmer Cost	$125,000
Cost per Week	$2,604
Price of Quantify	$1,398
Maintenance of Quantify per Year	$250
5× Performance Tuning Productivity Savings (days)	9.6
Dollar Value of Improvement (per year)	$5,000
Payback Period (months)	3.63
Quantify Return on Investment (3 years)	295%
Net Present Value (at 10% rate)	$9,447.11

One way of collecting test program benefits is via a survey that is distributed to the various groups that were involved throughout the test life cycle. Test teams can conduct their own surveys to inquire about the potential value of testing process and tool changes. Individuals participating in such a survey may include business analysts, requirements management specialists, developers, test engineers, and selected end users. These surveys can help gather benefits information on effectiveness of the test life-cycle process as well as the test tools and the improvement activities implemented.

A sample survey form is provided in Figure 10.1 that could be used to solicit feedback on the potential use of requirements management tools, design tools, and development tools. Surveys are helpful in identifying potential misconceptions and gathering positive feedback.

Automated Tool Feedback Survey

Project Name/Business Area:_____   Date: _____

1. Have you incorporated any of the following into your project schedules/
    development process?

Regression testing	Tests that compare the latest build of the application-under-test to the baseline established during the test development phase. Regression testing reveals any differences that may have been introduced into the application since the last build.
Performance or load testing	Tests using production loads to predict behavior and response time.
Stress testing	Tests that subject the system to extreme (maximum) loads. No delays are placed on the data submission to see what breaks first, fix system, and repeat.
Integration testing	Tests that are conducted in a production-like environment to increase the probability of a smooth transition of software from development into production.

1a. If the testing identified above was not incorporated into your project schedule,
    please explain why. If incorporated in the past and performed, describe the value
    it added, if any.

    _____

    _____

    _____

    _____

2. Have you or do you currently use an automated tool?   Yes _____   No _____
    Why or why not?

    _____

    _____

    _____

    _____

continued

Figure 10.1 Feedback Survey

continued from page 399

3. Are you using an automated tool? Which one(s)?

Business Modeling Tool	Requirements Management	Test Procedure Generators	Performance Testing
Configuration Management	Requirements Verifier	Unit TestTools	GUI Capture/Playback
Defect Tracking	Use Case Generators	Test Data Generators	Usability Measurement
Documentation Generator	Design	Test Management	Other

4. What are your future plans (if any) for automated test tool usage?

   _____ Expand usage to other projects   _____ The same usage for other projects

   _____ Expand usage throughout   _____ Do not plan to use a testing tool
   development process

5. Do you need any of the following services?

   Product training _____   Testing training _____   Consulting support _____
   Other _____

6. Briefly describe your perception of automated tools.

   _____

   _____

   _____

7. Do you feel that the usage of an automated tool adds value?   Yes _____   No _____
   Please explain.

   _____

   _____

   _____

8. Is it difficult to establish a process for using an automated tool?
   Yes _____   No _____   Please explain.

   _____

   _____

   _____

9. Do you have a success story, or summary of lessons learned, regarding automated tools
   that you would like to share with others?

   _____

Sometimes the results of surveys can be an eye-opener. Consider the following testimonial concerning a survey conducted to review the use of test plans on projects:

> When I was at Apple, my team conducted a review of 17 test plans in use by our department. Our findings were that none of the plans [was] actually in use, at all. Some of them were almost pure boilerplate. In one case the tester wasn't aware that his product had a test plan until we literally opened a drawer in his desk and found it lying where the previous test engineer on that product had left it! [2]

Remember that test automation is software development. It is necessary to implement a process, such as the automated test life-cycle methodology (ATLM), when automating the test effort. The test team also needs to be conscious of the benefits offered by a strategy that accepts *good enough* test automation. To execute an effective test program, it must adopt test design and development guidelines that incorporate proven practices. The test personnel may also need to obtain test tool expert support to get off the ground and running with test automation. Test personnel may also require formal training on the use of one or more automated test tools.

Chapter Summary

- ○ Following test execution, the test team needs to review the performance of the test program to determine where improvements can be implemented to benefit the next project. This test program review represents the final phase of the ATLM.

- ○ Throughout the test program, the test team collects various test metrics. The focus of the test program review includes an assessment of whether the application satisfies acceptance criteria and is ready to go into production. This review also includes an evaluation of earned value progress measurements and other metrics collected.

- ○ The test team needs to adopt, as part of its culture, an ongoing, iterative process composed of lessons learned activities. Such a program encourages test engineers to suggest corrective action immediately, when such actions might potentially have a significant effect on test program performance.

- ○ Throughout the entire test life cycle, a good practice is to document and begin to evaluate lessons learned at each milestone. The metrics that are collected throughout the test life cycle, and especially during the test execution phase, help pinpoint problems that should be addressed.

- ○ Lessons learned, metrics evaluations, and corresponding improvement activity or corrective action need to be documented throughout the entire test process in an easily accessible central repository.

○   After collecting lessons learned and other metrics, and defining the corrective actions, test engineers need to assess the effectiveness of the test program by evaluating the test program's return on investment. Test engineers capture measures of the benefits of automation realized throughout the test life cycle so as to perform this assessment.

○   Test teams can perform their own surveys to inquire about the potential value of process and tool changes. A survey form can be employed to solicit feedback on the potential use of requirements management tools, design tools, and development tools. Surveys also help to identify potential misconceptions and gather positive feedback.

References

1. Used with permission of Sam Guckenheimer, Rational Software. www.rational.com.
2. Bach, J. *Process Evolution in a Mad World*. Bellevue, WA: Software Testing Laboratories, 1997.

Part V

Appendixes

Appendix A

How to Test Requirements

A.1 | Requirements Testing Approach

Testing needs to verify that requirements are relevant, coherent, traceable, complete, and testable. The tests have their starting point with the criterion that each requirement have at least one quality measure. This measure is used to determine whether a given solution satisfies or does not satisfy the requirement. The following article by Suzanne Robertson, entitled "An Early Start to Testing: How to Test Requirements," outlines an approach for testing requirements [1].

Abstract

We accept that testing the software is an integral part of building a system. However, if the software is based on inaccurate requirements, then despite well-written code, the software will be unsatisfactory. The newspapers are full of stories about catastrophic software failures. What the stories don't say is that most of the defects can be traced back to wrong, missing, vague, or incomplete requirements. We have learnt the lesson of testing software. Now we have to learn to implement a system of testing the requirements before building a software solution. Appendix A describes a set of requirements tests that cover relevance, coherency, traceability, completeness, and other qualities that successful requirements must have. The tests have their starting point with the criterion that each requirement has at least one quality measure. This measure is used to test whether any given solution satisfies, or does not satisfy, the requirement.

Requirements seem to be ephemeral. They move quickly in and out of projects, they are capricious, intractable, unpredictable, and sometimes invisible. When gathering requirements we are searching for all of the criteria for a system's success. We throw out a net and try to capture all these criteria. Using Blitzing, Rapid Application Development (RAD), Joint Application Development (JAD), Quality Function Deployment (QFD), interviewing, apprenticing, data analysis, and many other techniques [6], we try to snare all of the requirements in our net.

The Quality Gateway

As soon as we have a single requirement in our net we can start testing. The aim is to trap requirements-related defects as early as they can be identified. We prevent incorrect requirements from being incorporated in the design and implementation where they will be more difficult and expensive to find and correct [5]. To pass through the quality gateway and be included in the requirements specification, a requirement must pass a number of tests. These tests are concerned with ensuring that the requirements are accurate, and do not cause problems by being unsuitable for the design and implementation stages later in the project. I will discuss each of the following requirements tests in a stand-alone manner. Naturally, the tests are designed to be applied to each of the requirements in unison.

Make the Requirement Measurable

In his work on specifying the requirements for buildings, Christopher Alexander [1] describes setting up a quality measure for each requirement.

> The idea is for each requirement to have a quality measure that makes it possible to divide all solutions to the requirement into two classes: those for which we agree that they fit the requirement and those for which we agree that they do not fit the requirement.

In other words, if we specify a quality measure for a requirement, we mean that any solution that meets this measure will be acceptable. Of course, it is also true to say that any solution that does not meet the measure will not be acceptable. The quality measures will be used to test the new system against the requirements. The remainder of this paper describes how to arrive at a quality measure that is acceptable to all the stakeholders.

Quantifiable Requirements

Consider a requirement that says "The system must respond quickly to customer enquiries." First, we need to find a property of this requirement that provides us with a scale for measurement within the context. Let's say that we agree that we will measure the response using minutes. To find the quality measure we ask: "under what circumstances would the system fail to meet this requirement?" The stakeholders review the context of the system and decide that they would consider it a failure if a customer has to wait longer than three minutes for a response to his enquiry. Thus "three minutes" becomes the quality measure for this requirement.

Any solution to the requirement is tested against the quality measure. If the solution makes a customer wait for longer than three minutes then it does not fit the requirement. So far so good: we have defined a quantifiable quality measure. But specifying the quality measure is not always so straightforward. What about requirements that do not have an obvious scale?

Nonquantifiable Requirements

Suppose a requirement is "The automated interfaces of the system must be easy to learn." There is no obvious measurement scale for "easy to learn." However, if we investigate the meaning of the requirement within the particular context, we can set communicable limits for measuring the requirement.

Again we can make use of the question: "What is considered a failure to meet this requirement?" Perhaps the stakeholders agree that there will often be novice users, and the stakeholders want novices to be productive within half an hour. We can define the quality measure to say "a novice user must be able to learn to successfully complete a customer order transaction within 30 minutes of first using the system." This becomes a quality measure provided a group of experts within this context is able to test whether the solution does or does not meet the requirement. An attempt to define the quality measure for a requirement helps to rationalize fuzzy requirements. Something like "the system must provide good value" is an example of a requirement that everyone would agree with, but each person has his own meaning. By investigating the scale that must be used to measure "good value," we identify the diverse meanings.

Sometimes by causing the stakeholders to think about the requirement we can define an agreed-upon quality measure. In other cases we discover that there is no agreement on a quality measure. Then we substitute this vague requirement with several requirements, each with its own quality measure.

Requirements Test 1

Does each requirement have a quality measure
that can be used to test whether any solution meets the requirement?

Keeping Track

Figure A.1 is an example of how you can keep track of your knowledge about each requirement.

Description: Short (1 sentence) description of the requirement.

Purpose: Why is this requirement considered to be important?

Owner(s): Who raised this requirement?

Quality measure: Unambiguous test for whether a solution meets the
    requirement.

Value: Customer value ranging from 1 (frill) to 10 (essential).

Type: Functional or nonfunctional?

Unique identifier: Tag for tracking the requirement.

Dependency: Existence/change dependencies on other requirements.

Figure A.1   This requirements micro-specification makes your requirements knowledge visible. It must be recorded so that it is easy for several people to compare and discuss individual requirements and to look for duplicates and contradictions.

By adding a quality measure to each requirement we have made the requirement visible. This is the first step to defining all the criteria for measuring the goodness of the solution. Now let's look at other aspects of the requirement that we can test before deciding to include it in the requirements specification.

Coherency and Consistency

When a poet writes a poem, he intends that it should trigger rich and diverse visions for everyone who reads it. The requirements engineer has the opposite intention: he would like each requirement to be understood in the same way by every person who reads it. In practice many requirements specifications are more like poetry, and are open to any interpretation that seems reasonable to the reader. This subjectivity means that many systems are built to satisfy the wrong interpretation of the requirement. The obvious solution to this problem is to specify the requirement such that it is understood in only one way.

For example, in a requirements specification that I assessed, I found the term "viewer" in many parts of the specification. My analysis identified six different meanings for the term, depending on the context of its use. This kind of requirements defect always causes problems during design and/or implementation. If you are lucky, a developer will realize that there is inconsistency, but will have to reinvestigate the requirement. This almost always causes a ripple effect that extends to other parts of the product. If you are not lucky, the designer will choose the meaning that makes most sense to him and implement that one. Any stakeholder who does not agree with that meaning then considers that the system does not meet the requirement.

<u>Requirements Test 2</u>

Does the specification contain a definition of the meaning
of every essential subject matter term within the specification?

I point you in the direction of abstract data modeling principles [7], which provide many guidelines for naming subject matter and for defining the meaning of that subject matter. As a result of doing the necessary analysis, the term "viewer" could be defined as follows:

Viewer

A person who lives in the area, which receives transmission of television programs from our channel.

Relevant attributes are:

Viewer name

Viewer address

Viewer age range

Viewer sex

Viewer salary range

Viewer occupation type

Viewer socioeconomic ranking

When the allowable values for each of the attributes are defined, it provides data that can be used to test the implementation. Defining the meaning of "viewer" has addressed one part of the coherency problem. We also have to be sure that every use of the term "viewer" is consistent with the meaning that has been defined.

<u>Requirements Test 3</u>

Is every reference to a defined term consistent with its definition?

Completeness

We want to be sure that the requirements specification contains all the requirements that are known. While we know that there will be evolutionary changes and additions, we would like to restrict those changes to new requirements, and not have to play "catch-up" with requirements that we should have known about in the first place. Thus we want to avoid omitting requirements just because we did not think of asking the right questions. If we have set a context [10, 11] for our project, then we can test whether the context is accurate. We can also test whether we have considered all the likely requirements within that context.

The context defines the problem that we are trying to solve. The context includes all the requirements that we must eventually meet: it contains anything that we have to build, or anything we have to change. Naturally, if our software is going to change the way people do their jobs, then those jobs must be within the context of study. The most common defect is to limit the context to the part of the system that will be eventually automated [3]. The result of this restricted view is that nobody correctly understands the organization's culture and way of working. Consequently, there is misfit between the eventual computer system and the rest of the business system and the people that it is intended to help.

Requirements Test 4
*Is the context of the requirements wide enough to cover
everything we need to understand?*

Of course, this is easy to say, but we still have to be able to test whether or not the context is large enough to include the complete business system, not just the software. ("Business" in this sense should mean not just a commercial business, but whatever activity—scientific, engineering, artistic—the organization is doing.) We do this test by observing the questions asked by the systems analysts: Are they considering the parts of the system that will be external to the software? Are questions being asked that relate to people or systems that are shown as being outside the context? Are any of the interfaces around the boundary of the context being changed?

Another test for completeness is to question whether we have captured all the requirements that are currently known. The obstacle is that our source of requirements is people. And every person views the world differently according to his own job and his own idea of what is important, or what is wrong with the current system. It helps to consider the types of requirements that we are searching for:

- *Conscious requirements.* Problems that the new system must solve.

- *Unconscious requirements.* Already solved by the current system.

- *Undreamed-of requirements.* Would be a requirement if we knew it was possible or could imagine it.

Conscious requirements are easier to discover because they are uppermost in the stakeholders' minds. Unconscious requirements are more difficult to discover. If a problem is already satisfactorily solved by the current system, then it is less likely for it to be mentioned as a requirement for a new system. Other unconscious requirements are often those relating to legal, governmental, and cultural issues. Undreamed-of requirements are even more difficult to discover. These are the ones that surface after the new system has been in use for a while. "I didn't know that it was possible, otherwise I would have asked for it."

Requirements Test 5

Have we asked the stakeholders about conscious, unconscious, and undreamed-of requirements?

Requirements engineering experience with other systems helps to discover missing requirements. The idea is to compare your current requirements specification with specifications for similar systems. For instance, suppose that a previous specification has a requirement related to the risk of damage to property. It makes sense to ask whether our current system has any requirements of that type, or anything similar. It is quite possible, indeed quite probable, that we might discover unconscious and undreamed-of requirements by looking at other specifications.

We have distilled experience from many projects and built a generic requirements template [12] that can be used to test for missing requirement types. I urge you to look through the template and use it to stimulate questions about requirements that otherwise would have been missed. Similarly, you can build your own template by distilling your own requirements specifications, and thus uncover most of the questions that need to be asked.

Another aid in discovering unconscious and undreamed-of requirements is to build models and prototypes to show people different views of the requirements. Most important of all is to remember that each stakeholder is an individual person. Human communication skills are the best aid to complete requirements [2].

Requirements Test 5 (Enlarged)

Have we asked the stakeholders about conscious, unconscious, and undreamed-of requirements? Can you show that a modeling effort has taken place to discover the unconscious requirements? Can you demonstrate that brainstorming or similar efforts have taken place to find the undreamed-of requirements?

Relevance

When we cast out the requirements gathering net and encourage people to tell us all their requirements, we take a risk. Along with all the requirements that are relevant to our context, we are likely to pick up impostors. These irrelevant requirements are often the result of a stakeholder not understanding the goals of the project. In this case people, especially if they have had bad experiences with another system, are prone to include requirements "just in case we need it." Another reason for irrelevancy is personal bias. If a stakeholder is particularly interested or affected by a subject then he might think of it as a requirement even if it is irrelevant to this system.

Requirements Test 6
Is every requirement in the specification relevant to this system?

To test for relevance, check the requirement against the stated goals for the system. Does this requirement contribute to those goals? If we exclude this requirement, then will it prevent us from meeting those goals? Is the requirement concerned with subject matter that is within the context of our study? Are there any other requirements that are dependent on this requirement? Some irrelevant requirements are not really requirements; instead, they are solutions.

Requirement or Solution?

When one of your stakeholders tells you he wants a graphic user interface and a mouse, he is presenting you with a solution, not a requirement. He has seen other systems with graphic user interfaces, and he wants what he considers to be the most up-to-date solution. Or perhaps he thinks that designing the system is part of his role. Or maybe he has a real requirement that he has mentally solved by use of a graphic interface. When solutions are mistaken for requirements, then the real requirement is often missed. Also, the eventual solution is not as good as it could be because the designer is not free to consider all possible ways of meeting the requirements.

Requirements Test 7
Does the specification contain solutions posturing as requirements?

It is not always easy to tell the difference between a requirement and a solution. Sometimes there is a piece of technology within the context and the stakeholders have stated that the new system must use this technology. Things like "the new system must be written in COBOL because that is the only language our programmers know," and "the new system must use the existing warehouse layout because we don't want to make structural changes" are really requirements because they are genuine constraints that exist within the context of the problem.

For each requirement, ask "Why is this a requirement?" Is it there because of a genuine constraint? Is it there because it is needed? Or is it the solution to a perceived problem? If the "requirement" includes a piece of technology, and it could be implemented by another technology, then unless the specified technology is a genuine constraint, the "requirement" is really a solution.

Stakeholder Value

There are two factors that affect the value that stakeholders place on a requirement: the grumpiness that is caused by bad performance, and the happiness that is caused by good performance. Failure to provide a perfect solution to some requirements will produce mild annoyance. Failure to meet other requirements will cause the whole system to be a failure. If we understand the value that the stakeholders put on each requirement, we can use that information to determine design priorities.

Requirements Test 8
Is the stakeholder value defined for each requirement?

Pardee [9] suggests that we use scales from 1 to 5 to specify the reward for good performance and the penalty for bad performance. If a requirement is absolutely vital to the success of the system, then it has a penalty of 5 and a reward of 5. A requirement that would be nice to have but is not really vital might have a penalty of 1 and a reward of 3. The overall value or importance that the stakeholders place on a requirement is the sum of penalty and reward—in the first case a value of 10, and in the second a value of 4.

The point of defining stakeholder value is to discover how the stakeholders really feel about the requirements. We can use this knowledge to make prioritization and trade-off decisions when the time comes to design the system.

Traceability

We want to be able to prove that the system that we build meets each one of the specified requirements. We need to identify each requirement so that we can trace its progress through detailed analysis, design, and eventual implementation. Each stage of system development shapes, repartitions, and organizes the requirements to bring them closer to the form of the new system. To ensure against loss or corruption, we need to be able to map the original requirements to the solution for testing purposes.

Requirements Test 9
Is each requirement uniquely identifiable?

In the micro-specification in Figure A.1, we see that each requirement must have a unique identifier. We find the best way of doing this is simply to assign a number to each requirement. The only significance of the number is that it is that requirement's identifier. We have seen schemes where the requirements are numbered according to type or value or whatever, but these make it difficult to manage changes. It is far better to avoid hybrid numbering schemes and to use the number purely as an identifier. Other facts about the requirement are then recorded as part of the requirements micro-specification.

Order in a Disorderly World

We have considered each requirement as a separately identifiable, measurable entity. Now we need to consider the connections between requirements and to understand the effect of one requirement on others. This means we need a way of dealing with a large number of requirements and the complex connections between them. Rather than trying to tackle everything simultaneously, we need a way of dividing the requirements into manageable groups. Once that is done, we can consider the connections in two phases: the internal connections between the requirements in each group, and then the connections between the groups. It reduces the complexity of the task if our grouping of requirements is done in a way that minimizes the connections between the groups.

Events or use cases provide us with a convenient way of grouping the requirements [8, 4, 11]. The event/use case is a happening that causes the system to respond. The system's response is to satisfy all of the requirements that are connected to that event/use case. In other words, if we could string together all the requirements that respond to one event/use case, we would have a mini-system responding to that event. By grouping the requirements that respond to an event/use case, we arrive at groups with strong internal connections. Moreover, the events/use cases within our context provide us with a very natural way of collecting our requirements.

Figure A.2 illustrates the relationships between requirements. The event/use case is a collection of all the requirements that respond to the same happening. The n-to-n relationship between Event/Use Case and Requirement indicates that while there are a number of Requirements to fulfill one Event/Use Case, any Requirement could also contribute to other Events/Use Cases. The model also shows us that one Requirement might have more than one Potential Solution but it will have only one Chosen Solution.

The event/use case provides us with a number of small, minimally connected systems. We can use the event/use case partitioning throughout the development of the system. We can analyze the requirements for one event/use case, design the solution for the event/use case, and implement the solution. Each requirement has a unique identifier. Each event/use case has a name and number. We keep track of which requirements are connected to which events/use cases using a requirements tool or spreadsheet. If there is a change to a requirement, we can identify all the parts of the system that are affected.

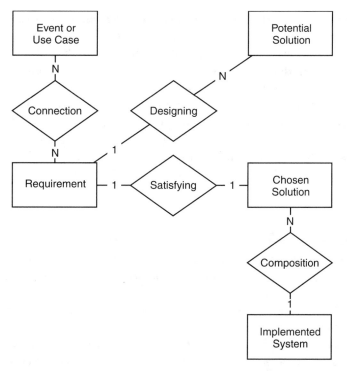

Figure A.2　　The event/use case provides a natural grouping for keeping track of the relationships between requirements.

Requirements Test 10

Is each requirement tagged to all parts of the system where it is used?
For any change to requirements, can you identify all parts of the system
where this change has an effect?

Conclusions

The requirements specification must contain all the requirements that are to be solved by our system. The specification should objectively specify everything our system must do and the conditions under which it must perform. Management of the number and complexity of the requirements is one part of the task.

The most challenging aspect of requirements gathering is communicating with the people who are supplying the requirements. If we have a consistent way of recording requirements we make it possible for the stakeholders to participate in the requirements process. As soon as we make a requirement visible, we can start testing it and asking the stakeholders detailed questions. We can apply a variety of tests to ensure that each requirement is relevant, and that everyone has the same understanding of its meaning. We can ask the stakeholders to define the relative value of requirements. We can define a quality measure for each requirement, and we can use that quality measure to test the eventual solutions.

Testing starts at the beginning of the project, not at the end of the coding. We apply tests to assure the quality of the requirements. Then the later stages of the project can concentrate on testing for good design and good code. The advantages of this approach are that we minimize expensive rework by minimizing requirements-related defects that could have been discovered, or prevented, early in the project's life.

References

1. Christopher Alexander. *Notes on the Synthesis of Form.* Harvard Press, 1964.
2. Donald Gause and Gerald Weinberg. *Exploring Requirements.* Dorset House, New York, 1989.
3. Michael Jackson. *Software Requirements and Specifications.* Addison-Wesley, Reading, MA, 1995.
4. Ivar Jacobson. *Object-Oriented Software Engineering.* Addison-Wesley, Reading, MA, 1992.
5. Capers Jones. *Assessment and Control of Software Risks.* Prentice Hall, New Jersey, 1994.
6. Neil Maiden and Gordon Rugg. Acre: selecting methods for requirements acquisition. *Software Engineering Journal,* May 1966.
7. Steve Mellor and Sally Schlaer. *Object-Oriented Systems Analysis: Modelling the World in Data.* Prentice Hall, New Jersey, 1988.
8. Steve McMenamin and John Palmer. *Essential Systems Analysis.* Yourdon Press, New York, 1984.
9. William J. Pardee. *How to Satisfy and Delight Your Customer.* Dorset House, New York, 1996.
10. James Robertson. *On Setting the Context.* The Atlantic Systems Guild, 1996.
11. James and Suzanne Robertson. *Complete Systems Analysis: the Workbook, the Textbook, the Answers.* Dorset House, New York, 1994.
12. James and Suzanne Robertson. *Requirements Template.* The Atlantic Systems Guild, London, 1966.

Note

Appendix B

Tools That Support
the Automated Testing
Life Cycle

B.1 | Introduction

Table B.1 indicates the various types of test tools available for use throughout the various life-cycle phases, supporting the automated testing process. This table provides the names of selected products associated with the various categories listed and is not to be construed as an exhaustive list of available products. Table B.1 lists tools that support the testing life cycle; it does not address development tools and tools supporting the other life-cycle phases, such as database tools, middleware connectivity and gateway tools, GUI builders, RAD development tools, and many others.

To avoid repetition, each tool is listed only once, even though some tools (such as defect tracking tools, configuration management tools, and test procedure generation tools) may be used throughout the entire development life cycle.

The in-depth descriptions of the tools that follow the table list many Web site URLs. The authors are aware that these URLs change often. If you find an outdated URL, please refer to the authors' Web site, http://www.autotestco.com, for an up-to-date list of these specific URLs.

Table B.1   Tools for the Testing Life-Cycle Phases

Life-Cycle Phase	Type of Tool	Tool Description	Tool Example
Business Analysis Phase	Business Modeling Tools	Allow for recording definitions of user needs and automating the rapid construction of flexible, graphical, client-server applications	Oracle Designer 2000, Rational Rose
	Configuration Management Tools	Allow for baselining important data repositories	Rational ClearCase, PVCS
	Defect Tracking Tools	Manage system life-cycle defects	TestTrack, Census, PVCS Tracker, Spyder
	Technical Review Management	Facilitate communication, while automating technical review/inspection process	ReviewPro (Software Development Technologies)
	Documentation Generators	Automate document generation	Rational SoDA
Requirements Definition Phase	Requirements Management Tools	Manage and organize requirements; allow for test procedure design; allow for test progress reporting	Rational Requisite Pro, QSS DOORS
	Requirements Verifiers	Verify syntax, semantics, and testability	Aonix Validator/Req
	Use Case Generators	Allow for creation of use cases	Rational Rose
Analysis and Design Phase	Database Design Tools	Provide a solution for developing second-generation enterprise client-server systems	Oracle Developer 2000, Erwin, Popkins, Terrain by Cayenne
	Application Design Tools	Help define software architecture; allow for object-oriented analysis, modeling, design, and construction	Rational Rose, Oracle Developer 2000, Popkins, Platinum, Object Team by Cayenne
	Structure Charts, Flowcharts, and Sequence Diagrams	Help manage processes	Micrografx FlowCharter 7
	Test Procedure Generators	Generate test procedures from requirements or design or data and object models	Aonix Validator, StP/T from IDE, Rational TestStudio

continued

continued from page 418

Life-Cycle Phase	Type of Tool	Tool Description	Tool Example
Programming Phase	Syntax Checkers/ Debuggers	Allow for syntax checking and debugging capability; usually come with built-in programming language compiler	Miscellaneous language compilers (C, C++, VB, Powerbuilder)
	Memory Leak and Runtime Error Detection Tools	Detect runtime errors and memory leaks	Rational Purify
	Source Code Testing Tools	Verify maintainability, portability, complexity, cyclomatic complexity, and standards compliance	CodeCheck from Abraxas Software, Visual Quality from McCabe & Associates
	Static and Dynamic Analyzers	Depict quality and structure of code	LDRA Testbed, Discover
	Various Code Implementation Tools	Depending on the application, support code generation, among other things	PowerJ, Jbuilder, SilverStream, Symantec Café
	Unit Test Tools	Automate the unit testing process	MTE from Integrisoft, Aprobe by OC Systems
Metrics Tools	Code (Test) Coverage Analyzers or Code Instrumentors	Identify untested code and support dynamic testing	STW/Coverage, Software Research TCAT, Rational Pure Coverage, IntegriSoft Hindsight and EZCover
	Usability Measurements	Provide usability testing as conducted in usability labs	ErgoLight
Other Testing Life-cycle Support Tools	Test Data Generators	Generate test data	TestBytes, Rational Performance Studio
	Prototyping Tools	Allow for prototyping of applications, using programming languages like Visual Basic or using tools like Access 97	VB, Powerbuilder

continued

continued from page 419

Life-Cycle Phase	Type of Tool	Tool Description	Tool Example
	File Compare Utilities	Allow for searching for discrepancies between files that should be identical in content	Often part of capture/playback tools such as Rational's Team Test. GMR Technologies' D2K/PLUS, and Software Research's EXDIFF
	Simulation Tools	Simulate application to measure for scalability, among other tasks	OPNET
Testing Phase	Test Management Tools	Allow for test management	Rational Suite TestStudio,Test Director from Mercury Interactive
	Network Testing Tools	Allow for monitoring, measuring, testing, and diagnosis of performance across the entire network	NETClarity, Applied Computer Technology ITF
	GUI Testing Tools (Capture/Playback)	Allow for automated GUI tests; capture/playback tools record user interactions with online systems, so they may be replayed automatically	Rational Suite Test-Studio, Visual Test, Mercury Interactive's WinRunner, Segue's Silk, STW/Regression from Software Research, AutoScriptor Inferno, Automated Test Facility from Softbridge, QARUN from Compuware
	Non-GUI Test Drivers	Allow for automated execution of tests for products without a graphical user interface	Aprobe by OC Systems
	Load/Performance Testing Tools	Allow for load/performance and stress testing	Rational Performance Studio
	Web Testing Tools	Allow for testing of Web applications, Java applications, and so on	Segue's SilkTest, ParaSoft's JTest, RSW e-Test Suite
	Environment Testing Tools	Various testing tools are on the market for various testing environments	Mercury Interactive's XRunner, Rational's Prevue-X

continued

continued from page 420

Life-Cycle Phase	Type of Tool	Tool Description	Tool Example
Year 2000 (Y2K) Testing Tools	Management and Y2K Test Planning Tools	Metrics reporting	DiscoverY2K, Rational Suite TestStudio, Revolve/2000
	Code Parsers, Inventory Analysis, and Code Analysis	Parse and report on mainframe or client-server source code for date impact	Revolve 2000 (mainframe), DiscoverY2K (client-server)
		Used to analyze Excel spreadsheets and Access databases	EraScan
		• nm: Displays symbol table information for Solaris binaries • ar: Used to check library dependencies	Solaris (standard system functions)
	Generation Tools	Support the baseline creation of Y2K test data	File-AID/MVSm, Abend-AID/XLS, Batch Abend-AID for DB2, CICS Abend-AID for DB2, DataVantage, Banner Software Datatect
	Data Agers	Allow for automatically setting the values of date fields in test data forward or backward to allow for Y2K testing	File-AID Data Ager, Princeton Softtech Ager 2000, ARESHET Systems Ageware 2000
	Date Simulation	Allow for data simulation and simulate the Y2K test environment	File-AID/MVS, Hourglass, HotDate 2000, FakeTime

B.2 | Business Analysis Phase

B.2.1 Business Modeling Tools

B.2.1.1 Oracle Designer/2000

Oracle Designer/2000 is a toolset for recording definitions of user needs and automating the rapid construction of flexible, graphical, client-server applications. When integrated with Oracle's Developer/2000, Designer/2000 provides a solution for developing second-generation enterprise client-server systems. For more information on Oracle Designer/2000, visit http://www.oracle.com.

Version 2.0 of Designer/2000 provides a fully integrated modeling and generation environment known as the Design Editor. The Design Editor provides a single-user interface for the design of both client and server applications, and a framework in which the cooperative generators share and synchronously maintain design information. During the design process, the test engineer records information in the Designer/2000 Repository. This design information is stored as design-level object definitions and is used by the generator products to generate databases and client applications.

The Design Editor provides test personnel with many different ways of performing tasks, allowing you to make your own choices as to how you want to work: design guides, which guide you through the entire process of creating client and server applications; design components, which are tailored to specific tasks, such as creating modules for application generation or setting preferences; or design wizards, which step you through specific tasks, such as defining module components. The Design Editor presents information in different views. The purpose of the views is to present you with only the information that you need to perform certain main processes, such as designing client applications or recording distribution details for a database design.

Design Components.   Using the different components in the Design Editor, you can create, edit, and delete the design-level objects that you require. Each component type, with the exception of navigator windows, has a specific purpose and can be used for manipulating object definitions that are related to that purpose only. For example, module diagrams can be used for defining client applications only; they cannot be used for tasks such as setting generator preferences or creating table definitions.

The types of components within the Design Editor include the Object Navigator, data diagrams, and module diagrams. The Object Navigator is used for managing and viewing all design-level object definitions that exist in the Repository. This component represents the relationships between objects, hierarchically. Data diagrams are used for designing databases; they graphically represent the relationships between the objects that make up the database design. Module diagrams are used for designing modules for application generation; they graphically represent the relationships between the objects that make up generated applications. The generator preferences palette is used for setting preferences to refine the behavior and appearance of generated applications. This component cannot be used to create object definitions. The Logic Editor is used for developing procedural logic code for client applications; the logic can be either server-side or client-side.

The action of selecting an object, such as a module, and dragging it onto the main Design Editor window opens the module diagram for the selected module.

This same drag-and-drop technique can be used to open a data diagram and the Logic Editor if the appropriate design object is selected. The Object Navigator and the other diagrams are designed to work together, allowing objects to be selected in one component and dropped in another. For example, a table and some columns can be selected in the Object Navigator and dropped on an open module diagram to automatically create usage of those tables and columns by that module.

Design Editor Views. Each view in the Design Editor is presented on a different tab in the navigator window. Each view relates to one of the following main design processes, and therefore displays Repository information that is relevant to that process only:

Designing a first-cut database

Designing client applications

Recording database administration details

Recording database distribution details

One Hundred Percent Generation. Designer/2000 Release 2.0 enables the 100% generation of client-server applications by the use of application logic and reusable module components. Application logic is custom code that may be recorded as part of the system design in the Designer/2000 Repository. Generators then incorporate this logic into the generated system, removing the need to modify generated programs other than through Designer/2000. Module components (parts of program specifications) can be reused and shared between modules; generators then create reusable objects as appropriate to the target environment.

Application Logic. Designer/2000 Release 2.0 provides the facility to record application logic or "custom code" within the Repository and to have the generators embed that code within the generated applications. This approach reduces the need for regeneration options or post-generation alterations to generated code, thereby improving the manageability and maintainability of systems developed using Designer/2000.

The reverse-engineering and design-capture capabilities of Designer/2000 also enable 100% reverse engineering of application logic as well as 100% generation. The Repository allows the storage and definition of application logic by holding the event model for each target language. For the Form Generator, logic can be defined at the form, block, and item levels for event points such as WHEN-VALIDATE-ITEM and PRE-INSERT. Each event point may have several pieces of code associated with it, including some user-defined (application logic) and some generated from declarative definitions (generated logic).

Designers can see the code that is to be generated from Repository definitions and sequence their own application logic within the generated code "chunks" as required. If necessary, users can also replace the generated application logic with their own. This concept is extended to the Server Generator for the definition of application logic in database triggers and commit time server-side procedures.

Application logic can be recorded against modules of all types and is fully supported by the generators for Developer/2000 Forms, Reports, and Graphics; WebServer applications; and Visual Basic. To permit this functionality, the Logic Editor supports the syntax of PL/SQL v2, Oracle Basic, Visual Basic, and Java.

Reusable Module Components. Designer/2000 enables increased productivity through reusable module components. A module component maps to a block in Forms, a group in Reports, or a zone in Visual Basic. In Designer/2000 terms, a module component typically consists of a base table and its lookup tables; it provides a logical "view" to the end user. All data input by any Designer/2000 tool at any stage of development are stored in a central Repository, enabling teamwork and project management. Designer/2000 supports a choice of development approaches.

Supported Environments.   On the server side, Designer/2000 supports the definition, generation, and design recovery of the following database types, via a native Oracle connection and ODBC connectivity: Oracle 8, 7.3, 7.2, 7.1, and 7.0; Personal Oracle Lite; Rdb; ANSI 92; DB2/2 and MVS; Microsoft SQL Server; and Sybase.

On the client side, Designer/2000 supports the following: generation of Form, Report, and Graphics components; generation of Visual Basic applications; generation of WebServer applications; generation of MS Help; and integration with other generated applications.

B.2.1.2   Rational Rose

Rational Rose is a business modeling tool, but also has many other uses during the testing life cycle. At a higher level, Rational Rose maps the business problems to requirements, and then maps requirements, logic, and code at the subsequent levels. For more details on Rational Rose, see Section B.4.1.1.

B.2.2   Configuration Management Tools

It is important that the final outputs of each life-cycle development phase be baselined in a configuration management tool (for the reasons described in Chapter 8). Many tools used throughout the development and testing life cycle come with built-in configuration management. For tools that lack this feature, it is important that all outputs are baselined. A configuration management tool such as Rational's ClearCase allows for version control, workspace management, build management, and process control.

B.2.2.1 ClearCase

Features of ClearCase include parallel development for teams:

- Automatic merging of as many as 32 contributors
- Additive and subtractive merging
- Graphical merge tools with editable, synchronized windows

Version control features include the following:

- Checkin/checkout development model
- Graphical display of version evolution
- Version directories, subdirectories, and file system objects
- Unlimited branching
- Interleaved delta compression and automatic caching
- RCS, SCCS, PVCS, DSEE, SourceSafe, and UNIX file conversion

Workspace management features are provided as well:

- Transparent access to all version objects
- Rule-based version selection
- Multiple, active views
- Dynamic workspace configuration and update
- Support for disconnected use (Windows only)
- Instant reconstruction of past configurations

Build management features include the following:

- Generation of a detailed bill of materials
- Compatibility with popular UNIX and Windows makefiles
- Automatic detection of makefile dependencies
- Network-wide binary sharing without copies
- Parallel builds on multiprocessor hosts
- Distributed builds and network load balancing

Process control features are as follows:

- Supports SEI Capability Maturity Model and ISO 9000
- Sets event triggers via user-defined programs or scripts
- Graphically manages logical process relationships

Specifications for ClearCase are as follows:

Hardware

- IBM or 100% compatible PC with a 486 or higher processor

Client Requirements

- 32MB RAM
- 35MB hard disk space

Server Requirements

- 64MB or more RAM
- 70 MB hard disk space (dependent on code base size)

Supported Environments

- Windows 95 and 98 (client only)
- Windows NT
- UNIX

B.2.3   Defect Tracking Tools

Defect tracking tools are used to manage the defects generated throughout the various life-cycle phases. Depending on your needs, you can select from a variety of defect tracking tools on the market (see Chapter 8 for a defect tracking evaluation checklist).

B.2.3.1   PVCS Tracker

PVCS Tracker is an enterprise-wide solution that captures, manages, and communicates the crush of feature requests, defect reports, and changes for a software development project. Using the I-NET interface, project team members anywhere in the world can directly capture all issues. They can easily establish priorities, assign ownership, manage hand-offs, and track issues from emergence to resolution. Tracker's automatic notification allows all team members to stay on top of changes that affect them. For more information concerning the PVCS product, see http://www.microfocus.com.

PVCS Tracker highlights include the following:

- I-NET (Internet and intranet), when enabled, allows you to choose your interface.

- Two interfaces are available for Tracker: traditional Windows and the Tracker I-NET Web interface. The Tracker I-NET interface allows access to Tracker via the Web, enabling you to use the Internet and intranets. Key capabilities are included in I-NET interface, including login, submit, in tray, query, and anonymous submit.

- Tracker associates revisions with problem descriptions.

- It automatically reports who, what, when, and why information for all module changes.

- It supports version labels for fixed modules to close a problem report.

- The in tray shows new or changed problem reports and change requests.

- Tracker automatically notifies users of ownership and status changes.

- PVCS Notify is integrated for automatic notification of Tracker and non-Tracker users through enterprise e-mail systems.

- Predefined reports and queries are available.

- You can generate custom graphical and text reports with fill-in-the-blank dialog boxes.

- You can customize report appearance by using the reporting toolbar.

- You can filter records with a conditional query.

- You can build custom queries with a point-and-click interface.

- Tracker provides an open architecture with an application program interface (API) and ODBC.

- It can link to other applications such as call tracking, help desk, automated testing, and Web systems.

- The open database support with ODBC technology works with dBASE, Oracle, SQL Server, and Sybase databases.

The Tracker I-NET Interface requires the following:

- Windows NT 3.51 or later

- Netscape Enterprise or FastTrack Server 2.0 or later

- Microsoft Internet Information Server 2.0 or later
- One of the following Web browsers: Netscape Navigator 3.0 or Microsoft Internet Explorer 3.0

Compatible databases are as follows:

- Oracle 7
- Microsoft SQL Server 4.21, 4.21a, 6.0, and 6.5
- Sybase System 10

Hardware and software requirements include the following:

- Personal computer with 386, 486, or Pentium-based processor
- Windows NT 3.51 or later: minimum of 16MB RAM, 32MB recommended; or Windows 95 or Windows 3.1: minimum of 8MB RAM, 16MB recommended
- Installation disk space: local—20MB, network—20MB on network file server, 3MB on workstations
- Compatible mail systems: Lotus cc:Mail, Lotus Notes mail, Microsoft Mail, or SMTP

B.2.3.2   TestTrack

TestTrack is a bug tracking software with many features, such as receiving bug reports via e-mail, sending e-mail notifications, handling duplicate bugs as single bug reports, automatically generating product release notes, attaching files to bug reports, and full cross-platform support. In addition to tracking bugs and enhancement requests, TestTrack tracks test configurations and team members. By tracking test configurations, you can match problem patterns related to specific computer software and hardware setups. By tracking team members, you can monitor workloads at a glance, determine which team members are overloaded, and reassign some of their work to other members. For more information concerning the TestTrack product, see http://www.seapine.com/.

Track Development Data

- Track bugs, feature requests, customers, users, user groups, and test configurations
- Identify your bugs and other development assignments in TestTrack's workbook
- Attach files to bug reports

- View attached pictures and text without leaving TestTrack
- Track estimates

Help Desk Support

- Access customer bug histories
- Search for and work with bug reports by customer

TestTrack Web

- Access TestTrack functionality from a standard Web browser
- Share existing databases with native TestTrack users
- Allow customers to check the status of previously reported support issues
- Automatically e-mail acknowledgments to customers who report support issues

Multiuser Support and Security

- Single- and multiple-user support in one package
- Security features that control data available to each user
- Password protection for single-user files
- Simultaneous access with automatic record locking

Customization

- Customize fields to meet individual product needs
- Customize the bug list to filter the fields displayed on the screen
- Specify required fields and field defaults
- Customize Solo Bug's field names to fit the project

Notification

- Automatically notify the development team of bug assignments, new bugs, changes, and so on using TestTrack's internal notification system and SMPT and MAPI e-mail
- Quickly identify new bugs, changed bugs, and assigned bugs by using Test-Track's indicators
- Provide a notification list with each defect

Queries and Sorting

- Track each bug's history
- Search for bugs by word or phrase
- USL date- and user-sensitive filters to query the database
- View user statistics such as how many bugs a user found or fixed
- Create and save custom filters/queries

Reporting

- Print or preview reports
- Customize detail, list, distribution, and trend reports
- Automatically generate release notes
- Save reports to text files
- Import data from tab- and comma-delimited files
- Export data to tab- and comma-delimited files

Simplified Bug Reporting

- Comes with Solo Bug, a stand-alone bug reporter for customers and beta sites so they can send bug reports directly to you via e-mail
- Automatically imports customer-reported bugs from an e-mail account

Cross-Platform Support

- Cross-platform support for Windows 95 and NT and Macintosh
- Solo Bug available for Windows 95, NT, and 3.1 and Macintosh

Supported Environments

- Windows 95 and NT 4.0, Macintosh 68K, and PPC

B.2.3.3   Census

Census is a defect tracking system with a graphical interface that offers predefined queries, reports, and more. For more information concerning the Census product, see http://www.metaquest.com/.

Defect Life-Cycle Model.   Census provides a defect life-cycle model for tracking defects from initial discovery to final resolution. Defects are either open or closed. Substates (new, to be verified, canceled, fixed, and more) define the different stages in the defect life cycle. You redefine the substates to tailor the life-cycle model software project.

Quick and Easy Access to Your Data. Census's data display can be customized. It has many predefined queries and reports, or you can build new queries (no SQL needed) and define custom reports (and graphs). You can add new queries and reports to the predefined lists so other users can access them.

Security and Privileges. Census's security restricts access to the system and to features. Different levels of functionality can be defined. Features not required for specific job functions can be disabled until needed.

Customization. Census provides a Template Editor for tailoring the defect record to your unique requirements. Set the choice values for fields like Product, Version, and Functional Area. Change labels and add new fields (select from nine field types). Set field attributes such as required, visible, and more. Indicate which groups can modify a field.

Powerful Architecture. Census is built around an innovative architecture composed of a core with a configurable template. The core provides the basic functionality required by any information tracking system—database access, queries, reports (and graphs), user/group privileges, print and mail support, automatic mail notification, and more.

Notifications and Electronic Mail. Census can send notifications, via electronic mail, when specific events occur—for example, when a defect is assigned to a new owner, when the status of a defect changes, or when the number of open defects exceeds a given threshold. Select from lists of predefined notifications or create your own. For each notification, specify the recipient and the contents. Mail defects (reports) from within Census using any MAPI-compliant mail system (Microsoft Mail, cc:Mail, and more).

Features

- Security—restrict user access to Census, define group privileges, restrict access to projects, and define who can modify fields
- Query Editor—edit existing queries (filters) and define new queries
- Sort Editor—edit existing sort criteria and define new sort criteria
- Organizer—share common styles between team members

- Report Editor—edit existing reports or create new reports
- Viewing of reports as text and graph (line, bar, and pie)
- More than 60 predefined query, sort, layout, and report styles
- Mail defect records or summary list contents as text or RTF
- Defects profile (set default values for new defects)
- Multiuser support (central database)
- Tracking of every change made to a defect using the revision history
- Construction of automatic e-mail notifications

System Requirements

- Windows 95 or NT
- 486 processor or higher
- Minimum of 25MB of hard disk space
- Minimum of 32MB RAM (additional memory will significantly improve performance)
- Disk space requirements for a Census server—dependent on database size (minimum of 50MB).
- Workgroup users—networking software, such as Microsoft Windows for Workgroups, Novell Netware, or Artisoft Lantastic
- Notifications—MAPI-compliant electronic mail system
- Power Customizations (replacement of Census template)—Microsoft Access license

B.2.4 Technical Review Management

B.2.4.1 ReviewPro

ReviewPro is a Web-based, software technical reviews and inspections tool. Technical reviews and inspections have proved to be an effective form of defect detection and removal. This tool automates this valuable process and prevents the migration of defects to later phases of software development. For more information on ReviewPro, visit http://www.sdtcorp.com.

Benefits of ReviewPro include the following:

- Automates defect detection and removal method
- Takes advantage of latest collaboration and Web technology for optimal productivity
- Provides everywhere access to the review process analysis and results

- Can be implemented with the existing IT infrastructure
- Offers quality and productivity improvements that make this tool an easy management sale.

ReviewPro supports the Windows NT and UNIX platforms.

B.2.5 Documentation Generators

Automated documentation generators such as Rational's SoDA can also aid in the testing life cycle.

B.2.5.1 SoDA

SoDA—Software Documentation Automation—is designed to reduce your efforts to create and regenerate development life-cycle documentation and reports. SoDA provides a common interface for extracting information from multiple tool sources, easing your ability to produce comprehensive project documentation. For more information, visit www.rational.com.

Highlights
- Provides WYSIWYG template creation for customization of documents
- Preserves data entered directly into the document from generation to generation
- Performs incremental document regeneration to reduce turnaround time
- Enables extraction of data from multiple information sources to create a single document
- Accommodates your choice of tools from which to extract information
- Maintains consistency between documents and information sources
- Can be integrated with a powerful publishing tool
- Provides a single documentation-automation solution across the software life cycle

Hardware and Software Requirements
- Microsoft Windows 95 or NT
- Microsoft Word 95 or Word 97
- 24MB RAM (48MB recommended)
- 25MB hard disk space
- PC with Pentium 90 processor (Pentium 150 recommended)

B.3 | Requirements Definition Phase

B.3.1   Requirements Management Tools

Requirements management tools allow you to manage and organize your requirements. A requirement is a condition or capability to which the system must conform [1]. Requirements management is a systematic approach to eliciting, organizing, and documenting the requirements of the system; this process establishes and maintains agreement between the customer and the project team on the changing requirements of the system [2]. There are many requirements management systems, such as Requiste Pro by Rational and DOORS by QSS.

B.3.1.1   RequisitePro

RequisitePro is a Windows-based tool that organizes any requirements (high-level business, functional, design, test) by linking Microsoft Word to a requirements repository and providing traceability and change management throughout the project life cycle. RequisitePro combines both document-centric and database-centric approaches and can be integrated with the development processes and tools. Key users for RequisitePro are all software or systems development team members—business analysts, project managers, product marketing managers, development managers, QA managers, developers, and so on.

One of the challenges in any project is managing the inevitable change in user requirements, software specifications, and test requirements and, more importantly, communicating those changes to everyone on the team. RequisitePro's automated traceability feature displays requirements relationships through a top-down, graphical hierarchy, so all team members can identify which requirements are affected by a change. Traceability relationships can be established within a single project or across multiple projects. Requirements and their changes are tracked all the way through implementation and testing to ensure that you deliver what you originally intended.

System Specifications
- Microsoft Windows 95 or NT 4.0
- 64MB
- 55MB hard disk space (minimum)
- Pentium 133 or better for optimal performance
- Any Windows-supported LAN
- Microsoft Word 95 or Word 97

B.3.1.2 DOORS

DOORS (Dynamic Object-Oriented Requirements System) is software for information management and traceability (IMT) needs. DOORS is used for managing requirements throughout the development life cycle. DOORS 4.0 is a project repository, adding a range of features that help individual users and corporations to capture, link, analyze, manage, and distribute key requirement data. Most requirements management tools allow for automatic tracing—for example, tracing of test procedures to requirements, design to requirements, and so on. For more information concerning DOORS, see http://www.qssinc.com/.

DOORS Wizards

- Project Creation Wizard
- Report Manager Wizard
- Page Layout Wizard
- View Wizard
- Impact/Trace Wizard
- Graph Column Wizard
- Iconizer Wizard

Capabilities

- Identifying requirements
- Structuring requirements within documents
- Accepting requirements from many sources
- Retaining a requirements change history
- Tracing between requirements in many documents
- Managing large numbers of changes
- Providing early risk analysis
- Providing life-cycle traceability and compliance
- Supporting the formal analysis process
- Generating documentation and traceability reports

Major Features

- Many import and export formats
- User-definable attributes
- User-definable views

- Sharable data and network compatibility
- Integrated, controlled change process
- Version history and baselines
- Traceability through link creation
- Customization through dxl (DOORS proprietary language)
- Full life-cycle and project support

DOORS is an X-Windows application with a Motif or OpenLook interface, depending on the host platform. It is also available for PC. The recommended UNIX configuration is 32MB RAM, 10MB disk space, and implementation on Sun SPARC, HP 9000, or IBM RS/6000 units.

B.3.2   Requirements Verifiers

Requirements verifiers are now available to support requirements management. For example, the Software through Pictures modeling tool from Aonix includes three checking functions: Check Syntax, Check Semantics, and Check Testability. Requirements that pass these functions are deemed unambiguous, consistent, and complete enough for testing [3]. Another example is Validator/Req, a powerful new requirements-driven validation and test generation tool. For more information, see http://www.aonix.com.

B.3.3   Use Case Generators

One method of modeling requirements is via use cases. The use case construct defines the behavior of a system or other semantic entity without revealing the entity's internal structure. Each use case specifies a sequence of actions, including variants, that the entity can perform, by interacting with actors of the entity.

One popular use case generator is Rational Rose (see Section B.4.1.1). Its Use Cases package is a subpackage of the Behavioral Elements package. It specifies the concepts used for definition of the functionality of an entity like a system. The package uses constructs defined in the Foundation package of UML as well as in the Common Behavior package.

The elements in the Use Cases package are primarily used to define the behavior of an entity, such as a system or a subsystem, without specifying its internal structure. The key elements in this package are UseCase and Actor. Instances of use cases and instances of actors interact when you work with the services of the entity. How a use case is realized in terms of cooperating objects, defined by classes inside the entity, can be specified with a Collaboration. A use case of an entity may be refined to a set of use cases of the elements contained in the entity. The interaction of these subordinate use cases can also be expressed in a Collaboration. The specification of the functionality of the system itself is usually expressed in a separate use case model (that is, a Model stereotyped "useCaseModel"). The use cases and actors in the use case model are equivalent to those of the system package.

UseCase. In the meta-model, UseCase is a subclass of Classifier, containing a set of Operations and Attributes specifying the sequences of actions performed by an instance of the UseCase. The actions include changes of the state and communications with the environment of the UseCase.

There may be Associations between UseCases and the Actors of the UseCases. Such an Association states that instances of the UseCase and a user playing one of the roles of the Actor communicate with each other. UseCases may be related to other UseCases only by Extends and Uses relationships—that is, Generalizations stereotyped "extends" or "uses." An Extends relationship denotes the extension of the sequence of one UseCase with the sequence of another one, while Uses relationships denote that UseCases share common behavior.

The realization of a UseCase may be specified by a set of Collaborations. That is, the Collaborations may define how instances in the system interact to perform the sequence of the UseCase.

Actor. An actor defines a coherent set of roles that users of an entity can play when interacting with the entity. An actor has one role for each use case with which it communicates.

In the meta-model, Actor is a subclass of Classifier. An Actor has a Name and may communicate with a set of UseCases and, at realization level, with Classifiers taking part in the realization of these UseCases. An Actor may also have a set of Interfaces, each describing how other elements may communicate with the Actor.

An Actor may inherit other Actors. The inheriting Actor will be able to play the same roles as the inherited Actor—that is, communicate with the same set of Use-Cases as the inherited Actor.

B.4 | Analysis and Design Phase

B.4.1 Visual Modeling Tools

An example of a visual modeling tool, Rational Rose, is described in this section. For more information concerning the Rational Rose product, see http://www.rational.com/.

B.4.1.1   Rational Rose

Rational Rose is an object-oriented analysis, modeling, design, and construction tool. It supports the Unified Modeling Language (UML), the standard notation for software architecture. The UML is the industry-standard language for specifying, visualizing, constructing, and documenting the artifacts of software systems. It simplifies the complex process of software design, making a "blueprint" for construction. The UML definition was spearheaded by Rational Software's industry-leading methodologists: Grady Booch, Ivar Jacobson, and Jim Rumbaugh [4].

Rational Rose, as a visual modeling tool, allows developers to define and communicate a software architecture, resulting in accelerated development, by improved communication among various team members. The tool also improves quality, by mapping business processes to software architecture. It increases visibility and predictability, by making critical design decisions explicit visually.

Component-Based Development

- Rational Rose users can model their components and interfaces through component modeling.

- Required components of a design can be reverse-engineered to explore the interfaces and interrelationships of other components in the model.

Multilanguage Development

- Rose 98 Enterprise Edition has multilanguage support—for C++, Java, Smalltalk, and Ada, as well as 4GLs such as Visual Basic, PowerBuilder, and Forté.

- Rose 98 generates Interface Definition Language (IDL) for CORBA applications and Data Description Language (DDL) for database applications.

Roundtrip Engineering

- Rose 98 allows you to move easily from analysis to design to implementation and back to analysis again, and thus supports all phases of a project's life cycle.

- Rational Rose 98 supports a change management process with forward engineering, reverse engineering, and model updating features that allow users to alter their implementation, assess their changes, and automatically incorporate them in their design.

Full Team Support

- Rational Rose 98 supports teams of analysts, architects, and engineers by enabling each to operate in a private workspace that contains an individual view of the entire model.

- Multiple engineers can work on complex problems concurrently; changes are made available to others by checking them into a configuration management and version control (CMVC) system. Having a protected workspace means that one person's changes won't affect the whole model until the time comes to share these alterations with the rest of the project.

- Rose 98 can be integrated with major CMVC tools, including Rational ClearCase and Microsoft SourceSafe, and is open to other CMVC systems.

Visual Differencing

- The Visual Differencing tool is a graphical comparison and merge utility that shows the differences between two models or controlled units.

Platforms Supported

- Windows 95 and NT
- Solaris 2.5 and 2.6
- HP-UX 10.2 and 11.00
- SGI IRIX 6.2 and 6.4
- AIX 4.1.4 and 4.2
- Digital UNIX 4.0B and D

System Requirements

Windows

- Microsoft Windows 95 or NT 4.0
- 486-based or Pentium-based PC-compatible computer system
- 24MB RAM (recommended)
- 25 MB hard disk space
- SVGA-compatible display (256 or more colors recommended)
- Any pointing device with at least two buttons

UNIX

- $32 + (16 * N)$ MB of RAM (where N is the number of users running Rose simultaneously on a given workstation)
- Midrange UNIX server or client UNIX workstation
- Any UNIX workstation or PC capable of displaying X Windows
- 200MB hard disk space for loading release + 1–3MB for each Rose model
- CD ROM reader
- Color display

B.4.2   Structure Charts, Flowcharts, and Sequence Diagrams

One tool that supports diagramming, Micrografx FlowCharter 7, is described in this section. For more information on the Micrografx FlowCharter 7 product, see http://www.micrografx.com/.

B.4.2.1   Micrografx FlowCharter 7

Micrografx FlowCharter 7 is a diagramming solution to manage business processes. It creates interactive diagrams of business processes, workflow, computer networks, Web sites, databases, and much more. It can create the following types of charts:

- Flowcharts
- Process Maps
- Organization Charts
- Network Diagrams
- Data Flow Diagrams
- Web Site Diagrams
- Project Timelines
- Decision Trees
- Deployment Charts
- SPC Charts
- "Swim Lane" Process Diagrams
- Total Quality Diagrams
- Auditing Diagrams
- Block Diagrams
- Cascade Diagrams

- Checklist Diagrams
- Comparison Charts
- Deployment Charts
- DrawBar Diagrams
- Pyramid Charts
- Circle-Spoke Diagrams
- Target Charts

Hardware and Software Requirements

- Microsoft Windows 95, 98, or NT 4.0
- Pentium or faster processor
- 24MB RAM (32MB recommended)
- 50–250MB hard disk space
- VGA or better video
- CD-ROM and mouse

B.4.3 Test Procedure Generators

Validator/Req from Aonix is an example of a test procedure (case) generator packaged with a requirements recorder. Validator applies heuristic and algorithmic means to requirements information to create test procedures. Aonix's Validator/Req tool includes a tracer as well as a requirements recorder, verifier, and test procedure generator. It can be used in Sun Solaris, HP-UX, UNIX, and Windows NT environments.

With the Validator/Req, you can

- Capture your specification in English
- Model your specification in test-ready use cases
- Prevent the most probable errors in specifications
- Generate industry-standard specifications
- Automatically generate test cases and scripts
- Automatically trace requirements to and from test cases

Designers who use Aonix's Software through Pictures modeling tools can record their requirements graphically in use cases. In addition, designers may record their designs as either object or structured models, depending on which methodology they follow. Then they can use Aonix's Validator/Req tool to generate test procedures from requirements and Interactive Development Environment's StP/T tool to generate test procedures from software design.

B.5 | Programming Phase

B.5.1 Syntax Checkers/Debuggers

Syntax checkers and debuggers usually are built into any third- or fourth-generation programming language compiler, such as C, C++, Visual Basic, or Powerbuilder. Even though this option is often taken for granted, syntax checkers and debuggers are important tools that improve the testing life cycle.

B.5.2 Memory Leak and Runtime Error Detection Tools

One runtime error and memory leak detector, Purify, is described here.

B.5.2.1 Rational Purify

Using Rational's patented Object Code Insertion (OCI) technology, Rational Purify runs after compilation and post-processes the object modules from which an executable is generated, producing an executable with runtime error checking inserted into the object code. As the code is executed, all memory accesses are validated to detect and report errors at the time of occurrence. Purify also reports memory leaks, showing where memory has been allocated but to which no pointers exist, so that the memory can never be used or freed [5].

Purify detects runtime errors with or without source code. It detects errors everywhere (third-party libraries, shared libraries, C code, + code, FORTRAN code, assembly code, C library, and system calls, for example). Errors identified include the following:

- Uninitialized local variables
- Uninitialized malloc'd memory
- Use of freed memory
- Freeing of mismatched memory
- Overwriting array bounds
- Overreading array bounds
- Memory leaks
- File descriptor leaks
- Stack overflow errors

- Stack frame boundary errors
- Static memory access errors

The intuitive graphical user interface offers the following features:

- Outline view for efficient error message browsing
- Color support for identifying critical errors quickly
- Point-and-click access to source code for editing
- Menu access to runtime options and suppressions
- Advanced debugging capabilities: pinpoints bug origin by stack trace and source line number, just-in-time debugging quickly isolates errors with the debugger, and New Leaks button instantly generates memory leak reports at any point in the program

Purify identifies and reports errors in multithreaded applications and memory allocated with custom memory managers. It can be used to create an integrated development solution with most common debugging tools and PureCoverage (for identifying untested code). It is easy to install and runs on multiple platforms.

Capabilities

- Identifies execution errors and memory leaks within your application everywhere they occur.
- Helps developers eliminate runtime problems before they reach the end user.
- Improves productivity and reduces development time by presenting accurate information in an easy-to-use and understandable interface. For today's complex software development projects, runtime or memory access errors are some of the most difficult problems to solve. Reading or writing past the boundary of an array, leaking memory unpredictably, or using uninitialized memory with random contents is a potentially disastrous error that can take weeks to find and fix. Purify solves these problems by combining runtime error checking and a graphical user interface.
- Uses OCI technology to intercept memory accesses by inserting additional instructions into the object code before every load and store operation. The major advantage to OCI is completeness: all code, including third-party and shared libraries, is checked in this manner. Even hand-optimized assembly code can be checked. OCI helps Purify precisely locate more types of errors in more areas of your application than any other similar tool. Thus bugs in

application code that manifest themselves in vendor or third-party libraries are detected.

- Provides automatic checking by adding one word, purify, to the application's makefile. The resulting program is a standard executable that can be executed or run under a debugger.

- Offers both interactive and batch reporting of error messages to make analysis easier. A graphical user interface allows the user to browse error messages. The hierarchical or outline display provides detailed information for specific error messages, focusing the user on the most critical errors first. Access to application source code or development processes such as run, make, and debug are only a mouse click away. This instant access makes correcting application errors simple and easy.

Supported Environments
- Sun SPARC workstations running SunOS 4.x
- Sun SPARC workstations running Solaris 2.3 through 2.5.1
- HP 9000 Series 700 workstations running HP-UX 8.07, 9.0.x, or 10.x
- HP 9000 Series 800 workstations running HP-UX 8.07, 9.0.x, or 10.x
- SGI workstations running IRIX 5.2, 5.3, or 6.2
- Windows NT (may be operating within Microsoft Visual Studio 6 development environment)

B.5.3   Code Checkers

One code checker tool, CodeCheck, is described in this section. For more information concerning the CodeCheck product, see http://www.abxsoft.com.

B.5.3.1   CodeCheck

CodeCheck (from Abraxas Software) measures maintainability, portability, complexity, and standards compliance of C and C++ source code. CodeCheck Version 8.0 is a programmable tool for managing all C and C++ source code on a file or project basis. CodeCheck is designed to solve many of your portability, maintainability, complexity, reusability, quality assurance, style analysis, library/class management, code review, software metric, standards adherence, and corporate compliance problems.

Features
- Maintainability—identifies and measures complex, sloppy, and hard-to-maintain code

- Portability identifies code that will not port between DOS, OS/2, UNIX, VMS, Microsoft Windows, and Macintosh environments or to 64-bit machines

- Complexity—measures program size (Halstead) object-oriented metrics, program cost, and program complexity (McCabe)

- Compliance—automates your corporate C/C++ coding and project specification standards for compliance validation

CodeCheck is input-compatible with all variants of K&R, ANSI C, and C++ (Microsoft, Metaware, Borland, Intel, Vax/Vms-Ultrix, HP/Apollo, Microtec, Watcom, Symantec, Apple MPW, CodeWarrior, AT&T, and GNU).

B.5.4 Static and Dynamic Analyzers

Examples of static and dynamic code analysis toolsets are LDRA Testbed by LDRA and Discover by Software Emancipation Technology. For more information concerning the LDRA Testbed product, see http://www.ldra.co.uk. More information on Software Emancipation's tools is available on the Internet at www.setech.com.

B.5.4.1 LDRA Testbed

LDRA Testbed is a unique quality-control tool for high-caliber program testing of computer software that is required to be reliable, rugged, and as error-free as possible. As a complete package of testing modules integrated into one automated software testing toolset, LDRA Testbed enables a greater degree of software testing to be attained.

LDRA Testbed's two main testing domains are Static and Dynamic Analysis. Static Analyzis analyses the code. Dynamic Analysis involves execution with test data, through an instrumented version of the source code, to detect defects at runtime. Within these two testing fields, LDRA Testbed analyzes the source code, producing report files in textual and graphical form that depict both the quality and structure of the code. This testing process enhances understanding of the source code and highlights areas of concern. These areas can then be either reworked or removed.

Static Analysis searches the source code for any programming standards violations.

LDRA Testbed's Static and Dynamic Analysis results are recognized by many international regulatory bodies as a clear indication of the quality of code and the extent to which it has been tested.

Windows Platforms Supported

- Windows NT
- Windows 95
- Windows 3.1x

UNIX Platforms Supported
- Sun OS
- Solaris
- HP-UX
- IRIX
- SCO
- AIX
- DEC UNIX (OSF/1)

Languages Supported
- Ada
- Algol
- C
- C++

B.5.4.2   Discover

Discover is a software development information system composed of a comprehensive, integrated set of applications and tools. It analyzes source code and creates a database of information (the Information Model) that captures the interrelationships between all entities in the code base, resulting in a detailed view and high-level architectural perspective of the entire application. The Information Model provides critical information for both management and the development team.

Discover captures detailed knowledge about the structure and operation of an organization's software that might otherwise reside only in the minds of individual programmers, thereby bringing precision, manageability, and predictability to the software development process. This tool enables software professionals to more thoroughly understand their large software systems, to more efficiently and accurately effect changes to a large body of source code, and to more easily reengineer or reorganize a complex software system.

Finding a solution to the year 2000 (Y2K) problem is only one of many applications of the Discover system (see Section B.8.6.1). More than 150 corporations worldwide already benefit from using Discover. A key advantage of using Discover-Y2K today is the benefit of automating the software development process and improving software quality well beyond the millennium date change. Discover will help organizations address the coming expansion of the telephone and social security number formats, as well as the European currency unification.

Discover supports C and C++ source code, Oracle embedded SQL and PL/SQL, and Java. It runs on SunOS, Solaris, HP-UX, SGI IRIX, and Windows NT.

B.5.5 Unit and Integration Test Tools

B.5.5.1 APROBE

Chapter 7 of this book briefly discusses white-box (or structural) testing. While white-box testing can consume up to 60% of the total cost of a testing effort, it is not as amenable to automation as black-box (or functional) testing, so the major focus of tool vendors has been to support the automation of black-box testing.

It is very difficult to get objective cost and defect figures for software development, but an excellent study on the matter is "Comparing and Combining Software Defect Detection Techniques: A Replicated Empirical Study", by Murray Wood et al. Proceedings of the 6th European Conference help jointly with the 5th ACM SIGSOFT Symposium on Software Engineering, 1997. What makes this paper even more credible is that the research was repeated twice as two independent experiments and both yielded essentially the same results.

Those results were pretty much as you would expect. The study considers three methods of finding bugs: code reading, white-box testing and black-box testing. White and black-box testing both contribute significantly to quality, code reading not quite so much. What is interesting is that either white or black-box testing will increase quality by about 40 percent. Both together will increase quality by a little over 60%. This implies that (by some measure) white and black-box testing are equivalent in terms of adding quality. Either will yield about a 40 percent increase in quality. Either will add 20 percent to the overall quality when used in combination with the other. To get high quality software, a combination of white and black-box testing techniques are needed.

Aprobe is a white box testing tool. It is designed to support testers and developers in white-box testing. It supports the specific white-box tests as discussed in Chapter 7, but perhaps more importantly, supports the creation and running of white-box tests that are application specific. Aprobe is perhaps the first general-purpose tool to address the general test area of white-box testing.

Summary of Capabilities

Aprobe provides certain white-box testing capabilities as described in Chapter 7 right out of the box. These have intuitive GUIs to guide the user in their operation:

1) <u>Test Coverage</u>. What source lines of the application have been executed during a given test? Certainly code that has never been executed has never been tested and is more likely to contain a bug than code that has been executed at least once.

Aprobe can also modify the program under execution to force conditions to allow execution to reach places that would normally be hard to reach. For example, Aprobe can easily simulate an I/O error so that the application code that handles the I/O error will be executed.

2) <u>Memory Checking</u>. Aprobe checks for memory leaks, double de-allocations of memory, freeing of non-allocated memory and certain memory common memory corruption errors.

3) <u>Performance Tuning</u>. Aprobe identifies the routines that are consuming the most CPU and wall clock time.

What makes white-box testing so expensive, however, is that most white-box tests require a software development activity, not just a test activity. Aprobe supports the development and running of white-box tests by supporting the insertion and deletion of arbitrary code into an application without even changing the executable file. Aprobe is unique in this capability.

Aprobe allows the insertion of ANSI C code into the executable memory image. These small portions of code comprise the white-box tests. These portions of code (called probes), have access to any and all portions of the application, so can reference and modify portions of the application without ever changing the actual executable file. Additionally, Aprobe provides a number of useful white-box support functions. Aprobe also includes a very sophisticated logging mechanism that can easily log and format large amounts of data with little affect on the application execution.

Platforms Supported:
Windows 2000
Windows NT
Solaris 2.5.1 and higher
AIX 4.1 and higher
OS/390

Languages Supported:
Ada
C++
C

White papers, download demos and more information concerning the Aprobe tool from OC Systems can be obtained from www.aprobe.com or via email at info@ocsystems.com.

B.5.5.2   Integrisoft MTE

Often to test and isolate a function from the main program, an engineer has to write a driver, stub(s), and specific test cases for each function. In some instances, the engineer needs to write multiple drivers and stubs to test a single function. The code for the driver and any stub(s) will typically be larger than the function itself. Therefore, having to write the driver and stub(s) might seem like moving one step backward for every step forward. This manual approach to unit testing is time-consuming, error-prone, tedious, and, in most cases, not repeatable.

The MTE product gives engineers the ability to automate the unit testing process. From its analysis of the source code, MTE has information on issues such as calling relationships and variable usage. Using this information, MTE will automatically build a test harness for automating the unit testing process.

MTE can automatically

- Generate the source code for a driver
- Generate the source code for stubs
- Generate the test case input file
- List global variables to initialize
- Generate a makefile
- Build a module test program
- Compile and execute the module test program
- Capture and display the global variable during the execution of the program
- Collect test coverage information during the execution of the program
- Verify that the expected output was achieved
- Save the results from running the program in a spreadsheet format for easy viewing
- Archive the test input files for future reuse

MTE is available for Windows NT, 95, and 98. For more information on MTE visit http://www.integrisoft.com.

B.6 | Metrics Tools

B.6.1   Code (Test) Coverage Analyzers and Code Instrumentors

Examples of code (test) coverage analyzers and code instrumentor tools are provided below.

B.6.1.1   TCAT

TCAT (Software Research) code coverage analyzers are available for C, C++, and Java. TCAT, Version 2.1 for Windows 95 and NT 4.x, features 32-bit native executables, advanced compiler-based, source-language scanning technology, improved runtime support, and full GUI access to a project's call trees, function and method digraphs, and current and past-test coverage data at both the branch (C1) and call-pair (S1) level. For more information concerning the TCAT product, see http://www.soft.com/.

Benefits
- Measure effectiveness of tests and test suites
- Identify untested code and reveal more defects
- Improve test efficiency

Key Features
- Combined branch and call-pair coverage for C and C++
- Annotatable call-tree displays with access to source
- Annotatable digraph displays with access to source

Applications
- Branch coverage: unit testing, integration testing
- Call-pair coverage: integration testing, system testing, test suite validation
- Graphical annotation: all levels of code test completion browsing, analysis

Supported Environments
- All major UNIX platforms
- SPARC SunOS 4.1.3
- Solaris 2.x
- x86 Solaris 2.x
- x86 SCO ODT 5.0 (3.0)
- SGI Irix 5.3, 6.2

- IBM RS/6000—AIX 4.2
- HP 9000–700 HP-UX 9.05
- DEC Alpha OSF/1
- 386/486 UNIX
- MS-DOS, Windows 95, Windows NT

B.6.1.2   Hindsight

Hindsight (from IntegriSoft) uses source code instrumentation for dynamic testing. HindSight analyzes (reverse-engineers) C, C++, and FORTRAN source code and produces charts, diagrams, and reports that aid in the process of program understanding. These visual representations of the user's program allow you to see program structure, logic, and variable usage. This product runs in UNIX.

Hindsight uses source code instrumentation for dynamic testing. Multiple levels of test coverage are measured, including segment, branch, and conditional coverage. The appropriate level of test coverage will depend on how critical your application is. To further extend test coverage, Hindsight simulates UNIX system functions so you can reach error-handling routines for functions such as malloc.

The product's Module Test Environment offers developers an automated environment for the generation of module test programs for software unit testing and verification. The Test Procedure Environment allows you to trace requirements to functions (or classes) and test procedures while making test coverage measurements. This approach supports impact analysis and allows you to determine which test procedures to run when a function changes, allowing you to rerun those test procedures immediately. A minimization algorithm determines a minimum set of test procedures while guaranteeing maximum test coverage.

Hindsight calculates source code measurements and software metrics for use in software quality assurance. The metrics calculated include cyclomatic complexity, data complexity, Halstead metrics, and design complexity. Metric reports such as Kiviat diagrams and metrics exception reports are presented for easy visualization of quality measurements. For more information concerning the Hindsight product, see http://www.IntegriSoft.com/.

B.6.1.3   EZCover

EZCover is a C/C++ test coverage tool from IntegriSoft. It allows engineers to see how effective their testing efforts are by showing which parts of the source code have been executed. Perhaps more importantly, it identifies which parts have not been tested. One of the biggest benefits that this tool provides is to help the customer to identify which test cases should be run again in the event that the source code is modified. No longer is it necessary to run an entire test suite just to test a small portion of the source code. One other helpful capability is the fact that the tool can show the engineer the minimum number of test cases and still achieve the same level of coverage. (Both of these features are the same in the UNIX-based Hindsight tool.)

EZCover calculates software measurements that can be used to identify complex or error-prone code, as well as difficult-to-test and difficult-to-maintain areas of code. It supports the following metrics:

- Cyclomatic complexity with and without case
- Modified complexity
- Data complexity
- Fan in
- Fan out/squared
- Number of blank, comment, declaration, and executable lines

EZCover runs in the Windows NT, 95, and 98 environments.

B.6.1.4   STW/C

STW/C (Software Testworks/Coverage) is a set of tools for coverage analysis to ensure that your test procedures thoroughly exercise your program in as many diverse ways as possible. STW/C analysis tools measure how well your test procedures exercise your program at the unit, system, and integration test levels. STW/C utilizes three measures to ensure your test procedures are as thorough as possible by performing the following operations:

- Measuring logical branch (CI) completeness at the unit test level with TCAT-II
- Measuring call-pair (SI) completeness at the integration or system level with TCAT-II
- Measuring the number of times each path or path class in a module is exercised (Ct) at the unit test level with TCAT-PATH

STW/C measures runtime coverage at the following levels:

- Logical branch: For unit testing, measures the number of times each branch has been exercised for both True and False conditions
- Call-pair: For integration and system tests, measures the number of times each function call has been exercised, as errors in parameters are extremely common

- Path: For critical functions, measures the number of times each path, which is a sequence of branches, was exercised

Features. STW/C can help to find a high percentage of software defects occurring from unexercised and dead code. You can then concentrate on building more efficient test procedures and fixing the errors that are discovered.

Coverage Metrics

- *CI* metric—TCAT provides logical branch coverage with the *CI* metric.
- *SI* metric—S-TCAT provides call-pair coverage with the *SI* metric.
- *Ct* metric—TCAT-PATH provides path coverage with the *Ct* metric.
- Complete coverage—STW/C provides the coverage solution for test procedure validation.
- Critical coverage—STW/C provides coverage for mission-critical applications, such as an application needing FDA certification.

Instrumentation

- Selective instrumentation—allows for instrumentation of isolated modules or exclusion of modules that have already reached a certain level of coverage
- Makefile support—integrates instrumentation steps into the user's existing makefile
- Control structures—recognizes and processes all control structures

Runtime Support

- Cross-development environments—performs coverage in cross-, remote, and embedded development environments
- Multiple concurrent processes—supports multiprocess programs
- In-memory reduction—optionally accumulates trace records in memory instead of being written to a disk

Coverage Reports

- Reports past, current, and cumulative test results
- Report types—provides hit, not hit, newly hit, newly missed, and linear and logarithmic histogram reports

Analysis Through Displays

- Directed graphs (digraphs)—uses call trees with graphic and color overlays to diagram a program's module dependencies

- Subtrees—isolates a subtree of a call tree relative to a specific module that the user wants to investigate further

- Path viewing—displays the paths individually for a selected module

- Color annotation—uses different color overlays based on lower and upper threshold values to indicate if a function call or logical branch has been unexercised or heavily executed

- Source viewing—allows navigation from a graph to a function call, logical branch, or logical path in the source code

- Statistics—summarizes information about the displayed call tree or directed graph

- Print option—prints directed graphs and call trees to PostScript output

Dynamic Visualization

- Execute program parts—generates logical branch and call-pair coverage data in real time

- Display selection—shows coverage obtained for logical branches through directed graphs, call pairs through call-tree displays, and an overall percentage through slider bars

Supported Environments

- Sun SPARC
- x86 Solaris
- SCO
- SGI
- IBM RS/ 6000
- HP 9000 and 700/800
- DEC Alpha
- UNIXWare
- MS-DOS
- Windows NT and 95

For more information concerning the STW/C product, see http.//www. ppgsoft.com.

B.6.1.5 PureCoverage

To locate untested areas of code, PureCoverage uses Object Code Insertion (OCI) technology to insert usage tracking instructions into the object code for each function, line, and block of code. OCI helps PureCoverage identify all portions of your application's code that have not been executed in testing, including code in vendor or third-party libraries. Thus all areas of the application can be tracked to identify gaps in testing quickly, saving precious testing time and ensuring that untested code does not reach end users [7].

Features

Detection of Untested Code with or without Source Code

- Detects untested code everywhere: third-party libraries, shared libraries, C code, C++ code, FORTRAN code, assembly code, C library calls, system calls
- Detailed data collection for coverage per function, line, basic block, application, file, library, or directory

Intuitive Graphical User Interface

- Outline view for efficient browsing of summary coverage information
- Customizable views for control of data displayed and sorting criteria
- Point-and-click access to line-by-line data via an annotated source view

Robust Reporting Mechanism

- Merge data over multiple runs and dynamically update coverage statistics
- Merge data from multiple applications sharing common code
- Generate difference reports between multiple runs or executables
- Generate difference and low-threshold reports
- E-mail nightly coverage data to development team
- Export data suitable for spreadsheets

Integrated Development Solution

- Works with most common debugging tools
- Works with Purify for runtime error detection

- Works with ClearDDTS for immediate coverage reporting with PureCoverage output
- Supports both C and C++ development environments

Benefits
- Improves overall application quality
- Helps ensure all code has been executed and therefore tested
- Prevents untested code from reaching the end user
- Helps deliver more reliable code
- Enhances developer productivity and testing efforts
- Reduces development time
- Fits into the existing development environment
- Provides tight integration with developer productivity tools such as debuggers, runtime error checking, and defect tracking systems to improve the efficiency of your software development process

Supported Environments
- Sun SPARC workstations running SunOS 4.x
- Sun SPARC workstations running Solaris 2.3 through 2.6
- HP 9000 Series 700 workstations running HP-UX 9.0.x or 10.30
- HP 9000 Series 800 workstations running HP-UX 9.0.x or 10.30

B.6.2 Usability Measurement Tools

It is important to mention usability measurements as part of the test tool discussion. Automated tools that check for usability need to ensure that usability factors are properly incorporated into development life-cycle documentation, such as requirement specifications, analysis and design results, application prototypes, and on-line application help functionality.

B.6.2.1 ErgoLight

ErgoLight solutions include tools for specifying the user's tasks, automatically logging the user's actions, logging observer's notes, on-line identification of operational difficulties, on-line solicitation of the user's intentions, backtracking the user's actions in sync with the user's problems and with the observer's notes, analysis decision making, and reporting. ErgoLight solutions integrate these tools in methodologies of software development, addressing the full development cycle, from product specification to development. The procedures that this tool automates support knowledge transfer from usability evaluators to team members who are in charge of functional specification, GUI design, user documentation, on-line assistance, and customer service. For more information on ErgoLight, see http://www.ergolight.co.il.

B.7 | Testing Support Tools

B.7.1 Test Data Generators

TestBytes, a test data generator, is described here.

B.7.1.1 TestBytes

TestBytes is a test data generation tool for testing your data management application. It can generate data to populate SQL database servers and PC databases quickly, whether you need data for application functionality testing, data-driven testing, or performance load testing. For more information on the TestBytes product, see http://www.platinum.com/.

Features

- Generates meaningful test data and populates the target database automatically without the need to write scripts or a single line of code
- Creates masked data within a column, making it possible for users to specify profiles for segments of a field (that is, values for titles such as Mr. or Ms.), one or more digits of a ZIP code, or area codes
- Supports referential integrity either directly from the database or from an ERwin model
- Generates data to multiple tables with one click
- Supports key unification and relationship cardinality
- Enables developers and testers to communicate their test data generation needs through standard reports
- Generates optionally to flat files, creating separated and delimited files that can be used to populate databases with large amounts of data quickly and easily
- Allows the definition of flat file formats that are independent of your database table definitions

- Allows less technical QA and testing team members to be productive early in the testing cycle
- Supports 32-bit Windows environments with an ODBC-compliant database

System Requirements
- Windows NT or 95
- Minimum 24MB hard disk space
- 32 MB RAM

B.7.2 File Comparison Tools

B.7.2.1   EXDIFF

EXDIFF is the extended file differencing system that operates as a stand-alone product or as part of the fully integrated TestWorks/Regression multiplatform suite of testing tools. EXDIFF extends commonly available file comparison utilities by comparing files of various logical structures. These structures include not only ASCII and binary files, but also bitmap image files saved with either TestWorks/Regression's capture/playback system (CAPBAK) or the standard X Window Dump utility (xwd). When used in conjunction with its TestWorks/Regression companion tools CAPBAK and SMARTS, the testing process is completely automated. For more information, see http://www.soft.com.

Supported Environments
- SPARC SunOS 4.1.3
- SPARC Solaris 2.3 through 2.6
- x86 Solaris 2.4 and 2.5
- RS/6000/AIX 3.2.5, 4.1.2, and 4.2
- HP 9000/7xx HP-UX 9.05 and 10.10
- HP 9000/8xx HP-UX 9.04, 10.01, and 10.10
- x86 SCO/ODT 2.0 and 5.0 (3.0)
- SGI Irix 5.3 and 6.2
- DEC-Alpha OSF1 3.2 and 4.0
- NCR 3000
- SCO/UnixWare 2.1.1

- DOS
- Windows 3.x, NT, and 95

B.7.3 Simulation Tools

Simulation tools can be used to simulate application-under-test models, so as to examine what-if scenarios, which are useful in predicting performance under varying conditions. An example of a simulation tool is OPNET.

B.7.3.1 OPNET

OPNET is a decision support tool to provide insight into the performance and behavior of existing or proposed networks, systems, and processes. (OPNET and MIL 3 are registered trademarks of MIL 3, Inc.) Specific tools are included with each OPNET license that assist users through the following phases of the modeling and simulation cycle.

Model Building and Configuration

- Network Editor—define or change network topology models
- Node Editor—define or change data flow (systems architecture) models
- Process Editor—define or change control flow (behavioral logic) models

Running Simulations

- Simulation Tool—define and run simulation studies using models constructed with the OPNET editors
- Interactive Debugging Tool—interact with running simulations

Analyzing Results

- Analysis Tool—display and compare statistical results
- Animation Viewer—watch dynamic behavior of models during simulation runs

The OPNET Model Library is included with OPNET Modeler and OPNET Planner, and contains a comprehensive set of networking protocols and analysis environments. Sample models included in the library are

- Ethernet
- Fiber Distributed Data Interface (FDDI)
- Client-Server Analysis Environment

- Circuit Switched Network Analysis Environment
- Transmission Control Protocol (TCP)
- Internet Protocol (IP)
- Open Shortest Path First (OSPF)
- Asynchronous Transfer Mode (ATM)
- Frame Relay
- AMPS Cellular Telephone System
- Cellular Digital Packet Data (CDPD)
- LAN Emulation

Supported Hardware
- Hewlett-Packard 9000/7xx HPPA
- Sun Microsystems Sun-4 SPARC
- Various PC-compatible Intel Pentium (or compatible)

Supported Operating Systems
- HP-UX 10.20
- Solaris 2.5.1
- Windows NT 4.0, 95, and 98

B.8 | Testing Phase

B.8.1   Test Management Tools

An example of a test management tool, TestStudio, is provided in Section B.8.3.1.

B.8.2   Network Testing Tools

NETClarity, a network testing tool, is described here.

B.8.2.1   NETClarity

The NETClarity suite of network performance management and diagnostic tools allows you, as the network manager, to monitor, measure, test, and diagnose performance across your entire network. The following products are available for network testing under the NETClarity suite. For more information on the NETClarity product suite, see http://www.lanquest.com/.

Network Checker+.   This set of network diagnostic tools allows you to check any LAN/WAN segments and the Internet for delays and broken links remotely via its Web browser interface.

Features

- Check Network is a response time and availability test between the NETClarity server and all Sentry Agents installed thoughout the network to verify connects.
- Remote Trace Route finds all hops between NETClarity Sentry Agents or between NETClarity Sentry Agents and a host/IP address on the Internet.
- Path Integrity Test sends a wide range of IP packet types between NETClarity Server and all Sentry Agents to verify path and successful transmission of data.

Remote Analyzer Probe

- Use a remote protocol analyzer probe
- Install remotes on Standard NT PCs
- Capture traces in Sniffer file format
- Use a browser to transfer trace files to the protocol analyzer

Server Requirements

- 200MHz Pentium computer
- 64MB RAM
- 1 GB hard disk space
- CD-ROM drive
- 10 Base-T, 100 Base-T, or Gigabit Ethernet NIC
- Windows NT 4.0 SP3

Sentry Agent Requirements

- Nondedicated 133MHz Pentium computer
- 32MB RAM
- 10MB hard disk space

- 10 Base-T, 100 Base-T, or Gigabit Ethernet NIC
- Windows NT 4.0 SP3

B.8.3 GUI Application Testing Tools

An example of a GUI application test tool is provided below.

B.8.3.1 Rational Suite TestStudio

Rational's TestStudio is an automated GUI client-server test suite that provides integrated programming and testing tools to simplify the creation of components and to replace expensive, tedious, and error-prone manual testing, resulting in higher-quality applications in less time with lower risk. This product can be used throughout the development process to create components more efficiently and to verify that the components work together properly when part of a complete application, that the resulting systems execute reliably, and that the system offers its users the intended level of performance. This suite includes requirements management; tools for testing Web and client-server application functionality, reliability, and application performance; defect tracking; system-wide reporting; and a knowledge base of software development best practices. The company that makes this product, Rational Software, has integrated solutions supporting a wide range of languages and platforms [8].

TestStudio is a seamlessly integrated product suite that includes Rational Robot, TestFactory, TestManager, RequisitePro, and ClearQuest for the automated testing of cross-Windows client-server applications.

TestManager.   This component lets you plan, manage, and analyze all aspects of testing cross-Windows client-server applications. This module accesses defect tracking, requirements tracking, testing progress reports, and other tools need to track test progress.

Rational Robot.   Rational Robot lets you create, modify, and run automated tests on Web and cross-Windows client-server applications. This test automation solution offers reusability and portability of test recordings across Windows platforms to provide one recording that plays back on all Windows platforms. The record and playback feature of the scripts gives you much flexibility during the test script development stage. The scripts use a Visual Basic–like language.

Example of Usage

- The user interface could be employed to enter a user name, address, phone number, age, and sex.

- The application has a Visual Basic front end that gets input from users.
- The application has a SQL Server back end.
- Add, edit, and update options are available on each user screen.

Benefits. A well-integrated suite touches on most of the test cycle. As Rational Software has aggressively sought to acquire and integrate different tools that aid in the test cycle, you can concentrate on tasks that require your intervention (such as designing new tests for changing requirements). Tracking the test requirements can begin during the requirements definition phase. Any issues or defects that are identified during this phase can be tracked using the defect tracker. This approach familiarizes the team with the defect tracker, which will be used extensively during the test cycle.

Use Rational Robot during unit testing. It forces the developer to test his or her modules thoroughly and aids in partially developing the scripts that can be used during testing. This action forces the development team to be a part of the test team and not to question the use of automated tools during the testing phase. The built-in reports that are provided with TestStudio aids in tracking the progress of the testing cycle. They also show how each team member is performing and identify the members who are overworked.

Other benefits of TestStudio include the following:

- *Flexibility of the scripting language.* The TestStudio scripting language is very close to Microsoft Visual Basic. There is also an option when you install the software to create test scripts in Visual Basic. It enhances your flexibility because of the popularity of Visual Basic.

- *Complexity of the scripting language.* The record and playback feature generates the script automatically. The user can also add programming logic to make intelligent scripts. The script language is as robust as any programming language. This feature helps in creating custom solutions for testing software that should conform to standards.

- *Compatibility with your current software and future integration.* This tool is compatible with a wide variety of software, including Java, PowerBuilder, Visual Basic, Oracle Developer/2000, SAP, and PeopleTools.

- *Tool performance over a network and sharing of the tool across networks among team members.* TestStudio is designed to work over a network. The choice of database for repository (where all of the test information is stored) is limited to either Microsoft Access or SQL Server. Microsoft Access is best suited for small teams on a LAN, whereas SQL Server is a perfect option for larger teams that need to share testing information on a server.

- *Clear and concise reporting and tracking of errors.* A defect tracking system is built into the TestStudio. It is easy to use and offers different levels of security to control the access of information. This feature will help in managing the errors and monitoring the progress of your testing effort. There are also many canned reports that help you communicate your testing efforts to management, as well as graphs and charts for visual reporting.

Hardware and Software Requirements
- PC-compatible with 486 processor (Pentium recommended)
- 130MB hard disk space (minimum)
- 139MB + 20MB free space (including all sample applications)
- Microsoft Windows NT 4.0 (service pack 3), 95, or 98

B.8.3.2   AutoScriptor Inferno

AutoScriptor Inferno is a nonintrusive, hardware-assisted, automated software test system for PC-based stand-alone and client-server applications. This comprehensive test system is designed to automate the unattended testing of multiple operating systems and environments with a single, unique solution. AutoScriptor Inferno tests both GUI and character applications running under any PC, network computer, or Macintosh operating system. For more information on AutoScriptor Inferno, visit, http://www.asitest.com.

By separating the testing software from the system under test (SUT), Auto-Scriptor Inferno is able to support the testing of any application running under any operating system without loading any special drivers or code on the SUT. This task is accomplished by connecting the SUT to the Inferno test system box. The Auto-Scriptor Inferno system is connected to each client (SUT) machine via the keyboard, mouse, and monitor. The AutoScriptor Inferno hardware consists of an external box that resides near each target machine. This external box intercepts the keyboard, mouse, and video of the target, permitting its simulation by a human test engineer.

In the capture (recording) phase, the test engineer exercises the AUT based on the system test plan. The Inferno test system captures keystrokes and mouse movements; the answers from the system, such as screen contents, are captured as well. This information is stored in an ANSI C++-based test script. In the subsequent play-back (execution) phase, the test script is executed on one or many clients directed over a network by the multiuser AutoScriptor Inferno Dashboard application. During playback execution, all application responses are captured and the true performance of the SUT is accurately measured. This phase runs unattended and automatically synchronizes to the AUT.

The power of AutoScriptor Inferno lies in its ability to capture reusable graphical objects (icons, push buttons, menu items, list boxes, hypertext links, and so on) and share them throughout all test cases. Either while recording or when the system is off-line, patterns can be captured, updated, or replaced. These patterns are stored in user-definable directory structures and can then be reused when recording future scripts. This technology drastically reduces the time spent on test script maintenance and allows for cross-platform script portability.

AutoScriptor Inferno communicates via a standard network connection enabling multiuser test playback across numerous client machines. It can support an unlimited number of simultaneous clients. One test scenario can control the same test or different tests on each client machine that is connected to the AutoScriptor Inferno test system. Multiuser testing is critical for network-based applications where stress, load, and performance testing are critical to success.

Changes in computer hardware, network versions, and operating systems can cause unexpected compatibility problems with existing hardware and software. Prior to a production rollout of a new application to a large numbers of users, AutoScriptor Inferno provides a clean method of ensuring that these changes will not adversely affect current applications and operating environments.

Nonstandard PC-based, network computer, and Macintosh operating systems such as NextStep, PC Solaris, GEOS, QNX, VENIX, Linux, PSOS, and MacOS are not supported by most software test tool vendors. In contrast, all of these operating systems and more are fully supported by AutoScriptor Inferno. This product works with Windows 3.x, 95, 98, and NT 3.x through 5.0, as well as QNX, DOS, Geoworks, OS/2, UNIX, NextStep, JavaOS, NCOS, MacOS, and other proprietary operating systems. Any Internet/intranet-based application is fully supported, including hyperlink verification and Java applet testing. Any application that resides on a PC, Mac, or network computer can be automated with AutoScriptor Inferno.

B.8.4 Load/Performance Testing Tools

Examples of load and performance testing tools are provided in this section.

B.8.4.1 PerformanceStudio

Rational Software's PerformanceStudio offers a method for load, stress, and multiuser testing of e-commerce, ERP, and Windows client-server applications. This automated network test tool for Windows allows complete multiple-machine test synchronization without programming. PerformanceStudio lets you test 32-bit and 16-bit Windows NT and Windows 95 client-server applications and 16-bit Windows 3.x client-server applications.

PerformanceStudio is fully integrated with TestStudio (see Section B.8.3.1). It also includes Web server testing. With powerful new features such as virtual user testing, DataSmart Recording, ClientSmart Pacing, LoadSmart Scheduling, ServerSmart Playback, and HTTP class error collection and analysis, PerformanceStudio provides the easiest and fastest method of ensuring the quality of your HTTP Web servers. PerformanceStudio also continues to provide the industry's only solution for complete cross-Windows testing by enabling you to test 32-bit Windows NT and Windows 95 client-server applications. Offering seamless integration with all the products in TestStudio, PerformanceStudio provides the easiest and most powerful method of ensuring that your Windows client-server and HTTP Web server applications are business-ready before deployment [9].

Features

- DataSmart Recording automatically generates parameterized scripta and randomized test data without programming.
- ClientSmart Pacing automatically maintains accurate user emulation timing during playback to provide meaningful, controlled test results.
- LoadSmart Scheduling models complex usage scenarios without programming.
- ServerSmart Playback automatically verifies server-under-test responses to ensure valid load.
- The 100% Visual Interface creates powerful client-server multimachine tests quickly and easily through a point-and-click interface; no programming is required.
- Comprehensive graphing and analysis allows you to graph any performance metric for in-depth analysis of test results.
- The Performance-metrics database accumulates statistical information across multiple test runs.
- User-defined standard graphs allow you to define your own graphs as default templates to create a reusable, standard analysis across projects.
- Multimachine synchronization allows you to use intermachine scheduling options, including delays, iterations, wait-for-machine, and more, to test sophisticated multiuser scenarios in your application.
- Automatic resource monitoring monitors every agent machine's resources automatically—for example, memory and disk space—for powerful stress and configuration testing.

Load Testing.   Load testing is the process of running a number of client machines simultaneously to "load" your client-server system and measure response times. It typically involves creating various scenarios to analyze how your client-server system responds under various loads. You must be able to easily control the starting and stopping of many machines at once, and precisely time the effects of each.

PerformanceStudio provides all the information you need to analyze your load tests. It reports automatically calculate statistics for elapsed times, including minimums, maximums, and averages. PerformanceStudio graphics provide rapid visual analysis of how the response times of different parts of your application vary with the number of users. This information gives you an indication of how your client-server application will perform when loaded end-to-end.

Stress Testing.   Stress testing is the process of running your client machines in high-stress scenarios to see whether they "break." Examples of stress conditions include running a client application for many hours continuously, running a large number of iterations of a test procedure, or running a large number of different test procedures. Stress testing is important for ensuring that your client application will be able to handle production conditions, where the ineffective management of machine resources can result in system crashes.

PerformanceStudio makes stress testing easy, yet powerful, through its automatic machine resource monitoring feature. By simply selecting which resources to test, this tool automatically monitors machine resources such as USER, GDI, global memory, DOS memory, free file handles, and disk space on every agent machine. Combined with Performance Studio's ability to iterate a test procedure thousands of times, automatic resource monitoring provides a method of measuring the stress that an application places on a client.

You'll quickly spot any client-side resource management problems with the information generated by PerformanceStudio. For example, reports will indicate which machines fail and when. Graphics highlight trends in resource usage to help you quickly detect common errors such as memory leaks and excess consumption of system resources and disk space.

Multiuser Testing.   Multiuser testing is the process of running multiple machines simultaneously to simulate the application workflow of a client-server system. For example, you might synchronize multiple stations so they access the same record in a database to check for problems with locking, deadlock conditions, concurrency controls, and more. Multiuser tests are typically difficult to do manually because they require precise synchronization between users.

PerformanceStudio's multimachine synchronization lets you easily define test scenarios in which test stations wait for conditions to be satisfied before they continue.

For example, you can have one station add a record to a database, and have the next station wait to read the record until the first station has completed its task. With PerformanceStudio, multimachine synchronization is easy and powerful, and can be accomplished through PerformanceStudio's point-and-click interface without any programming.

You'll be able to spot any multiuser problems in your client-server application through the results displayed in the PerformanceStudio Test Log Viewer and automatically generated reports. PerformanceStudio's reports will help you identify machines that experience inordinate delays or "hang" indefinitely due to deadlock conditions. The Test Log Viewer's color-coded display will highlight any functional problems arising from errors in shared data or database updates. This feature will help you ensure your client-server application operates properly when multiple users are running it.

Configuration Testing.   Configuration testing lets you determine how your client-server application works on different machines. For example, you can run the same set of tests simultaneously on many test stations with different hardware and software configurations. You can also measure the response times of each station to determine the minimal and optimal configurations for your client machines. This consideration is important because incompatible software, insufficient memory, or too-slow processor speed may cause your application to crash.

With PerformanceStudio, you can validate the operation of your client-server application on a variety of client machines at the same time. By assigning the same test to a number of different client machines, you can determine how each part of your application performs on each machine. In addition, you can use the automatic resource monitoring capabilities of PerformanceStudio as a powerful method of configuration testing.

For example, you'll quickly be able to determine how well and how fast your client-server application runs on different client machines. The reports in PerformanceStudio include statistics about the elapsed times of each test procedure on each machine. Graphics help you visually compare the performance of all your test stations. In addition, PerformanceStudio's graphics will highlight any resource management problems that you may have on specific client configurations. With PerformanceStudio, it is easy to determine which machines are best suited for your client-server application.

With a recording agent, PerformanceStudio captures user activities—including keystrokes, mouse movements, and SQL requests—to automatically generate scripts that represent a realistic multiuser load. Using one driver machine to simulate as many as thousands of users, PerformanceStudio reveals an application's true behavior, including any performance bottlenecks that emerge during the application development process. Problems induced by multiuser load can then be fixed prior to deployment. PerformanceStudio is available for testing client-server, Web-enabled, and ERP applications.

PerformanceStudio's recording technology saves time in other ways as well. Because user transactions are captured or freeze-framed, there is no human intervention and, therefore, no margin for error.

Benefits

- Fully automated recording of scripts
- Accurate, clear, and concise script generation
- Efficient reporting tools that quantify response time and throughput within seconds following a test
- Extensive monitoring tools to track and debug scripts during tests
- Complete documentation, including a reference manual with script commands and a user guide
- Options to test client and server separately or simultaneously
- Ability to add looping, branching, and randomization to scripts
- Simulated think time, typing time, and mouse delays
- Dynamic adjustment of throughput during test execution to model all types of user loads
- Multiple scripts that read data from a common set of input files
- Centralization control and synchronization, including launching, stopping, tracking, and synchronizing while collecting performance data and monitoring the application
- Full synchronization of scripts, passing of data among scripts, and queuing of scripts when entering critical regions
- Access to data returned from the AUT
- Ability to drive the client and the server from the same script
- Script execution that utilizes minimal driver resources to allow emulation of many users from small driver machines
- Easy-to-learn, simplified interface
- SQL recording in client-server scripts that is embedded in high-level script statements

B.8.5   Web Testing Tools

An example of a Web test tool is provided in this section.

B.8.5.1   Silk Tools

The Silk family of Web testing tools consists of SilkTest, SilkPerformer, and Surf! This automated software testing tool suite is specifically designed to meet the challenges of testing Web applications [10]. For more information concerning the Silk family of Web testing tools, see http://www.segue.com/.

SilkTest uses Segue's Universal Testing Architecture to offer functional and regression testing to ensure the reliability of both Internet and intranet applications. SilkPerformer simulates real-world Web traffic to measure the capacity and scalability of a Web server. By gauging server performance, you can predict and tune the overall performance of your Web applications before they deploy. Surf! automatically tests applications developed for both intranets and the World Wide Web. You can use Surf! to automatically generate functional regression tests to validate all links in Web applications—without any recording or coding.

SilkTest Features

- Test the mix of technologies commonly found in Web applications (Java applets, HTML, ActiveX, images, and more). SilkTest is not tied to any vendor API, so the SilkTest scripts can be reused as more technologies are adopted.

- Test applications that run in multiple browsers. Universally accessible Web applications run under multiple and increasingly dissimilar browsers, and must be tested in each environment. A single SilkTest script can be used to test the Web application under multiple browsers (Netscape Navigator, Microsoft Internet Explorer, and so on).

- Test the entire Web application. SilkTest scripts drive clients and servers—Web, database, and application—from a central point of control, even when they are on entirely different platforms. This feature gives you an accurate picture of how your system components perform together.

- Automate the testing process. The need to test as many as possible access methods and scenarios dramatically increases testing complexity and the amount of testing that must be done—making automated testing the only viable alternative for Web applications.

SilkPerformer Features

- Simulate real-world traffic to measure true Web server capacity and avoid performance problems

- Validate performance and scalability requirements in your Web application to minimize software risk

- Predict Web server bottlenecks and problems before your application deploys to ensure the reliability of your software

- Pinpoint errors and report testing results

- Retest performance improvements without the cost and effort of completely rebuilding your Web application

- Ensure end-to-end software performance and reliability of Web application with a fully integrated test tool suite

Hardware and Software Requirements

- Windows NT 4.0 and 95

- Pentium or better

- Any browser or Internet/intranet application using standard Internet protocols

B.8.6 Year 2000 Testing Tools

It is difficult for an organization to test all of its software for year 2000 compliance with a single tool. Many Y2K testing tools are on the market. This section describes two tools that support common platforms and Y2K testing.

B.8.6.1 DiscoverY2K

DiscoverY2K is an end-to-end solution for managing year 2000 compliance projects for client-server applications. Leveraging the Discover system (see Section B.5.4.2), DiscoverY2K enables companies to complete their year 2000 software conversion efforts for a fraction of the cost and time than would otherwise be possible. With its robust audit trail capability and its ability to offer rapid assessment and change, DiscoverY2K also provides a powerful insurance policy and backup plan, post-millennium, to minimize potential year 2000 liability.

DiscoverY2K provides software development organizations with the technology to assess the full scope of the year 2000 problem, understand the effect of this non-compliance, execute the necessary changes, and test the applications. It supports any conversion methodology chosen by the customer and addresses all four phases of the conversion: asset inventory, impact analysis, remediation, and testing.

Software Emancipation's DiscoverY2K/SET is a development information system that, when used across an entire development organization, allows teams to rapidly evolve, reengineer, and reuse legacy software. It consists of four components: Y2K Base, Y2K TPM Filter, Y2K TaskFlow, and Y2K Trace.

Supported Platforms/Operating Systems

- Sun OS
- Solaris
- HP-UX
- SGI IRIX
- Windows NT

Supported Languages

- ANSI C/C++
- K&R C
- Visual C++
- VAX C
- Oracle Embedded SQL
- Java
- PL/SQL

B.9 | Other Test Tool Vendors

This appendix lists only a few of the many tools available on the market today. For further detail on the various test tools, see product vendor Web sites or visit http://www.methods-tools.com.

Software Quality Engineering (800-423-8378; sqeinfo@sqe.com; http://www.sqe.com) sells an extensive survey of test tools.

Revision Labs publishes *A Guide to Automated Testing Tools,* which contains information on over 30 different capture/replay tools. (http://www.revlabs.com).

Ovum Ltd. publishes and sells a large number of reports on a wide range of computing and communications technology topics, including testing tools. (info@ovum.mhs.compuserve.com; http://www.ovum.com; Compuserve: MHS: INFO@OVUM).

Rodney C. Wilson, *UNIX Test Tools and Benchmarks* (Prentice Hall, 1995, ISBN 0-13-125634-3) is a primer on testing and tools to help with the task.

References

1. http://www.rational.com.
2. Oberg, R., Probasco, L., Ericsson, M. *Applying Requirements Management with Use Cases.* Rational Software Corporation, 1998.

3. Poston, R. "A Guided Tour of Software Testing Tools." www.aonix.com.
4. See note 1.
5. See note 1.
6. See note 1.
7. See note 1.
8. See note 1.
9. See note 1.
10. http://www.segue.com.

Appendix C

Test Engineer Development

In part of their attempt to do more with less, organizations want to test their software adequately, but as quickly and thoroughly as possible. To accomplish this goal, they are increasingly turning to automated testing. The shift to automated testing has had a major effect on the software industry and test professionals interested in furthering their career in software testing would be well advised to take note. Changes in the software industry stemming from the growth of automated testing include a greater demand for test engineers who are also software professionals and the migration away from manual testing methods. Additionally, the job market is rich with entry-level test positions for new computer science and information systems college graduates.

In the past, the tasks of performing software testing and the effort to develop software were often viewed as totally different responsibilities requiring vastly different skill sets. Today's test engineer, however, needs to be a software professional with programming skills and knowledge of networks, databases, and operating systems. The division of skills between software test engineers and software developers will continue to become less significant.

The evolution of automated test capabilities, together with recent emphasis on quality standards and software maturity guidelines, has given birth to new career opportunities for software engineers. Within the job market, there has been an explosion in the demand for automated software test professionals. Many software engineers are choosing careers in the automated test arena because of the different kinds of tasks involved and the variety of applications for which they are introduced. Additionally, experience with automated test tools can provide a career lift. It provides the software engineer with a broader set of skills and perhaps a competitive career development edge.

The test effort associated with today's two-tier and multitier client-server and Web environments is complex, so test engineers need a broad range of technical skills. Test engineers and test teams, therefore, need experience across multiple platforms, multiple layers of supporting applications, interfaces to other products and systems, different types of databases, and application languages. In an automated test environment, the test engineer also needs to know the script programming language of the primary automated test tool.

Given the breadth and depth of skills required by the test engineer to perform in a test engineering role, what might a test engineer expect in terms of a career path? Table C.1 portrays a possible test career progression.

In the first several years, the person could take on either a test engineering or a programmer analyst role. With more experience and the development of additional skills, he or she could move into a team or test/programming lead position. Eventually, the individual might assume a management position.

As a test engineer, you might ask, "What should I do to improve my chances of moving up through these progressive steps?" You might also ask, "What might a career development program plan look like?" Table C.2 outlines a six-step test engineer career development program. This development program is aimed at identifying the different kinds of skills and activities at each stage or level on which test engineers should focus time and attention so as to improve their capabilities. If you are already performing in a management capacity, then Table C.2 serves as a guideline on how to approach training and development for your staff.

Table C.1   Test Career Progression

Career Progression	Description
Junior test engineer	Entry-level position. Develops test scripts.
Test engineer/programmer analyst	1–2 years of experience. Programs automated test scripts.
Senior test engineer/programmer analyst	3–4 years of experience. Defines processes and mentors junior test engineers.
Team lead	2–6 years of experience. Supervises 1–3 personnel on a task. Supports size/cost estimation.
Test/programming lead	4–10 years of experience. Supervises 4–8 personnel. Schedules and leads tasks. Develops technical approach.
Test/QA/development/project manager	8+ years of experience. Responsible for 8 or more personnel performing on one or more projects. Full life-cycle management responsibility.
Program/business manager	15+ years experience. Responsible for personnel performing on several projects. Project direction and profit/loss responsibility.

Table C.2 Career Development Program

Development Stage	Time-frame	Development Program Activities
Technical skills	Years 1–2	• Become familiar with overall test engineering life cycle • Initital introduction to business areas of applications under test • Evaluate/experiment with automated test tools • Develop and execute test scripts • Learn test automation programming techniques • Further develop technical skills in programming languages, operating systems, networks, and databases
Test process	Years 3–4	• Improve understanding of the test engineering life cycle • Review, develop, or improve upon test and/or development standards and defined processes • Participate in requirements, design, and code inspections, walkthroughs, and reviews • Mentor more junior test engineers or programmers • Refine test automation programming techniques • Learn business areas of applications under test • Further develop technical skills in programming languages, operating systems, networks, and databases
Team effort	Years 4–5	• Supervise 1–3 test engineers or programmers • Perform task scheduling, tracking, and reporting • Develop size/cost estimations • Maintain technical skills, attend leadership courses, and attend test conferences • Further develop skills in life-cycle support tools, such as test tools, requirements management tools, defect/issue tracking tools and configuration management tools
Technical stewardship	Years 5–6	• Supervise 4–8 test engineers or programmers • Perform task scheduling, tracking, and reporting • Improve ability to develop size/cost estimations • Develop technical approach for test or development effort • Perform test planning and produce test plans • Maintain technical skills and spend considerable time mentoring other test engineers on test process, planning, design, and development • Maintain skills in life-cycle support tools • Begin to deal with customers and make presentations
Test/project management	Years 6–12	• Supervise 8 or more test engineers or programmers • Manage test effort on one or more projects • Obtain advanced college degree in related engineering or management discipline • Deal with customers and make presentations • Maintain technical and life-cycle support tool skills
Business/product management	Years 12+	• Identify and cultivate business opportunities and partnerships • Provide project and/or product development direction • Grow business/improve product sales • Take on profit/loss responsibility

C.1 | Technical Skills Stage

The first career development stage focuses on the development concerns for an individual performing in an entry-level or a junior test engineering position. The focus of development during this stage is the improvement of technical skills. Test engineers will need to enhance their skills by becoming more familiar with test tools and test techniques, as well as with programming languages, operating systems, networks, and databases.

If new to the workforce, the test engineer will need to become familiar with the overall test engineering life cycle and will need to learn the business areas of applications under test. If the test engineer has several years of experience and is making a transition to a test career, then the person may have already developed this business area knowledge. Commonly, individuals performing in the areas of software development, system administration, network management, and software quality assurance rotate into the software test discipline. Often out of necessity, these individuals become responsible for software testing because of the variety of work involved in software testing, the opportunity to work with automated test tools, and the chance to apply programming skills during the performance of test script development.

To become more knowledgeable on test tools and test techniques, the test engineer can read periodicals and journals such as software development magazines, read books on software development and testing, and surf the Web for test information. Other avenues to learn more about testing and to obtain answers to questions include local test tool user groups, test and software conferences, and quality assurance or process improvement-related seminars and associations.

It is important to develop skills and understanding of automated test tools. Obtain evaluation copies of automated test tools and experiment with the tools to become familiar with how they work and what they can do. If your organization has a license for an automated software test tool but may not be using it on a project that you are supporting, then experiment with the test tool.

Test engineers can augment their technical knowledge by enrolling in technical training courses offered by universities, community colleges, and technical training centers. Training on test tools and test methodology is valuable. Some organizations that offer such training are listed in Table C.3. Also see http://www.autotestco.com/ for updates to this list.

The test engineer's employer may also offer training. The types of technical training courses that are helpful for the test engineer include those addressing software programming, network engineering, database modeling and development, operating systems, and other technical issues.

As a first priority, the test engineer should become more proficient in the use of any test tool being used on a current project or a tool planned to be used on an upcoming project. It is also worthwhile, where possible, to receive training on tools

Table C.3 Test Training Organizations

Training Organization	Location	Contact Information
Andrews Technology, Inc.	San Francisco	www.andrewstech.com
Bender and Associates	San Francisco	www.softtest.com
DC Systems	Oakbridge Terrace, IL	www.dcsys.com
Dynamic Software Technologies Inc.	Cincinnati, OH	www.expertest.com
ETEC	Atlanta, Dallas	www.asketec.com
Expertest, Inc.	West Chester, OH	
Godhead Consulting	Houston	www.godhead consulting.com
Greenbrier and Russel	Atlanta, Dallas, Denver, Milwaukee, Phoenix	www.gr.com
Interface Design Group	San Francisco	www.interfacedesign.com
Internet Connection Services and Solutions Inc.	St. Louis	www.icss.net
NobleStar Systems	Washington, DC	www.noblestar.com
Real Time Technology Solutions	Tuckahoe, NY	www.rttsweb.com
Revision Labs	Portland, Seattle	www.revlabs.com
SoftGear Technology Inc.	Los Altos, CA	www.softgeartech.com
Software Quality Engineering	Washington, DC, Tampa, Portland	www.sqe.com
Software Testing Laboratories	Bellevue, WA, Boise, Los Angeles, Baltimore	www.stlabs.com
STA Group	Bellevue, WA, Boston, Santa Clara, CA	www.stagroup.com
Visual Systems Development Group	Montreal	www.visual.com
Waterfield Technology Group	Boston, New York	www.wtgi.com
Winmill Software	New York, Boston	www.winmill.com
XXCAL Testing Laboratories	Los Angeles	www.xxcal.com

other than one with which the test engineer is already comfortable. This kind of training helps the test engineer develop the ability to look at test requirements and test engineering challenges from a multitude of different perspectives. With these different perspectives, the test engineer has more latitude to explore creative solutions to test program work.

C.2 | Test Process Stage

The second career development stage focuses on understanding the software development and test life-cycle process. The test engineer must first become familiar with the organization's overall test life-cycle process. The Automated Test Life-cycle Methodology (ATLM) can be adopted to help define an organization's methodology for implementing and performing automated testing. The test engineer must also develop a comprehensive understanding of the different test strategies and the types of test tools that are available.

Beneath the organization's overall test life-cycle process, the test team should develop lower-level defined processes (test procedures) for performing test activities. The organization's process asset repository should include a standard (template) test plan, the top-level test life-cycle process, and the detailed test procedures, together with applicable development and test standards.

The overall software development process has been defined as "the set of activities, methods, practices and transformations that integrate managers and software engineers in using technology to develop and maintain software" [1]. Evidence suggests that improvement in the overall software development process to include the test life-cycle process provides increased productivity and product quality [2]. Sixty-nine percent of companies don't have a measurable, repeatable software testing process. Seventy-four percent of companies say the best way to meet software quality demands is to "build a process that sets goals and [begins] testing in the beginning of the development life cycle" [3].

For test process assets to be meaningful, they must be used. For test process assets to be used, they must be effectively implemented. Implementation requires that processes not only be defined, but also be established, incorporated into the system, made the norm, and eventually adopted as a standard. Implementation also means that test engineers are trained on the test process assets and assume ownership of them.

One effective approach for implementing the test process is to initiate a process brief program. The *process brief program* represents a timely and efficient way to achieve process definition. It requires that test team personnel develop presentations for each defined process area. Each presentation follows a prescribed format, with the test engineer outlining essential process elements such as entry/exit criteria, inputs, process steps, process participants, relevant tools, and outputs. The test team realizes several goals by undertaking this approach. Test engineers performing presentations take ownership and learn the process, other test team members are trained on the defined process, and improvements on the process become possible because the process has been both defined and baselined.

The test team should first require that a process brief be performed on the overall test process for the organization. Within this top-level process definition, 5 to 10 primary test steps (procedures) would be defined. Test engineers would then be assigned responsibility for the defined test procedures, and process briefs would be constructed for each test procedure.

The process brief is designed to simplify process definition by having the test engineer prepare presentation slides that detail the primary ingredients of the standard process definition. That is, the process brief consists of simple text and diagrams. The time required to develop the presentation slides should be minimal.

The process brief serves as a vehicle to define a test process; it also represents a way to obtain management and project team consensus on the defined process. In addition, the conduct of the brief serves to train other test team personnel on the process. Table C.4 gives a suggested format for the process brief slide presentation. The structure for the process context diagram (slide 3 of the process brief) is depicted in Figure C.1.

Table C.4   Process Brief Format

Slide Number	Title	Contents
1	Introduction	Definition of the process objective, process scope, test goals and strategies, and process participants, and identification of tools and methods
2	Process Overview	Graphic (bubble chart) of the top-level process.
3	Process Context Diagram	Structured format that specifies entry/exit criteria, inputs, process steps, and outputs
4	Process Flow	Bullets of text describing each significant activity (step or procedure) for the process
5-7	Detailed Process Diagrams	Detailed (bubble chart) process diagrams for each of the top-level process steps
8	Process Outputs	Table identifying outputs, output purpose/value, and repository for the output
9	Issues/ Recommendations	Bullets of text providing the test engineer with an opportunity to communicate perceived issues and improvement recommendations

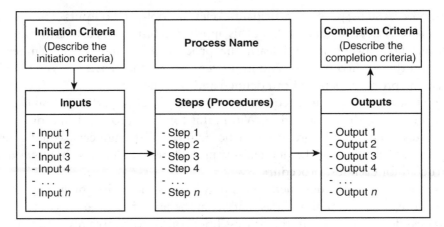

Figure C.1   Process Context Diagram Format

The test process stage of test engineer career development should also focus on activities other than the knowledge of the test process and involvement in process briefs. The test engineer should participate in requirements, design, and code inspections, walkthroughs, and reviews. He or she should begin mentoring other, more junior engineers within the test team. Project and test managers need to avoid the temptation of steering junior test engineers toward test process and test tool documentation, when these less experienced personnel request help. Mentoring is more beneficial to the junior test engineer, and the test engineer providing the mentoring generally learns from the experience as well.

During the test process stage of development, the test engineer will need to take his or her test automation skills to the next level. The test engineer needs to view test automation activities as requiring their own, separate development effort, complete with strategy and goal planning, test requirements definition, analysis, design, and coding. He or she must learn to appreciate the fact that effective automated test development requires careful design and planning, just like any software application development effort.

The test engineer needs to develop test automation programming techniques so as to create test scripts that perform such tasks as testing of different data values, testing of a large number of different user interface characteristics, or volume testing. Automated test scripts need to be developed that invoke looping constructs to exercise a script repeatedly or that call conditional statements to exercise a statement only under a specific condition. In addition, test scripts need to be developed that take advantage of application programming interface (API) calls or use .dll files, use files, and libraries. Eventually, the test engineer needs to apply his or her evolving skills to help establish test script programming standards and frameworks.

C.3 | Team Effort Stage

In the team effort stage of development, the test engineer needs to improve his or her verbal communication and writing skills. This person must develop the ability to effectively organize thoughts, concepts, and ideas within written correspondence, such as e-mail messages and reports, and during speaking engagements, such as meetings and presentations. Without these communication skills, the test engineer's career progression may be needlessly delayed. The team lead, test lead, and test management positions all require that the individual be able to communicate assignments, conceptualize and discuss complex test strategies, and talk through difficult technical challenges. Strong communications skills are also necessary to be able to assure supervisors, through written status reports, that proper actions are being taken to mitigate test program risks and resolve technical problems.

The test engineer should inquire about communication skill development courses to improve his or her verbal and writing skills. It is also important to gain experience by giving formal presentations in front of people. Where possible, the test engineer should join clubs and organizations, such as Toastmasters (www.toastmaster.org), that offer opportunities for the test engineer to polish his or her public speaking skills.

In addition to developing communication skills, the test engineer should become involved in the exercise of sizing a test program. The test team member might initially volunteer to help develop a work breakdown structure for a new test effort. The work breakdown structure provides a way of identifying the various types of test activities that are expected to be performed on a test effort (see Section 5.2). The test engineer can also offer to help with timekeeping activities, which maintain a historical record of the effort expended to perform the various test activities on projects. The maintenance of historical records helps support the test effort sizing exercise, by allowing test team members to better judge the amount of effort that will be required for a new project. The test engineer should become familiar with the different sizing methods for determining the necessary size of the test team (see Section 5.3.1). Where possible, the test engineer should learn about and become involved in test task scheduling, tracking, and reporting.

The personal software process (PSP) is an education program that supports development of sizing and estimation skills together with task scheduling, tracking, and reporting skills. Test engineers should read Watts Humphrey's *A Discipline for Software Engineering,* which explains the PSP program [4]. Test engineers can also obtain classroom and on-site training on the PSP through an organization called Advanced Information Services (AIS) [5] For more information on PSP training offered by AIS, see the Web site http://www.advinfo.net/.

Another way to continue to progress as a test professional during this stage is to become more involved in the test activities outlined in Section 5.3. The test engineer, for example, might become involved in new activities in which he or she has not yet gained experience, such as support for the test bed environment, development and maintenance of test data, and the maintenance of the test script reuse library.

In addition, the test engineer can further develop his or her skills in life-cycle support tools, such as test tools, requirements management tools, defect/issue tracking tools, and configuration management tools during this stage. It is important that the test engineer understand the application and capabilities of these tools. It is also beneficial for him or her to become familiar with ways to integrate and share data between these tools.

C.4 | Technical Stewardship Stage

In the technical stewardship stage of development, the test engineer needs to begin performing management support activities. Management support activities include test engineer recruitment, development of relationships with test tool vendors, staff supervision, customer relations, and oversight of test tool evaluations and introductions. It is important during the technical stewardship stage that the test engineer take responsibility for developing test effort estimations as well as performing task scheduling, tracking, and reporting activities.

The test engineer must provide technical leadership on each test program. This leadership includes providing guidance to subordinate test engineers with regard to test planning, design, development, and execution activities. The test engineer must stay current with the latest test approaches and test tools and must be able to transfer this knowledge to the rest of the test team. He or she also needs to display leadership in the area of test process implementation and test process improvement. Test process leadership may involve reviewing test metrics, lessons learned, and the results of test program benefits surveys in a meeting setting with the rest of the test team. It could also be evidenced by the assignment of subordinate test engineers to the tasks of reviewing existing test procedures and developing new test process briefs that improve the test procedures.

To effectively demonstrate the necessary leadership skills, the test engineer might need to undergo personal effectiveness training. This training includes courses and seminars that improve the test engineer's ability in the areas of leadership, team building, and public speaking. The goal for the test engineer is to deal with people more effectively, while also being more capable in overcoming tough technical challenges. Important skills in this stage include diplomacy, creativity, and conceptualization.

At this stage, the test engineer can begin to stand out as an exceptional software professional by making clear distinctions about problems and remaining focused on options and solutions. The ability to make clear distinctions stems from an improved ability to listen and understand what is being said, listen for how it is being said, and sometimes listen for what is not being said. The test engineer needs to be very honest when dealing with fellow project personnel—but not brutally honest. "Being honest" implies that the test engineer can ask questions and state observations in a constructive, nonthreatening, and respectful way.

Staying current with the latest test approaches and test tools may require that the test engineer attend software, quality, and test conferences. Where possible, he or she can practice public speaking skills by offering to make presentations at these conferences. During the development of a presentation topic and the preparation of presentation slides, the test engineer stands to become more knowledgeable on the particular topic. During the actual presentation and discussions following the presentation, this individual will learn even more.

C.5 | Test/Project Management Stage

During this stage, the test engineer needs to evolve from a technical leadership role to one in which he or she becomes responsible for a test program and perhaps even a complete development project. In a test management role, the test engineer must ensure that each project test plan is complete and accurate. (See Chapter 6 for more information on test plan development.) The test manager is also responsible for enforcing the cohesive integration of test and development activities.

The test manager needs to ensure that the acquisition of required hardware and software is performed correctly and within the necessary timeframe, that the test environment is developed and maintained properly, that test product configuration management is performed, and that the test process is defined and maintained. Likewise, he or she must ensure that the test program remains on schedule and, in doing so, obtain accurate measures of test progress.

Given the increased number of personnel being supervised, the test manager needs to be concerned about employee motivation. It is a good practice to acknowledge good performance, publicly where possible. The test manager should also use a bonus program to reward personnel who put in extra effort to ensure the success of a test program and promote the credibility of the test team.

As the manager and leader for the test team, this individual is responsible for cultivating a good reputation for the entire test team. The test team must be viewed as an organization that performs professionally and provides value to each project. By maintaining its good reputation, the test team will be able to influence business decisions made by senior management, such as whether to purchase a new test tool. The test manager must also be careful to protect test team members from unwarranted or harsh criticism. Issues and criticisms should go through the manager rather than having the particular test engineer be approached in person.

Because the test manager may be responsible for directing and juggling test efforts across more than one project, he or she must be able to rely upon skilled and capable test leads to assist on each project. The test manager, therefore, needs to make good hiring decisions and then motivate and further develop each test lead. The ability to delegate is an important skill that involves the establishment of an honest and trusting relationship with each test lead. In fact, having a competent staff to perform the various test program activities is essential.

A primary concern for the test manager involves the need to maintain an overall level of test capability. Thus the test manager must identify potential single points of failure and take corrective action. A single point of failure involves a situation where only one member of the test organization has a particular test tool or technology skill. When this skill is vital to the credibility of the test team and the ability to successfully perform on projects, then the loss of the individual represents a significant risk.

To develop a clear picture of the different kinds of test tool and technology skills that reside within the test team, the test manager should develop a test team capability profile. Such a profile lists the name of each member of the test team together with the skills in which he or she has proficiency. Somewhere on the profile sheet, the test manager needs to list the top 10 or so most critical test tool and technology skills required of the test team. Where deficiencies exist, the test manager should implement mentoring relationships, on-the-job training, and formal training mechanisms to bolster the team's capability. It is worthwhile to ensure that the test team is at least two deep in the most important test tool and technology skill areas.

If the test manager is to move up further within the organization, an advanced college degree may be necessary. The manager should investigate the post-graduate education programs available from colleges and universities in the vicinity. He or she is in a position where close coordination and dealings with senior management and possibly with a client or customer are required. In this environment, an understanding of office politics becomes crucial to job security and career advancement.

One significant aspect of office politics is the notion that the test manager may be technically correct on a subject, but present the information to senior management in an ineffective way. The test manager needs to be sensitive to the political environment and savvy enough to remain focused on the desired end result. It is important to respect others and allow them to hold different opinions. Your opinion may be correct given all the knowledge and information that you have at your disposal. Another person's opinion may be correct given all the knowledge and information that he or she has. The test manager may lose a few battles, but must understand that the cherished end result is to win the war.

C.6 | Business/Product Management Stage

In the next stage of development, the test engineer evolves out of a test management role and into being concerned with the business health and well-being of a part of the organization or for a product line. In this environment, the manager must begin to shift his or her focus from concerns within the organization and to activities and concerns involving people and organizations outside of the organization. Business opportunities must now be identified and partnerships with outside organizations cultivated and reaped.

As a business or product manager, the individual must be able to develop a vision for the future of the business or product line and to obtain and organize resources necessary to support the vision. He or she must now focus less on how to get the job done, but instead be more concerned about identifying the kind of job that needs to get done. The individual now needs to be surrounded by people who can understand the kinds of jobs that need to be done and who know what is necessary to complete each job.

References

1. Curtis, B. "Software Process Improvement: Methods for Modeling, Measuring and Managing the Software Process." Tutorial notes, 15th International Conference on Software Engineering, May 17–21, 1993.

2. Curtis, B., Kellner, M., Over, J. "Process Modeling." *Communications of the ACM,* 1992; 35:75–91.

3. The 1996 CenterLine Survey.

4. Humphrey, W. *A Discipline for Software Engineering,* Reading, MA: Addison Wesley, 1995.

5. Pauwels, R. E-mail message dated May 4, 1998.

Appendix D

Sample
Test Plan

WALLSTREET FINANCIAL TRADING SYSTEM

Delivery 2

Test Plan

(Date)

PREPARED FOR:

FINANCIAL TRADEWINDS CORPORATION
City, State

PREPARED BY:

AUTOMATION SERVICES INCORPORATED (AMSI)
Street Address
City, State

Contents

D.1 | Introduction

D.1.1 Purpose

This test plan will outline and define the strategy and approach taken to perform testing on the WallStreet Financial Trading System (WFTS) project. It is intended for use by WFTS project personnel in understanding and carrying out prescribed test activities and in managing these activities through successful completion. This document defines the details of test responsibilities and activities and describes the tests to be conducted.

This test plan has been developed to fulfill the following objectives:

- To lay out the management and technical effort necessary to support testing throughout the system development life cycle

- To establish a comprehensive test plan that identifies the nature and extent of tests deemed necessary to achieve the testing objectives for the WFTS project, including software and hardware requirements.

- To coordinate an orderly schedule of events, identify equipment and organizational requirements, describe test methodologies and strategies to be used, and identify items to be delivered

- To provide a plan that outlines the contents of detailed test procedure scripts and the execution of those test procedure scripts (that is, which testing techniques will be used)

To help standardize the test effort and make it more efficient, test procedure development guidelines are provided in Appendix D.A. These guidelines have been adopted and are being implemented by the AMSI test team for the WFTS project. The test team will take advantage of testing tools to help improve and streamline the testing process. For further detail on the test strategy, see Section D.3.3 of this plan.

Test procedures are identified and tracked using the Dynamic Object-Oriented Requirements Management System (DOORS) requirements management tool. This approach will allow for easy management of test progress status. Once a test is performed, the test procedure status is revised within DOORS to reflect actual test results, such as pass/fail. Appendix D.B provides a test verification summary matrix that is generated using DOORS; it links the test procedures to test requirements so as to measure test coverage. Test procedures and test scripts supporting system acceptance test (SAT) are provided in Appendix D.C.

D.1.2 Background

The WFTS project was initiated in response to management's recognition of the need for improvement within the service management operations at Financial

Tradewinds Corporation (FTC). A mission element needs statement was developed and approved that authorized the establishment of a new system called the Wall-Street Financial Trading System (WFTS).

The project consists of several deliveries. Delivery 1 of the WFTS, which was implemented recently, provided system foundation applications. Delivery 2 involves the development of mission and support applications, which will enable FTC to trade securities and various assets on Wall Street more effectively.

The test requirements definition for the WFTS project is driven by detailed requirements/use cases/use case scenarios (see Section D.3.6) and by the evolutionary nature of additional user input. Use case requirements are maintained within the (DOORS) requirements management tool. Detailed WFTS use case requirements have been established for Delivery 2 and define test requirements and test procedures. Test documentation—test plans, test procedures, and test results—is captured and stored within DOORS. Additionally, PVCS Tracker will be used to manage software problem reports.

D.1.3 System Overview

This section provides an overview of the WFTS and identifies critical and high-risk functions of the system.

System Description. WFTS presently consists of a suite of hardware and software, including nondevelopmental items (NDI)/Commercial off-the-shelf (COTS) and developmental software. WFTS will provide FTC with daily trading and executive decision-making support. Automation Services Incorporated (AMSI) developed WFTS Delivery 1 and is under contract to develop and test Delivery 2. Figure D.1.1 depicts the WFTS Delivery 2 software architecture. Each block represents a software component (configuration item) of the system. Table D.1.1 summarizes the WFTS software components and their estimated COTS composition.

Critical and High-Risk Functions. During system requirements analysis and requirements specification development, the AMSI test team participated in the review of use case analysis results and WFTS joint application development (JAD) sessions. Critical success and high-risk functions of the WFTS system were identified. These functions include those most critical to the mission of the system and those that help mitigate the greatest risk to successful system operation. These functions have been ranked in priority sequence, as shown in Table D.1.2. This understanding of functional importance serves as an input to test team prioritization of test activities.

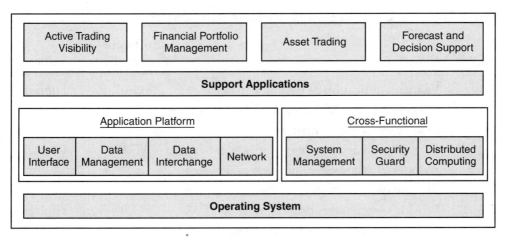

Figure D.1.1   WFTS Delivery 2 Software Architecture

Table D.1.1   WFTS Software Components

ID Number	Description	DI	NDI/ COTS	D1	D2
OS-01	Operating system	—	COTS	D1	—
UI-02	User interface	—	COTS	D1	D2
DM-03	Data management	DI	—	D1	D2
DI-04	Data interchange	DI	—	D1	D2
NW-05	Network	—	COTS	D1	—
SM-06	System management	20%	80%	D1	D2
SG-07	Security guard	—	COTS	—	D2
DC-08	Distribution computing	30%	70%	D1	D2
SA-09	Support applications	80%	20%	—	D2
TV-10	Active trade visibility	25%	75%	—	D2
FP-11	Financial portfolio management	20%	80%	—	D2
AT-12	Asset trading	DI	—	—	D2
DS-13	Forecasts and decision support	DI	—	—	D2

Table D.1.2   Critical and High-Risk Functions

Rank	Function	Software Component	Indicator
1	Verify identification of trading partner account prior to any automated exchange of asset trading information	SG-07	High risk
2	Sort through asset trade opportunities and identify the best-value trade and close the deal on this trade	AT-12	Critical
3	Provide communications and flow of information between software components operating at different levels of security classification	SG-07	High risk
4	Monitor exchange rates and primary economic indicators for changes in the securities market and the worldwide economy	DS-13	High risk
5	Monitor securities and the most significant securities movement	TV-10	Critical
6	Provide simulation modeling that produces extended forecasts, analyze future of evolving trends, and provide long-term executive decision support	DS-13	Critical

D.1.4   Applicable Documents

Documents that are pertinent to the WFTS Delivery 2 test program are listed in this section.

Project Documentation

- System Requirements Specification, Delivery 2
- Use Case Scenario Document, Delivery 2
- Software Design Document, Delivery 2
- Interface Design Document, Delivery 2

- WFTS Statement of Work (SOW)
- Concept of Operations
- Management Plan
- Software Development Plan
- Security Test Plan, Delivery 1
- Test Plan, Delivery 1
- Test Report, Delivery 1
- Security Certification Test Report, Delivery 1
- Delivery 2 Kick-Off Meeting Presentation Slides
- Security Requirements and Design Review Meeting Materials, Delivery 2
- Security Review Meeting Report
- User Interface Review Presentation Slides, Delivery 2
- System Implementation Plan, Delivery 2
- Security Plan, Delivery 2 (draft)
- Security Test Plan, Delivery 2 (draft)

Standards Documentation

- Automated Test Life-Cycle Methodology (ATLM)
- Test Procedure Design and Development Standards
- IEEE/EIA 12207 Information Technology Software Life-Cycle Process
- AMSI Standards and Procedures (standard process supporting business analysis phase, requirements phase, design phase, development phase, testing phase, and maintenance phase)
- AMSI Code Inspection Process
- AMSI Programming Style Guide
- AMSI GUI Style Guide
- AMSI Usability Style Guide

Tool Documentation

- TeamTest (Test Management Tool) User Manual
- PVCS Tracker Documentation
- Performance Studio Documentation
- DOORS (Requirements Management Tool) User Manual

- PVCS (Configuration Management Tool) User Manual
- SystemArmor Security Guard Software Documentation
- UNIX Operating System Software Documentation
- InsitFul Securities Trade Visibility Software Documentation

D.1.5 Master Schedule

This section addresses the top-level schedule for the WFTS test program. The test program schedule contains the major events, activities, and deliverables involved in the test program. Activities performed by the test team include the design, development, and execution of tests, as well as inspections of project documentation and software products. The test team will also produce test documentation consisting of the items listed in Table D.1.3.

Table D.1.3   Test Documentation

Test Program Document	Description	Due Date/Timeframe
Test plan	Test planning document	(date)
Test verification summary matrix	A requirements traceability matrix that maps test procedure coverage to test requirements and specifies a test qualification method for each system requirement	(date)
Test procedures	The scripts used to perform/execute testing	(timeframe)
Test and integration working group meeting minutes	Minutes from test and integration working group meetings	Periodic
Test development progress reports	Metrics reports outlining the progress status of the test procedure development effort	Biweekly
Test readiness report or presentation slides	Report or presentation that outlines the readiness of the test program to conduct user acceptance testing	(date)
Test execution progress reports and other progress and quality metrics	Reports that outline the status of test execution	Biweekly
Defect tracking reports	Reports that outline the number and severity of outstanding software problem reports	Biweekly
TPM status reports	Reports that outline the progress of the system toward meeting defined technical performance measures (TPM)	Biweekly
Test report	Report documenting the outcome of the test	(date)

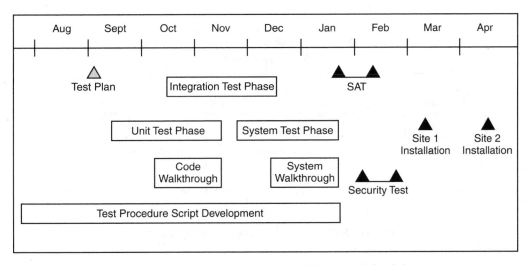

Figure D.1.2 Test Program Milestone Schedule

The major events, activities, and documentation to be performed or prepared in support of the WFTS test program are outlined in the test program milestone schedule depicted in Figure D.1.2.

D.2 | Roles and Responsibilities

Roles and responsibilities of the various groups are defined in this section.

D.2.1 Project Organization

Figure D.2.1 depicts the WFTS project organization. Reporting to the WFTS project manager are four line supervisors: the software development manager, the systems engineering manager, the product assurance manager, and the functional requirements manager. The software development manager is responsible for software and database design and development, as well as unit- and integration-level software tests. The systems engineering manager leads the system architecture design effort and is responsible for new COTS product evaluations. This manager maintains the network that supports the system development and test environments, and is responsible for database administration of the deployed Delivery 1 WFTS system. The product assurance manager is responsible for test, configuration management, and quality assurance activities.

The test manager is responsible for system test and user acceptance test activities supporting the WFTS system. The functional requirements manager is responsible

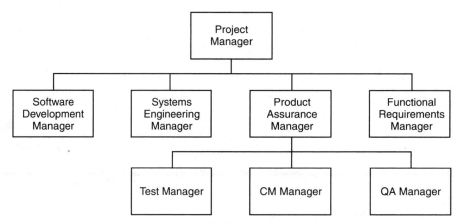

Figure D.2.1   WFTS Project Organization

for requirements analysis, system requirements specification, and maintenance of the requirements baseline. Functional analyst personnel also support development and review of detailed design activities.

D.2.2   Project Roles and Responsibilities

D.2.2.1   Project Management

The project manager is responsible for client relations, project deliverables, schedules, and cost accounting. He or she coordinates with the particular line manager with regard to each technical task performed. The staff of project management specialists maintain project plans, schedules, and cost accounting information. Project management is responsible for ensuring that standards and procedures are followed and implemented appropriately.

D.2.2.2   Functional Requirements

The requirements group is responsible for requirements analysis and system requirements specification and for the derivation of subsequent use cases. This group also supports development and review of detailed design activities.

D.2.2.3   Software Development

The software development group is responsible for software development, as well as unit and integration software tests. It must develop software products in accordance with software development standards and conventions as specified in the software development plan (SDP). The software development group also performs unit and integration test phase planning. The results of unit and integration test phase planning are then provided as input to Section D.3 of the test plan.

For software development items, each developer will maintain a systems development folder (SDF) that contains the design documentation, printed copies of lines of code and user screens generated, development status of the item, and test results applicable to the item.

Test support responsibilities of the software development group include those described here.

Software Product Design and Development. When designing and developing any software or database product, the developer will comply with the software development standards and conventions specified in the SDP. Certain SDP provisions are automatically enforceable, such as the use of system development folders and compliance with the procedures associated with the use of the product development reuse library. Testability will be incorporated into the software as defined in the SDP. The third-party controls (widgets) defined for the development of this system must comply with the list of third-party controls that are compatible with the automated testing tool. The test team will be informed of peer reviews and code walkthroughs initiated by the development team.

Development Documentation. The development team will maintain SDFs. Embedded within the lines of programming code will be documentation in the form of comments. The embedded comments facilitate understanding of software structure and define the purpose of software routines. They will trace or correlate to pseudocode so as to facilitate software design traceability from the actual source code to the design document.

Unit Test Phase. Developers will test individual software units with respect to their function and integrity. Software unit program code will be analyzed to ensure that the code corresponds to functional requirements. Tracing tools will minimize code volume and eradicate dead code. Memory leakage tools will be applied, and code coverage tools will be used to verify that all paths have been tested. The system test team will perform unit testing in accordance with AMSI standards and procedures.

Integration Test Phase. Integration testing will be conducted to demonstrate the consistency between the software design and its implementation in accordance with AMSI standards and procedures. Its results will be recorded in the SDFs and inspected for software quality assurance. When software modules are ready to support the integration and system test phases, the source code and all files required for proper generation of the executables will be baselined within the software configuration management tool. Each software build will be generated using the source code products maintained within the software configuration management tool. The system test team will perform integration testing and verify completeness according to integration test procedures.

The software development group is also responsible for database design and development and all data migration and synchronization activities. Additionally, it helps the test group in setting up a test environment. The database group develops the database in accordance with database development standards and conventions as specified in the SDP.

D.2.2.4   Systems Engineering

The systems engineering group is responsible for the development of the system architecture design, integration of COTS products, research of COTS products, and evaluation of COTS products. As part of COTS integration, the systems engineering group will be responsible for the design and development of software modules as well as testing of the integrated COTS products. The systems engineering group will develop and maintain a simulation model of the WFTS using the OPNET simulation tool. The WFTS simulation model will simulate the major functions of the system and provide information on bottlenecks and queue buildups.

The systems engineering group maintains the network and hardware that work with the system development and test environments, and is responsible for database and system security administration of the deployed Delivery 1 WFTS system. The group installs and configures COTS products as required to integrate them with the rest of the system. The necessary parameters are defined for COTS products by this group and then set to work in the target environment. Hardware is installed and configured to reflect a typical end-user site. Upon receipt of the new system equipment that is destined for deployment at an end-user site, the appropriate hardware and system software configurations are installed.

D.2.2.5   Product Assurance

The product assurance group implements test, configuration, and quality assurance activities. The system test team performs various test activities supporting the WFTS system by following the ATLM. It takes responsibility for system test and user acceptance test activities supporting the WFTS system; it also carries out the unit and integration test phases described in Section D.3.

The system test team develops the test plan and procedures, and it performs the tests necessary to ensure compliance with functional, performance, and other technical requirements. Test program activities include the maintenance of test automation reuse libraries, planning and execution of tests, and the development of test reports. These responsibilities are detailed below.

Test Procedures Development. Test procedures will be prepared for system-level testing that provide the inspector with a step-by-step (test script) operational guide to performing each test. They will exercise both system software (COTS and developmental items) and hardware.

Test procedures will include the test procedure title, test description, references to the system specification, prerequisite conditions for the test, test execution steps (script), expected results, data requirements for the test, acceptance criteria, and actual results. Those test procedures to be used for site acceptance testing will be identified as a result of input from end users.

Unit and Integration Test Phase. The system test team will witness unit and integration test activities.

System Test Phase. The system test team is responsible for system testing; the scope of this testing is described in Section D.3. The test team will document results within the requirements management tool and produce progress reports, as detailed in Section D.1.5.

System Acceptance Test (SAT) Phase. The system test team performs user acceptance testing, as described in Section D.3. The test team will document the results within the requirements management tool and produce progress reports as specified in Section D.1.5.

Test Reports. Raw test data and reports will be kept to indicate the specific pass/fail results of all system hardware and software tests. The test team will prepare a test report at the conclusion of system and user acceptance testing, which will include the raw test data, reports, and a test results summary, together with conclusions and recommendations.

Field/Site Acceptance Testing. This step will involve checkout and performance testing to ensure that equipment and software are installed correctly. Test activities will include verification that the system performs in accordance with specifications and is capable of meeting operational requirements. Site acceptance tests will consist of a reduced set of confirmation tests providing a reasonable check that the system is ready for operation.

D.2.3 Test Task Structure

Table D.2.1 indicates the types of test tasks that may be performed by the system test team for the WFTS test program. This task structure represents the work breakdown structure (WBS) that will be used by the test team to support cost accounting activities on the project.

Table D.2.1   Test Program Work Breakdown Structure

Number	Work Breakdown Structure (WBS) Element
1	**Project Start-Up**
1.1	Scope. Outline preliminary test goals and objectives.
1.2	Sizing. Perform test effort sizing.
1.3	Team composition. Undertake test team composition analysis and test engineer job description development.
1.4	Recruiting. Develop test engineer recruiting advertisements and conduct interviews.
2	**Early Project Support**
2.1	Goals/objectives. Further define test goals and objectives and review goals/objectives with project management, development group, and test engineers to develop understanding and acceptance of test goals and objectives.
2.2	Constraint examination. Review project constraints, such as short time to market or limited resources.
2.3	Testability review. Assure that testability is designed into the application.
2.4	Requirements review. Ensure that requirements are specified in terms that are testable.
2.5	Review of standards. Identify and become acquainted with applicable standards.
3	**Decision to Automate Test**
3.1	Test objectives/strategies. Refine definition of test objectives for the project and develop test strategies.
3.2	Test tool value. Outline the value/benefits derived from incorporating an automated test tool.
3.3	Test tool proposal. Develop a test tool proposal.
4	**Test Tool Selection and Evaluation**
4.1	Systems engineering environment. Review organization's systems engineering environment.
4.2	Test tools available. Review types of test tools available.
4.3	Test tool candidates. Research, evaluate, and score test tool candidates.
4.4	Evaluation domain definition.
4.5	Hands-on tool evaluation.
4.6	Test tool evaluation report. Document tool selection and results of evaluations.
4.7	Test tool purchase. Develop purchase order and coordinate with the purchasing department.

continued

continued from page 504

Number	Work Breakdown Structure (WBS) Element
5	**Test Tool Introduction**
5.1	Test process. Implement (or modify existing) testing process, methodologies, and "life-cycle" approach to testing to allow for the introduction of automated testing tools. Assure that the test effort is performed in parallel with the development effort. Maintain test tool introduction process.
5.2	Defect detection activities. Attend inspections and walkthroughs.
5.3	Test tool expertise. Participate in formal test tool training, review test tool tutorials, and practice with test tool.
5.4	Test tool validation. Validate new test tool releases to ensure that the tool performs according to specification and that it works in the particular operating environment.
5.5	Test consultation. Create a test support hotline, answering questions within the organization pertaining to the test process and tools. Provide mentoring and coaching on automated software test discipline.
5.6	Test tool orientations. Provide presentations and demonstrations to orient projects and personnel on the use and application of test tools.
5.7	Relationship building. Develop a working relationship with the development group and facilitate communications among project team members.
5.8	Network environment setup. Consult on the setup of an automated test tool repository on the local area network. Request additional network storage space where necessary.
5.9	Defect management process. Establish process (workflow) for defect reporting and resolution for a project. Outline applicable standards and formats.
5.10	Defect management training. Provide training on the process for defect reporting and resolution.
5.11	Test tool reporting. Determine the types of automated test reports applicable to the project.
6	**Test Planning**
6.1	Test requirements. Document application-under-test (AUT) test requirements.
6.2	Examination of constraints. Identify and outline constraints such as short time to market and limited engineering resources.
6.3	Test goals/objectives. Document goals and objectives for testing (for example, scalability, regression) within the test plan. Include goals pertaining to end-user involvement in the test process.
6.4	Test strategy. Document the test strategies and the types of test tools that apply on the project.
6.5	Test program activities. Develop a test strategy that incorporates test activities early within the development life cycle.
6.6	Deliverables. Identify the product deliverables on the project that will be reviewed or tested by test personnel.

continued

continued from page 505

Number	Work Breakdown Structure (WBS) Element
6.7	Critical success functions. Work with project team and business users to identify critical success functions and document them within the test plan.
6.8	Test program parameters. Define test program parameters such as assumptions, prerequisite activities, system acceptance criteria, and test program risks and document them within the test plan.
6.9	Level of quality. Work with project team and business users to determine the level of quality for the project and document it within the test plan.
6.10	Test process. Document the test process within the test plan, including the test tool introduction process and the defect management process.
6.11	Test training. Document test training requirements and plans within the test plan.
6.12	Decision to automate test. Document the assessment outlining the benefit of using an automated test tool on the project, and the ability to incorporate an automated test tool given the project schedule.
6.13	Technical environment. Document the technical environment in which the AUT will be developed and eventually operate. Identify potential application design or technical automated testing tool issues that may need to be resolved.
6.14	Test tool compatibility check. Document results of the test tool compatibility check. Where an incompatibility problem arises, document work-around solutions and alternative test methods.
6.15	Quality gates. Plan for the incorporation of quality gates.
6.16	Risk assessments. Perform risk assessments in support of project management reviews and reporting requirements.
6.17	Test readiness reviews. Perform planning and analysis activities necessary for test readiness reviews. Develop presentation slides and perform presentations where required.
6.18	Test plan document. Assemble and package the test-planning documentation into a test plan. Incorporate changes to the test plan as a result of test plan reviews by project management and end users or customers. Maintain the test plan document throughout the test life cycle.
6.19	Test data. Document test data requirements and plans for developing and maintaining a test data repository.
6.20	Test environment. Identify requirements for a test laboratory or test environment and identify the personnel who are responsible for setting up and maintaining this environment.
6.21	Reporting requirements. Define reporting requirements and document them within the test plan.
6.22	Roles and responsibilities. Define and document roles and responsibilities for the test effort.
6.23	Test tool system administration. Outline the requirements for setting up and maintaining the automated test tools and environment, and identify the personnel who are responsible for setting up and maintaining the test tools. Administration includes setup of tool users and various privilege groups.

continued

continued from page 506

Number	Work Breakdown Structure (WBS) Element
7	**Test Design**
7.1	Prototype automated environment. Prepare and establish a test laboratory environment to support test design and development.
7.2	Techniques and tools. Identify test techniques/strategies and automated tools to be applied to the project application and its interfaces.
7.3	Design standards. Prepare and establish test procedure design standards.
7.4	Test procedure/script design. Develop a list and hierarchy of test procedures and test scripts. Identify which procedures and scripts are to be performed manually and which will requre an automated test tool.
7.5	Test procedure/script assignments. Assign test team personnel to the various test procedures and scripts.
7.6	Inputs/outputs. Develop test procedure/script design inputs and expected outputs.
7.7	Test automation script library. Identify test automation scripts contained with the organization's script library that can be applied to the project.
8	**Test Development**
8.1	Best practices/standards. Develop and tailor best practices and standards for test development for the project.
8.2	Script creation standards. Implement test procedure script creation standards (for example, comment out each automated testing tool scripting step, fill in test procedure header file information, provide modularity, and so on).
8.3	Script execution standards. Implement test procedure execution standards (for example, a consistent environment, test database backup, and rollback).
8.4	Test setup. Implement test procedure script strategies during the various testing phases (for example, regression test phase, performance test phase).
8.5	Test procedure pseudocode. Prepare step-by-step pseudocode for the test procedures.
8.6	Work-around solutions. Develop work-around solutions for tool/AUT incompatibility problems.
8.7.1	Unit test phase test procedures/scripts. Witness execution of unit test procedures and scripts.
8.7.2	Integration test phase test procedures/scripts. Witness execution of integration test procedures and scripts.
8.7.3	System test phase test procedures/scripts. Develop test procedures and automate scripts that support all phases of the system test cycle (that is, regression, performance, stress, backup, and recoverability).
8.7.3.1	Develop a test procedure execution schedule.
8.7.3.2	Conduct automated test reuse analysis.
8.7.3.3	Conduct analysis to determine which tests to automate.
8.7.3.4	Develop a modularity relationship matrix.

continued

continued from page 507

Number	Work Breakdown Structure (WBS) Element
8.7.4	Acceptance test phase test procedures/scripts. Develop and maintain test procedures and scripts.
8.8	Coordination with the database group to develop test database environment. Baseline and maintain test data to support test execution.
8.9	Test procedure peer reviews. Review test procedures against the script creation standards (comments for each test tool scripting step, header file information, modularity, and so on).
8.10	Reuse library. Develop and maintain a test procedure reuse library for the project.
8.11	Test utilities. Support the creation or modification of in-house test support utilities that improve test effort efficiency.
9	**Test Execution**
9.1	Environment setup. Develop environment setup scripts.
9.2	Testbed Environment. Develop testbed scripts and perform testbed development logistics.
9.3	System test phase execution. Execute test procedures as part of walkthroughs or test demonstrations.
9.4	Acceptance test phase execution. Execute test procedures as part of walkthroughs or test demonstrations.
9.5	Test reporting. Prepare test reports.
9.6	Issue resolution. Resolve daily issues regarding automated test tool problems.
9.7	Test repository maintenance. Perform test tool database backup/repair and troubleshooting activities.
10	**Test Management and Support**
10.1	Process reviews. Perform a test process review to ensure that standards and the test process are being followed.
10.2	Special training. Seek out training for test engineers for special niche test requirements that become apparent during the test life cycle. Continue to develop technical skills of test personnel.
10.3	Testbed configuration management (CM). Maintain the entire testbed/repository (that is, test data, test procedures and scripts, software problem reports) in a CM tool. Define the test script CM process and ensure that test personnel work closely with the CM group.
10.4	Test program status reporting. Identify mechanisms for tracking test program progress. Develop periodic reports on test progress. Reports should reflect estimates to complete tasks in progress.
10.5	Defect management. Perform defect tracking and reporting. Attend defect review meetings.
10.6	Metrics collection and analysis. Collect and review metrics to determine whether changes in the process are required and to determine whether the product is ready to be shipped.

continued

continued from page 508

Number	Work Breakdown Structure (WBS) Element
11	**Test Process Improvement**
11.1	Training materials. Develop and maintain test process and test tool training materials.
11.2	Review of lessons learned. Perform this review throughout the testing life cycle and gather test life-cycle benefits information.
11.3	Metrics analysis and reporting. Analyze test process metrics across the organization and report the results of this analysis.

D.2.4 Test Team Resources

The composition of the WFTS test team is outlined within the test team profile depicted in Table D.2.2. This table identifies the test team positions on the project together with the names of the personnel who will fill these positions. The duties to be performed by each person are described, and the skills of the individuals filling the positions are documented. The last two columns reflect the years of experience for each test team member with regard to total test program experience as well as years of experience with the designated test management tool for the project.

The WFTS test team includes both full-time resources and personnel who aid in testing on a part-time basis. The phases supported by each test team member and the availability during each test phase is outlined in Table D.2.3.

The WFTS test team will need to have a working knowledge of several tools for its test program. Table D.2.4 outlines the experience of the test team members with the test management, requirements management, configuration management, and defect tracking tools. The last column indicates the training required for each test team member.

D.3 | Test Program

D.3.1 Scope

The WFTS test program is aimed at verifying that the Delivery 2 WFTS system satisfies the requirements/derived use cases and is ready to be deployed in the FTC's production environment. The test program involves the implementation of a number of test strategies across several test phases, including unit, integration, system, user acceptance, and site acceptance testing.

System-level test effort consists of functional testing, performance testing, backup and recoverability testing, security testing, and verification of system availability

Table D.2.2   Test Team Profile

Position	Name	Duties/Skills	Test Experience (years)	Test Tool Experience (years)
Test manager	Todd Jones	Responsible for test program, customer interface, recruiting, test tool introduction, and staff supervision. Skills: MS Project, SQA Basic, SQL, MS Access, UNIX, test tool experience.	12	1
Test lead	Sarah Wilkins	Performs staff supervision, cost/progress status reporting, test planning/design/ development and execution. Skills: TeamTest, Purify, Visual Basic, SQL, SQA Basic, UNIX, MS Access, C/C++, SQL Server.	5	3
Test engineer	Tom Schmidt	Performs test planning/design/ development and execution. Skills: Test tool experience, financial system experience.	2	.5
Test engineer	Reggie Miller	Performs test planning/design/ development and execution. Skills: Test tool experience, financial system experience.	2	1
Test engineer	Sandy Wells	Performs test planning/design/ development and execution. Skills: Financial system experience.	1	—
Test engineer	Susan Archer	Responsible for test tool environment, network and middleware testing. Performs all other test activities. Skills: Visual Basic, SQL, CNE, UNIX, C/C++, SQL Server.	1	—
Junior test engineer	Lisa Nguyen	Performs test planning/design/ development and execution. Skills: Visual Basic, SQL, UNIX, C/C++, HTML, MS Access.	—	—

Table D.2.3　**Test Team Personnel Availability**

Position	Name	Test Phases	Availability
Test manager	Todd Jones	Unit/Integration Test	100%
		System Test/Acceptance Test	100%
Test lead	Sarah Wilkins	Unit/Integration Test	100%
		System Test/Acceptance Test	
Test engineer	Tom Schmidt	System Test/Acceptance Test	100%
Test engineer	Reggie Miller	System Test/Acceptance Test	50%
Test engineer	Sandy Wells	System Test/Acceptance Test	50%
Test engineer	Susan Archer	Unit/Integration Test	100%
		System Test/Acceptance Test	
Junior test engineer	Lisa Nguyen	Unit/Integration Test	100%
		System Test/Acceptance Test	

Table D.2.4　**Test Team Training Requirements**

Team Member	Test Management Tools	RM Tool	CM Tool	Defect Tracking Tool	Training Required
Todd Jones	✓	✓	✓	✓	None
Sarah Wilkins	✓	✓	✓	✓	None
Tom Schmidt	✓	✓	✓	✓	None
Reggie Miller	✓	✓	✓	✓	None
Sandy Wells	—	✓	✓	✓	TestStudio
Susan Archer	—	✓	✓	✓	PerformanceStudio
Lisa Nguyen	—	—	—	—	All four tools

measures. Separate security testing is applied to ensure that necessary security mechanisms perform as specified. Site acceptance testing will be performed in association with site installation and checkout activities.

Tests will be comprehensive enough to cover the network, hardware, software application, and databases. Software tests will focus on NDI/COTS and developmental software. The unit and integration test phases will involve tests of newly created or modified software as well as COTS products incorporated in WFTS Delivery 2 development effort, as noted in Table D.1.1. System and user acceptance tests will exercise Delivery 2 development products and perform a regression testing on the existing Delivery 1 application software. Thus the complete WFTS system will be reviewed.

D.3.2   Test Approach

When developing the WFTS test approach, the test team reviewed system requirements/derived use cases and use case scenarios; it also studied the system description and critical/high-risk function information described in Section D.1.3. Using this information, the test team performed a test process analysis exercise to identify a test life cycle. In addition, it analyzed the test goals and objectives that could be applied on the WFTS test effort. The results of these analyses appear in Table D.3.1.

Table D.3.1   Test Process Analysis Documentation

Process Review

- The project will use the organization's standard test process that adopts the ATLM.
- To ensure a smooth implementation of the automated test tool, the project will take advantage of the ATLM test tool introduction process.

Test Goals

- Increase the probability that the AUT will behave correctly under all circumstances.
- Detect and support the removal of all defects in the AUT by participating in defect prevention activities and conducting defect detection activities, as defined in the test strategy.
- Increase the probability that the AUT meet all defined requirements.
- Perform test activities that support both defect prevention and defect removal.
- Be able to execute a complete test of the application within a short timeframe.
- Incorporate a test design that minimizes test script rework following changes to the application.

Test Objectives

- Ensure that the system complies with defined client and server response times.
- Ensure that the most critical end-user paths through the system perform correctly.
- Identify any significant defects in the system, track software problem reports, and verify closure of all significant software problem reports.
- Ensure that user screens perform correctly.
- Ensure that system changes have not had an adverse effect on existing software modules.
- Use automated test tools, whenever possible, to provide high test program return.
- Incorporate test design and development that minimizes test script rework following changes to the application.

In addition to identifying test goals and objectives, the test team documented test program parameters, including its assumptions, prerequisites, system acceptance criteria, and risks.

D.3.2.1 Assumptions

The test team developed this plan with the understanding of several assumptions concerning the execution of the WFTS project and the associated effect on the test program.

Test Performance. The test team will perform all tests on the WFTS project with the exception of those unit and integration phase tests, which are performed by the system developers and witnessed by the system test group.

Security Testing. System security tests, designed to satisfy the security test requirements outlined within the security test plan, will be executed during system testing and will be incorporated into the test procedure set constituting the system acceptance test (SAT).

Early Involvement. The test team will be involved with the WFTS application development effort from the beginning of the project, consistent with the ATLM. Early involvement includes the review of requirement statements and use cases/use case scenarios and the performance of inspections and walkthroughs.

Systems Engineering Environment. The suite of automated tools and the test environment configuration outlined within this plan are based upon existing systems engineering environment plans outlined within the WFTS management plan and the software development plan. Changes in the systems engineering environment will require subsequent and potentially significant changes to this plan.

Test Team Composition. The test team will include three business area functional analysts. These analysts will be applied to the system test effort according to their functional area expertise. While these analysts are on loan to the test group, they will report to the test manager regarding test tasks and be committed to the test effort. They will support the test effort for the phases and percentages of their time as noted in section D.2.4.

Test Limitations. Given the resource limitations of the test program and the limitless number of test paths and possible input values, the test effort has been designed to focus effort and attention on the most critical and high-risk functions of the system. Defect tracking and its associated verification effort, likewise, focus on assessing these functions and meeting acceptance criteria, so as to determine when the AUT is ready to go into production.

Project Schedule.   Test resources defined within the test plan are based upon the current WFTS project schedule and requirement baseline. Changes to this baseline will require subsequent changes to this plan.

D.3.2.2   Test Prerequisites

The WFTS test program schedule depicted in Figure D.1.2 includes the conduct of a system walkthrough. This walkthrough involves a demonstration that system test procedures are ready to support user acceptance testing.

The conduct of this walkthrough and subsequent performance of SAT requires that certain prerequisites be in place. These prerequisites may include activities, events, documentation, and products. The prerequisites for the WFTS test program execution are as follows:

- The full test environment configuration is in place, operational, and under CM control.
- The test data environment has been established and baselined.
- All detailed unit and integration test requirements have been successfully exercised as part of the unit and integration test phases.
- Materials supporting test-by-inspection and certification methods are on hand. Materials representing evidence of test-by-analysis are on hand.
- The system test procedure execution schedule is in place.
- Automated test procedure reuse analysis has been conducted.
- A modularity-relationship model has been created.
- System test procedures have been developed in accordance with standards.
- The WFTS system baseline software has been installed in the test environment and is operational.

D.3.2.3   System Acceptance Criteria

The WFTS test program within the AMSI test environment concludes with the satisfaction of the following criteria. In accordance with the test schedule depicted in Figure D.1.2, two site acceptance tests are performed following completion of these criteria.

- SAT has been performed.
- Priority 1–3 software problem reports reported during SAT and priority 2–3 software problem reports that existed prior to SAT have been resolved.

The test group has verified the system corrections implemented to resolve these defects.

- A follow-up SAT has been conducted, when required, to review test procedures associated with outstanding priority 1–3 software problem reports. Successful closure of these software problem reports has been demonstrated.

- A final test report has been developed by the test team and approved by FTC.

D.3.2.4 Risks

Risks to the test program (see Table D.3.2) have been identified, assessed for their potential effects, and then mitigated with a strategy for overcoming the risk should it be realized.

D.3.3 Test Strategies

Drawing on the defined test goals and objectives and using the ATLM as a baseline, the test team defined the test strategies that will be applied to support the WFTS test program. The test team will utilize both defect prevention and defect removal technologies as shown in Table D.3.3.

The AMSI test team will execute the SAT. It will develop test threads to exercise the requirements specified in the detailed requirements/use case documents. The test procedures will specify how a test engineer should execute the test by defining the input requirements and the anticipated results. The detail of this information is controlled through the DOORS test tool and is available on-line. The DOORS database serves as the repository for system requirements and test requirements.

The DOORS requirements management tool is used for managing all systems requirements, including business, functional, and design requirements. It is also used for capturing test requirements and test procedures, thus allowing for simple management of the testing process. Using the DOORS scripting language and the associated .dxl files, the test team can automatically create a traceability matrix that will measure the coverage progress of test procedures per test requirements. In turn, test procedures will be derived from the detailed business requirements and use cases and stored in the DOORS database.

The highest-risk functionality has been identified, and the test effort will focus on this functionality. Reuse analysis will be conducted of existing test procedures to avoid rework of automated test procedures available from previous testing efforts. If the automated test tool is not compatible with some of the functionality and no feasible automation work-around solutions can be found, tests will be executed manually.

Table D.3.2   Test Program Risks

Number	Risk Title	Description	Effect	Mitigation Strategy
1	COTS Testing	Method of testing requirements that will be supported by the COTS tool InsitFul has not been resolved. Issue: certification versus test qualification method. Also unclear whether automated test tool is compatible with InsitFul GUI.	150 additional test hours $12,000 cost 2 weeks schedule slip	Producer of InsitFul has been cooperative. Plans in place to test compatibility of product. Additional help by supplier is under negotiation.
2	Security Testing	Security plan and security test plan are both in draft form. Security requirements not finalized.	50 hours test rework $4,000 cost 2–4 weeks schedule slip	Potential system developer lined up to support test procedure rework and peak load period.
3	Require-ment Changes	Requirements pertaining to the Asset Trade component experienced late changes. Development staff behind schedule on this component.	2–4 weeks schedule slip	Monitoring situation. No mitigation strategy identified.
4	COTS Docu-menta-tion	The Financial Portfolio COTS product slated for use is a beta version, and no product documentation exists.	40 hours test rework $3,200 cost 2 weeks schedule slip	Test team working from documentation for the previous release of the product and attempting to identify differences over the phone.
5	Require-ments Defini-tion	Requirements definition for the Asset Trade component is at a high level, and test requirements are unclear.	60 hours test rework $4,800 cost 2–4 weeks schedule slip	Test team working with functional analysts to attempt to obtain greater definition through more detailed use case analyses.
.	.	.	.	.
.	.	.	.	.
.	.	.	.	.

Table D.3.3   Test Strategies and Techniques

Defect Prevention Technologies

➤ Examination of Constraints
➤ Early Test Involvement
➤ Use of Standards
➤ Inspections and Walkthroughs
➤ Quality Gates

Defect Removal Technologies

➤ Inspections and Walkthroughs
➤ Testing of Product Deliverables
➤ Designing Testability into the Application
➤ Use of Automated Test Tools
➤ Unit Test Phase: Error Handling, Memory Leak, Path Coverage, Fault Insertion, Decision Coverage
➤ Integration Test Phase: Integration Testing
➤ System Test Phase: Functional, Security, Stress/Volume, Performance, Usability
➤ Acceptance Test Phase: Functional, Security, Stress/Volume, Performance, Usability
➤ Strategic Manual and Automated Test Design
➤ Execution and Management of Automated Testing
➤ Random Testing
➤ Test Verification Method
➤ User Involvement

A modularity model will be created that depicts the relationships among the test procedures. Test procedures will be broken down and assigned to the various test engineers, based on the requirements category and the test engineer's business knowledge and expertise. Progress will be monitored and test procedure walk-throughs will be conducted to verify the accuracy of test procedures and to discover any discrepancies with the business requirement.

The WFTS system will be modeled for scalability using the simulation modeling tool OPNET. This model will simulate the major functions of the WFTS system and provide information about bottlenecks and queue buildups. Inputs to OPNET include arrival rates of the various transactions, the sizes of the transactions, and the processing times at the various stages of the process flow. After the model is built, it must be validated against the test data obtained from the performance testing process. Once this validation is complete, the model can be used to examine what-if scenarios and to predict performance under varying conditions.

D.3.4   Automated Tools

The test team for the WFTS project will use the automated test tools listed in Table D.3.4. The development team uses the PureCoverage and Purify tools during unit testing. During system acceptance testing, the test team will use TestStudio. The application will be analyzed for functionality that lends itself to automation. This strategy will streamline the process of creating and testing certain redundant transactions. Test scripts will be developed following the test procedure development guidelines defined in Appendix D.A.

If software problems are detected, the team will generate defect reports. Software problem reports will be reported to system developers through PVCS Tracker. The DOORS database supports the FTC repository for system requirements, test requirements, and related software problem reports.

TestStudio will be used as the GUI automated test tool. DOORS will serve as the requirements management tool. Performance Studio will be used for performance and stress testing. TestStudio Test Procedure (Case) Generator will be used to create a baseline of test procedures.

Table D.3.4   Automated Test Tools

Activity/Task	Automated Test
Business Modeling	Rational Rose
Simulation Modeling	OPNET
Requirements Management	DOORS
Load Testing	Performance Studio
Test Management	TestStudio
Configuration Management	PVCS
Defect Tracking	PVCS Tracker
GUI Testing	TestStudio

D.3.5 Qualification Methods

For each test requirement, a testability indicator/qualification method will be used. The following qualification methods will be employed in test procedure steps to verify that requirements have been met:

- *Inspection.* Inspection verifies conformance to requirements by visual examination, review of descriptive documentation, and comparison of the actual characteristics with predetermined criteria.

- *Demonstration.* Demonstration verifies conformance to requirements by exercising a sample of observable functional operations. This method is appropriate for demonstrating the successful integration, high-level functionality, and connectivity provided by NDI and COTS software. NDI and COTS products are certified by vendors to have been developed and tested in accordance with software development and quality processes.

- *Tests.* Testing verifies conformance to requirements by exercising observable functional operations. This method is generally more extensive than that used in demonstrations and is appropriate for requirements fulfilled by developmental items.

- *Manual Tests.* Manual tests will be performed when automated tests are not feasible.

- *Automated Tests.* When automation analysis outcome is positive, the test procedures will be automated.

- *Analysis.* Analysis verifies conformance to requirements by technical evaluation, processing, review, or study of accumulated data.

- *Certification.* Certification verifies conformance to requirements by examination of vendor (or supplier) documentation attesting that the product was developed and tested in accordance with the vendor's internal standards.

D.3.6 Test Requirements

Test requirements have been derived from requirements/use cases/use case scenarios developed for the application. In the requirements traceability matrix maintained within the DOORS database, system requirements are mapped to test requirements. The test team worked with the project manager and development team to prioritize system requirements for testing purposes. The test team entered the priority values within DOORS, as shown in the test verification summary matrix depicted in Appendix D.B.

D.3.7 Test Design

D.3.7.1 Test Program Model

Armed with a definition of test requirements and an understanding of the test techniques that are well suited to the WFTS test program, the test team developed the test program model, which depicts the scope of the test program. The model includes test techniques that will be employed at the development test and system test levels as well as the applicable static test strategies, as shown in Figure D.3.1.

D.3.7.2 Test Architecture

Having defined a test program model, the test team next constructed a test architecture for the WFTS project. The test architecture depicts the structure of the test program, defining the way that test procedures will be organized in the test effort. Figure D.3.2 depicts the test architecture for the WFTS project, where development-level tests are design-based and system-level tests are technique-based.

The design components shown in Figure D.3.2 were retrieved by the test team from the project's software architecture. Five components are being tested at the development level: System Management (SM-06), Security Guard (SG-07), Distributed Computing (DC-08), Support Applications (SA-09), and Active Trade Visibil-

---

Test Program Model

Static Test Strategies	**Other Qualification Methods**
• Requirements Review	• Demonstration
• Product Deliverable Test	• Analysis
• Design Review Participation	• Inspection
• Inspections and Walkthroughs	• Certification
Development-Level Techniques	**System-Level Techniques**
• Error Handling	• Functional Testing
• Memory Leak	• Security Testing
• Path Coverage	• Stress/Volume Testing
• Fault Insertion	• Performance Testing
• Decision Coverage	• Usability Testing

Figure D.3.1 Test Program Model

Test Architecture Development Test Level				
SM-06	**SG-07**	**DC-08**	**SA-09**	**TV-10**
Error Handling	Error Handling	Error Handling	Error Handling	Error Handling
Memory Leak	Memory Leak	Memory Leak	Memory Leak	Memory Leak
		Path Coverage	Path Coverage	Path Coverage
		Fault Insertion	Fault Insertion	Fault Insertion
		Decision Coverage	Decision Coverage	Decision Coverage

System Test Level				
Functional	**Security**	**Stress/Volume**	**Performance**	**Usability**
SM-06	SM-06	TV-10	TV-10	SM-06
SG-07	SG-07			SG-07
DC-08	and			DC-08
SA-09	Security Plan			SA-09
TV-10	Requirements			TV-10

Figure D.3.2   Sample Test Architecture

ity (TV-10). For each of these design components, the test techniques that will be applied are noted.

D.3.7.3   Test Procedure Definition

A preliminary step in the test design process involves the development of the test procedure definition, which aids in test development and helps to bound the test effort. The test procedure definition identifies the suite of test procedures that must be developed and executed for the test effort. The design exercise involves the organization of test procedures into logical groups and the allocation of test procedure number series for each set of tests required.

Table D.3.5 depicts a sample test procedure definition for development-level tests. Column 1 of this table identifies the series of test procedure numbers allotted for testing of the particular design component using the particular technique. Column 2 lists the software or hardware design components to be tested. The design components referenced are retrieved from the test architecture. The test technique is listed in column 3, and the number of test procedures involved in each set of tests (row) is estimated in column 4.

Table D.3.5   Test Procedure Definition (Development Test Level)

TP Numbers Allocated	Design Component ID	Test Technique	Number of Test Procedures
100–150	SM601–SM634	Error Handling	35
151–199		Memory Leak	35
200–250	SG701–SG728	Error Handling	30
251–299		Memory Leak	30
300–350	DC801–DC848	Error Handling	50
351–399		Memory Leak	50
400–599		Path Coverage	200
600–650		Fault Insertion	50
651–849		Decision Coverage	200
850–899	SA901–SA932	Error Handling	35
900–950		Memory Leak	35
951–1150		Path Coverage	200
1151–1199		Fault Insertion	35
1200–1399		Decision Coverage	200
1400–1450	TV1001–TV1044	Error Handling	45
1451–1499		Memory Leak	45
1500–1699		Path Coverage	200
1700–1750		Fault Insertion	45
1751–1949		Decision Coverage	200
1950–1999		Integration Test	25
			Total = 1,745

Table D.3.6 depicts a sample test procedure definition for system-level tests. Column 1 of this table identifies the series of test procedures allotted for each particular test technique. Column 2 lists the test technique.

Columns 3 through 5 provide information to specify the number of test procedures involved at the system test level. The number of design units or functional threads required for the tests is given in column 3. Four functional threads are planned to support stress and performance testing. Note that usability tests will be conducted as part of functional testing; as a result, no additional test procedures are needed for this test technique. The number of system requirements involved in the tests is identified in column 4, and the number of test requirements is given in column 5.

Table D.3.6   Test Procedure Definition (System Test Level)

TP Numbering Convention	Test Technique	Number of Units or Threads	Number of System Requirements	Number of Test Requirements	Number of Test Procedures
2000–2399	Functional	186	220	360	360
2400–2499	Security	62	70	74	74
2500–2599	Stress	4	12	24	96
2600–2699	Performance	4	14	14	56
—	Usability	186	4	4	—
					586

Table D.3.7   Test Procedure Naming Convention

TP Naming Convention	Design Component/ Test Technique	Test Level	Test Procedure Estimate
WF100–WF199	Systems Management (SM)	Development	70
WF200–WF299	Security Guard (SG)	Development	60
WF300–WF849	Distributed Computing (DC)	Development	550
WF850–WF1399	Support Applications (SA)	Development	505
WF1400–WF1949	Active Trade Visibility (TV)	Development	535
WF1950–WF1999	Integration Test	Development	25
WF2000–WF2399	Functional/Usability Tests	System	360
WF2400–WF2499	Security	System	74
WF2500–WF2599	Stress	System	96
WF2600–WF2699	Performance	System	56
WF2700	System Test Shell	System	1

The last column estimates the number of test procedures required for each test technique listed. For functional and security testing, there may be one test procedure for every test requirement. For stress and performance testing, four threads are planned that will need to be altered for each test procedure to examine different system requirements.

D.3.7.4   Test Procedure Naming Convention

With the test procedure definition in place for both the development and system levels, the test team adopted a test procedure naming convention to uniquely identify the test procedures on the project. Table D.3.7 provides the test procedure naming scheme for the WFTS project.

With the various tests defined, the test team identified the test procedures that warrant automation and those that can be performed most efficiently via manual methods. Table D.3.8 depicts a portion of a traceability matrix that is maintained using DOORS, which breaks down each test procedure required for system-level testing. Each test procedure in Table D.3.8 is cross-referenced to several other elements, such as design component and test technique. The last column identifies whether the test will be performed using an automated test tool (A) or manually (M).

D.3.8   Test Development

Tests are automated based on the automation analysis outcome of the test design phase, as shown in Table D.3.8. They are developed in accordance with the test pro-

Table D.3.8   Automated versus Manual Tests

TP Number	Design Component	Test Technique	SR ID	SWR ID	TR ID	A/M
.	.	.	.	.	.	.
.	.	.	.	.	.	.
.	.	.	.	.	.	.
2330	TV1016	Functional	3.2.3c	TV029	2220	A
2331	TV1016	Functional	3.2.3c	TV030	2221	A
2332	TV1016	Functional	3.2.3c	TV031	2412	M
2333	TV1017	Functional	3.2.3d	TV032	2222	A
2334	TV1017	Functional	3.2.3d	TV033	2412	A
2335	TV1018	Functional	3.2.3e	TV034	2223	A
2336	TV1018	Functional	3.2.3e	TV035	2412	M
2337	TV1019	Functional	3.2.3f	TV036	2224	A
2338	TV1019	Functional	3.2.3g	TV037	2412	A
2339	TV1019	Functional	3.2.3g	TV038	2225	A
.	.	.	.	.	.	.
.	.	.	.	.	.	.
.	.	.	.	.	.	.

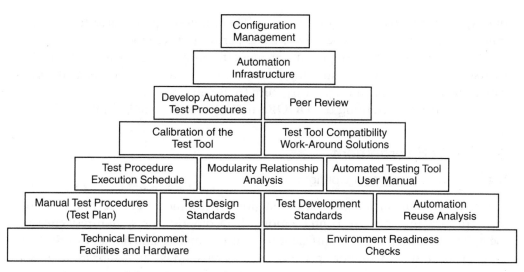

Figure D.3.3   Test Development Architecture

Table D.3.9   Automation Reuse Analysis

TP Number	Design Component	Test Technique	SR ID	SWR ID	TR ID	A/M	Reuse Asset
2330	TV1016	Functional	3.2.3c	TV029	2220	A	—
2331	TV1016	Functional	3.2.3c	TV030	2221	A	MMS2079
2332	TV1016	Functional	3.2.3c	TV031	2412	M	—
2333	TV1017	Functional	3.2.3d	TV032	2222	A	—
2334	TV1017	Functional	3.2.3d	TV033	2412	M	—
2335	TV1018	Functional	3.2.3e	TV034	2223	A	LW2862
2336	TV1018	Functional	3.2.3e	TV035	2412	M	—
2337	TV1019	Functional	3.2.3f	TV036	2224	A	—
2338	TV1019	Functional	3.2.3g	TV037	2225	A	ST2091
2339	TV1019	Functional	3.2.3g	TV038	2226	A	ST2092
.	.	.	.	.	.	.	.
.	.	.	.	.	.	.	.
.	.	.	.	.	.	.	.

cedure execution schedule and the modularity-relationship model. Test development must be consistent with the test development guidelines provided in Appendix D.A. Additionally, test procedures will be developed using the automatic test procedure generation feature of the TestStudio test tool.

The test team prepared a test development architecture, depicted in Figure D.3.3, that provides a clear picture of the test development activities (building blocks) necessary to create test procedures. The test development architecture illustrates the major activities to be performed as part of test development.

To conduct its test development activities efficiently, the test team performed an analysis to identify the potential for reuse of existing test procedures and scripts within the AMSI automation infrastructure (reuse library). The results of this reuse analysis are maintained using the DOORS tool and are depicted in Table D.3.9.

D.4 | Test Environment

D.4.1   Test Environment Configuration

The test environment mirrors the production environment. This section describes the hardware and software configurations that compose the system test environment. The hardware must be sufficient to ensure complete functionality of the software. Also, it should support performance analysis aimed at demonstrating field performance. Information concerning the test environment pertinent to the application, database, application server, and network is provided below.

Application

Visual Basic 5.0

Iona's Orbix V2.3

Microsoft's Internet Information Server

Neonet V3.1

MQ Series V.20

Windows NT V4.0 service pack 3

Application Server

Dual-processor PC, 200MHz Pentium processors

256MB Memory

4–6GB hard disk, CD-ROM drive

2 Syngoma 503E SNA boards

Microsoft SNA Server 3.0

Digital DCE 1.1C with Eco patch

Encina 2.5 with patches

Windows NT 4.0 with service pack 3

Database

Sybase 11 Server V11.x.1 application server

Microsoft's SNA Server V4.0

Digital DCE Client and Server with Eco patch V1.1c

Encina V2.5 with patches

Workstation

Windows NT V4.0 service pack 3

Iona's Orbix V2.3

Sybase Configuration

Application: Sybase 11 Open Client CT-Lib V11.1.0

Database: Sybase 11 Server V11.x.1

Sun Solaris for the database server

Network Configuration

Ethernet switched network

Baseline test laboratory equipment for WFTS central site configurations was acquired for development and testing performed in support of Deliver 1 WFTS system. Delivery 2 requirements involve additional functionality, and as a result of the scope of the test effort must be modified accordingly. Two site configurations must be added to the WFTS test lab configuration. The procurement of additional hardware and software resources is reflected in the test equipment list given in Table D.4.1.

D.4.2 Test Data

Working in conjunction with the database group, the test team will create the test database. The test database will be populated with unclassified production data. The configuration management group will baseline the test environment, including the test database. Additionally, during performance testing, test data will be generated using Rational's Performance Studio tool. These data will be baselined in the PVCS configuration management tool. To assure adequate testing depth (volume of test database of 10 records versus 10,000 records), the test team will mirror the production-size database during performance testing. To assure adequate testing

Table D.4.1   Test Equipment Purchase List

Site	Product Requirement	Product Description	Vendor	Quantity	Unit Cost	Annual Mainte-nance
Site 1	Application server	Compaq ProLiant 6500	Compaq	1	(cost)	(cost)
Site 1	Communication server	Compaq ProLiant 1600	Compaq	1	(cost)	(cost)
Site 1	Database server	Sun Workstation	Sun	1	(cost)	(cost)
Site 1	Server operating system	Windows NT	Microsoft	2	(cost)	(cost)
Site 1	Server operating system	Sun Solaris	Sun	1	(cost)	(cost)
Site 1	Database management system (DBMS)	Sybase Server	Sybase	1	(cost)	(cost)
Site 1	CORBA server	Iona Orbix	Iona	1	(cost)	(cost)
.	.	.	.	.	.	.
.	.	.	.	.	.	.
.	.	.	.	.	.	.

Table D.4.2   System Test Data Definition

TP Number	Design Component	Data Requirement	Description
.	.	.	.
.	.	.	.
.	.	.	.
2330	TV1016	Database tables	Screen inputs
2331	TV1016	Variable input	Range of data values (see test requirement)
2332	TV1016	Variable input	Range of data values (see test requirement)
2333	TV1017	Data object	Requires a bitmapped TIFF data object
2334	TV1017	Variable input	Range of data values (see test requirement)
2335	TV1018	Database tables	Screen inputs
2336	TV1018	—	Printer output test using existing data.
2337	TV1019	Data object	Requires a bitmapped TIFF data object
2338	TV1019	Variable input	Range of data values (see test requirement)
2339	TV1019	Database tables	Screen inputs
.	.	.	
.	.	.	

breadth (variation of data values), it will use data with many variations, again mirroring the production data environment. Test data will use the procedure data definitions, whenever possible.

Table D.4.2 is a matrix that cross-references test data requirements to each individual test procedure that is planned for system testing.

D.5 | Test Execution

D.5.1 Test Program Reporting

An earned value management system will be used to track test program progress, including cost and schedule measures. Earned value involves tracking of the value of completed work relative to planned costs and actual costs, so as to provide a true measure of cost status and to enable AMSI's personnel to define effective corrective actions. Four primary steps make up the earned value process:

1. Identify short tasks (functional test phase).
2. Schedule each task (task start date and end date).
3. Assign a budget to each task (task will require 3,100 hours using four test engineers).
4. Measure the progress of each task (schedule and cost variance).

The primary tasks to be performed by the test team have been identified consistent with the work breakdown structure outlined in Table D.2.1. A detailed test schedule has been prepared identifying each task. For each task, timeframes have been determined and hours and personnel have been allocated. The SAT test execution schedule is detailed in Section D.6.

After a test procedure has been executed, the test team will undertake evaluation activities to assure that the test outcome was not the result of a false-positive or false-negative condition. The test procedure status is then revised with the requirements management tool to reflect actual test results, such as full, partial, or failed demonstration of compliance with the expected outcome, as defined in the test procedure.

D.5.2 Test Program Metrics

Table D.5.1 shows the test progress metrics that will be collected and reported. The quality assurance group will report on the quality metrics.

Table D.5.1   Test Program Metrics

Metric Name	Description
Test procedure execution status	Number of executed test procedures versus total number of test procedures. This test procedure execution metric will indicate the extent of the testing effort still outstanding.
Error discovery rate	Number of total defects found versus number of test procedures executed. The error discovery rate metric uses the same calculation as the defect density metric. It is used to analyze and support a rational product release decision.
Defect aging	Date defect was opened versus date defect was fixed. The defect aging metric provides an indication of turnaround of the defect.
Defect fix retest	Date defect was fixed and released in new build versus date defect was retested. The defect fix retest metric provides an idea of whether the testing team is retesting the fixes fast enough to get an accurate progress metric.
Defect trend analysis	Number of total defects found versus number of test procedures executed over time. Defect trend analysis can help determine the trend of defects found. Is the trend improving as the testing phase is winding down?
Problem reports	Number of software problem reports broken down by priority. The problem reports measure counts the number of software problems reported, listing them by priority.

D.5.3   Defect Tracking

To track defects, a defect workflow process has been implemented. Defect workflow training will be conducted for all test engineers. The steps in the defect workflow process are as follows:

1. When a defect is generated initially, the status is set to "New." (Note: How to document the defect, what fields need to be filled in, and so on also need to be specified.)

2. The tester selects the type of defect:
    - Bug
    - Cosmetic
    - Enhancement
    - Omission

3. The tester then selects the priority of the defect:
    - Critical—fatal error
    - High—needs immediate attention

- Medium—needs to be resolved as soon as possible but not a showstopper
- Low—cosmetic error

4. A designated person (in some companies, the software manager; in other companies, a special board) evaluates the defect and assigns a status and makes modifications of type of defect and/or priority if applicable).

   The status "Open" is assigned if it is a valid defect.

   The status "Close" is assigned if it is a duplicate defect or user error. The reason for "closing" the defect needs to be documented.

   The status "Deferred" is assigned if the defect will be addressed in a later release.

   The status "Enhancement" is assigned if the defect is an enhancement requirement.

5. If the status is determined to be "Open," the software manager (or other designated person) assigns the defect to the responsible person (developer) and sets the status to "Assigned."

6. Once the developer is working on the defect, the status can be set to "Work in Progress."

7. After the defect has been fixed, the developer documents the fix in the defect tracking tool and sets the status to "fixed," if it was fixed, or "Duplicate," if the defect is a duplication (specifying the duplicated defect). The status can also be set to "As Designed," if the function executes correctly. At the same time, the developer reassigns the defect to the originator.

8. Once a new build is received with the implemented fix, the test engineer retests the fix and other possible affected code. If the defect has been corrected with the fix, the test engineer sets the status to "Close." If the defect has not been corrected with the fix, the test engineer sets the status to "Reopen."

Defect correction is the responsibility of system developers; defect detection is the responsibility of the AMSI test team. The test leads will manage the testing process, but the defects will fall under the purview of the configuration management group. When a software defect is identified during testing of the application, the tester will notify system developers by entering the defect into the PVCS Tracker tool and filling out the applicable information.

AMSI test engineers will add any attachments, such as a screen print, relevant to the defect. The system developers will correct the problem in their facility and implement the operational environment after the software has been baselined. This release will be accompanied by notes that detail the defects corrected in this release as well as any other areas that were changed as part of the release. Once implemented, the test team will perform a regression test for each modified area.

The naming convention for attachments will be defect ID (yyy), plus Attx (where $x = 1, 2, 3 \ldots n$) (for example, the first attachment for defect 123 should be called 123Att1). If additional changes have been made other than those required for previously specified software problem reports, they will be reviewed by the test manager, who will evaluate the need for additional testing. If deemed necessary, the manager will plan additional testing activities. He will have the responsibility for tracking defect reports and ensuring that all reports are handled on a timely basis.

D.5.4 Configuration Management

The CM department is responsible for all CM activities and will verify that all parties involved are following the defined CM procedures. System developers will provide object code only for all application updates. It is expected that system developers will baseline their code in a CM tool before each test release. The AMSI test team will control the defect reporting process and monitor the delivery of associated program fixes. This approach will allow the test team to verify that all defect conditions have been properly addressed.

D.6 | Detailed Test Schedule

A detailed SAT test schedule (portion of schedule) is provided in Table D.6.1.

Table D.6.1 Test Schedule

Task ID	Task Description	Duration	Start	Finish
.	.	.	.	.
.	.	.	.	.
.	.	.	.	.
22	Develop SAT test responsibilities	1d	11/25	11/25
23	Develop review and reporting methods	1d	11/26	11/26
24	Develop management of test sessions	1d	11/27	11/27
25	Verify CM activities	1d	11/27	11/27
26	Verify change-control activities	1d	11/27	11/27
27	Develop issue/problem reporting standards	1d	11/30	11/30
28	Develop SAT test procedures	59d	12/12	2/12
29	Develop functional/usability test procedures	55d	12/12	2/8
30	Develop security test procedures	15d	12/22	1/7
31	Develop stress/volume test procedures	16d	1/7	1/23
32	Develop performance test procedures	14d	1/23	1/27
33	Develop system test shell procedures	3d	2/9	2/12
.	.	.	.	.
.	.	.	.	.
.	.	.	.	.

Appendix D.A | Test Procedure Development Guidelines

AMSI's standard test procedures development guidelines for the WFTS project are outlined below. These guidelines are available in the AMSI CM library.

Table D.A.1   Test Development Guidelines

Development Guideline Topics	Description
Design-to-development transition	Specify how design and setup activities will be translated into test development action
Reusable Test Procedures	Test procedures need to be reusable for highest test program return on investment
Data	Avoid hard-coding data values into scripts, rendering them not reusable
Application navigation	Standard navigation method needs to be deployed for reusable test scripts
Bitmap image recording	Addresses the use of bitmap image recording method for test procedure development
Automation wildcards	Development guidelines supporting reusable test procedures
Capture/playback	Outlines on how to apply the use of capture/playback recording
Maintainable Test Procedures	Test procedures whose defects are easy to remove and can easily be adapted to meet new requirements
Cosmetic standards	Standards defined to promote test program code that is easy to read and comprehend
Test script comments	Specifies where and how comments are used within procedures and scripts
Test script documentation	Specifies that test script documentation is important for test procedure maintainability
Test/application synchronization	How to synchronize server/GUI/AUT with test script
Test procedure index	Guidelines supporting the maintenance of an index to find test procedures of interest
Error handling	Guidelines for how test procedures will handle errors
Naming standards	Defines standard naming convention for test procedures
Modularity	Guidelines for creating modular test scripts
Looping constructs	Looping constructs support script modularity
Branching constructs	Branching constructs support script modularity
Context independence	Directs development of test procedures given test procedure relationships

continued

continued from page 534

Development Guideline Topics	Description
Global files	Globally declared functions are available to any procedure and support maintainability
Constants	Guidelines addressing use of constants to support maintainable test procedures
Other Guidelines	Other test development guidelines
Output format	Users need to define the desired appearance of the test procedure results output
Test procedures/verification points	Guidelines can specify which test procedure to use most often and which ones to avoid
User-defined verification	Addresses the use of script programming for user-defined verification
API calls, dynamic link libraries (.dll)	Addresses test automation using APIs and .dlls as part of the user-defined verification methods

Appendix D.B ｜ Test Verification Summary Matrix

A description of the columns contained within the test verification summary matrix is provided in Table D.B.1, and the actual test verification summary matrix for WFTS Delivery 2 is provided in Table D.B.2. The test verification summary matrix represents an example of the type of requirements traceability matrix that can be generated using DOORS. This matrix links the test procedures to test requirements, enabling the test team to verify the test coverage.

Table D.B.1　Test Verification Summary Matrix Terminology

Column Title	Description
Para ID	The paragraph number of the particular requirement from the WFTS system specification document
Text	The text of the requirement statement
Key	The unique requirement identification number generated by the requirements management tool for that requirement statement
Method	The verification (qualification) method to be used to verify that the requirement has been satisfied by the system solution
Pri	Identifies the priority of the requirement: CR = critical, HR = high risk, PM = technical performance measure, NN = noncritical
D1/D2/D3	Identifies the system delivery (either D1, D2, or D3) in which the solution to the requirement has been implemented
Test Procedure	Identifies the test procedure that exercises a test of the requirement

<u>Table D.B.2</u>   **Test Verification Summary Matrix**

Para ID	Text	Key	Method	Pri	D1	D2	D3	Test Procedure
3.2.1a	System shall perform software installation and upgrades	178	Test	NN	D1	—	—	SM2012
3.2.1b	System shall perform software system load balancing for WFTS system servers	179	Test	NN	—	D2	—	SM2013
3.2.1c	System shall perform a recovery of the system and data in the event of a system failure	180	Test	HR	—	D2	—	SM2014
3.2.1d	System shall manage disk and file structure and allocation, including the ability to determine the amount of disk space used and available	181	Test	NN	—	D2	—	SM2015
3.2.1e	System shall be able to configure electronic mail and manage directory service capabilities	182	Test	NN	D1	—	—	SM2016
3.2.1f	System shall monitor the software configuration of critical system components and workstations, including checks for outdated versions	183	Test	NN	—	D2	—	SM2017
.	.	.	.	.	.	.	.	.
.	.	.	.	.	.	.	.	.
.	.	.	.	.	.	.	.	.

Appendix D.C | Test Procedures and Test Scripts

Manual test procedures supporting SAT are documented within the DOORS database. Automated test procedures and test scripts supporting SAT are maintained using the TeamTest test tool.

Appendix E

Best Practices

Following the ATLM, as outlined in this book, constitutes the adoption of a set of proven practices. This appendix summarizes these best practices and gives additional recommendations and suggestions that constitute a set of best practices for the development and execution of automated testing. These best practices are aimed at helping the test team to avoid the kind of test program missteps that consume test engineers' time and increase test program effort. General practices that have served as ongoing themes in this book include the notion that not all test requirements can be supported by test automation. Other general practices include the performance of thorough test planning and related management activities, such as tracking test environment development activities.

Good planning adheres to the philosophy that the test effort must be approached from a systematic, structured, and step-by-step perspective. Each test activity should be valuable in and of itself, and it should support the next step in the test life-cycle process. In some cases, patience is a virtue, especially when the application-under-test (AUT) is unstable and constantly undergoes change. During such a timeframe, the test team needs to postpone the automation of black-box test procedures, and instead, focus its time and effort on other test activities.

Test automation should be a professional discipline, performed much like software development. Best practices and standards for test automation should be developed and applied just like a software development effort. Several test automation best practices are described in Table E.1.

E.1 | Documented Process

The test team cannot automate a process that is not defined. Automated test tools do not impose a process on the test engineer; rather, they support a test process. Tools also do not offer application expertise. As a result, technical problems can obscure process issues.

The test team should start by documenting the current test life-cycle process used by the organization and then modify this process to reflect the incorporation of

Table E.1   **Best Automated Testing Practices**

Document the process

Manage expectations

Use a pilot project

Verify test tool compatibility

Verify test tool upgrades

Baseline the system setup and configuration before installing a new
tool

Avoid incompatible test tools

Avoid unnecessary software installation in an already-baselined
testing environment

Understand the overall test program objectives

Remember that not everything should be automated

Keep automation simple

Follow test procedure design and development standards

Conduct automated versus manual test analysis

Conduct reuse analysis

Encourage test team partnership with all teams involved in the
system development life cycle

Keep the communication flowing

Ensure schedule compatibility

Involve the customer from the beginning of the system
development life cycle

Document and report defects

Use an automated test expert or tool advocate to sell the benefits of
the automated tool within the project team

Clarify test team assignments

Participate in user group meetings and testing discussions on the
Web

Suggest test tool improvements to the vendor

Become a beta tester

Take advantage of the knowledge of the specialty topic experts (tool
experts)

automated test tools. For a detailed discussion of test process definition, refer to Chapter 4.

E.2 | Managing Expectations

The long-term success of the test team depends upon its ability to obtain the capital, training, and personnel resources needed to adequately perform test activities on projects. The political leverage required to obtain these resources is achieved by test team performance that is consistent with senior management expectations within the organization. Chapter 2 covers the establishment of expectations, communication of the benefits of test automation, and the salesmanship of test automation to management—all important facets of a winning political strategy.

E.3 | Pilot Project

The test team needs to obtain experience with an automated test tool and test automation practices on a small project before undertaking automated testing on a large project. It is beneficial to identify an application in development that could be used as the pilot project on which to apply test automation or a new test tool for the first time.

A good strategy is to first apply test automation in an isolated test environment (test lab) and then a pilot project before initiating test automation on a wide scale across two or more projects concurrently. (Refer to the pilot application selection guidelines outlined in Chapter 3.) Ideally, the test environment and pilot project will be similar enough to projects typical for the organization that the test team can be adequately prepared for a larger-scale test effort. Note also that the test performance within the pilot project environment constitutes an evaluation aimed at assessing the test tool's actual performance on a first project.

E.4 | Test Tool Compatibility Checks

It is desirable to have candidate test tools checked out within an isolated environment before they are installed within the target test environment. If part of the target application exists in some form at the time of test tool consideration, then the test team should install the test tool or tools along with the application and determine whether the two are compatible. Once a compatibility check has been performed and a few problems arise, the test team will need to investigate whether work-around solutions are possible. See Chapter 4 for further discussion of compatibility checks.

When third-party controls (widgets, OCX, or ActiveX) are used to develop the application, the development team needs to know in advance whether the automated tool is compatible with each third-party control. It is a good idea to ask the tool vendor to provide a list of third-party controls with which the tool is compatible and to hand this list to the developers who are planning on implementing these various controls.

Also note that test tools need to be compatible with both the current software application and future development environments. The primary test tool adopted by the test team organization should be compatible with primary development tools in the market. The test team should keep abreast of the evolution of development tools and environments, enabling it to anticipate the environment in which testing will be applied in the near future.

One special concern is the availability of memory to support both the application and the automated test tool.

E.5 | Test Tool Upgrades

A test team may have extensively tested a test tool in an isolated environment and then applied the test tool on one or more projects. As a result, the test team may be familiar and capable with the particular test tool and confident that it works as specified within product literature. Suppose that the test tool vendor announces a bigger and better version of the test tool product as part of a product upgrade. Should the test team immediately adopt the new version and apply it to the project at hand?

The test team will want to make sure that the scripts created in the old version of the tool still work with the new version of the tool. Most vendors promise backward compatibility, meaning that scripts created in the current version of the tool can be reused in the new version of the tool, without any changes to the existing scripts. Past experience, however, indicates that these promises are not always fulfilled.

For example, one test engineer named Neil worked on a project that had invested as much as $250,000 in an automated test tool. When the new version of the test tool was implemented in the test environment, Neil discovered that it supported MS Exchange as the mail engine; the previous version of the tool and Neil's company, on the other hand, employed MS Mail. A work-around solution was identified that required the installation of both MS Mail and MS Exchange on desktop computers that were outfitted with the automated test tool. This approach allowed MS Mail to be used to support e-mail requirements, while MS Exchange supported defect notification and coordination requirements. This elaborate effort could have been avoided if the test tool vendor had brought this major change to the attention of the test team.

Any test team needs to approach the use of a new product release with caution. Some tests should be carried out to ensure that test team activities can still be performed with the new version in the same manner as with the previous test tool release. The test team also needs to make sure that the test tool upgrade doesn't adversely affect the current system setup. One valuable check is to ensure that the new version of the test tool remains compatible with the organization's systems engineering environment. Without these types of checks, the test team may suddenly discover that the test tool upgrade has disrupted its ability to perform activities with other tools within the test environment. When discoveries are made that part of the test tool no longer functions in the same way, the test team may need to identify or develop an extensive work-around solution.

E.6 | Baselined System Setup and Configuration

To ensure the integrity of the current system environment, it is a good practice for the test team to back up the current system setup/configuration baseline before installing any new automated test tool or new version of an automated test tool. Specifically, it is beneficial to back up .dll files prior to new installations to ensure that these files are not overwritten. This precautionary activity should be performed even when the test team has successfully tested the new test tool software within an isolated test environment.

E.7 | Software Installations in the Test Environment Baseline

It is a good practice to avoid the installation of unnecessary new software within the target test environment once the test environment becomes operational and has been baselined. On one occasion, a test engineer installed a product called Microsoft Plus! that provided elaborate new mouse icons and screen savers. Test scripts that had worked perfectly prior to the installation of Microsoft Plus! no longer worked, however. The test environment had changed, and the change affected test integrity.

E.8 | Overall Test Program Objectives

The test team needs to be careful to avoid the trap of becoming consumed with the development of test scripts that distract the test engineer from his or her primary mission—finding errors. Specifically, the test engineer should not overautomate tests and should resist the impulse to automate a test that is more effectively performed manually. An obvious example would involve the situation where three days were consumed automating a test that could have been performed manually within a few minutes.

Remember to analyze what should be automated. It is not necessary or feasible to automate everything. Why take days to automate a feature that can be tested by hand in five minutes, is used frequently through normal use of the program, and will be tested heavily only at key milestones?

E.9 | Keep Automation Simple

The most elaborate testing script is not always the most useful and cost-effective way of conducting automated testing. When using a table-driven approach, the test team should keep in mind the size of the application, the size of the test budget, and the return on investment that might be expected from applying a data-driven approach. Consider the example of the test engineer named Bill, who demonstrated an elaborate table-driven approach at a test tool user group meeting. Bill had developed a significant number of scripts to support a data-driven approach, even though the application's functionality that he was trying to test in an automated fashion was quite basic—that is, simple record add, delete, and update functions. It would have been much more efficient to use a data file to enter the various records, which amounted to a test development effort of no more than a half an hour. The resulting script also could be reused as often as necessary. The table-driven approach that Bill presented took him two weeks to develop.

Test engineers, for example, might find a way to use a GUI test tool to circumvent the GUI entirely through the use of API or RPC calls. This elaborate effort may produce an elegant test automation solution, but at what cost? Test engineers should be careful not to spend more time on programming the automation code than is available in the test schedule and budget or than it would take to develop the AUT.

E.10 | Test Procedure Design and Development Standards

Test engineers need to take a disciplined approach to test procedure design and development. Specifically, they need to rigorously adhere to design and development standards so as to promote maximum reusability and maintainability of the resulting automated testing scripts. Test engineers need to flag those test procedures that are repetitive in nature and therefore lend themselves perfectly for automation. Initially, the test team should focus on the augmentation of manual tests through automation. Test development should be a natural extension of the detailed test design activities performed consistently with the guidelines described in Chapter 7.

In particular, high-risk and mission-critical functionality should be addressed early within the test development and execution schedules.

E.11 | Automated versus Manual Test Analysis

Part of the test design effort outlined in Chapter 7 involves an analysis intended to determine when to automate and when to test manually. The test team should realize that not everything should be automated immediately. Instead, it should take a step-by-step approach to automation. It is wise to base the automation effort on the test procedure execution schedule, with one goal being to not duplicate the development effort.

E.12 | Reuse Analysis

As described in Chapter 8, the test engineer needs to conduct reuse analysis of already-existing testing scripts, in an effort to avoid duplication of automation efforts. Test resources are limited, but expectations of test team support may be greater than budgeted for. As a result, the test team cannot afford to squander precious time and energy duplicating the test effort. Measures that can be taken to avoid duplication include performing a disciplined test design. Consider the example of test procedure scripts being allocated according to functional areas of testing. Such an action can magnify the number of automated tests produced. In this situation, the test design should include a strategy for having the test procedures cut across several functional areas.

E.13 | Test Team Communication with Other Teams

The test team cannot work in isolation. Instead, it needs to be involved from the beginning of the system development life cycle and partner with all teams involved in the life cycle so as to implement an efficient test program. The test team needs to clarify any automated test tool add-on or code intrusion up-front with developers. When source code must be expanded or augmented by inserting probes, wrappers, or additional statements around source code statements and functions, the tool can be considered intrusive and the developers need to be advised of this potential problem.

For example, one test team deployed a test tool, which requires an add-on product when testing applications developed in a particular version of Visual Basic. The test team routinely informed the developers during test execution (late in the process) that an add-on product was being used and that the cause of defect might be attributable to the add-on product. The developers, however, were surprised to learn of the add-on product. Afterward, the development team asserted that the add-on product produced several reported defects. The test team realized that it would have been better to advise the developers earlier in the test process of the use of this add-on.

E.14 | Schedule Compatibility

The project schedule should include enough time to accommodate the introduction and use of automated test tools. An automated test tool is best introduced at the beginning of the development life cycle. Early introduction ensures that the test team has adequate lead time to become familiar with the particular automated test tool and its advanced features. Sufficient lead time is also necessary so that system requirements can be loaded into a test management tool, test design activities can adequately incorporate test tool capabilities, and test procedures and scripts can be generated in time for scheduled test execution.

Without a review of the project schedule, the test team can find itself in a no-win situation, where it is asked to do too much with too little time. That is, expectations of test team performance may be greater than that which the test team can demonstrate. Friction and animosity often result. The test team or the automated test tool may bear the brunt of the blame for schedule slippage and cost overruns. Test automation needs to be embraced by the project early in the development life cycle to be truly effective. Also, the test team needs to be selective when identifying which tests will be supported by test automation and which would be more effectively performed manually. Chapter 4 discusses the test team's review of the project schedule when contemplating the use of automation on the test effort.

E.15 | Customer Involvement

When establishing the test environment, the test team needs to be conscious of how test results will ultimately be presented to senior management and to customers. The test engineer can gauge management and customer reaction early to report formats and test result output to obtain a feel for how well the test tool output is understood. The test team may need to port test output to different office automation tools that allow test results to be more clearly understood and conceptualized.

The form and appearance of test output constitute an extremely important issue with regard to satisfying the application customer or end user. Although the test team could have the most wonderful script for producing test results, the customer or end user may not like the format and appearance of the output.

Another customer involvement issue pertains to the end user's or customer's understanding of the particular test strategies and test design implemented. This consideration is particularly important when the end user or customer did not participate or was not involved in the project during the time that system and test requirements were developed. The best solution is to obtain customer involvement early in the life cycle and throughout the test effort.

E.16 | Defect Documentation and Reporting

During test procedure development and even before official test execution has begun, the test team may identify defects. If so, the team should document the defects and share them with the development team. It should avoid postponing defect documentation and reporting until the official start of test execution.

E.17 | Automated Test Advocates and Experts

Before deciding to develop automated test procedures to support test requirements, the test team needs to be sure that personnel on the team are proficient in test automation. Ideally, the project manager should act as an automated testing advocate. Given the many misconceptions about automated testing (see Chapter 2), an automated testing advocate is necessary to resolve any misunderstandings surrounding the test effort.

For example, successful automated test efforts require that test engineers become familiar with the application early in the life cycle and that enough time in the schedule be allocated to the development of test procedures. Project management personnel who are not familiar with these requirements may not allocate enough time in the schedule for the test effort. When the test effort then falls behind schedule, the test tool may be viewed as the problem, causing test automation to be abandoned on the project. To overcome this obstacle, there needs to be one or more automated testing advocates on a project who understand the value and the requirements for an automated test effort and who can effectively communicate the automated test life-cycle process to management and the rest of the test team.

E.18 | Test Team Assignments

Just as it is important to include an automated testing expert and advocate on the test team, not everyone on the test team should be focused on performing test automation. When the entire test team focuses on automation, no one is left to perform test evaluation activities, manual tests, and other test analyses. It is best to separate these assignments, with one test engineer focusing on the automation of test scripts while another concentrates on the business issues associated with the AUT.

It is not uncommon for test engineers to become so involved in trying to automate one or more test scripts and develop the best automated testing library that they lose sight of the testing objective—to find defects. The test procedures may take longer to execute because the test engineer is trying to automate each one; problems that could have been discovered earlier through the use of manually executed scripts are therefore not found until each test procedure has been automated. Even with automation, the manual test effort is still a very valid approach for some tasks. The test engineer thus needs to conduct automation analysis and reuse analysis, and not lose sight of the fact that not everything can be automated.

E.19 | User Group Participation

Numerous user groups have been established for leading test tools. The test team should ask the particular test tool manufacturer about user groups for the tool that operate within the particular metropolitan area. At the user group meetings, the test team can find out how others are using the tool, learn tips and tricks, and gather other good information about the tool and its future.

Additionally, the test team can participate in many testing discussion groups or testing newsgroups to expand its collective testing knowledge.

E.20 | Test Tool Improvement Suggestions

During the design of a test procedure, the test engineer may think of a better way to develop tests, provided that the test tool would support the idea. In these situations, the test engineer should send in an enhancement request to the test tool manufacturer. Companies welcome such suggestions. There are often places on the company Web site where test engineers are encouraged to submit their enhancement requests on-line.

E.21 | Become a Beta Testing Site

Another great way of learning about the latest and greatest developments of the test tool vendor is to volunteer to become a beta tester. As a beta tester, the test engineer can discover problems specific with his or her AUT that can be elevated and fixed in time for the official release of the tool.

E.22 | Specialty Topic Experts

No matter which tool that the test team elects to use, some test automation experts will have thought of ways to improve upon the use of the tool. The test team should surf the Internet to identify free add-on utility software, automation ideas, and expert and mentoring support; these resources will increase the team's return on its automation investment. See the authors' Web site (http://www.autotestco.com/) for information on test tool expert support and links to various test tool training avenues.

Index

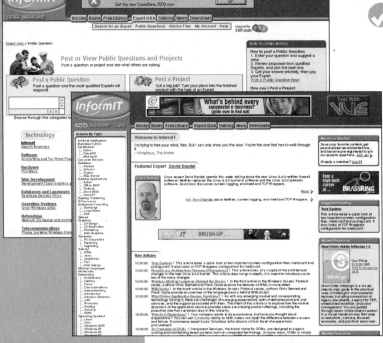